THE ONTARIO MUNICIPAL BOARD:

From Impact to Subsistence 1971-2016

PETER H. HOWDEN

 FriesenPress

Suite 300 - 990 Fort St
Victoria, BC, V8V 3K2
Canada

www.friesenpress.com

ISBN
978-1-4602-9905-0 (Paperback)
978-1-4602-9906-7 (eBook)

1. *Law, Administrative Law & Regulatory Practice*

Distributed to the trade by The Ingram Book Company

An indispensable insider's view of the much-maligned, often misunderstood, but absolutely necessary, Ontario Municipal Board."

—*John Mascarin, B.A. and M.A.(Toronto); LL.B.(Osgoode Hall); Editor-in-Chief, Municcipal & Planning Law Reports and Digest of Municipal &Planning Law).*

"The most valuable, incisive, in depth scrutiny and candid exposition of Canada's oldest land use tribunal."

—*(Ian James Lord, B.A.(Queen's); MSc.Pl (Toronto); LLB (Osgoode Hall).*

TABLE OF CONTENTS

INTRODUCTION

... Not here
not here the darkness, in this twittering world,
from Four Quartets, Burnt Norton
—T.S. Eliot, Faber, 1943

The Ontario Municipal Board (also called the "OMB" and "the Board") is a tribunal of several faces: it depends upon the viewer which face that person may see. For the person who was wrongly refused a minor variance because the local counsellor intervened in the local committee's process on behalf of a well-connected neighbour, the OMB's face is a welcoming and impartial one. It promises a tribunal that will listen. For a neighbour beside what has been a vacant grassed open area used by the neighbourhood as a park to play local ball games – a lot now proposed for construction and use as three blocks of low-rise condominiums peopled by innumerable strangers – it is a threat of unwanted change. While the city is supporting the neighbours' opposition, it appears to be both threat and hope: hope if the municipality should continue to oppose the development and threat that the tribunal would allow the development if the municipality became satisfied and settled, leaving the costs to the residents to fight alone and probably lose.

> It is usually those seeing the black prince whose negative views get heard by the general public.

For others without a direct interest but who either see the Board as an integral part of the democratic process or who see it as a needless intervention by a provincial appointee into the local process, the OMB appears either as the knight on a white charger ready to settle wrongs, or the black prince whose only aim is to consolidate power by overturning the democratically elected council's decision. It is usually those seeing the black prince whose negative views get heard by the general public.

Because of the extreme polarization of views of this tribunal today, it is time to look at it again, in a somewhat less academic, more pragmatic, and slightly more memoirist approach than the recent two publications on different aspects of the OMB.[1]

Actions of the Province of Ontario in proclaiming planning policy since the last published examination of the Board in 2002 have been aggressive and comprehensive to a degree unknown before 2002. That fact alone changes the dynamics of the OMB's role. Together with the rising cost of lengthy hearings, these factors complicate it by elevating the importance of consistency and predictability in interpreting policy, not only for outcomes. This book is more necessary now because the 2002 publication, *A Law Unto Itself*, looked only at the Board's decisions during three periods and their relation to public policy set by the Province. Unlike this book, it was not a holistic scrutiny of the Board's working conditions and its work, and the degree to which performance meets or does not meet the Board's public mandate.

The Foreword will provide to the non-professional reader an understanding of the various processes and parts of the *Planning Act* involved in the overall planning process in the Ontario *Planning Act*, and the relevant provisions of the *Expropriations Act*. This tribunal is also the provincial adjudicator of claims for compensation where persons have suffered the taking or disturbance of their land for public use. [Planning professionals can skip the Foreword].

Chapter I looks back briefly at the history of the OMB, where it came from and why it was formed. This is not a history text but it is important to appreciate how this tribunal began and the original purpose for it. By 1946, the OMB was a powerful regulatory and adjudicative tribunal involved in all phases of municipal planning and financing of works and projects. The Spadina Expressway hearing in 1971 became emblematic of the attention that this tribunal was attracting as the centre for municipal development and works.

In the late 1960s and early 70s and forward to 1990, municipal government in Toronto and other centres had come under scrutiny. Some councils gave the impression of a closed shop. But for the developers with big ideas, the shop was wide open. City decisions in the development field favoured large urban renewal schemes, ones that were designed to re-order large chunks of downtown neighbourhoods. They threatened destruction of some older neighbourhoods and the historic buildings that went with them. Chapter II will bring those days to life. The reform movement led by David Crombie and John Sewell brought the operations of municipal government to public attention. It was municipal government that most attracted serious critical public scrutiny then, not the OMB. It continued to be recognized or criticized only for the work it was doing across the province, seldom as a body lacking credibility in the planning field.[2]

Chapter II also walks through a contextual history of the OMB within the administrative arms of government, and the attitudes within the OMB to the new environmental movement in the 1970s. The concerns over the narrowing of views of the environment within the OMB resulted in an eco-planning process for municipal and provincial projects separated from the regular planning process. Internally, the change from appointment to term employment of Board members, its perceived loss of independence, and the effects of changes in government related to changes within the Board take the narrative and issues about the OMB to 2003 when the McGuinty Liberals gained power from the Harris/Eves Conservative party.

Chapters III and IV will look more closely at the very serious decline of public faith in the OMB from about 1995 and 2000 to the present. The empty polemics against, and serious criticism of, the OMB will be examined and separated so that the real problems of this tribunal may be laid bare. The alleged pro-developer bias is scrutinized and another more serious imbalance is found.

Chapter V looks at the purpose and mandate of the OMB within the planning process, apart from the performance of that mandate. It is the end of the first part of the book.

Entitled "Shake-up", Chapter VI pulls together the provincial position on the OMB, the resulting issues internally, aggravated by the less than demanding selection process. The laissez faire attitude in government toward the OMB ended and in the case of municipalities, is reversed; they are now officially recognized as a level of government that is accountable and responsible for all matters within their jurisdiction. The issues discussed, in addition to probable transfer of minor variance appeals to the municipalities from the OMB, include restricting appeals from Official Plans (OPs) to grounds relating to policy conformity and OP compliance with the *Planning Act*.3 It is a chapter marking a plateau of uncertainty from which the OMB could either rise or fall.

Chapter VII looks at the current literature regarding the OMB, whether the OMB has met and is meeting the demands of its mandate, and ideas for change to the process including removal of its *Planning Act* jurisdiction from the OMB. The criticisms warranting serious attention are identified.

In the following three chapters, the examination focusses on the causes of the current problems at the OMB and the extent to which the criticism of the Board as a democratically illegitimate tribunal is borne out or is not borne out. This analysis will range from the administrative reorganization of some tribunals with others into groups or clusters and its effects on the OMB, to difficulties caused by the OMB's own deficiencies in decision-making. The question of the OMB's inclusion in this reorganization of tribunals, the grounds or lack of grounds for so doing and the risks being run are analyzed with the advantages as known so far. New developments in the law and potential avenues to be taken in the future are considered against a backdrop of current law under the *Planning Act* and the *Expropriations Act*.

Chapter XI deals with the elusive goal of principled consistency in decision-making and with the sharp decline in numbers of members, the early use of part-time members, the problems of timely decision-making, the writing of decisions and the surprisingly questionable competence of a Board granted deference due to its specialized expertise. I look at the legitimate expectations of the OMB's stakeholders, and the degree to which the problem is either the irrelevance of the tribunal's mandate in today's context or the failure of the OMB to live up to its mandate. The mandate is well supported by stakeholders. I find that it is more relevant today than ever. It is a problem of government and tribunal wounding the tribunal and thus failing the mandate of both.

Finally, in Chapter XII, I propose changes for the future to provide a focus for the tribunal that is more consonant with community participation and serious consideration of options by all parties, assisted by expert mediators, planners and lawyers of related experience and trained in conflict resolution. They are also aimed at allowing municipalities some room to determine their own planning structure as a level of government recognized now to be responsible and accountable by the *2001 Municipal Act*, subject to compliance with provincial planning statements and the *Planning Act*. Provincial adjudicative oversight would continue to be a function of the same, or a new, tribunal. Expropriation claims would carry on with a new, properly staffed tribunal delivering decisions within sixty to ninety days of being heard.

Throughout the text, I will be providing accounts of several cases decided by the Ontario Municipal Board. They represent decisions over the last fifty years where the OMB has performed its duty, led the process, and cared for the public interest with which it was charged. They provide a picture of the tribunal and what it can do when it performs well.

I was a member and vice-chair of this tribunal in the 1980s until 1992. Others have written about the Board from the outside. Bruce Krushelnicki, also a former member and vice-chair, now the new Executive Chair of the tribunal cluster that includes the OMB, has written a helpful introduction titled *A Practical Guide to the Ontario Municipal Board* that is valuable as a text and guide for anyone who is contemplating involvement in the process. There are two other books on the OMB I will consider in some detail later. They are: A Law Unto Itself: How the OMB has Developed and Applied Land Use Planning Policy, by J. G. Chipman, a formative monograph published in 2002, and the more recent Planning Politics In Toronto: The OMB and Urban Development, by A. A. Moore, published in 2013.

I felt that it was time that someone with knowledge of the OMB from the inside should write about the Board and what has happened to it over the last twenty years, together with a look at how the law has changed with public and judicial opinion. Whether you may be a planning/municipal law practitioner, political policy aficionado, person affected by the Board's rulings, or general reader, the trip should interest and benefit you. The exercise will come full circle to focus on what I propose as a final coherent program of ideas for the future.

There are several process issues I will deal with as the book proceeds. They include:

- the standard of review used by the OMB
- the role of the OMB as an appellate tribunal, which hears evidence
- the end of de novo hearings, to be replaced by a true appeal hearing on the soundness of any grounds for disturbing the decision under appeal
- new guidelines for focused hearings and mandatory mediation
- a new duty to show the OMB up front that there is potential merit to the appeal
- a new consulting requirement for the Province to follow in section 3 in order to open up new policy statements to prior due process by AMO and the OMB
- the changed role of the OMB when it considers a compensation claim from a taking of land or disturbance, and
- need to improve efficiency and timeliness of compensation and planning decisions.

This is a book that can be read by those wanting to know where the OMB came from and the role it played at different ages, at times supplementary to and, where necessary, a directive towards municipal government when it fails to act in the public interest. It can also be read as an informative guide to what to expect at an OMB hearing and why party status before council and evidence disclosure to the municipality are vital to an appeal. It should assist practitioners to understand, by the weaknesses shown here, what is expected of them at a hearing and before a hearing. Careful outlines of submissions, position papers on practice points that are likely to arise, and requests for written submissions to supplement oral argument are several ways in which well-prepared counsel and planners could assist their clients and themselves. You will find answers to the mandate of this Board as it should be and the route through the process of choice.

You can learn from this book a lesson in public administration and a caution to bureaucratic uniformity. It is a story of how structural change that fails to consider the needs and goals of each organ to which it applies may result in loss of an important function through suffocation and a subsistence diet. It is also an investigation that, out of administrative deficiencies and mistakes, unearths clues to antidotes that point a different way to something exciting, where proper sustenance, care in selection, and brilliant leadership can be a game-changer.

FOREWORD

THE *PLANNING ACT* TERMS: OFFICIAL PLANS, ZONING BY-LAWS, SITE PLANS, AND SUBDIVISION CONTROL

Before we proceed further, I should level the knowledge playing field right now about what is needed to understand the Ontario Municipal Board's mandate – that is, the role that the Ontario Municipal Board is authorized to play in the planning process in Ontario. [For those familiar with the process, you can simply skip this section.]

The best way to explain the Board's role in the Ontario planning sphere is to start by thinking of the whole system of land use provisions in the *Planning Act* as expressing different levels of land use control. The ultimate source of planning policy is the Province through the Ministry of Municipal Affairs and the Provincial Policy Statement, issued from time to time by the minister. The vehicle used to implement provincial and local planning policy is the municipality; mediating between the two and overseeing policy implementation in contested cases is the OMB, the provincial land use appeals tribunal.

For each municipality, the official plan, the OP for short, is the source document of planning policies, future land use plans and zoning controls for a municipality. Its policies and goals must agree with the Provincial Policy Statement (2014) and Growth Plan, where one is in force. (The Greater Golden Horseshoe Growth Plan covers much of the area around the west end of Lake Ontario.) All municipal by-laws, including a by-law amending the zoning by-law, and the zoning by-law itself, in turn must conform to the governing OP, both local and regional (also called upper tier) within 10 years of a new OP. The official plan is described in the *Planning Act* as clearly a policy document but one with some teeth.

The Board used to act on referral from the responsible minister to it of an OP and/or zoning application; it could approve, reject, or approve as modified part or all of an OP or amendment (an OPA) to the OP; its duty was to see that the party not before the Board, the public and the public's welfare, convenience and health, was taken into account in any decision. The Board did, and still does, stand in the shoes of the Minister in determining the planning acceptability of an OP or an amendment to an OP and accompanying zoning change and in applying public interest considerations to them. Now, of course, an OP comes to the OMB if someone files an appeal from part of it but the Board retains much the same powers and duty.

The Official Plan is not only a policy document for the future. It sets land use categories for the whole municipality. Within those broad categories, an OP may well form a ground for disallowance of a building permit where the OP classifies a certain site as being, say, in an area designated for residential use and the zoning has not been updated by the lower tier municipality to conform with its new OP, still permitting only industrial uses. This zoning once would have been interpreted to allow a building application for a low rise industrial plant on the basis that the OP is not an effective restrictor of land use; it is a policy document. However, it has been held in a similar situation that a regional OP's land use designation could preempt the landowner's right to a building permit where the use applied for was within the lower tier zoning by-law. The bright line differentiation between OP as policy only, and zoning by-law as the effective land use control, has dimmed somewhat.[5]

In broad terms, land controls descend from the OP and tighten into law in the zoning by-law, which carries out the policies in the OP on the ground. It sets out in each zone the permitted uses and those not permitted, and the regulations such as minimum frontage on the street, maximum area and depth, and maximum gross floor area, either in gross figures or as a proportion of the lot.

From there, the next detailed level of control is the site plan. It sets the menu for placement of all planting, noise sources, light and traffic mitigation measures, and built forms on the site, outbuilding location, curbs, driveway and traffic flow through the site, especially important for commercial uses. Minor variances are intended to take in only discrepancies from the legal limit, which comes within the intent of the zoning by-law and the OP. And finally, the creation of new lots is controlled by consents or grants of severance, and plans of subdivision for larger numbers of lots, with controls or standards to which all services are to be completed. The Board hears appeals from either the successful or the unsuccessful party and others given standing by the Act or the Board, at each level of control.

All of the development appeals in Ontario where there is public controversy end up at the OMB for final resolution. And they all entail some form of development or rules for development or protection from development that will last for generations.

In addition, the OMB is the tribunal that hears all appeals regarding development charges and all claims arising from expropriation proceedings in Ontario remaining unresolved after early attempts at resolution through the assistance of Ontario's Board of Negotiation or private mediation. Expropriation in law covers all instances of the taking of land without the consent of the owner by public authorities pursuant to a statutory power. The OMB also hears claims for damages for interference with, or disturbance of, an owner's rights caused by construction arising out of an expropriation. The relevant provisions granting these powers to the OMB are:

> 29(1) The Board shall determine any compensation in respect of which a notice
> of arbitration has been served upon it under section 26 or 27, and, in the absence

of agreement, determine any other matter required by this or any other Act to be determined by the Board.

(2)   All oral evidence submitted before the Board shall be taken down in writing and, together with such documentary evidence and things as are received in evidence by the Board form the record. (R.S.O. 1990, c. E.26, s. 29(2).)

(3)   The Board shall prepare and furnish the parties to an application with written reasons for its decision.

A claim under the *Expropriations Act* can even include claims for interference due to construction of works by a public authority where the interference is unreasonable. The issue is: whether an interference with the private use and enjoyment of land is unreasonable when it results from construction that serves an important public purpose. The answer, as I see it, is that the reasonableness of the interference must be determined by balancing the competing interests, as it is in all other cases of private nuisance. (Antrim Truck Centre Ltd. v. Ontario (Transportation), 2013 SCC 13, [2013] 1 S.C.R. 594.)

The Board operates at all its hearings within its own founding statute, the *Ontario Municipal Board Act*.[6] In the Act, the Legislature has provided the Board with some indications that signify an intent that it should make the decisions, not the court. The *OMB Act* provides a narrow right of appeal, limited to questions of law only. The Act provides the Board with power to decide all questions of law or fact and to customize its orders to the imperatives of the case. There is no excuse for a Board member not ensuring that the design that a proponent uses to convince the Board of only minimal impacts on neighbouring development shall be the design insisted upon by use of strict terms in the order.

One additional term that will be used a great deal is the Provincial Policy Statement (PPS). That is the declaration of provincial policy that covers virtually all major features, natural and manmade, as well as future development or areas of no, or limited, development. The PPS must be issued under section 3 of the *Planning Act*. It is the same section that requires both municipalities and the OMB, in any decision, to be consistent with the PPS and the local OP. Subsections 3(1) and (2) provide for the PPS. Sections 3(5) and (6) deal with consistency of Board and municipal decisions with the PPS and with comments on planning matters in the following terms:

3(1)   The Minister, or the Minister together with any other minister of the Crown, may from time to time issue policy statements that have been approved by the Lieutenant Governor in Council on matters relating to municipal planning that in the opinion of the Minister are of provincial interest.

(2)   Before issuing a policy statement, the Minister shall confer with such persons or public bodies that the Minister considers have an interest in the proposed statement.

(5)   A decision of the council of a municipality, a local board, a planning board, a minister of the Crown and a ministry, board, commission or agency of the government, including the Municipal Board, in respect of the exercise of any authority that affects a planning matter,

    (a) shall be consistent with the policy statements issued under subsection (1) that are in effect on the date of the decision; and

    (b) shall conform with the provincial plans that are in effect on that date, or shall not conflict with them, as the case may be.

(6)   Comments, submissions or advice affecting a planning matter that are provided by the council of a municipality, a local board, a planning board, a minister or ministry, board, commission or agency of the government,

    (a) shall be consistent with the policy statements issued under subsection (1) that are in effect on the date the comments, submissions or advice are provided; and

    (b) shall conform with the provincial plans that are in effect on that date, or shall not conflict with them, as the case may be.

These are the basic terms that I will be commenting on as the book proceeds. They are all you will need to understand what follows. Any additional statutory provision that may be referred to will be supplied so that you will be in the same framework of laws that experienced lawyers and planners are.

CHAPTER I

THE HISTORY

Try to remember when life was so tender
that no one wept except the willow
from The Fantasticks
—Harvey Schmidt/Tom Jones

BIRTH OF A NEW ENTITY

Originally, a rather loosely formed commission was sent out during the 1880s by the Ontario government in answer to a political problem. As trains became more and more popular for their speed in delivering goods across large regions and the vastness of this continent, many found the noise and soot in their towns distressing. And U.S. state capitols and Canadian provincial capitals heard their complaints. That first commission was simply a number of men who travelled around Ontario to hear complaints by citizens and report back to the government. There was no name. It was little more than a quick attempt by politicians to be able to say that they had done something about the complaints.

By 1906, it was clear that more than an occasional sounding board for complaints was needed. In those days, when an activity had become too large for the traditional government departments to manage, there was an option at hand – the example in Canada was the federal Board of Railway Commissioners and in the United States, regulation of rail and other land based transport by the newly-created Interstate Commerce Commission. One person who has written on this process, John Chipman, described the process succinctly:

> It was believed that placing such matters in the hands of specialized agencies would serve to remove these time-consuming and contentious matters from the political arena, and that such agencies would develop expertise in their

areas of jurisdiction, and would, as nonpartisan bodies, ensure that the interests of all affected parties were fairly addressed.[7]

In a more targeted examination of the origin, a Toronto practitioner in municipal law examined the Ontario Municipal Board's root jurisdiction in its original form and its actual beginning in 1906.[8] At that time, the accounting rules and format of records were in the hands of another office, the Provincial Municipal Auditor. That office began in 1897 and there are those who believe that the origins of the OMB went back to the Municipal Auditor's Office. But its responsibilities, as well as the auditor himself, were folded much later into the Bureau of Municipal Affairs in 1917. Those powers did not come to the OMB until 1932.

The author's conclusion is that in 1906, a new creature of government was born. In his words, the Ontario Legislature conceived "the historic, groundbreaking creation of a distinctly new form of provincial governance." He summed it up succinctly in the following words:

> Its quintessential core, being that of an independent, quasi-judicial administrative tribunal, set it apart from the earlier provincial supervisory offices to such a degree that an entirely new [but not original] entity commenced on that date.[9]

The date was June 1, 1906. And it became known as the Ontario Railway and Municipal Board (ORMB).

It was then that partial financial supervision over municipalities was given to the then ORMB. Over time, the ORMB was given many disparate areas to deal with under a myriad of laws. In the early decades, it appears that most of the Board's time was taken up with supervision of Ontario railways. From the beginning, and more so since the Second World War, as land use planning became more and more sophisticated amid the post-war boom in population and development, the legislature added to the Board's jurisdiction considerably.

In proceeding in this way, governments were handing over growing sectors of the economy to boards or commissions and giving them very broad powers to deal with those sectors. No one knew how they would employ these wide powers and so an older agency like the OMB grew into a strong centralized group directed, in Ontario's case, from a Toronto base office. That growth and accretion of power to the OMB in the planning area occurred in 1932 with the Ontario Municipal Board Act, 1932; the Bureau of Municipal Affairs, later the Ministry of Municipal Affairs, temporarily merged under the supervision of the Ontario Municipal Board to the extent that the Cabinet was empowered to select one member of the OMB to have charge of all municipal matters, known as the Commissioner for Municipal Affairs. By 1946, planning in Ontario was ready for the next step.

TRANSITION TO LAND USE PLANNING TRIBUNAL AND REGULATOR

With the *Planning Act* of 1946, the Province created the first comprehensive planning framework in law for Ontario. The year 1946 was the significant starting point when:

> The original *Planning Act* established a framework for provincial and municipal involvement in statutory master planning. The piecemeal local planning powers that had accumulated in the first half of the century were consolidated into a comprehensive piece of enabling legislation that provided all authority for land use planning and development in the province."[10]

Much of the implementation was assigned to the local municipalities, but the OMB had to approve all zoning by-laws and all official plans referred by the Minister before they could come into force. A municipal zoning by-law had no effect at all without the Board's approval. The uses legally permitted on each lot or the site regulations for yards and gross floor area and height had no effect in law until the OMB's approval gave them life.

By this time, the OMB had become the regulatory and adjudicative tribunal for municipal financial and planning decisions. No municipal project could proceed and no OP or zoning by-law had any effect in law without approval by the OMB. OPs were technically to be approved or rejected by the Minister of Municipal Affairs but wherever there was an objection, the OP or the OPA would be referred to the OMB for a de novo hearing and any zoning by-law passed or refused by a municipality associated with an OP or OPA that was also objected to would be heard with it.

By the 1960s and early 1970s, the attention paid to the OMB bore no resemblance to the attacks of today. Then, there was much more a feeling in the air that this was a tribunal that made things happen and that was not worried about taking on municipal and pro-development decisions where planning principles had been lost. This was well before my time on the Board but I remember how much a part of media coverage the OMB became in those years when I was completing my qualifications for entry to the bar and starting into practice in Toronto.

Planning in Ontario reached a new sophistication then and this same tribunal became headline news in decision after decision. The Annual Report for the year 1969 did not overstate the situation when it described the Board as a tribunal of "wide-ranging jurisdiction and the image created by daily reports of its work and decisions in the public press" had established it as a centre of power and justice in Ontario.

The writer of that report and the main axle around which the tribunal's public image revolved was a gruff, somewhat remote gentleman named Joseph A. Kennedy, Chair of the Ontario Municipal Board from 1960–1972. He and his co-members brought the Board into the modern era as an administrative tribunal. He was the Chair of one of the best known hearings before the Board, a decision that rocked the Metro Toronto Traffic Department and absorbed the attention of front pages of the largest Toronto dailies.

The Spadina Expressway hearing forms the first subject of the case reports because it exemplifies the era when the OMB was a highly respected part of the municipal process, when daily reports of its work and decisions were part of the public scene. Its mandate was broader in those days as a virtual regulatory tribunal for municipal finance and planning decision review, but it was much the same in principle as it is now under the *Planning Act*.

BEING THERE 1: THE 1971 EXPRESSWAY HEARING[11]

When you open a road map of Toronto today looking for major expressway routes, one stands out in the centre: the Spadina Expressway, or as it is now known, Allen Road. It extends out as a slightly drooping, insensate limb, hanging south from above Sheppard Avenue down to Eglinton Avenue. It is hard now to recall the incredible emotions that this road aroused as it reached its present terminus in the midtown area. Because where it ends now was far from where it was meant to go. The Spadina Expressway was slated to continue south ripping through several established neighbourhoods, tearing out houses and evicting residents caught in its swath, as an access-controlled freeway to connect to another, the Crosstown Expressway from an extended 400 Highway east to the Don Valley Parkway.

It was a time in the wake of the turbulence of the '60s social revolution when Toronto's professional and academic classes joined an anti-urban expressway movement sweeping across the continent. And the centre of their attention soon became that small group led by Joseph A. Kennedy, called collectively the Ontario Municipal Board.

Kennedy became a legend. He was one chair of an administrative tribunal who led by example by developing his own philosophy of what that tribunal was about, and by trying to impose it on the tribunal. At the time, the Board had power to approve or halt most municipal projects by means of its oversight duties toward municipal debt instruments, as well as the power to bring into effect or kill zoning by-laws and municipal policy expressed in an OP. The statutes granting the Board power provided virtually no criteria to limit its discretion in the municipal field. So when Metro Council's[12] Transportation Committee once more reviewed the Spadina Expressway as it neared Eglinton Avenue from January to June 1970 and voted in favour of the Expressway, the leaders of the growing movement against it announced that they would take it to the Ontario Municipal Board.

They hired one of the foremost legal counsel in the city, John J. Robinette. Robinette promptly went before Metro Council to ask them to halt all construction until the OMB heard the case. He cited the doubling of its cost, as well as design changes since the initial OMB approval back in 1963 and interim financing approval in 1965 and 1967. The very breadth of power possessed by this Board had intermittently caused a few to call for its abolition as undemocratic and unaccountable for its decisions. It was the power concentrated in this one tribunal that attracted the Stop Spadina leaders to the OMB. And when Robinette made his pitch to Metro to call an interim halt, Metro withdrew its prior opposition to the OMB review, asked the OMB for approval of a further cost increase, and closed down all further construction of the Expressway until OMB approval was provided.

A preliminary hearing was scheduled for September 15, 1970. It was at this pre-hearing that the Board Chair and the two members could ascertain and deal with any problems regarding the witnesses to be called, time limits, any willingness to resolve certain issues, and the parameters of the hearing. In this instance, the members of the OMB assigned to this case were two experienced lawyers, with Mr. Kennedy, also a former lawyer, as the Chair.

Metro Toronto attempted to argue that the hearing should be confined to the financial ability of the Metro government to pay for the remaining upgraded cost. At this point, the OMB signaled that this was not to be just another expenditure application. The Chair ruled against Metro, pronouncing that this would be a full inquiry into all matters related to the Expressway including the necessity and the potential pluses and minuses it would likely bring to Toronto should it continue south to Bloor St. as planned.

On January 4, 1971, the entrance door for the panel opened. The noise level immediately lowered as William Shub and Robert McGuire took their seats on each wing, the Chairman in the centre. It was a decisive moment for each of them. There was no going back; they were seized, as they say in the courts, meaning this panel must now hear the case to the end. There was no Board reporter to keep a transcript. As would be the case in the later decades of the twentieth century, hiring a reporter to make a transcript record of proceedings before the OMB is left to the parties to arrange. Neither side did so nor was there ever anything in the Board's budget to cover that cost.

Metro called the first witness. It was the Commissioner of Roads and Traffic for Metro Toronto. The first point that Metro counsel went for was to establish the unquestionable legitimacy of the Expressway, and at the same time infer the illegitimacy of this hearing, by having the witness declare that it had been approved by Metro Council with the full support of the provincial government. Immediately, the Chair spoke up:

> "You can say that, and that is so. But here it is limited to a persuasive effect on this Board in its consideration of the expenditure of money, it does not have a binding effect."

He continued, "I like to think that as long as section 64 of the *Ontario Municipal Board Act* stands as the law laid down by the Legislature, that any arm of the government, or even the government itself, in giving approval, would not be bypassing the provisions of section 64 at least (unless) they expressly said so."

Section 64 of the *Ontario Municipal Board Act* is not an easily understood provision. It dealt with municipal debentures and the restriction on dispensing with the inhabitants' assent to a debt issue to the sole determination by the OMB. In referring to that section, he was saying that under his leadership the OMB would be the sole determiner of the scope of the hearing and it would be a full and legitimate hearing of all the issues.

In the meantime, a trap was waiting. One of the Stop Spadina leaders had been meeting with a planner one day in the Metro offices. At one point, the planner had to leave the office. Left behind and spread in front of him was a consultants' report that, in the seconds he had to look at it, seemed highly relevant to the hearing. They were able to pass news of it to one of the lawyers and he obtained it through a mutual discovery process prior to the hearing. It was a study of Travel Demand some twenty to thirty years in the future, should the expressway network including the Spadina be built, commissioned by Metro Roads Department.

Counsel for the expressway opposition cross-examined the witness on his support for the expressway system. Immediately the witness distanced himself from the Traffic Demand report, denying he had ever read it. The reason for this answer was immediately clear – as Ian Milligan wrote in his seminal article on the Spadina Expressway, "This Board Has a Duty To Intervene: Challenging the Spadina Expressway through the OMB, 1963-71", on which I have relied for much of this account:

> The most significant piece of evidence, especially in light of the OMB's subsequent decision, was the Keats Peat Marwick & Co. Travel Demand Study for 1995 (then twenty-four years into the future). Commissioned by (Metro Roads), the study showed the catastrophic consequences for citywide traffic flows if the expressway network was built.

The hearing began to enlarge into a debate on the whole notion of urban expressways. Various well-known expert witnesses from the United States and Canada attended and testified. The Toronto Board of Education, the Association of Women Electors and other citizens' and neighbourhood organizations brought petitions against the expressway's completion and the corresponding destruction of residential neighbourhoods. At one point, the number of expressways not yet fully known became public through the hearing. On a graphic map, they resembled a city-wide Rube Goldberg machine, a great network of freeways throughout Toronto forming a closed system of connections with each other and never with the city street system, each with destructive consequences for the neighbourhoods they would have cut through but with benefits to traffic movement in the city. This was used, as were other graphic depictions, by the legal counsel for the parties to try to persuade the Board. And then, suddenly, the door behind the desk closed for the last time.

After sixteen days, it was all over. The chair and the two members of the OMB withdrew from the public glare and the clash of ideas generated at the hearing.

For those sixteen days and the weeks before and after the OMB hearing, it was the talk of Toronto. The Board even then inspired heated arguments over its legitimacy and existence. It also brought to front and centre as no other body could, the pressing urban force for neighbourhood destruction, against which many felt disfranchised and powerless. This was the meaning that Chairman Kennedy had brought to this disparate and, until then, unknown group of men — that this Board was a necessary part of a democracy, one place where the outnumbered and the voiceless facing loss of their neighbourhoods could be heard and could succeed against a powerful majority from the outer city and the suburbs. Under Kennedy, the Board would protect the last significant green space in Toronto, its great ravine network, from the insatiable demands of development along the edges and inner banks; and it was where those Metro traffic engineers with all the numbers had to prove that their proposal, considered holistically in the cold light of a winter's day, would be of benefit to the city as a whole.

> Under Kennedy, the Board would protect the last significant green space in Toronto, its great ravine network, from the insatiable demands of development …

The OMB decision upheld the completion of the Spadina Expressway by two to one. Both Mr. Shub and Mr. McGuire saw the importance of concerns expressed by those opposed; they understood and accepted them but they saw the decision of the Metro Council as having been made some seven years before and approved by the Board. They saw the Board as essentially a place where serious problems should be aired publicly. But it was not its role to take over the role of the council to put in place a vision of the City different from that of the councillors. As Mr. Shub wrote: "It is suggested that the Board, when making its determination should be governed by the face of Toronto it is desired to achieve. I cannot agree. This is precisely the function of council."

Few remember them. It was Chairman Kennedy's eloquent echo of the fears and concerns of many people that they remember. Kennedy saw the Board as a body put in place to consider the minority interest, those without power who must face the impacts from development projects, be they buildings, a gravel pit, or roadways. He saw the minority interest in the case as represented by all those people whose homes in the Expressway's path would be destroyed or would be affected by being isolated beside a major roadway giving off constant traffic fumes and noise. He saw that parts of the irreplaceable ravine system would be lost forever to the expressway. He found that there would be considerable damage and that the general public interest in the common good of the city had not been shown to benefit. As Ian Milligan wrote, citing Kennedy's own words:

> The most forceful section of his ruling focused on the role of the OMB and seriously weighed the merits and disadvantages of intervening in the democratic process: "I have said in past decisions that this Board should not presume to interfere with the exercise of discretion by local elected representatives within the limits of powers conferred upon them by the Legislature without some cogent reason, some serious reason for so doing. In my opinion there are cogent reasons, serious reasons for so doing in this case. I do not believe that

citizens have a right to overrule their elected representatives, but I do believe this Board has a duty to intervene in cases such as this one."

While expressing respect for the democratic process, Kennedy had been convinced by the Expressway opponents on two grounds: firstly, there would be considerable damage to minority interests, but secondly he was not fully convinced that the overall public interest would benefit from the Expressway. Indeed, Kennedy declared that while the "fundamental duty of government is to protect the greatest common good ... these needs should prevail over minority and individual rights and interests only if the project proposed in the public interest can be justified and supported."

The decision was appealed to the Ontario Cabinet. On June 3, 1971, only five months after the hearing before the OMB commenced, Premier William Davis rose in the Ontario Legislature and announced the end of the Spadina Expressway. The terminus remains to this day at Eglinton Avenue. The name disappeared with the rest of it, replaced by Allen Road, in memory of a former Metro chairman, William Allen. The way toward that decision was paved by the dissent of Mr. Kennedy and his view of the OMB as a place where power was granted to make decisions in the public interest and to refuse to capitulate to powerful interests where the long-term interest of all in maintaining a humane environment were being severely threatened. In his view, the case for the Expressway was not proven.

This case carried with it the seeds for controversy in the future for the OMB. The difference ultimately between the chairman and the two members was part of the controversy that lives on today.

Should one tribunal continue to have the authority to go beyond findings on the evidence to overrule the elected council of the municipality in question? Or should the tribunal serve more as a planning court whose role in the end is to see that proper procedure was followed, an unbiased hearing was granted before the Board, the duty of fairness was met, and the proposal was compatible with its surroundings?

The issue whether an appointed body should have the power to set aside a decision of an elected municipal council was before the 1972 select committee of the Ontario Legislature within one year after the Spadina hearing. That committee had a wide mandate to examine all aspects of the Board's work, including whether the OMB should continue its oversight role over planning and other decisions of elected councils. For one point, some of its members were authorized to visit Manitoba and British Columbia to observe the system in each province. Manitoba had a Municipal Board with some similarity to Ontario's. British Columbia functioned then, and still does function, without any provincial body like the OMB. The committee had a wide mandate but seemed constricted in time. It appears that way because of the breadth and number of subjects it recommended for study instead of making its own recommendation. One was the very question that separated the majority and minority of the OMB panel the year before.

The select committee said in its report that it "explored" the basic question: what role, if any, should an appointed body such as the OMB play in the process of legislative decision-making? Its answer? The OMB should continue, "as an independent appeal tribunal to review municipal legislation, subject to the changes recommended in this report." (Those changes were all procedural, dealing with matters such as limiting it to an appeal tribunal with no more de novo authority, and setting a general rule of two members on a decision panel where the hearing was not a preliminary or pre-hearing conference and where it was not an appeal from a minor variance or severance decision.)

As for the basic question, the committee left it to a vague review at a later time by persons unknown of all functions of the OMB not dealt with in the report and to determine whether each power should be left with the OMB, transferred or abolished. In other words, it ducked the issue.[13]

CHAPTER II

FROM THE PALMER-STEWART YEARS (1972-1989) TO THE HARRIS-MCGUINTY SUCCESSION (1995-2005)

And we must take the current when
it serves, Or lose our ventures.
from Julius Caesar
—W. Shakespeare

THE INDIVISIBLE DIVIDE: PLANNING AND ENVIRONMENT

An issue arising from this period was the post-Kennedy attitude of the Board to environmental matters and its public cost due to the OMB's perceived hostility to environmental evidence and issues.

The description of the content of an "official plan" in the *Planning Act* did not expressly refer to the "environment" in the 1970s. It spoke of policies to "secure the health, safety, convenience or welfare of inhabitants." Before 1972, the Board nevertheless did deal in its hearings and decisions with environmental impact, for example sewage or waste disposal and effects on natural systems, air and water quality relating to compatibility of residential with heavy industrial uses. One of the major interests of the Kennedy-led OMB was the preservation of the large ravine areas of the city as open natural areas important to the health and quality of life in a large city. After the Kennedy period as Board Chair, W.H. Palmer assumed the position. A much reduced interest and little aggressive concern toward environmental concerns took over at the OMB. It was a temporary takeover but it had consequences.

A community of prominent environmentalists composed of lawyers and advocates, environmental engineers and planners, public sector consultants and directors, as well as interested and committed lay people, had little respect for the way in which the OMB dealt with environmental matters. As 1972 passed into early 1973, the trend at the Board was increasingly to downgrade or ignore serious concerns over environmental issues and measures to remediate negative environmental impacts. As a result, meetings and seminars on environmental matters would be held without any representative of the OMB being present. Environmental papers and conferences failed to refer to the OMB as a relevant factor regarding environmental issues and environmental review.

Professionals and middle level government bureaucrats involved in the environmental movement, which took over Canada in the early 1970s, wanted reform. Their aim was a broad and idealistic one: the betterment of the people of all of Ontario by providing for the protection, conservation, and wise management of the environment.

At roughly the same time, there began to be accepted what became known as the OMB's "traditional" position. That traditional attitude and approach was to separate environmental evidence and issues from pure planning evidence and issues and admit only evidence on the planning issues. Some members of the OMB, going up to the Chair himself, as well as some planners and lawyers saw environmental issues as of lesser importance, or as irrelevant to planning principles. Embedded in that stance is the assumption that there is a clear line between environmental and strictly planning evidence, a line which has not been satisfactorily drawn in any decision of the OMB.

In 1974, a story was published in a major newspaper in Toronto on the OMB's Chair W.H. Palmer, which, if true, confirmed the hostility of key persons at the OMB toward environmental matters. The newspaper piece included some "impressions" that Mr. Palmer said he had formed. Referring to the backlog of cases at the OMB, Mr. Palmer's view was that too many cases were taken up with "days and days of stuff." His view was that environment and environmental engineering issues were for other departments of government; the Board was there only to hear "planning issues." At hearings, the presiding member would often rule out evidence of, for instance, guidelines for measuring and remediating particular environmental impacts – e.g. noise or groundwater quality guidelines – stating that it was not planning evidence.[14]

This issue came to a head in 1974 before the Divisional Court. The Court issued its decision in Westminster (Township) v London (City)[15] on September 24, 1974, a unanimous decision of a strong panel, which included Justices Houlden and Van Camp, and Dalton Wells, Chief Justice of the High Court. The case involved an application for judicial review brought by the Township of the Board's direction that the Board would not listen to evidence on environmental matters. The application before the Board concerned the application of the City of London to locate a waste disposal facility, a sanitary landfill site, in the Township of Westminster, which shares a common boundary with the city. The issue that went to the Divisional Court was one of several proceedings by neighbouring owners protesting against the city's effort to locate the landfill in Westminster Township. There had been an environmental hearing by an Environmental Hearing Board and so this record was affected by there having been another proceeding that had already heard evidence regarding compliance with the *Environmental Protection Act*. However, the decision does not depend on that fact. The Court stated, on the issue of the relation of environmental and planning evidence:

The next submission of counsel for the applicant was based on the ruling of the OMB dealing with environmental matters. In the course of the hearing, the OMB ruled that it would not listen to evidence pertaining to such matters as they had already been dealt with by the Ministry of the Environment. The OMB stated that it was only concerned with planning matters and did not wish to hear evidence on environmental matters. Counsel for the applicant submitted that as a result of the Board's ruling, the applicant would be denied a full hearing before the OMB.

Both counsel agreed that it is most difficult to make a distinction between evidence which relates to environmental matters and evidence which relates to planning matters. We can understand the reasons for the reluctance of the OMB to listen to evidence bearing on environmental matters in view of the lengthy hearing before the Environmental Hearing Board. But we think the ruling of the OMB was wrong, and when the hearing is recommenced, we believe the OMB should listen to the evidence presented to it without attempting to distinguish between environmental matters and planning matters.

This was acceptance of the obvious as we look back on those days – that a planning case must deal with all relevant and current issues and questions of land use cannot be decided in an enclosed shell remote from the conditions surrounding, under, and over the site in question. Those conditions and the issues of impact from the proposed use of the site in question and impact of existing uses on that proposed site must include satisfaction of concerns proven regarding environmental issues.

As I stated to a conference of planners and lawyers involved in environmental and planning law in the mid-1980s:

> Planning and environment cannot be separated, and it is not correct, legally or philosophically, to attempt to do so.

Since the *Westminster v London* decision by the Divisional Court, we have learned the same simple fact, in Toronto, North York, Ottawa-Carleton, Calabogie, Bedford Township, Niagara, Kitchener and other places. Planning and environment cannot be separated, and it is not correct, legally or philosophically, to attempt to do so. Building separations, built density, height, waste disposal, view corridors, acoustics, air, sun, water quality, health, welfare – how is one to disconnect some of these from others where all are part of the real situation, real life, and a liveable environment, and say they do not count in a planning process of any soundness?

The dichotomy between planning and environmental evidence and the supposed irrelevance of the latter to planning matters that became scripture among influential planning purists and some members of the OMB occurred at a time that proved to be most unfortunate. It was in this same period that decisions were made about a planning approval process for provincial and municipal projects that would represent "thoughtful, transparent planning in the public sector ... Such undertakings would, in future, be subject to careful, upfront valuation and scrutiny, including an examination of the rationale or need for the undertaking." The projects would include not only site-specific ones but whole programs and plans to apply across Ontario.

In 1976, the *Environmental Assessment Act* (EAA) came into effect and the Environmental Assessment Board (EAB) was born as the adjudicative tribunal for the new process. Those decisions froze the mindset of some in government of "environment" as a set of issues in a special planning process separate and apart from the planning process for private and public undertakings. The Environment Review Tribunal [now within the administrative cluster called the Environmental and Land Tribunals Ontario (ELTO) like the OMB] continues as the successor of the EAB to this day. Despite the aim of transparency and opportunities for public input, the EAA authorized the Minister of Environment (MOE) to approve or reject any proponent's environmental assessment. He could refer the assessment, where the Minister decided not to make the final decision, to the EAB, or to a joint board composed of members of the EAB and the OMB where a project required approvals under more than two Acts.[16]

We continue to pay for those years of separation of environmental requirements from other necessary requirements of government included in the planning process and its approvals. Both processes have suffered from time to time from exemptions granted by government and chronic underfunding, and a resulting inability to respond adequately to applications requiring approvals.

The greatest area of deficiency in my experience was enforcement of MOE guidelines that were incorporated in by-laws and approval conditions, due to shortages of staff. That problem continues.

Since 1983, the *Planning Act* has expressly referred to the environment. All approvals now must consider environmental issues by reason of the statutory purpose to promote sustainable development and the provincial interest stated in related matters in section 2(a), (b), (c), (d), and (q) of the *Planning Act*. Section 2 requires as a statutory duty that the OMB and municipal councils must have regard to those environmental and other listed elements of provincial interest in its hearings, deliberations and decision-making. The environmental assessment (EA) is now a process commonly required of development applicants by official plan policy and/or provincial policy under the *Planning Act*.

The *Planning Act* uses the words "have regard to" when it speaks in section 3 of the OMB's duty towards the decision of the municipal council when the Board is considering an appeal from council. A case that dealt at some length with the meaning of that phrase deserves close scrutiny because it was decided when the *Planning Act* required the Board and council to have regard to provincial policy. (The Act has since been amended to require that municipalities and the Board make decisions consistent with provincial policy.)

The "have regard to" language still applies to the Board when it is considering an appeal from a decision of the municipal council. The same case is apposite here because it does show how well considered matters of the natural environment are when the Board deals with them in terms of provincial policy. It also shows how a party can use an appeal under the *Planning Act* to request a changed, more restricted zoning on a property owned by another person if the appellant has evidence to support it. Land ownership is not a prerequisite to bringing an appeal to the OMB under the *Planning Act* provisions.

I will return to this subject and the relation in future of the OMB and the Environmental Review Tribunal, the successor to the Environmental Assessment Board, when we come to Chapter VIII on the Environment and Land Tribunals Ontario, the name of the cluster or grouping of tribunals in which the OMB now is positioned. Now, enjoy the damn case.

BEING THERE 2: THE CASE OF THE WATERY GRAVE

(Material Handling Problem Solvers Inc. v Essex (Town) 44 OMBR 364)

Before getting into this story, you should remind yourself that we live in a democracy where each of us has rights. And one of those rights is that if you own a piece of land, you cannot be stripped of its value by government unless you are compensated for it. Isn't that right? But what if you buy land in Florida without knowing it, and later you find you paid good money for land that was largely a swamp, without anyone telling you part of it was a swamp? What was that old saying? *Caveat emptor.* In English, let the buyer beware. It was a golfer Ben Hogan who expressed in biblical terms the ultimate wish of all golfers, and no doubt the wish of the owner of the tract of land we are about to read about: may thy ball lie in green pastures and not in still waters.

In the 1990s, a fellow named Don Hearn had done well in business in Windsor, Ontario. His company, mysteriously named Material Handling Problem Solvers Inc., made a bold move one day and bought a large property of about two hundred acres. Hearn probably saw the property from his sleek black convertible as he sped by it with friends a few times, his hair blowing over his eyes as he kept pushing it back. He could see it had a large area, at least 150 acres, covered with a fine stand of trees, and in one corner, there were about twenty acres cleared for a farm field. There is no indication that he checked the zoning or walked the site prior to buying. He told his buddies that he was going to develop a golf course. By 1998, Don's company had applied to the Town of Essex to change the Town's OP and zoning by-law to allow it. The OP marked it for agriculture and so it was zoned to permit only agricultural use.

Within a short time, word about this application got round and a few farmers concerned to preserve the area for agriculture use and some rural people with a concern for the environment got together and put in a notice opposing the golf course. They saw the land Hearn had bought as part of an important habitat for certain bird life and they believed that not only was the large woodlot worth preserving, the land was part of what could be significant marsh or wetland that might have provincial significance.

The Town did not embrace Hearn's application for the golf course immediately and so he and his legal team took it by appeal to the Ontario Municipal Board. The Board placed it under case management and attempted a resolution by mediation as the hearing was approaching in the summer of 2000. This did not work.

Around the same time, Hearn's people started cutting trees and began to prepare the site for development. Friends of Marshfield Woods, as the opposition had become known, went to the Town, then to the OMB, pleading that they put a stop to Hearn's activity but to no avail. The County had no tree preservation by-law. However, this got another person involved, a Dr. Spellman who was a researcher and had had experience with wetland identification and with the OMB before. He agreed to get involved and he acted immediately with foresight. Spellman hired a wetlands expert to study and evaluate the land in the area surrounding and including Hearn's property. Within a month in April 2000, Spellman received the result. There was no doubt. The area he studied, which included the treed part of the Hearn land, constituted a forested swamp. Not only that, the evaluation showed it to be of provincial significance.

Spellman submitted the evaluation to the Ministry of Natural Resources. The Ministry found the study to have been completed within its guidelines and accepted the conclusion that it was a woods wetland complex that had provincial significance. Its letter to Spellman was dated May 18, 2000. By June 2, 2000, Hearn's legal team knew of this identification. The hearing came on in the second week in June. Hearn attended with his lawyer. He proceeded to withdraw his applications and appeals. The hearing ended with that abandonment.

Hearn then had new applications filed on August 15, 2000. The Town this time approved the by-law to rezone his land for the golf course. However, the application to the Province for the OPA failed to get the necessary approval of the Ministry of Municipal Affairs and Housing; it was denied in February 2001. Hearn then appealed from this refusal to the OMB. However, before this occurred Dr. Spellman did something that many do not realize can be extremely effective, particularly if you have the evidence to back it up. Spellman filed a counter-application and appeal asking for an OPA and a zoning amendment to re-designate Hearn's land and the remainder of the identified area as Marshland Wetland Complex, meaning that if they were approved, the Hearn land and the rest could not be developed for a golf course. The Town refused to take Spellman's application seriously because it was not Spellman's property and it did nothing. That delay allowed him to appeal after the requisite time to the OMB. Nothing in the *Planning Act* prevented Spellman's move; it is an Act concerned with land use and with process, not with ownership.

Since this all happened, the Ministry of Municipal Affairs and Housing joined in the proceedings at the OMB, opposing the golf course and providing evidence to support the Spellman appeals. In addition, the region's Conservation Authority recognized its mandate to protect the environment by supporting Spellman and "the Friends" against Don Hearn.

One member was assigned to this case, an exceptional member but he had no co-panelists from a rural land use or environmental engineering background to contribute to the workload and stress of this case. The Board was faced with a multi-sided and complex hearing with serious emotional undercurrents. Those feelings surfaced once in a while in the form of tree-cutting and drainage threats by local farmers afraid of what they saw as something that could happen to them. The town and Don Hearn with his company Material Handling Problem Solvers Inc. (MHP) supported the rezoning for the proposed golf course. The Province and the Conservation Authority were there to protect each one's mandate, the Ministry to support the Spellman appeals and the Authority to protect the wetland that it designated. Both were opposed to the Hearn proposal as a consequence. A group of landowners with large holdings in the County opposed the position of Dr. Spellman, that allowed a third party to apply to down-zone one's land without one's consent and a public authority could recognize the downzoning and resulting devaluation of the property. To them, this was a taking without compensation and if it succeeded, they would knock over their bush: in other words, they would cut the woodlots and drain the land of water for farming. This was a threat repeated several times throughout the hearing by local farmers and other owners.

The first problems identified by the Board members were whether the identification of the Forested Wetlands Complex breached the rules of fairness and the related issue, whether the wetland's status was to be considered as of the date of the original application when it was not identified as a provincially significant wetland, or was it to be considered as of the date of the second hearing and the renewed application by Don Hearn. By the time Hearn applied a second time, the Ministry had, to the knowledge of Hearn the owner, recognized the lands as having provincial significance as a rare protected resource and subject to the provincial policy statement discouraging development. If the wetlands status was considered as of the original application, the Board could proceed on the basis that the status of the Hearn land was as a valued woodlot but nothing more.

First, there was no doubt that the Board was bound by a ruling by the Divisional Court to the following effect – each development proposal is to be considered by the Board as subject to the policies as they stood on the date of the application. The binding case was called *Clergy v Mississauga (City)*.[17] The original application to the Town for approval of the golf course was in July 1998. At that time, there had been no identification of the Hearn land as part of the Wetland Complex and therefore it would not be subject to the policy protecting significant wetlands. Hearn withdrew his original application in early June 2000. His second application for similar relief to allow his golf course idea was filed in August 15, 2000. Hearn's counsel submitted that for purposes of the *Clergy* principle, the effective date of Hearn's application was July 1998, because Mr. Hearn never abandoned his idea to proceed with the golf course. He merely withdrew the formal application, renewed it in August in his second application and all that happened effectively was that the matter was adjourned to August 2000.

As the Board ruled, however, it was clear that in June of 2000, Hearn had abandoned his appeal and withdrew his application. There was no adjournment of the same proceeding; he agreed to take back his development application and the hearing on it and his appeal ended that day; there was no live application or appeal after the hearing ended in early June. The Board therefore had to apply the provincial policies and the status of the Hearn land for purposes of the provincial policy statement as of the date of the filing of the second application. That was in August 20, some three months after the wetland complex was identified and notice given to Dr. Spellman on May 18 of that identification. Hearn's team and Don Hearn himself had actual notice of the wetlands designation by June 2, 2000, only days before the aborted hearing of the first application was to start.

There is a slippery part to the Board's decision and that is the fact that the Ministry gave notice of its identification of the Hearn and other lands as significant wetlands only to Dr. Spellman. It is somewhat shocking that the Ministry of Natural Resources never thought that the owner of the land should be formally notified of its decision despite the potential loss of development rights that decision implied. However, the Board found as a fact that the owner and his counsel had actual notice before the first application was heard and withdrawn. There is no doubt that as of that withdrawal, Don Hearn certainly knew well that this had happened, a fact that played a part, I venture to say, in his withdrawal of his first application only days after Hearn had learned of the Ministry's acceptance of the wetlands evaluation.

These are not easy issues. They require judgment, knowledge of case law, and fairness and consistency in principle. These are the types of issues that it is difficult visualizing several municipal councils (out of the total of 444 in Ontario) facing without guidance from a provincial oversight tribunal. Each would have its own take on how to respond in policy terms. The next issue is an even more difficult one, an issue that could have gone either way no matter the ruling on the effective date of application of the provincial policy statement.

Having found that the Hearn lands had been correctly identified as Forested Wetlands Complex, a provincially significant wetland, the next issue to be wrestled with was this – what is the effect of the language in section 3(5) of the *Planning Act* in these circumstances where it says that the OMB "shall have regard to policy statements" issued under the Act? The Act no longer read as it did in 1995, or as it does now, that the OMB's decision "shall be consistent with policy statements" issued under the Act. The "have regard to" language is in the low range of the continuum between absolute conformity and agreement at the high end and mere awareness of the policy at the low end.

Like the evaluation of justification for purposes of the Food Land Guidelines in the Ottawa-Carleton case, this type of interpretation issue, involving the weighing of several factors, needs a carefully reasoned approach with no local axe to grind and some degree of policy consistency.

The principle of equal justice where circumstances are similar and the ability to understand the uniqueness needed for a solution to a special situation must each be recognized and dealt with by planning tribunals. At the same time, decisions like these must involve, and be seen to involve, a concern for the principled application of provincial policy.

Different municipalities bordering on each other, often with similar land use and policy choices, acting without any oversight guidance, would each make their own land use choices. The problem is that those choices would be acted on by development companies and by organizations and individuals wanting the status quo preserved with very different results that would impact on each other down the road, with results that neither wanted. This happened in the County of Simcoe where two townships bordering on the city of Barrie each made policy choices, one by allowing numerous residential severances, and the other by choosing to go with a number of large commercial developments. In one case, the township lost its commercial area and more to the designated growth centre in Barrie. Subsequently, it lost its ability to exist as a viable municipality and disappeared in a governmental restructuring of the region. The other saw most of its former agricultural area get sliced up by residential lots and eventually most of it became part of the urban area.

Madame Justice Claire L'Heureux-Dubé J. of the Supreme Court of Canada wrote the following thoughtful comment on the struggles for justice and consistency, citing *Tremblay v Quebec* (*Commission des Affaires Sociales*) [1992] 1 SCR 952:

> Ordinarily, precedent is developed by the actual decision makers over a series of decisions. The tribunal hearing a new question may thus render a number of contradictory judgments before a consensus naturally emerges. This of course is a longer process; but there is no indication that the legislature intended it to be otherwise. Bearing this in mind, I consider it is particularly important for the persons responsible for hearing a case to be the ones to decide it.

> ... Recognizing the existence of a conflict in decisions as an independent basis for judicial review would, in my opinion, constitute a serious undermining of those principles. This appears to me to be especially true as the administrative tribunals, like the legislature, have the power to resolve such conflicts themselves.[18]

It is through the difficult decisions like the Essex case and others that a tribunal must come to grips not only with the ruling in the case but its members must look to the tribunal's own jurisprudence, with a view to the application or not of a provincial policy statement in a similar circumstance in the future and decide the present case on its own merits while articulating for future cases why the member is deciding as she is. Any tribunal takes time to work through its developing case law to arrive at a consistent approach to an issue.

What does the *Planning Act* mean when it said that the Board and municipalities, in making planning decisions, must have regard to government policy? The member in this case looked for guidance first to reasons in earlier OMB cases. The tribunal must "have regard to" government policies like the *Food Land Guidelines*,19 which remained the pre-1983 adopted statement on agriculture, or post-1983 statements like the Flood Plain Planning adopted under section 3 of the 1983 Act. It doesn't say that the Board must follow them; however, the Board is required to have regard to them. In other words, to consider them carefully in relation to the circumstances at hand, their objectives and the statements as a whole, and what they seek to protect. The Board is then to determine whether and how the matter before it is affected by, and complies with, such objectives and policies, with a sense of responsible consistency in principle.

In the Essex case, the presiding member then considered another approach to the same words, which went beyond consideration to circumstances that made it inappropriate or impossible to meet the policy. This last element seems well beyond the direction to have regard to a policy statement; it goes so far as to treat the policy statement like a statutory requirement with a rigid borderline saying, beyond this line be dragons. The member's sensible reworking of that approach encapsulated more clearly than either of these earlier approaches what I think the direction means. He restated the meaning of the words "have regard to" as requiring careful consideration of the words, the objectives and intended outcome(s) of the policy, the existence or not of ameliorating circumstances that make departure from its strict application fair and reasonable, and some consistency in applying its essential principles in similar situations.

The presiding member decided that in the Essex case, one of the objectives of the policy was to value and preserve large high quality wetlands, natural assets rare in Ontario. It was public policy not to allow development in the very type of wetland that he had before him, on a substantial portion of the Hearn property. He could see no way that he could rule against applying the policy statement. He was correct in deciding as he did.

There is much good sense and fair consideration in this decision. In the end, Hearn had lost nothing from what he had purchased – land in a high quality protected class of farmland, a woodlot and a forested swamp, which he had never bothered to check out for land restrictions, all of which was zoned to prohibit any use other than agricultural uses; one of those permitted uses could be the siting of one residence on the non-swamp land. The only difference now was that most of it was zoned to protect from development the forested wetlands instead of prime farmland. It was there to be enjoyed, as it had been when he bought it, for hunting, observation of marsh wildlife and hiking and perhaps for one residence. It just is not allowed to be a golf course or any active use that would prejudice its use for agricultural and conservation purposes. Nor was it when Hearn purchased it.

> ... an example of high quality reasoning and problem-solving of complexity and sensitivity.

This case engaged in a serious way what the proper planning principles should be in face of a declared public interest, in this case protection of a disappearing natural asset of provincial significance, a large forested wetland, and private rights of land ownership. Looked at in its entirety, it does not amount to, or engage the Board's policy against downzoning to the point of sterilizing land without due compensation. This was an example of high quality reasoning and problem-solving of complexity and sensitivity.

In presiding over a complex case, equal in difficulty to any in the court system, there is an art to it. The trick is to have the patience, the mental capacity, and the sensibility, together with knowledge of the law in the municipal field and equally important, the insight and logical creativeness to set it down in writing understandably for future use as part of the jurisprudence of the Ontario Municipal Board. A tall order, yes, but one that the best on this Board have risen to in difficult cases at least in my lifetime since the chairmanship and passionate leadership of Joseph A. Kennedy from 1960–72 and for some twenty years thereafter. The problems of today stem from the shake-ups caused by political changes in government and management decisions that have affected the selection process. These internal changes will be discussed in later chapters.

THE AMENDMENTS OF 1983 AND MERGER

The late 1960s and 1970s were a time of great discontent with municipal government. Centred in Toronto, a movement developed around the opposition to the Spadina Expressway. The Expressway became a symbol of the profound unhappiness many younger people felt, coming out of the freedom of the '60s, toward the 'business as usual' attitude of Toronto Council. The city bureaucracy and the executive committee were more familiar than was usual and the suspicion was of secret meetings where the real decisions were taken, the vote in public being only a gesture to democracy.

There were two directions where the reform movement attacked. One was the old boys' club attitudes at city hall and the closed nature of decisions at the council level. The second was the largescale urban renewal projects and apartment projects that were to replace older homes and whole residential areas causing people of lesser means to lose their only source of housing. Restoration of neighbourhoods and protection for old buildings that lent the aura of a different age replaced the demolition and destruction that the reformers saw the city allowing, and certain developers were perpetrating it without any real regard for those to be displaced.

From 1972 to 1980, David Crombie and later John Sewell headed Toronto Council as mayor, both ardent reform leaders. They conveyed a suspicious attitude about their predecessors and the present councillors in municipal government that some were not in it for the betterment of the city but to get their way at the expense of the city's older residential neighbourhoods. They succeeded in opening up city government to more receptiveness toward persons affected by city policies, particularly those in the development and planning areas. The crusade increased the already suspicious attitude most people had toward municipal politicians. Some of that came out of press coverage of the Drapeau mayoralty in Montreal and a sense that similar conspiracies were at work in Ontario municipal government as well.

Land use planning and conservation became the major way in which the reform movement took on city hall in the 1970s. They saw a parallel between the threat the Expressway posed to older city neighbourhoods and the destruction of other neighbourhood homes for large urban renewal projects like Trefan Court. The reformers saw these projects and the mindset behind them as deals between the city's inner governing group and developers without any public debate. Throughout the 1970s, restoration of neighbourhoods and of older structures and protection for heritage buildings and older residential areas in the city core became the concerns of city council. This change in priorities was mirrored in other municipalities in the province to a greater or lesser extent. It was a time when there was acceptance of the Board's role and mandate and of its value as a source of needed oversights. It was a time when the Board had sufficient numbers and diversity to match skill sets to the demands of particular hearings, a subject in which the chair Henry Stewart (1980–1990) took a personal interest on a daily basis. There were over thirty members at that time and multiple member panels on major hearings were the norm.

> Throughout the 1970s, restoration of neighbourhoods and of older structures and protection for heritage buildings and older residential areas in the city core became the concerns of city council.

When it came to media coverage of large-scale OMB hearings, the attitude of most parties who participated and of the reporters who covered those hearings was a sense of fairness with which all sides were treated, and that most parties received the attention their concerns warranted.

For instance, in September 1986, the Board completed a fifteen-week hearing into a detailed plan to develop the Railway Lands and to erect a dome stadium. Some two billion dollars was the estimated value of the development rights. The coverage in both the Toronto Star and the Globe & Mail stuck very much to the facts of the proposed development and to the patience of the panel throughout the summer long hearing. When the decision appeared, the unsuccessful parties commented only upon the detail and that they felt "incredulous" over the decision to approve with modifications but accepted it and hoped for better from the remainder of the decision, which was reserved. The railways did not get all they wanted but professed to be satisfied. Not one remark was reported questioning the bona fides of the Board, its place in the planning process or that it was an anti-democratic proceeding by an illegitimate Board.

Other major hearings in the 1980s included the Palladium case in Ottawa where coverage was, if anything, most complimentary and detailed by reporters who understood what had gone on during the hearing and the basics of the decision. The downtown North York plan decision concerning development rights of close to two billion dollars was regarded in the *Globe & Mail* of May 11, 1988 as "a reasonable trade-off, more protection for neighbouring residential areas for higher density development on Yonge St." A statement from the head of one residents' group, which had settled with the city on terms they were satisfied with – "The

Board has endorsed our accord. It shows you that cooperation with the city on planning is to everyone's advantage. Confrontation gets you nowhere."

A ground-breaking hearing under the *Rental Housing Protection Act* resulted in a refusal by the Board to approve a conversion from rental to condominium. The reporter for the *Star* on May 15, 1987 stated: "We now know – thanks to a clear logical ruling by the Ontario Municipal Board – that Bill 11 makes it next to impossible for landlords to escape rent control and make a fast buck selling apartments as condominiums." Later in the same article, written as a letter to the Premier: "The Board turned down the conversion. In a decision that runs for just 22 pages, the Board clarified the wording – in effect plugged the holes — in Bill 11 and blew away years of bull manure propaganda churned out by landlords." In not one of these examples was there any bitterness expressed or an attack levelled at the Board's role in the process. It was not only accepted but treated as an asset to the process. The Board had become the source and continuing authority on the planning process and solutions to any problems that came along.

In 1983, amendments had been made to the *Planning Act* and the *Municipal Act*, in company with other legislation related to municipal financing supervision; they changed the Board from a regulatory tribunal with its hand in virtually every municipal planning and financing decision to an appeal board with an enlarged jurisdiction to hear all matters from the beginning. It retained its independent authorization to deal with, approve, and modify or reject OPs, plans of subdivision, and OP amendments in place of the Minister of Municipal Affairs and its hearings continued to be de novo – from the beginning in each case.

At about the same time, in 1983 or 1984, the Land Compensation Board merged into the Ontario Municipal Board. Its numbers were not large but they were used to handling significant and difficult claims. The marriage of skill sets from the two boards made the whole a uniquely empowered and naturally suited group of talents. The OMB became responsible for expropriation matters, including issues of need for the expropriation and the hearing to fix the compensation for loss of and/or damage to land. As a whole, it retained power under a still innumerable number of statutes to authorize a myriad of matters – some in government still estimate the number at about one hundred statutes.

With these events, the Ontario Municipal Board became a truly unique tribunal in terms of late twentieth century Canada. The abilities of the members covered a great range of intersecting disciplines. A synergy developed through the enriching experiences of panels of people from differing careers yet all were associated with aspects of municipal governance. A lawyer would be deciding cases with an architect and a municipal administrator where building articulation, density mixes and evidentiary issues all moved through the same multi-handled sieve, or on another panel an ecologist would sit with a former municipal engineer on a case with flood plain and servicing issues.

It was a case of clustering of governmental bodies to the final degree before we knew the name as shorthand for reorganization; it was complete merger. I saw the OMB's evolution to a tribunal that could run an efficient hearing process that was nonpolitical, impartial and transparently public. One expropriation compensation practitioner from Toronto told me that we had no idea how admired the Ontario process was in the United States. American lawyers faced cases of expropriation claims where the court at trial would be of one political persuasion, and on appeal, the court would be dominated by judges from the other party, in each case with different scales of evaluation.[20]

One of the Board cases referred to above as exemplifying the image and treatment of the OMB in the late 1980s and early '90s was the so-called Ottawa Senators hearing. There have not been many where two sides took positions so strongly opposed; as the hearing commenced, they were virtual polar opposites.

BEING THERE 3: THE OTTAWA-KANATA HEARING, 1991

[Ottawa-Carleton (Reg. Mun.) Official Plan Amendment 8 (Re) (1991), 26 OMBR 132]

Out of the early 1990s, this case became a significant decision for the way the Board dealt with the problem of policy guidelines without a statutory development/urban line to mark a firm barrier to encroachment on agriculture. How the conflict between the abutting agricultural and urban mixed use areas, each with significant local cultural and historical significance behind them, was not clear at all. It also had to face the issue of incompleteness of the applications when they were before, and approved by, the regional and city councils.

The regional council of Ottawa-Carleton and the city of Kanata had approved amendments to the regional OP and the local zoning by-law for a multi-use centre with related hotel, office and retail facilities on a 100-acre block of land adjoining and inside the western urban area boundary of Kanata. But this was only part of what Bruce Firestone and his band from Terrace Investments Ltd. were working on. Their dream was to develop a whole town on six hundred acres and sell it lot by lot at a high profit. This entertainment centre/arena would be a central part of the new town.

And it was now more than a dream. Terrace and its partners had assembled the land for this purpose on both sides of the major expressway connecting Ottawa and Montreal to the south, Highway 417. They applied to develop the entire six hundred acres to establish the new town.

RETURN OF THE OTTAWA SENATORS

It was well known what one hundred acres of this overall proposal was for, immediately next to Highway 417. It was proposed to be the site of a new hockey arena-entertainment centre called the Palladium. Firestone required it as home ice for the planned return of the Ottawa Senators to the National Hockey League. So it was decided that the development applications to the region and to Kanata for the one hundred acres would be separated from the town idea and within nine months of the filing, by August 29, 1990, both the regional council and Kanata had approved the rezoning and both OP Amendments for the 100-acre site.

These council decisions were appealed under the provisions of the *Ontario Planning Act* to the Ontario Municipal Board. Those who appealed had no less riding on this hearing, both of themselves and their desire to stop the continuing reduction of the agricultural land base. They included the Ontario Ministry of Agriculture and Food (now the Ministry of Agriculture, Food and Rural Affairs), The Ontario Institute of Agrologists, the Federation of Citizens' Associations of Ottawa-Carleton and a number of individuals, supported by numerous farmers and other persons and institutions concerned about the loss of what was prime farmland including the United Church of Canada, and Senator Herbert Sparrow, a former Chair of the Senate Agriculture, Fisheries and Forestry Committee. For, while this 100-acre lot was within the western boundary of the city of Kanata, it formed part of an outer corridor, which was rural and farmed actively. The land was classed as high priority agricultural land.

The Ontario Ministry of Agriculture and Food (OMAF), unlike other objectors who came on their own, had the mandate and the knowledge to seek out able representation, expert witnesses to counter the benefits claimed by the proponents in infrastructure addition by a new interchange to serve the arena, economic benefits due to the draw in the market to the arena for hockey and other name entertainment, and extension of services to the site. The Ministry's counsel had studied his case, knew all the details about every alternate site in the Ottawa-Carleton region and had mastered even the page references to everything in the ministry's statement of provincial policy. He and his clients and their supporters would be ready for their arguments.

The experienced counsel recruited late in the process by the Terrace proponents had been brought in to take over a case that was incomplete at best. He was under severe pressure from Firestone and others to march to their drum of economic benefits and hockey mania, knowing that it was not the way to succeed at this level. He was too well aware that not enough planning and preferred site evidence had been provided to the regional and city councils to form a complete record on which their approvals were based. He knew that opposing counsel knew that too. In most hearings, that kind of gap before the municipal counsel alone could end it. This was probably one example of a case that would not have responded to mediation, had it been available. The tribunal was faced with a clash of forces, both with emotional, ecological or cultural rightness on their sides.

A FIRST FOR REGIONAL PLANNING?

The auditorium was full that first day. And unlike most other hearings, their numbers persisted and reached a crescendo in the final days of the eight-week hearing when the unrepresented public participants gave their evidence and the lawyers made their final submissions. There was daily television transmission from a spot in the hall designated by the OMB. Somehow that was not good enough; people had to come, to be there for at least part of a day or more. And of course many of the themes spoken of later by the people who came unrepresented were given full statistical treatment and planning rationales from the expert evidence called by the proponent and the agriculture ministry, the Agrologists and the Regional Municipality of Ottawa-Carleton.

Echoes of the same clash of views about the role of the OMB from the Spadina hearing resounded through the hall, as did some unexpected ideas. For instance, one individual, the head of a local firm that conducted public surveys, suggested that the Board should take into account the data from a sample poll of Ottawa public opinion. Many who supported the proposed facilities simply saw the Board as some strange body visited upon them by some alien power posing a real threat to interfere with the decisions of the local councils. Others who opposed seemed to accept that this kind of public hearing was a fair way of honouring democratic rights but the decision was clear to them – it had to be rejection of the Palladium proposal on the basis that a line in the sand must be drawn in order to preserve inviolate the rest of the agricultural land base.

> The OMB is in fact accountable to the legislature for ... conducting public hearings into development proposals and for determining their fate based on the evidence before it, provincial policy and the public interest.

There were few who knew that this Board had had a presence in the planning process from the beginning of community planning law in Ontario between 1906 and 1921. The OMB is in fact accountable to the legislature for conducting public hearings into development proposals and for determining the fate of those proposals based on the evidence before it, provincial policy, and the public interest. It must make its determinations by ensuring that they are consistent with provincial policy statements; before 2006 its decisions were measured in relation to provincial policy by the less strict test that they must "have regard to" it. The Board must also follow the common law and the procedures and principles in the *Planning Act*.

The OMB must judge for itself through the members assigned to the hearing what is in accordance with the principles of good planning. And it is not in the habit of interfering with decisions of elected councils unless they fail the test of consonance with good planning principles. This became a signature point for most of the Board after the Spadina hearing to the early 1990s. When the Board could not agree with the council's decision, the Board generally dealt with it specifically, showing exactly why the council decision could not stand. This was well before the 2006 amendments expressly requiring the Board to have regard to a council's decision on any appeal. The problem came from a minority of Board members who did not recognize the municipality's decision. The 2006 amendments made that clear: the Board "shall have regard to any decision that is made under this Act by a municipal council" (*Planning*

Act, section 2.1). It was already clear in law ever since 1965 and Hopedale Investments Ltd. v Oakville (Town).[21]

The planning process in Ontario establishes a policy of planning principles and independent review rather than political, economic or other forms of power and influence as the sole determining factors. It is the Board's job to understand and apply these principles in the wider public interest.

There is no doubt that OMAF and the Institute of Agrologists and their supporters made a persuasive case for protecting the good quality farmland in this case. But somehow, in little over a month of preparation time ahead of the hearing, any gaps in the proponent's case were plugged. All the proposed alternate sites were answered. But was it too late?

In the end, there were three elements that convinced the Board that it was not a case for intervention by the Board:

> i.   The preservation of at least five hundred acres of good agricultural land for continued consolidation as a viable farming area with the rest of the area west of Kanata and north and south. The threat was there, and very real, of this facility attracting to it a new urban area that would not have stopped at five hundred acres

> ii.   Nowhere in the regional OP was there a process in place, or an up-to-date bank of sites suitable, for this new major public building or attraction to locate, and there were no others available within the strict time limits Firestone and his team had to work with

> iii.   There are sometimes intangible matters or elements of a proposal, which speak beyond the perimeter of the specific proposal to the community's sense of itself and which evoke a deep sense of history, continuity and identity for that community.

As the Board's decision stated:

> The need for this facility consists of a particular combination of social, historical, and economic factors and circumstances whereby fundamentally and on balance the Board cannot find the Councils were wrong or acted against any planning principle in seeking to secure such (unique) benefits for this area. (Decision, p. 72)

Under cross-examination, the Ministry's expert witness on alternate sites had to concede that the earlier unsatisfactory record before the councils was now complete as it stood before the OMB. These lacunae in the Plan – the lack of a Major Facility process and no bank of available sites for one – left an entrepreneur like Firestone, or anyone else needing guidance on siting of a major facility and facing serious time limits on his own, with no policy guidance or bank of suitable sites to consider. In the end, even on OMAF's search evidence, there was no other site that could meet the time and site constraints for this proposal to work.

The other arm of the proponents' efforts came from the NHL requirements and time was a strictly limited commodity in that process. There must be a first time for everything and this sudden opening for a major community facility with wide support appeared to be a first for regional planning.

The large problem on which the issues were joined was whether the proposal failed to regard the *Food Land Guidelines,* the provincial statement of policy on agriculture. When it came to the siting for a Major Community Facility, the Guidelines did not close the door on it if there was evidence sufficient to justify locating it in a non-urban centre. In this case, no other suitable site was available and capable of readiness within the time set by the organizing agency, the NHL. The Board had no reason to second guess the regional and city councils who approved it; the site would receive no re-designation from Agriculture Resource Area in either the upper or lower tier OPs until the proponent had proven full NHL membership and unconditional guarantee of the franchise. This decision would form no precedent for introduction of urban uses into a rural area; the region must amend its OP to institute a buffer zone designation as an urban separator where the uses shall be maintenance yards and agricultural uses, with no rezoning allowed to permit residential or any other nonfarm use. In addition, the piped service extension to the Palladium would be sized only to service this one development. The Council was to designate it as a facility of major significance to, and part of the evolution of the regional community. No other urban use would be able to make such a claim and as such, justification for use under the Food Land Guidelines was demonstrated by the planning and agricultural experts called by the proponent Terrace Investments Ltd.

As matters have turned out, the resolve of the Regional government has remained firm and the land to the west, north and south continues to be farmed to this day with no indication of any immediate change in the future. In fact, it appears the Senators may now be looking to move to another site more centred near the downtown of the City of Ottawa where, for traffic reasons, it was regarded that this use was not a good fit due to the concentration of so many other attractions in that one area.

In the end, in a lengthy decision, the Board had to face numerous interesting and challenging issues. These included:

1. Putting an end to the parties' support and participation in the West Urban Community Expansion Study (which involved considerably more agricultural land than one hundred acres and the proponent's original town concept on six hundred acres)
2. Critical weighing of the claimed economic and social benefits
3. The intent and purpose of the *Food Land Guidelines*
4. Justification issues, alternative sites alleged

5. Urban options and timing
6. Site servicing without providing encouragement to others to stop farming
7. Sufficiency and provision of the transportation infrastructure without any funding from regional municipalities
8. Traffic impacts and requirements to meet them
9. Capacity of the arena entertainment centre in line with infrastructure capacity
10. Storm water management plan
11. Market capacity and need for the mixed use/arena facilities
12. Potential effects on agricultural uses
13. Inevitability and sustainability of neighbouring agricultural lands within the surrounding agricultural area
14. Assessment of regional plan criteria on conformity
15. Assessment of alleged alternative sites
16. Complexity of conditions to ensure net benefits to the region to be as promised
17. Five modifications to the Official Plan Amendment (OPA) and ten draft subdivision plan conditions
18. Meaning of the "have regard to" clause relating to the weight to be given provincial policy.

Having sat on complex matters in Superior Court, Divisional Court, and the OMB, decisions like this one are as difficult as, or even more difficult than, issues many judges must deal with. This decision is not, by any stretch, less challenging than many other decisions.

This was a hearing with a strong and important provincial interest supported by the presence of the lead Ministry to assist the Board in interpreting the *Food Land Guidelines* and to impress on the Board and the public the importance of protecting agricultural land under urban pressure. The action of the Ministry to lead the opposition to the arena for the Ottawa Senators is not one that is emulated by many. It is hard to understand why this is the case. The *Planning Act* in section 17(51) authorizes the Minister of Municipal Affairs and Housing to give the required notice at least thirty days before the commencement of the hearing of a provincial interest in the Board hearing. That interest may be part of the mission of any ministries provided it is an interest recognized within section 2 that is likely to be affected by the plan being put forward at the OMB. The Minister must identify the provisions of the plan by which the provincial interest is, or is likely to be, adversely affected, and the general basis for the opinion.

The notice conditions were not in the Act when the Ottawa hearing occurred. It is not an onerous process. They also were not in the Act when the OMB embarked on the Etobicoke Motel Strip Secondary Plan in 1991. Because of the wasted time that the Province caused, all parties at that hearing due to a late invocation of the provincial interest and no notice as to what exactly the provincial interest was, the Board levelled some direct criticism at the ministries involved and suggested several changes to the procedure including a minimum notice period and identification of the interest involved being two of those recommendations. The amendments to the provincial interest procedure followed belatedly, in 2004.

The effect of this kind of action by the Minister serves, together with the active participation of the ministry in charge of the subject area at the hearing, to dramatize the actual interest to be protected and to provide standing in order to bring evidence to the Board and to make submissions on the contents of the order at the end of the hearing. This occurred in the Etobicoke Motel Strip Secondary Plan hearing (the interest of the MOE in the common area and a special installation to protect the shoreline and the public using it) and in a subdivision hearing in Grey County to make immediate the concern of the MOE over subdivision practices and allowances where prominent river and groundwater systems were involved and needed protection. In the few cases where the Province has shown leadership like this, the evidence from the Province was generally helpful, in the subdivision test case crucial; it clarified the real interest at stake behind the policy words like nothing else can. The final benefit it provides is control of the result. The OMB decision is not final until the Lieutenant Governor in Council decides either to reverse it or approve it with or without changes as it touches on the provincial interest identified in the notice.

The policy of the Province toward agricultural issues, the *Food Land Guidelines*, was fully considered. The fact that the large erosion of agricultural land into urban use that was planned by the proponents of the Palladium and the area study contemplating several hundred more acres of urban sprawl were terminated was a positive result to the Ministry and to those interested in agricultural protection. The OMB decision was accepted and confirmed later by the Ontario Cabinet.

GOVERNMENTAL CHANGES: EFFECTS ON INDEPENDENCE AND CONSISTENCY

We started this trip into the heart of this administrative tribunal with the Spadina Expressway hearing and the words of the founder of the modern OMB, Joseph Kennedy. His decision was a minority opinion but its essential power harmonized with the temper of its time and paved the way for what followed. The chairpersons since then have been men and women of different times and style. Each has left a mark on the Board. No one has led the Board with the same drive and the same sense of the dramatic moment that Mr. Kennedy had. Though I never knew him, I understand from persons who did that no one could dominate the Board in the same almost dictatorial manner as he was able to. All of the chairpersons have understood, I think, the importance to the Board of its ability to make its own institutionally independent decisions through its members.

In urging the need for consistency in practice and in principle, I am in no way suggesting that independence is not important; I am simply suggesting that that independence is, or should be, a cultural and an institutional dynamic that informs the essential credibility of the organization. Independence does not match up with each member as it does with a Superior Court judge.

Independence is, or should be, an institutional and collective characteristic and status – sharing both a subjective and an objective state of mind – that each member shares in as part of the whole. Nothing is more important to the Ontario Municipal Board and performance of its mandate under the *Planning Act* than the ability in each case to hear evidence, make findings of fact and law, and interpret and apply government policy free of government pressure, direct or indirect, in each case. Each member should be free to discuss and be able to collectively come to general administrative and adjudicative policies freely but having a sense of what is necessary in the public interest and to best serve the Board's mandate. Any such policies should be publicly known as rules, practice directions, rulings in cases, and/ or best practices of the tribunal.

> " ... what has happened to and within the Board since the late 1980s and more so since 1995 is so damaging."

When Board members sit as a panel of the OMB on a compensation case under the *Expropriations Act* that panel acts and must be seen to occupy much the same position as a judge. The ability of the member or members making up a panel of the Board on a compensation case to act judicially, impartially and according to law must be uncompromising. It is not the same as sitting on a planning case. The adjudicators in a compensation case must in themselves be able to preside and rule in such cases with the required knowledge, authority and integrity, independent of any governmental pressure or influence.

The quality of independence that the OMB should bring to its decision-making within a policy-led process or on a hearing under the *Expropriations Act* should be seen to be transparent and real. It is precisely for this reason that what has happened to and within the Board since the late 1980s and more so since 1995 is so damaging.

We are coming now to a consideration of the road and the bumps in the road as the Board tried to find its way through the post-Kennedy years. The mandate of the Board, as a past Chair reminded me, is not necessarily the same as the actual role played by it. The mandate of the Board changed dramatically in 1983 when it ceased to be the municipal regulator, involved in every financial and planning initiative of local government, to act as an adjudicative planning appeals tribunal. At the same time, it was still performing its role as an independent tribunal existing within the executive branch of government.

In carrying out this mandate from its position within a government ministry, the Board's adjudicative duty was to interpret and apply government policy and the law to the facts of each case that came before it. It also assumed its duties at this time under the *Expropriations Act* to adjudicate compensation issues. In this role, it acted most closely to a civil court, hearing expert evidence, submissions of counsel on admissibility of evidence and making the decisions on how much money should be paid by government to individual landowners for loss of their land, injury to any remaining land by factors such as the irregularity of what was left, and disturbance damages.

In assuming these duties from the former land tribunal, it would be dealing with a different kind of claimant. In compensation cases, the claimants are virtually unique in the justice system. They have done absolutely nothing to attract or undergo an expropriation. And cases like this need a mechanism that can work quickly to try to resolve the matter through what is now the Board of Negotiation, a specialized group of appraisal-related professionals working part time. And for the ones that do not settle, a hearing is needed as soon as the preparatory work is completed. The OMB has been able to provide judicial services to this standard within its process, and it has been able to do so perhaps more effectively than the former board because its members have a familiarity with the planning process. Factors like the steps required and the kind of time various planning processes can take where the development potential of the land and comparative sales must be considered, in order to find the highest and best use of the land, are helpful in understanding the expert evidence on that subject. And time, in the sense of the distance in time from the expropriation date, is an important component of that exercise.

On the land use planning side, the Board began to deal more with government policy in the 1980s and '90s because a few ministries had started to issue such policies in a comprehensive form. Until the late '70s, the Board heard of government policy more in relation to individual initiatives and in a variety of ways. Sometimes the evidence of what policy was on a particular subject came from a minister's statement in the legislature. In one case, the announcement of policy took place right in the hearing room when the Provincial Treasurer and Minister of Economic Affairs had one of his officials deliver a letter on the projected population in 2010 to be accommodated by Barrie's annexation of land from neighbouring townships. By 1991, three comprehensive statements of policy were in use: the agriculture ministry's Food Land Guidelines (FLG), the Natural Resources ministry's aggregate policy, and the housing statement on affordable housing strategy. In applying government policy, the OMB was claiming to be, and acting as, an independent agency and yet was functioning from a ministry within the executive arm of government, the Ministry of the Attorney General. Chairman Kennedy put into words his approach to this part of the Board's mandate. In a decision in 1970, he used these words, which have a renewed resonance now that the setting and publishing of government policy is more comprehensively formalized:

> To say that the Board follows government policy is certainly not to say that it would or should seek to ascertain the wishes of the government, the executive branch, in a particular case and then decide as the executive council may request, or as any member of that council may request or suggest. No ...

> This Board applies (government) policy by considering and interpreting the statement of policy with the assistance of counsel after making findings of fact on the evidence before it much the same way as the Courts apply the law by

considering and interpreting the pertinent law after making findings of fact on the evidence before them. The Government states its policy as of general application and this Board interprets and decides how that policy applies to the facts of the particular case without assistance from the Government or any member and applies that policy for reasons which are given in writing and which are subject to appeal to the courts on questions of law and to the executive council on any question.[22]

The Board is duty bound to apply and interpret government policy as it sees it in light of the public interest and how the proposal may affect, or not, the public's convenience, health, or safety. It is not a court bound to follow precedent. It applies government policy as the Board interprets it within the factual matrix established by the evidence without assistance from anyone in the executive branch of government. This understanding of the distinction of the tribunal from the Courts and the Board's independent role of applying and interpreting government policy has since been a central principle of its operation. Its relation to the Ministry of the Attorney General and the officials of that office is maintained at arm's length.

The role is incredibly more important and complex now in this time of all-ministry-generated policy statements covering everything of significance in the Province from development patterns and economic prospects to aggregate water quality, urban boundaries and intensification of development within them, agricultural protection and archaeological/cultural heritage. And layered over that are the growth plan for the Golden Horseshoe Area as amended twice to date, the Greenbelt Plan and the Oak Ridges Moraine Plan for specific targeted geologic and hydrogeological formations. Slightly beneath the layers of provincial and growth policies lie the local and regional OPs.

> The Board is in no way bound to follow the interpretation of policy given it by a Ministry witness …

One of the paradoxes that the Board has had to live with is that, as a tribunal appointed by the executive branch of government, not by the Legislature, it is expected at least to pay attention to, interpret and apply government policy to the facts as it finds them. It must do so to the extent that the decision is to be consistent with the objectives, the intent and the meaning of the policy applied within the factual frame of the particular case. But the decision is to be the independent decision and reasons of the OMB. The Board is in no way bound to follow the interpretation of policy given it by a Ministry witness, though that witness's evidence would be scrutinized carefully.

Until the 1990s, members of the Ontario Municipal Board were basically appointed for life, or until the member decided to leave for another career. It was, by statute, a full-time job. Now, there are part-time and full-time members. In 1988, the appointment of members changed. At first, appointment changed to employment of members by a term contract of three years.

The present policy has evolved to appointing the member to a two-year term, followed by a three-year term and finally a term of five years. There is no tangible assurance that reappointment will occur but the expectation of the government and the appointee at the time of appointment is that, presuming the member does their job satisfactorily, the member is making a career move that will probably last ten years and will terminate at that time. However, many things can happen, especially in government where elections occur at least every four to five years and a change of government means all "assurances" from the prior government disappear.

The idea of term appointments for Board members means that near the end of each term, there is some degree of uncertainty as to the member's future. That may be slightly less so now because of the ten-year template but that template is not a contract for ten years; after two years, the tenure could be over, or after five years. This means that the member is beholden to the government of the day for his or her livelihood, presuming, as with most of us, that one's career provides one's principal income and interest. Most professional people in mid-career have no pension unless they are saving personally toward their retirement, something most intend to do but many do not in fact. Members of the OMB do become part of group pension and dental/medical plans.

The tenure by fixed term of Board members, who must of necessity work within and with government policy, is the most serious issue that the Board must cope with. It is difficult for anyone who consciously thinks about it to see this Board as independent where members are dependent on the same government to renew their term each two to three to five years. Even if the member is on the final five-year term, that member may realize that she needs an additional one to three years to take her to the next stage in life, such as retirement and starting on a pension income, or a company not ready to offer them a position at the moment of expiry of the term but can later. So the member must ask the government for an extension and is dependent on it for that extension. Several law practitioners spoke to me during interviews of a perception that Board members no longer act independently, given their lack of tenure.

The idea of term appointments was introduced by the Peterson Liberal government in 1988. Until then, members were appointed "at pleasure," a status that appeared from the literal words to place the appointee in a position of courting the Crown's or the government's favour to keep one's job. That was far from the truth. In practical terms, it was an appointment for life if you wanted it to be and the Board was treated as an independent agency. No government would dare to approach a Board member or discipline a member by sacking him or her if a decision did not go the way the government wanted it to. It just would not, and did not, happen. Government had too much to lose if it were seen to attempt to fix a case this way.

In 1988, Ian Scott, the Attorney General, proposed the idea of term appointment – actually, employment subject to a fixed term to be more accurate. He announced it to the Board as a corrective to the so-called insecurity of a job at pleasure. Three years was the original idea for the term of employment as a member.

Mr. Scott attended a dinner that the Ministry held as part of the Board's annual retreat. I remember it well. I had known Ian Scott since the days when we were both young lawyers and both of us were friends with members of the Brewin family. Scott worked in the Brewin law firm in the mid '60s. Andrew Brewin ran and won more times than I can remember in the east Toronto riding of Greenwood. In 1967, John Brewin decided to run as a candidate for the NDP in Don Valley, a riding held by a senior Conservative minister, Tom Wells. There were some upper/middle class wards in the riding and as young lawyers, Ian and I were assigned to canvas those areas for John Brewin, I think because we each were used to wearing a suit and tie and looked clean. The amazing thing about that race was that, as a first-time candidate, John ran more strongly than most observers thought he would. He almost upset Wells. And the area Ian Scott and I canvassed was either very close or the NDP may have won a poll or two there. It was a thrill to be part of that kind of campaign where the candidate appeared to have no chance and came so close to pulling off the upset of the night.[23]

At the dinner, Ian came around to each table. I give him full marks for bringing the news personally and talking to each of us to see if we had questions or comments. When he came to our table, he sat opposite me. After the usual pleasantries, and probably a witty remark from Scott, we talked about the term appointment concept. I tried to convince him that, if he were going to change the appointment scheme, he should make them for life because the position was a sensitive one, members made ministerial decisions on referral of OPs and plan amendments by the Minister of Municipal Affairs, and should not be treated liked hired hands. The talk was amiable to a point. But when I told him that he must think about this some more and not continue with the term employment idea, he became visibly angry. He hit the table with his right hand and declared, as best I can remember his words now: "This is not a matter for debate. We are the government. We set the policies. And you need to understand that we intend that you will carry out those policies."

And with that, he rose, excused himself and left to go to the next table. There was no doubt from the commencement of the term appointments to the Ontario Municipal Board that this was an exercise of government power.

The employment of members by term contract has played a part in the overall decline of respect, talent, diversity of professional experience, and of comparative

> "The employment of members by term contract has played a part in the overall decline of respect, talent, diversity of professional experience ..."

remuneration and benefits that set in since the late 1980s and early1990s. And it was only seven years after that dinner and the inception of term employment that a government displayed the power and flashed the message that failure to renew can send – either you get a sense of what we expect or you will be looking for a job.

The problem of political independence became more acute during the two changes in government at the provincial level from 1995 to 2003. It was not a factor during the Rae NDP government. In 1995, the Harris-led Conservatives won the election, ousting the Rae government. Shortly after that changeover, a member who had been appointed by the NDP saw his term approaching the time for renewal. The fact that he was appointed by the NDP was well known inside and outside the Board. There was no better person to choose in order to make a statement.[24]

It was late 1995 and early 1996. The first news that he received after he had broached the subject of renewal was that things were looking favourable and he should apply, the renewal was likely. Subsequently, a senior Board official asked to see him. He was told that there was a problem. The problem came from "an external source." By then, word was spreading through government and the tribunals that Mr. Harris wanted to clean house of prior appointments. This was an obvious one.

There was trouble from another direction by this time, too, and it was also political in origin. The member had presided over a hearing near Toronto at which two aldermen attended. They were members of the Conservative party. The subject of the hearing was a publicly funded housing project, which the two town councillors were opposing, at least partly on ideological if not somewhat delusional grounds. They complained to the Board and the upper echelons of government, accusing him of being a Marxist. They charged that he was biased against those opposing the project and them. They saw the fact of housing being funded by the government as a socialist idea that should not be supported. In fact, the real problem was that the Town had led no planning evidence whatsoever to support its opposition to the project. The member had delivered a decision supported by evidence-based reasons allowing the project to proceed. They complained in writing, letters that he saw. A few weeks later, it was quietly suggested to him that he should not request a renewal of his appointment. He did not take the suggestion. He was not renewed. As a result, he sued the government; the litigation was settled but on terms protected by a non-publication clause.

Since then, he has become an associate and now a partner in a highly successful development and planning law firm where he remains to this day. But the message was not too subtle and it was clear. If you want a future here, you had better have your antennae out before you make a decision on anything controversial. And for those dealing with the Board, the perception given by the term employment of members became stronger.

For instance, how can it be seen to act independently where a first or second year member who has left a career in the private sector, or a member in her fifth year, is alone on a hearing, knowing that that person is subject to renewal within one year? And the same pressures are there during the third term, especially in the final year before the fifth year starts. All the assurances that were given four years earlier mean little now as the fifth year renewal approaches. For something like a sports arena in a small city or an affordable housing project in a quiet well to do neighbourhood in North Bay or Toronto with sizeable neighbourhood opposition whose government connections are unknown but possible, or a development control by-law affecting one of the major development companies, it would not be wise to court disapproval in a close case during, for instance, the Harris government's time in office.

When the McGuinty-led Liberals gained power in 2003, according to a development lawyer who remembers, one of the first things they initiated was planning reform. This meant that they wanted to clean house at the OMB because the people they would want would simply not agree with the appointees of the Mike Harris government. A number of new members were appointed by the McGuinty government as others retired. The political instability resulting from the changes on the Board and the huge changes in planning policy and legislation from 1990 to 2010 has "led to a degree of uncertainty on the Board and lack of tenure of members does nothing to solve that problem." As one development lawyer put it to me in graphic terms:

> I regard the OMB as useful and necessary to the planning process. It allows people who have an interest or a concern to appeal and that is an important right. But the most important development in the last few years is the degree to which hearings before the Board go into mediation. The reason for this is that the parties are so afraid of the outcome that they prefer mediation. The outcome is so unpredictable. The cost of a Board hearing is so high that the threat of having to go through it has a real bite.

> This part (lack of tenure) of the system does not work well. There is no question that the shortness of the term makes Board members nervous. It leads to instability and uncertainty in decision-making. The bigger question stands from the way in which the Board was treated during the last couple of changes in government at the provincial level. When the Liberals got in, one of the first things they reached for was planning reform. This meant that they have to clean house at the OMB because the people they would want would simply not be the appointees of the Mike Harris government. The political instability resulting from the changes on the Board and the huge changes in planning policy and legislation has led to an unfortunate degree of uncertainty on the Board and the term appointments do nothing to solve that problem. The government must know that these members live in fear and there is one obvious reason for that – they want the Board members to toe the line.[25]

Others within the planning and legal professions have talked to me about the issues over independence and tenure. A sampling of their views follows.

> "The main problem is that the Board is underfunded and while I do not want to say that the members or some of them are not competent, they are overworked and face a very demanding job. One possible problem could be political influence, I am not sure. I hope that the Board will continue to be objective, it has to be, to do a proper job, but there is a serious concern about possible political influence."[26]

"The term of appointment is too short. I was against this type of appointment when the Attorney General Scott brought it in. It puts the Board members under a subtle pressure to act as the government would want."[27]

"I think the most important role the Board has is to provide an independent arbiter using planning grounds and it acts as an interpreter of planning policy. The problem is that it is not perceived today as independent and the root cause of that is the limited tenure of members. That is the single largest credibility issue that the Board has. The Bar Association for years has been trying to persuade the province to change the tenure but it refuses."[28]

"The three-year term is very much unacceptable to me. It leaves open the likelihood that the member will be influenced in his/her decision-making by their perception of what the government wants."[29]

"About independence, I think when it is a close decision, the member is influenced to decide in the way that member sees as preferred by the government. I read some decisions and really cannot understand how the particular decision was reached. When you question the decision with others, you often hear that that member was up for renewal at that time."[30]

"About the term of three years, there is too much risk of political influence or bias playing a part because of the shortness of the term. Because of the importance of the Board, there should be some process of appointment like that of judges where the members of the bar and other professional groups of which the applicants are members may comment on their abilities, competence, and suitability for the job. There should be some emphasis in attempting to get a better mix of racial and cultural minorities on the Board because of different customs which will come up."[31]

The Liberal government changed the policy of term employment of members. However, it changed the terms in law not at all. They government stated that tribunal members appointed to any tribunal would hold the job for ten years, the terms in law being two years, three years followed by five years. At each interval, there was no assurance that was legally binding to insure that the member was not refused a renewal and so the terms remained in effect.

The perception remains that members of the Board are subject to pressure not to go too far from what they sense would be the disposition expected by the government. No member has said as much, except for an anonymous member talking about this subject with a law practitioner of experience before the Board.[32] The member is reported to have told him that he was not comfortable in the dying days of his term with making difficult or unpopular decisions.

Practitioners who were asked about independence of the Board all agree that they believe members are influenced to decide in the direction that member sees as preferred by the government, especially in the three to six months before their term is to expire. The important point is that most advocate practitioners of law who frequently appear regularly at the Board perceive that members are affected by it to some degree, some more, some less, when the member is close to term's end. And that is a very serious problem for a Board whose strongest characteristic used to be its independence from government.

This is one area to which the government should give serious consideration. The tenure issue has to be faced and corrected to preserve some credibility for the Board in the long term. A strengthening and targeting of suitable candidates in the appointment process, wedded to longer terms with some tangible expectation of renewal, absent cause for dismissal, or lifetime appointments, should be a priority of the 2016 governmental review. The problem with lifetime (to sixty-five) appointments is obvious. Not all persons who are appointed make a satisfactory adaptation from their past careers. Sometimes, the person who is appointed has been marked as a favoured person for political reasons. Appointees who have no inclination or drive to work at this job must be axed early before they have a chance to hurt the tribunal, a neighbourhood or parties. With appointments, that is easier said than done because some people have a political protector who is well placed in the government in power. On the other hand, in order to secure qualified people of some distinction for what is a quasi-judicial and mediating role of serious demands in time and days and weeks away from home, a first term of two years with no assurance of renewal is simply not sufficient. On the tenure issue, a number of practitioners were concerned enough to give me their opinions.

> "The tenure issue has to be faced and corrected to preserve some credibility for the Board in the long term."

- "What you want are candidates in mid-career who have energy and enough experience to have the ability and you cannot get those people when there is no security of tenure and you are faced with the rule that on leaving, you cannot practice before the Board for two years and the problem is about to get extremely serious. The government has made it known that it is going to remove everyone from the Board who has been there for ten years or more. This means that some of the best members will be lost soon. That will leave only four members who have more than five years of experience. Another part of the problem is the rate of pay ... the remuneration keeps being frozen as it has been for many years."[33]

- "The province is not doing enough to educate the public about the difficult task that the Board has and the respect that it is due ... The Board's term is much too short. It is like tying one hand behind your back when you are really trying to obtain capable people."[34]

- "I would like to see lifetime appointments, like a judge. That gives you a lot of experience, history and context instead of losing members and their experience regularly ... there should be some checking on their abilities, the way that enquiries are made before a judge is appointed. Board members are making decisions on matters worth far more money than most judges have to decide. They should be treated more like judges."[35]

- "People are not getting three year terms necessarily; some are being renewed for only one year or part of a year."[36]

- "First of all, the government must start staffing the Board fully. Its membership is sadly depleted. I like the idea of having members who are trained in mediation techniques ... The principal ways to improve the Board are new members, proper funding, more mediation, more staffing and have the government explain adequately to the public what the OMB is about and why it deserves respect for what it does."[37]

- "Members must be appointed for life and they must be appointed to a properly resourced body. That means that there must be access to research and there has to be a sufficient number of qualified members to provide the kind of mixed panels at hearings that are required."

Q. Do you think that the current closed process of appointment by an office of the Ontario cabinet is in tune with the requirements of the Ontario of 2015?

- "No. It is not. Whatever the process will be, it must provide the assurance that the members are competent and can do the job ... one thing I wanted to add was that whether they use clustering as in ELTO, there must be standards of appointment and a properly resourced board to do the job. One last thing that should be added is that the Board can only send one member to a hearing now and so there is no combination of job experience which can be brought to bear in a complicated planning issue. Often, planning issues involve matters of architecture, engineering, and environmental expertise, together with land use planning, and the need for legal experience to run the hearing. The former practice of sending members of different job experience was very helpful to the credibility of the decision and those kinds of planning issues."[38]

To the public who read the local and regional news, the OMB has become a controversial and largely pro-developer tribunal, which is responsible for the many ills of the planning process, from the continued urban sprawl out from Toronto to an anti-democratic agenda and anti-resident mindset. Municipal councils' decisions escape much criticism now because they have legitimacy with the public: they are elected by the inhabitants of their town or city. That is in sharp contrast with the informed public views of the OMB and of municipal government in the 1960s and early '70s and forward into the 1990s.

THE COURTS' NEW GENEROUS APPROACH TO MUNICIPAL POWER

In the 1990s, a new attitude of heightened understanding toward municipalities and the powers needed to govern at the local level began to take hold in the courts in Canada. It was not anything extreme, an attitude more than an ideology. A court would not interpret the words of a statute as if they were different words, but the courts would look harder at the purpose of legislation to try to ensure that if an activity was to be regulated municipally, the powers needed to do so should follow. Since the 1990s, municipalities in Ontario have been accorded more latitude than ever before by the courts to govern themselves and find their own solutions. Present Chief Justice McLachlin wrote the following in what was a dissent in 1994, but now her words have become one of the most cited excerpts from any court judgment over the last thirty years:

> Recent commentary suggests an emerging consensus that courts must respect the responsibility of elected municipal bodies to serve the people who elected them and exercise caution to avoid substituting their views of what is best for the citizens for those of municipal councils. Barring clear demonstration that a municipal decision was beyond its powers, courts should not so hold. In cases where powers are not expressly conferred but may be implied, courts must be prepared to adopt the "benevolent construction," which this Court referred to in Greenbaum, and confer the powers by reasonable implication. Whatever rules of construction are applied, they must not be used to usurp the legitimate role of municipal bodies as community representatives.[39]

And seven years later, Justice L'Heureux-Dubé wrote along similar lines for the Supreme Court majority, dealing with a municipal by-law restricting the use of pesticides in the Town of Hudson, Quebec:

> The case arises in an era in which matters of governance are often examined through the lens of the principle of subsidiarity. This is the proposition that

lawmaking and implementation are often best achieved at a level of government that is not only effective, but also closest to the citizens affected and thus most responsive to their needs, to local distinctiveness, and to population diversity.[40]

In 2003, the Court of Appeal applied these authorities to a *Planning Act* case involving land use policies.[41] The City of Toronto approved an amendment (OPA 2) to its official plan, which established a series of policies aimed at preserving, maintaining and replenishing the supply of rental housing throughout the city. Several property owners, developers and associations of owners of rental residential property, including Goldlist Properties Inc. (Goldlist) appealed the adoption of OPA 2 to the Ontario Municipal Board. The OMB found that OPA 2 was illegal and invalid on the grounds that: (1) it was outside the powers conferred upon the city by the *Planning Act*; and (2) it conflicted with the *Tenant Protection Act*. The city appealed. The judgment, co-written by Morden and Sharpe JJ.A,. held that OPA 2 was within the city's authority under the *Planning Act*, section 16 to adopt OPA 2 and that there was no conflict. In addition, the court ruled that it was beyond the powers of the OMB to declare the city by-law invalid but it was within its jurisdiction to answer whether OPA 2 was an official plan as meant by the Act. The court stated unanimously:

> 55] In our view, given the overall framework of the Act and the purpose of official plans, this specific legislative directive that the municipality should address the adequate provision of a full range of housing provides strong statutory support for the City's authority to adopt OPA 2. The legislature and the Minister have both made it clear that attending to the housing needs of its residents is a matter requiring the attention of the municipality in the exercise of its statutory powers related to land use planning. It follows, in our view, that when defining the planning "goals, [page 460] objectives and policies" that are to govern its planning decisions, a municipality is entitled to include "goals, objectives and policies" related to ensuring an adequate supply of rental housing.

> 57] We are fortified in our reading of the scope of the City's authority with respect to OPA 2 by recent jurisprudence that has emphasized the importance of enhancing local decision-making and avoiding narrow and technical readings of municipal powers. In 114957 *Canada Ltée (Spraytech, Société d'Arrosage) v. Hudson (Town)*, [2001] 2 S.C.R. 241, 200 D.L.R. (4th) 419, at para. 21, the Supreme Court of Canada stated that the courts should accord municipal powers a liberal and benevolent interpretation, and that only in the clearest of cases should a municipal by-law be held to be ultra vires, and approved the dictum of McLachlin J. in *Shell Canada Products Ltd. v. Vancouver (City)*, [1994]

1 S.C.R. 231, 110 D.L.R. (4th) 1, at para. 19, "barring clear demonstration that a municipal decision was beyond its powers, courts should not so hold."

There is no doubt in all this that the power of municipalities to act is to be considered generously by the courts. "Barring clear demonstration that a municipal decision was beyond its power" means the onus is on the person asserting ultra vires to so demonstrate. This judicial revision concerns the interpretation of municipal powers. It does not mean that all municipal decisions, including those that are not questioned as being ultra vires like a municipal decision on a zoning amendment, are to be treated in the same way. Under the *Planning Act*, the Board is directed only to have regard to municipal decisions, the lower level of deference. However, even that level does mean some respect is to be shown their decisions; such decision may not be simply written off as beyond a council's collective understanding as the OMB did in the Waterloo Official Plan decision in 2013.

The new 2001 *Municipal Act* in fact recognizes municipalities as a level of "responsible and accountable governments" with "powers and duties under this Act and many other Acts for the purpose of providing good government" with respect to matters within their widened jurisdictions. The Association of Municipalities of Ontario (AMO) is given constitutional status as the representative organization for Ontario municipalities. The Province obligates itself to "consult with municipalities in accordance with a memorandum of understanding entered into between the Province and the Association of Municipalities of Ontario."[42]

By this time, some municipal governments had become restless and wanted to take on more decision-making in the planning process without being answerable to a provincial tribunal like the OMB. The *Municipal Act*, 2001, in expressly granting recognition to municipalities as a level of responsible government, and by bestowing on municipalities wide spheres of jurisdiction within which they are given the power to regulate and prohibit conduct, have recognized wide areas within which they have some freedom to regulate and prohibit without having to make sure each item of action is authorized by the Province. Later in the new *Municipal Act* some of the minutiae have crept back in but the fact remains that the Act bestows power in wider chunks than ever before and no longer subjects municipalities to the prohibition of discrimination. It allows municipal governments much the same freedom that the Provinces have to act within their spheres of authority and they do so. It is a recognized level of government that the Province must confer with on an official intergovernmental level.

It was not clear what the judicial change in approach to municipal powers and discretion meant for tribunals like the OMB that regularly faced appeals from municipal decisions. That dichotomy of thinking between the courts and the OMB remained quiet until an appeal by development companies from parkland policies adopted by Richmond Hill, a case of discretionary authority granted to municipalities, which the Board saw fit to cap at a maximum dedication or cash in lieu. It was appealed successfully by the municipality to the Divisional Court, reported as Richmond Hill (Town) v Elginbay Corp., 2016 ONSC 5560. It now is under appeal to the Ontario Court of Appeal. The seminal issue is whether the OMB has the authority, as part of its power to modify official plans in what it sees as the public interest in commercial certainty, to place a finite limit on a discretion granted the municipalities in the *Planning Act* over the amount of parkland dedication or cash in lieu to be exacted on subdivision applications.

CHAPTER III

THE ALLEGATIONS

These words are like razors, they come not singly...
from Titus Andronicus, Act 1, Scene 1

The following paragraphs comprise excerpts from comments of individuals, councillors, press reports and editorial remarks, and documented works with conclusions about the Ontario Municipal Board. I think this list captures much of the current disillusionment, upset and cynicism that continues about the OMB.

MEDIA CRITICISM

From The Toronto Sun, September 2014 "Time to take some of Ontario Municipal Board's power away"[43] by Christina Blizzard, Queen's Park Columnist

TORONTO – The Ontario Municipal Board is unaccountable, out-of-control and too often bows to developers, say its critics.

It's adversarial in nature, costly for communities to fight and arbitrary in some of its decisions, they claim.

And its wreaking havoc on local decision-making, say planners, politicians and local resident groups who've tried battling highhanded decisions by the unelected body.

The OMB routinely overrules decisions made by local councils and has thwarted municipalities in their attempts to slow urban sprawl.

Toronto has a large, sophisticated planning department that's more than capable of deciding on densities and other planning needs for the city's unique neighbourhoods.

Former New Democrat MPP Rosario Marchese is a long-time critic of the OMB. Marchese says the OMB has become a law unto itself.

"The OMB has tremendous power not just to adjudicate, but to create its own policies which I believe is wrong," Marchese said.

It often overrules or ignores the province's own *Places to Grow Act* that sets out rules for development.

I believe more and more cities want to have the power to do their own planning," Marchese said ... Premier Kathleen Wynne mentions OMB reform in her letter to Municipal Affairs Minister Ted McMeekin. She asked McMeekin to review the 'scope and effectiveness' of the OMB."

Marchese isn't optimistic. He says a previous promise to reform the OMB resulted only in changes that were favourable to developers.

McMeekin, a former small-town mayor, agrees the OMB is too adversarial. "We would like to see more conciliation, negotiation and less of an adversarial approach," McMeekin said.

From the National Post, April 10, 2014, "Urban Sprawl: Time to scrap quasi-judicial unelected and unaccountable Ontario Municipal Board" by Josh Matlow and Kristyn Wong-Tam, Toronto city councillors

The Ontario Municipal Board (OMB) is a quasi-judicial, unelected and unaccountable provincial body that has the final say on all planning decisions in Ontario. The tribunal's powers to overrule decisions made by elected municipal representatives are anti-democratic and often lead to planning decisions that support the development industry over our communities and our official plan ...

Toronto is growing quickly. Our city's planning staff should spend their time designing complete neighbourhoods with access to transit, vibrant business areas, green space and social supports. Unfortunately, they spend too much time defending appeals by developers at the OMB. It's time to free Toronto from the OMB.

From Toronto Star, August 27, 2013, "How the OMB stifles democracy in Ontario"[44] by Martin Cohn, Politics columnist

The Senate isn't the only unelected, unaccountable body that likes to second-guess our democratically elected representatives.

Perhaps you've heard of the Ontario Municipal Board? The OMB may lack the high profile of the Senate, and its appointees don't make headlines for bogus expense claims.

But the OMB's legacy of meddling makes it no less notorious. After decades of overruling city councils across the province to side with powerful developers, it has a reputation for favouring special interests over the public interest.

Now the OMB is itself getting a second look. A creature of Queen's Park, it has just picked a fight with the province that it probably can't win.

Last week, after months of public musings, the Liberal government announced a review of OMB operations. It will seek public feedback and try to streamline the way this quasi-judicial body – unique in North America – overrules city halls and overreaches into provincial governance ...

... In a closely watched move, Waterloo Region is taking the OMB to court over a bizarre ruling that granted developers access to more than 1,000 hectares of prime farmland. Waterloo's OP had restricted future development to 85 hectares of urban lands designated for intensification – in line with the provincial Places to Grow Act but land-hungry developers appealed to the OMB and won. Hence the pushback from city hall, and the call for public feedback out of Queen's Park. In a rare move, the government has also joined Waterloo's formal court challenge against the OMB."

Critics argue that the OMB too often serves as a surrogate planning board, allowing developers with deep pockets to do an end-run around Toronto's planning department. That's antidemocratic.

From Toronto Life, September 2015, "The Ossington strip is getting a mid-rise, whether it wants one or not"[45] by Steve Kupferman

After more than two years of opposition by neighbourhood residents, the inevitable has happened: the Ontario Municipal Board has given its go-ahead to 109OZ, a six storey, 87 unit condo building planned for the site of a former auto repair centre on the Ossington strip, near Argyle Street. The OMB's decision preempts any attempt by city council to scale back the project, meaning Ossington dwellers have little choice but to get used to it.

From Waterloo Region Record, August 13, 2013, "Region alleges bias in OMB decision on future development"[46] by Jeff Outit

Regional council is now alleging bias by the provincial tribunal that ruled against it, in a deepening dispute over suburban growth. Politicians made the rare allegation Tuesday, announcing they will ask a court to rule if the Ontario Municipal Board acted unfairly in ruling against council earlier this year. The planning dispute turns on the amount of land available for development by 2031. Council wants 80 hectares preserved. In a controversial ruling, the tribunal sided with developers in endorsing up to 1,053 hectares.

The allegation of bias turns on the involvement of consultant Jeannette Gillezeau. Council says she testified for developers on methodologies involving land budgets, and that tribunal members relied on her evidence. At the same time, council claims Gillezeau helped train tribunal members on land budget methodologies in a private session. This causes "many, many questions for us," regional planning commissioner Rob Horne said. In a release, council said "this has serious implications for procedural fairness" based on the potential for "inappropriate interaction" between the tribunal and a key witness for developers. The Ontario Municipal Board would not comment.

Regional Chair Ken Seiling could not say how much the court action will cost taxpayers. "It's not cheap, but it's such an important principle," he said. Critics assert the tribunal's ruling contradicts provincial legislation and undermines council's plan to restrain suburban growth. "I think the stakes are very high," Horne said.

POLITICAL AND ACADEMIC CRITICISM

(a)   Waterloo Chronicle, May 28, 2014, "Proper Planning."[47] Statement by Catherine Fife, MPP Kitchener-Waterloo, Ontario New Democratic Party

"... It is clearly time for sensible, accountable OMB reform. In 2009, the Liberals inexplicably gave up the power to review OMB decisions. In 2013, it exempted the OMB from the Land Use Planning Review. They have made the OMB accountable to no one, left Ontario as North America's only jurisdiction in which local government can be overruled by an unelected body, and wasted an immense amount of tax dollars on appeals and court cases."

(b)   Waterloo Chronicle, May 28, 2014, "Proper Planning." Statement by Stacey Danckert, Ontario Green Party

"Clearly, the OMB needs to be revamped to emphasize the needs and desires of municipalities. This includes providing a clear mandate in line with the Places to Grow Act, which also needs to be strengthened to limit exemptions that allow for urban sprawl..."

From Passing The Buck: The Ontario Municipal Board and Local Politicians in Toronto, 2000-2006,[48] by Aaron A. Moore

(Excerpt from a paper presented for the Canadian Political Science Association 2009 Annual Conference Ottawa, Ontario, 27–29 May 2009)

The Ontario Municipal Board is an extraordinary gift to politicians. Though never designed for the purpose, it now has the role of deciding many of the difficult planning issues which elected representatives are glad to shirk (Cullingworth 1987, 436). J. B. Cullingworth made this comment, concerning the effect of the Ontario Municipal Board (OMB) on Ontario's municipal politicians, in his survey of Canada's planning institutions. He also added that the Board "nicely allows politicians to abrogate the responsibilities which properly fall on them" (Cullingworth 1987, 440). Cullingworth is not alone in suggesting that local politicians in Ontario will use the Board as a means to avoid decision-making on land-use issues. Toronto's media increasingly has identified such behaviour among the city's local politicians...

Even former councillor Paul Sutherland suggests that "many councillors have complained about the OMB, even though when they have finished complaining, they are wink winking: 'Thank God, it was there'" (quoted in Rusk 2005, A26). If such anecdotes are true, then local politicians in Canada's largest city may be using the existence of the Board to negotiate what Paul Kantor describes as the "explosive dilemma," a political system increasingly open to citizen input in conjuncture with an erosion of municipal governments' leverage over businesses (Kantor 1988, 5). This paper examines whether and how the OMB influences the behaviour of local politicians in Toronto.

I hypothesize that the OMB erodes a vital resource for local politicians by removing their power of final decision-making on planning issues, but in so doing, actually allows local politicians more flexibility in tackling what Kantor so ominously calls the "explosive dilemma." The OMB allows local politicians in the city to avoid making a decision between the wealth of developers and the support of the electorate.

From A Law Unto Itself: How the Ontario Municipal Board Has Developed and Applied Land Use Planning Policy,[49] by John Chipman

... a clear conclusion arising from this study is that the Ontario Municipal Board has outlived its usefulness as a planning review tribunal. Underlying the conclusion that the review of local planning decisions is preferably carried out by a tribunal is the assumption that a review is required at all. It appears evident from the analysis of the OMB's decision-making, however, that it no longer performs a necessary role in Ontario's planning system; that, if anything, it makes the planning process more complex, time-consuming, and expensive. Most importantly, it places the ultimate decision-making authority for land use planning which is in its essence a political process, in the hands of appointed non-accountable officials...

Most of the province's population ... are now found in large municipalities whose councils are regularly dealing with planning policies and development proposals and with the conflicts these can generate.

These municipalities have considerable planning expertise available to them. Nor is this experience and expertise limited to larger municipalities, as the administration of planning controls has become customary throughout the province. As the board has not been contributing something beyond this, such as ensuing that provincial policies are being followed, resolving inter-municipal disputes, or considering the implications of major planning or development patterns, it is making decisions that many municipalities are equally well equipped to make.

... This leads us to consider a legal rationale, frequently given for retaining the OMB's planning review function, namely that a tribunal functioning in a quasi-judicial manner is required to ensure that the rules of natural justice are applied in determining the rights of property owners ... But other provinces have achieved the same result by establishing public hearing requirements prior to the adoption of official plans and zoning by-laws which are considerably more stringent than those found in Ontario's Planning Act.

"Rethinking the Role of the OMB in the Planning/Development Process in Toronto"

This white paper proposal for a changed process in Toronto using an independent and diverse set of professionals on area Planning Advisory Committees suggests that where the planning staff, the Planning Advisory Committee (PAC) and City Council each vote for or against a proposal and all three agree, in those cases, no appeal will be allowed to the OMB. The authors suggest the following:

> The Current financial, regulatory, governance and community environment in which city planning operates generally creates conflict and can often result in the need for adjudication at the OMB putting at risk the prospect for achieving maximum opportunities for positive city building.

> But there is still a place for a re-formed oversight body with stronger emphasis on resolution, consistency and accessibility, for major cases where development engages provincial and Official Plan policies that have regional consequences and, for site specific matters, limited to cases where the key Toronto decision-makers cannot reach consensus.

> We need a modus operandi for Planning that enhances the decision-making process through meaningful dialogue... in an open and transparent setting and not within the rigid confines of a "judicial tribunal".[50]

-oooooo-

In addition to published criticisms, there is another aspect to the dark side of the OMB that is remembered but not documented. That is, the bullying and rude behaviour of several male members in the 1980s and before. I observed some of these episodes as a lawyer and as a colleague between 1975 and 1989 approximately. This does not apply to current members. This dark side was touched on as early as 1972 by the Select Committee of the Legislature because of complaints about certain members' behaviour. The Committee described the behaviour as lacking in

"This does not apply to current members."

patience and courtesy. It stated that this kind of behaviour triggered a right of any citizen to complain to the Attorney General.

For instance, take the case of a rezoning of a site from Institutional-H to remove the holding symbol and allow the construction of a school. A middle-aged woman comes forward when the public were invited to voice their objections. She speaks of why she wanted the site to stay as a green site and that if a school was built there, she would lose a natural area and she could no longer have a view of the rise of land beyond. The place obviously meant a lot to this person for meditation and periodic need for solitude. One of the Board members might say, loudly and impatiently, something to this effect:

> This is ridiculous. You have no right to have someone else provide a park for your personal pleasure for free. And why do you think you are entitled to a view where it is over someone else's property. How dare you come here and take a position like this. Everything is fine while someone else has to provide for your personal happiness."

This gives the flavour of what this kind of dressing down sounded like. And it would be said with a sarcastic edge to the member's voice. Of course, the substance of what is being said is correct but the arrogance of the tone and the language obscures the point needlessly and hurtfully.

There were not many members who would act this way but they are remembered, not well, by too many of the public who had genuine concerns that they wanted to express and were not listened to, nor was their dignity as human beings respected. To them, the OMB became an arrogant, anti-democratic tribunal, which could not have had the public interest in their hearts or minds.

Today, the behaviour that attracts negative comments and encourages critical attitudes is of a different variety. Some members, not many and definitely a minority, simply do not fully understand the role of the Board in the planning process and are less than knowledgeable about the tribunal's importance and the powers that the Board has. Their decisions are often short, to the point of not telling those who came to the hearing what exactly it was that caused the member to accept certain evidence over their own.

Most importantly, a judicial or tribunal decision should tell the parties, particularly the losers, how the decision was arrived at and the steps taken and the evidence tested to ensure that the result was the only just verdict. It continues to be an ongoing problem, which the Board must fix, if it is to continue to exist as a planning review tribunal. There is no great solace to anyone when the presiding member, who has been seen apparently noting evidence throughout the hearing on his computer, is seen at the end to take a few minutes to complete his typing. Then it is printed off on one or two pages and read out as the member's decision. This is a tribunal member who has really considered seriously what he has been hearing? Yet within fifteen to twenty minutes he dismisses the losing parties' evidence in a few sentences that show no real capture of the meaning of what they thought they had told him. And a structure that will last a lifetime is ratified, or lost in ten to twenty minutes.

Expressing the reasons for decisions in direct, comprehensible language is not easy but the duty of fairness, in requiring an open transparent process, requires the effort to be made. It requires work from the newly-appointed Executive Chair of ELTO to ensure that members now and in the future get this. Chapter XI yokes together decision-making and reasons for decisions as an important and interrelated team of subjects that have not attracted the interest that they should from government. Chapter XII relates selection procedures to both, in recommending a package of reforms that are interdependent and mutually reinforcing.

THE WATERLOO REGION OFFICIAL PLAN HEARING AND FALLOUT: NEED FOR EDUCATION

A recurring situation that requires a Board response and action stems from the high conflict, major policy hearings that result in a decision that lacks any reasonable public explanation, at least from what the media decide to report. This is an example of the type of troubled waters created by the Board's failure to explain in its decision, or through a spokesperson to the media, how it was dealing with provincial policy and yet appearing to mollify developers in the Waterloo Region OP hearing referred to scathingly above.[51]

The Board was accused of the most serious conduct for a provincially-appointed appeals Board, part of whose role and responsibility is to have regard to important statements of provincial policy. In effect, it appeared to have compromised its duty to oversee the implementation of provincial policy objectives for no good reason. To the public, through the filter of the media, a number of large development companies hired good lawyers and got their way over a region that was trying to implement provincial policies intended to protect prime agricultural land by establishing a secure boundary for the urban area and intensify development in the urban area. Furthermore, the Board members were alleged to have attended a training session, at which the expert witness retained by the appellant developer was one of the presenters, a ground for apprehended bias. That is the way it seemed from what was made public.

> The Board ... appeared to have compromised its duty to oversee the implementation of provincial policy objectives for no good reason."

Regional officials must have believed that something essential in the OP had been lost; to this extent the Board had not appeared to them to have acted with any good reason because those regional municipal officials normally would say nothing and go back to work. A regional staff planner felt strongly enough to say it publicly. This was not business as usual.

When this decision was to be released, it must have been known that this was a major decision for a key region in southwestern Ontario. Yet apparently no meaningful summary from the Board members who wrote the decision was prepared for insertion at the end of the decision to explain directly how this decision went beyond an appreciation of good lawyering to the long term future, to provincial policy, and to the deference required to the decision of an elected body, the latter above all. If of course there was no good reason for the decision, then one wonders why it was not held for the panel to reconsider the policy issue carefully.

The practice of the Board has been for the chair or a vice-chair to edit and review the decision before release. As a duty vice-chair, if I saw an obvious inconsistency in findings or an error in stating the law or a lack of clarity in the findings and order, I would bring it to the attention of the member and review the problem area again when it came back. So did other vice-chairs. Often the members would say that they had some questions of their own over that section but decided to keep them to themselves. I had never encountered a problem from a member about this exercise.

It was not as if there were sections in that decision that were not controversial and misleading. For instance, the deference of the OMB to the decision of the Regional Council was expressed in a manner that would undermine deference to any municipal decision. Following *Ottawa (City) v. Minto Communities Inc.* [2009] O.J. No.4913 (Div. Ct.), the Board cited the words of a Superior Court judge, Mr. Justice Aston:

> The words "have regard to" do not by themselves suggest more than minimal deference to the decision of Municipal Council ... The Board does not have to find that Council's decision is demonstrably unreasonable to arrive at a different conclusion.

The Board went on to say:

> [84] In this case, the minutes of Regional Council dated June 6, 2012 reflect that boundary expansions can be determined in the context of the Region's five year reviews, at least in the opinion of one Council member. Furthermore, it is undeniable, in our estimation, that a land budget exercise for purposes of the Growth Plan is an inherently detailed, complex and arduous process. To expect Council members to completely and assiduously appreciate each and every assumption made, statistical projection given and nuance associated with a particular methodology, would be unrealistic in the circumstances.

> [85] In our view, we have, as required, carefully considered Council's decision in relation to the appropriate methodology to be employed. However, based upon our comments in relation to the Determining Factors and in light of the fact that we, and not Regional Council, had the benefit of hearing extensive

evidence and submissions with respect to each of the methodologies used, we do not agree with Regional Council that the Region's methodology should be endorsed.[52]

The Board allowed the development group's appeal over the decision of regional council. Facially, there is reason to doubt the correctness of the Board's judgment for at least two reasons:

1. The Board had the lesser deference language to direct it in its attitude toward the council's decision, it is true. That language is now "shall be consistent with." When the Waterloo Region OP was before the Board, the language directing the Board was to "have regard to" the council's decision, a test regarded as toward the lower end of the deference continuum. With respect to the court, however, having regard to something is not minimal deference as suggested. There is a whole room of difference between "minimal deference" and "demonstrably unreasonable". In any event, even granting use of the term "minimal deference," to have regard to a decision as one of an elected council means more than merely reading it carefully. To "have regard" to a council decision means, consider the words carefully, and consider also the objectives and intended outcome(s), and be cognizant of the fact that the decision is by an elected level of government among other things, and whether the decision carried out or exceeded provincial policy. Some analysis as to how the Board was having regard to the council's decision and yet overturning it, in addition to merely not agreeing with some points of methodology, were in order.[53] The assumptions that a council could not understand the finer points and that the view of one councillor somehow represents the view of council, should not have sufficed, in my view, if this matter had proceeded further to the Court of Appeal.

2. The Board may have been in error in applying to a policy document a rule for construing statutes. This occurred where the Board was considering the meaning of the Growth Plan in section 2.2.7.3 and the words "planned to achieve" rather than "will achieve" or "will be achieved." This occurs in paragraph 73 of the Board decision and the provision under review is a part of the Growth Policy, not a statute. The proper approach to the interpretation of policy is to follow the approach to policy in *Bele Himmel*, quoted in the *Goldlist* decision. That approach is a much more self-reinforcing and broad one, as one would expect with a document intended to be part of an operating system. As explained by Saunders J. in *Bele Himmel Investments Ltd. v. City of Mississauga et al.* (1982), 13 O.M.B.R. 17 at 27:

Official plans are not statutes and should not be construed as such. In growing municipalities such as Mississauga, official plans set out the present policy of the community concerning its future physical, social and economic development.[54]

Like an official plan, a growth plan is a policy document, not a statute. To then add the rather dismissive clauses, which the Board did, was, in my experience, the opposite behaviour of any tribunal directed to pay attention to a decision of another – what the Board said undercuts completely what is left of the direction in the *Planning Act*.

In addition, to read into the language "planned to achieve" by a certain date something quite different from the words "will be achieved" by a date is somewhat minor. The words were being used in a planning document so either way, it means we are planning on the assumption that the housing target will be achieved by 1931.

I would have expected that the Board's internal edit/review practice would have brought to light any inconsistency with provincial policy on agricultural protection and urban boundaries and intensification. But assuming it was facially defensible, the silence from the administrative side of the Board and from the Ministry of Municipal Affairs and Housing and the Ministry of the Attorney General whose ministry includes the OMB, was deafening. It left the position critical of the OMB as a default and so only the region's comments were heard in the media and by the public. The Province must realize that decisions like this are difficult and require patience to understand but once understood, no doubt a spokesperson could release to the media a pre-approved explanation of the issues, the necessary legal background, and why the decision went the way did so that it was known that there were reasons for this decision. Or, this decision should have been held by the edit/review process until the members talked out the issues, with the Chair as mediator.

As the following press excerpt reveals, this controversy was resolved and the land to be made available for development was considerably scaled back from that allowed by the Board panel that heard the case. In the end, the Board was left with another black eye.[55]

It is past time for the provincial tribunal responsible for policy consistency to consider its public face and stop producing decisions subject to later review and correction, or that lack cogent principles that convert to reasons and a decision that flows logically and that really explains its rationale.

"It is past time for the provincial tribunal responsible for policy consistency to consider its public face and stop producing decisions subject to later review and correction ..."

This will be a matter for future attention and work as we continue this drive through the entrails as well as the public passages of this tribunal. It is important for any tribunal to be aware of its public face. It is vital that it ensure that all of its members strive for excellence in their written work and in their communication skills, written and oral. It is equally important that members understand their position as major decision-makers within the provincial policy framework but not part of the provincial government. People do not need to like difficult decisions but they need a reason to respect and accept them. The public's trust is a worthy goal that any institution must continually strive for in a democracy. It is particularly so for the Ontario Municipal Board, which must deal daily with the interface between administrative principle and policy and elected levels of government.

Lack of public trust is most serious. The repeated criticism of the Board, decision after decision, with no answer or explanation from the government, is a huge error on the government's part. If it felt that there was a real problem, the 2016 review would be complete and out for debate by now. Otherwise, its job should be to educate the public on what it is trying to do through the planning process. Or does it see its job in a different way? As to urban sprawl, for instance, could it be that the government knows that its own intensification target is weak (only forty per cent of all development is to occur in already developed urban areas), and it simply does not want the context of these intensification-related decisions to get out because it knows that the target is indefensible? And this is the province's contribution to the global warming issue and to protection of agriculture? Back to that black eye...

> WATERLOO REGION — Six years to the day since it was approved by regional politicians, the plan guiding growth here to 2031 is finally in effect.
>
> "It's been a long journey, and what happens in the Region of Waterloo quite regularly is there's a lot of innovation that occurs, and I think what we saw in this case is the innovation we put forward just wasn't readily accepted ..." said Kevin Eby, director of community planning. "When all is said and done we achieved what we set out to achieve."
>
> At a hearing Thursday, the Ontario Municipal Board, which decides land planning disputes, accepted a comprehensive settlement of several developer appeals to the Region of Waterloo's OP.
>
> The boundary was the region's attempt to curb urban sprawl and encourage intensification in city cores.[56]

-oooooo-

The Waterloo Region plan officially came into effect on June 18, 2015, with some sense that the provincial policy statements had been paid attention to and a defensible urban boundary was set after the event, and not by the OMB.

When this and other media accounts of the public disillusionment with this Board are reviewed over years, in my view there is a recurring set of themes and a case that requires a substantial answer, absent which this tribunal's continued existence as a land use review tribunal should be in severe doubt. Those themes include, from a provincial perspective, the OMB's alleged anti-democratic power and wide area of discretion to overturn lower and upper tier councils' decisions, a pro-development bias, and record of favouring special interests over the public interest. They also include the failure to date of the procedural reforms of 2006 to harness the OMB's *de novo* jurisdiction and reduce hearing time and cost. There is also the rationale provided by the OMB's mere existence and authority that allow councillors to abdicate their democratic choice between "the wealth of developers and support of the electorate."

Regarding the defence of the OMB as the assurance of a fair hearing, there are the allegations by John Chipman in *A Law Unto Itself* that: (i) the OMB is no longer required to ensure that the rules of natural justice are applied to protect the rights of property owners; BC and some other provinces have covered off that protection by enforcing more strict notice and public hearing requirements than those required in Ontario; and (ii) many large municipalities have sophisticated administrations to implement planning controls, to ensure policies adopted in the provincial policy statements are followed, and to see that private interests do not overcome public policy. Chipman believes the OMB as of 2002 had not been contributing to the matters in (ii) consistently and that it had done the reverse by favouring private over public interests.

It is time that some coherent comment and sense of reality is brought to bear on this field of alleged broken faith. You will note that I do not use the word defence because that is not what this is about. But it *is* about making the choice about the future of this tribunal a more rational and informed one.

CHAPTER IV

UNEQUAL, ANTI-DEMOCRATIC

Democracy is comin'
from "Democracy",
—*Leonard Cohen, 1992*

The accusations most commonly made by critics are that the OMB is an unelected and unaccountable provincial tribunal that is given the final say on all planning decisions in Ontario and cases brought before it on appeal. It has the power to overrule elected municipal councils in doing so. And it has no political legitimacy to do so.

There is no disputing two of these charges. The OMB is not elected. And it has the power to make its own decisions. It does not have a say in all planning decisions. It can decide only those that are appealed to it.

THE OMB IS NOT ELECTED: IS ITS DISCRETION UNLIMITED?

So the charges that the OMB is unelected and has the power to make its own decisions are quite right. But to the critics, each of these characteristics raises a concern. Let's deal with the first fact conceded here – the OMB is not elected. Why is that a problem?

Most officials who are given the power of decision to deal with conflicts and controversies that need some finality are not elected. It is also charged that the OMB is anti-democratic for the same reason. This charge is not one repeated by informed commentators in their critical appraisals of the Board and that is for good reason. Because in any democracy, where people disagree or become involved in a dispute situation, a court or a tribunal or a person respected in the community is given the job of bringing finality to the dispute. That may occur by the judge or the tribunal talking to both sides, trying to work out a compromise and, failing that, making a decision based on what the person or persons heard from both sides. The judge or tribunal is usually appointed, whether it be in Canada or the U.S. (where certain state judges and tribunal members are elected and the rest – all federal judges, for instance – are appointed), to carry out that decision-making function.

It is said that the Board is not accountable. That is simply not the case at least in the formal institutional sense. The Board is accountable to the government for the manner, the efficiency and the completeness with which it does its work. Each appointed board or commission is accountable to the agency or office that appoints them. Local tribunal members are accountable to the local council or regional council in the case of planning advisory committees who appointed them; the terms are often annual or coterminous with the council that appointed them. In the case of the OMB, it is accountable to the Ontario government through the Ministry of the Attorney General.

> "The Board is accountable to the government for the manner, the efficiency and the completeness with which it does its work."

The OMB accounts for what it has done each year through its annual report in a very general and numeric sense. The reports are public and set out a comment by the Chair about the past year's performance, usually in terms of the challenges the Chair faced. The reports contain charts of numbers of files dealt with, hearing dates scheduled, that sort of thing. The principal reins that the government hold on tribunal members is the power to renew or not renew their terms of appointment. The government has no authority or power to order the Board to make a certain decision or to alter anything in the reasons for decision on a case before it. Any attempt by a government official to interfere in that way amounts to serious misconduct if not a criminal offence if a certain intent and incentive was operating. It does not happen. But government does have the right to expect members to carry out the Board's mandate, which includes carrying out government policy declared under section 3 of the *Planning Act*. On any individual case, the Board maintains its independence of decision as to how it interprets and applies government policy, but it cannot ignore or treat it lightly where facts as found make it relevant.

TWO IMPORTANT ELEMENTS TO COMBAT PUBLIC CYNICISM

I understand that it is not simply institutional accountability that is in play, where people charge the Board with being unaccountable by election or otherwise. In reality, I think that this complaint has to do with the exercise of the wide discretion by members in cases day to day and the fear that there is no oversight holding them accountable for the performance of their duties including the exercise of that discretion. That is not so in law. In *Cloverdale Shopping Centre v Etobicoke (Township)*,**57** the court discussed at some length the jurisdiction, duties and discretion of the Board when an OP was referred to the Board with or without an accompanying zoning amendment. When the Minister referred a matter to the Board, the

Board had all the functions and authority granted the Minister by the *Planning Act*. The court distinguished a civil trial from a hearing before the Board in holding that the decision of the Board at the hearing is unlike that made in a civil trial between two or more parties. In its decision, the Board must take into account the party that is not in the room: the public interest. The Board must hear all objections but it is not making only a decision on whether they are valid or not, important though they may be. The Board's decision takes those matters into account but, in the words of the court: They may, however, be over-ruled upon the larger considerations of administrative policy.

Those considerations include public safety, health, convenience and welfare of the inhabitants as well now as the broad matters of provincial interest listed in section 2. However, these matters do have limits.

The first set of limits is caught by the following paraphrase of the Court of Appeal decision in *Cloverdale Shopping Centre*:

> If it can be demonstrated that the Minister or the Board has exceeded the jurisdiction conferred upon him or it by the Acts, such excess as a matter of law is open to correction; again if it be demonstrated that the order of the Minister or of the Board does not conform with the provisions of the Act, the order as a matter of law is open to review but within his or its jurisdiction and always assuming a full and fair hearing to those directly concerned, the grounds upon which the Court may interfere with the decision are limited by the administrative nature of the function performed.

Discretion is not unrestricted though it admittedly is assumed to be wide. The limits vary according to the subject matter but we will take the widest example, that of an OP or OPA hearing. For an OPA, and zoning amendment, the limits are wide but far from providing an unbridled discretion. The evidence for and against is a major part of the Board's consideration of an OPA but it can also take into account the broader public interest as described and how the proposal affects and is affected by the public health, safety, convenience and welfare generally.

The Board cannot allow or dismiss an appeal simply because the member did not like the lawyer for a party or a witness or how someone parted their hair. These are completely extraneous matters, which the member cannot use as part of the reason for acting on the matter. But can the member decide for some extraneous reason and dress it up as a decision on the evidence in light of the public interest? These are broad terms, I know, but they cannot be manipulated that way without something in the evidence or submissions that fail to address the public interest. The member is confined to those considerations in the governing Act and to go beyond those will end up with the decision being set aside or quashed as one beyond the jurisdiction of the Board.

The Board's exercise of discretion is also constrained by the principles of natural justice, those tenets that are shared by most civilized societies, regarded as self-evident since Roman times in broad outline. They are also referred to as principles of procedural fairness, of "fair play in action" as Dickson CJ stated in *Kane v Bd. of Governors of U.B.C.* and they include:

i.   a party has a right to be heard by a tribunal acting fairly; a party is entitled to know the case against him or her before being called upon and must be given fair opportunity to present that party's case and question witnesses;

ii. a hearing should be on reasonable notice to the parties and should be heard by person(s) who are impartial, whose minds are open to being persuaded and who are seen to be impartial by a reasonably well informed person;

iii. the persons who heard the case must decide it; a decision cannot be delegated to a third party once the hearing starts;

iv. the decision must be based on evidence, not speculation, and the decision must indicate what was used in arriving at the decision.**58**

In addition, there is authority for the proposition that the adjudicator(s) have a duty to listen fairly to all sides and, on an OPA and zoning proposal appealed to the Board, to hear submissions on the public interest that are engaged by the proposal. If there is evidence of reasonable apprehension of bias, the result may well be a quashing of the decision.

Beyond the law and legal concepts, this is a subject with a history. In the '60s, the speculation was that the OMB was overly critical of development. Then in the '70s, those who "knew" said the Board was biased in the owner-developer's direction and from the Comay report believed that members had a discretion that allowed them to be influenced by extraneous considerations.**59** However, as we have seen, this was a period in which the overwhelming show of public distrust was toward municipal government, its closed attitudes and its broad partnerships with builders and developers to rip out whole areas of aged housing for new large apartment towers or large neighbourhood redevelopment projects.

The '70s saw a more serious phenomenon develop, which had ramifications for the way government would structure environmental review adjudication. After Mr. Kennedy retired as OMB Chair, there crept through the planning world the mindset that the OMB saw a divide between planning evidence and issues, which the Board would properly deal with and environmental issues, which the OMB would not. A kind of veil dropped over any evidence dealing with air, water or other issues relating to the environment as different and set apart from proper planning evidence, which the Board would accept.

In the 1980s, the most important thing was to ensure the public felt the member listened and understood their concerns, because many people believed no one in government paid attention to them. I would attempt to describe their issues as accurately as possible and at least provide a special setback or architectural feature that the evidence established would lessen whatever the impact was likely to be on their property where I knew there was no reason to deny the appeal by a developer or homeowner. Otherwise, if the evidence failed to support the matter under appeal and if the grounds on which the municipal planning position favouring the project were shown to be counter to established policy or lacking in any planning merit, and I mean that in the sense of a politically inspired or pressured decision without planning merit, the appeal would be allowed and the OP adoption and/or zoning by-law would be rejected.

By the '90s, with the NDP government in power, social issues and politically correct standards became important, including always being gender neutral and never implying that a woman was influenced by things a man would not be. Then the Harris years began and appearances counted for nothing as people had become too smart; they became highly judgmental, mere words were no longer enough, and controls on development were looked on by government less favourably. Generally, decisions of municipal councils were exempt from this cynicism.

Recently, developer influence, unchecked autonomy, and decisions made by an unelected and unaccountable body have returned as the chief complaints but this time without any scrutiny of municipal decisions made for reasons of re-election within four years. In this cycle, the only constant is a sense that the system cannot be trusted, that somebody with an in group in government is always going to harm you in some way or fail to act in your interests. There is an increased sophistication, a more discerning sense, in the public generally. Everyone is less tolerant of the occasional jolts in life. To everything, there must be a reason and someone must be to blame. When a tribunal makes a decision, who benefits? And whom does it hurt?

Now, and in the years since 2000, the public sees members of the Board as decision-makers without an evident code, oversight, direct control over even guidelines that can assist in pointing toward predictability in decisions, or subject to some principled benchmark. Without such overt mechanisms, why should members be trusted not to favour a developer or to have a dislike for homeowners or to refuse to believe a council decision counts for much. They are unknown entities, people largely without any public profile who seem to do whatever they want without criteria, limiting elements, or ability to define why one group won and the others lost.

The outcry over the OMB is not loud these days but it is there. In the issue of a St. Catharines newspaper of May 18, 2016, there is a report of a growing movement among municipalities across Ontario, according to a Welland councillor. The movement is called the OMB Reform Working Group. The news came out of the group's summit meeting in Markham in May 2016 where over one hundred representatives from municipalities across Ontario discussed their concerns about the OMB. The Minister of Municipal Affairs and Housing was asked to attend the meeting. He declined but urged the group by letter to report to the Ministry what its concerns are and they will be taken into account by the review aimed at reforming the OMB. This is the same review about which the premier had written to me in April 2016. So far, eighty municipalities have committed support for a motion originally drafted by the councillor who heads the working group. That motion calls for the government to cut the authority of the

OMB down to ruling on objections to by-laws and other municipal planning instruments based only on questions of law or process. The motion is alleged also to insist that the government require the Board to uphold decisions of municipal councils unless they are contrary to the "processes and rules set out in the legislation."

This motion has support in the Niagara region from seven municipalities including Niagara Falls and Welland north to Grimsby. When it came down to the reason behind this serious dilution of the OMB's authority to virtual meaninglessness, only one development was referred to as a problem and that was by a Niagara Falls councillor. The development was a gas station. The residents objected to it when it was first proposed, the local council turned it down and now it is in place. The councilor quoted a typical comment to her: "I can't believe you passed that bloody gas station near my kid's school." She said the council turned it down and the OMB overruled the council and so it is built. One councillor did not directly add to the criticism. Instead he supported the notion that the OMB can always do its job better, and that he hoped "the Province would do a better job of appointing OMB representatives – people with a planning background and an understanding of the law."[60]

COUNTERING PUBLIC CYNICISM

The problem is: most people feel somehow that the "system" can't be trusted. I guess this is the reason I am so insistent on targeted recruitment using open and transparent characteristics needed particularly on this tribunal and not as strictly anywhere else in the ELTO cluster. This approach to selection should be carried out in order to increase the number and diversity of members with people with proven records of excellence and discernment in their career performance. And they must be people with the power to communicate in a meaningful way, to convey the reasons for a decision, and to know how to stress the public interest aspects of it that mean everyone has some benefit, whether the decision be pro or con or a compromise. They must be persons who have the planning competence and legal acumen to demonstrate clearly how the Board order can ensure that all conditions of a decision would happen, or the proposal will not happen.

> "... they must be people with the power to communicate in a meaningful way, to convey the reasons for a decision ..."

The parties must be able to see that there are principles at work that directed the decision, consistent with other decisions on the same or similar policy or fact situation. I will return to the importance of the selection and recruitment process and the significance of writing effectively. These elements must form the key to a credible tribunal in the future. The public do not have to like a decision-making body but their respect is winnable if that tribunal trusts them to tell them exactly why a decision was made so they feel their part in the hearing was understood. They need to know that no favour is being bestowed because there are good and understandable reasons for the decision that it is important they know and comprehend.

A selection process targeted to mediator-planners and others in related fields who have ability and command of themselves and the principles and practice of mediation, coupled with the ability to produce work that expresses a transparent rationale, are the two most important elements necessary to combat public cynicism.

In cases of complaints about behaviour or competence of a member, the complaint would go to the Chair. Until December 2015, it was Associate Chair, Mr. Wilson Lee, who acted in that capacity. Dr. Bruce Krushelnicki has recently been appointed as Executive Chair, which means he would be the one to whom a member would be answerable for inappropriate behaviour. If the complaint is found to be correct, the member could receive a reprimand and be compelled to get further training in the area complained about. The member may not survive the next term renewal when the term has ended.

Travel expenses, a problem for other levels of government, are closely monitored. If a member went over an allowance for a meal, for instance, the member would receive a call about it and be warned that the overage would not be paid by the government. And it normally would not be repeated. There would never be an issue over expenses as the rules are clear and a member would be held personally accountable for any amounts spent that did not qualify.

The two faults that cannot be tolerated at the Board are the failure to be responsible for work undertakings and opaque or gratuitous reasoning for decisions. At least one career and perhaps a few others ended for the former cause.

If there was serious misbehaviour that embarrassed the Board and the government that appointed him or her such as dishonesty or taking benefits for favourable treatment, the member could be suspended from further work temporarily pending investigation or the member could be terminated without pay and, where the behaviour warrants it, charged with a criminal offence. Each member is accountable to the tribunal Chair and to the government. Of course, the tribunal as a whole is accountable for its performance to the Legislature and the government of the day. This is why, in 2016, the provincial government is reviewing the performance and the jurisdiction of, and its exercise by, the Ontario Municipal Board.

APPOINTED OR ELECTED: A COMPARATIVE SEARCH IN CANADA AND THE UNITED STATES61

All courts in Canada and all tribunals are appointed bodies. Election of judges can bring with it additional serious baggage – allegations of corruption, for instance, where the judge makes a decision that favours a contributor to the judge's campaign or makes it a condition of being heard that counsel contribute to the judge's campaign.

For some examples of planning boards or commidssions in the United States, the Oregon Land Conservation and Development Commission has seven members all appointed by the

Governor and confirmed by the state Senate, serving four-year terms limited to two consecutive terms. Oregon's Land Use Board of Appeals (LUBA) has three members appointed by the Governor and confirmed by the Senate. It is referred to by Aaron Moore in his latest book *Planning Politics* as the most similar to the OMB and I think he is correct. It can make overturn decisions of local councils on zoning and other development matters though it has to accept the state plan.

California's powerful Coastal Commission has twelve voting members and three nonvoting members. It has jurisdiction over a wide swath of land along the California coast. All members are appointed either by the Governor, Senate Rules Committee, or the Speaker of the Assembly; each appoints four commissioners, two public members and two elected officials. It can overrule a local municipal decision, make its own and enforce it.

In Hawaii, the Land Use Commission is appointed by the Governor. Same for Vermont's state environmental board and the district commissions, which assist it with the state development permit system.

In Florida, land use appeals are dealt with by administrative law judges in the Department of Administrative Hearings (DOAH). All are appointed by the Governor. The DOAH has the power to overrule a local council decision on zoning. Maryland's so-called Smart Growth plan seems to operate by the state enacting certain standards that the county and district boards that administer the system incorporate into their ordinances; there is no state land use tribunal in Maryland. In the rest of the United States, the local municipalities administer the planning and zoning program. For the states that have a state level land use commission or tribunal, all are appointed.

Typically, in most states, the municipality either appoints the members of the local commission or planning or zoning board or it is elected locally. This commission or board considers amendments to zoning and whether the variance is minor and within the local plan. The appeals are to a board of adjustment or to the council. The appeal board is either appointed or elected. Any appeal from the board of adjustment is to the court on legal grounds.

The same is true of all six similar provincial land use tribunals: the Alberta Municipal Board, Saskatchewan Municipal Board, the Manitoba Municipal Board, the New Brunswick Assessment and Planning Appeal Board, the *Commission municipale du Québec* (CMQ), and the Nova Scotia Utility Review Board. In each case, the tribunal is appointed by government.

In Alberta, the Municipal Government Board has a narrow jurisdiction municipally over certain subdivision appeals depending on their proximity to things like a landfill site, sewage treatment plant, a body of water, or a highway allowing speeds over 80kph, to name a few. It also can hear inter-municipal disputes over land use by-laws, make recommendations on annexations, and hear appeals regarding conflicts between municipal and provincial approvals. Apart from subdivision appeals, it cannot decide the fate of a development application by overruling a municipal decision as most of the others can. It is appointed by the Alberta government on recommendation by the Minister of Municipal Affairs.

The Quebec CMQ is unlike the other Boards in the severe limits on its jurisdiction. It provides conflict resolution services to municipalities having a dispute, provides mediation services, and has extensive investigatory and managerial capability, but its principal planning function is to give its opinion on the conformity of a law with the planning program and the development plan of a municipality. It does not hold appeal hearings and decide the fate of development applications. Its members are appointed.

The New Brunswick Assessment and Planning Appeal Board (APAB) and the Nova Scotia Utility Review Board (NSURB) are closest to the OMB in jurisdiction and practice, though the former disposes of appeals on legal rather than land use planning grounds.

The Nova Scotia Board is a super board dealing with everything from electrical power regulation to municipal planning. In its planning jurisdiction, it is similar to the OMB; it decides zoning appeals and appeals from plans of subdivisions and development agreements. It can amend and rescind zoning by-laws but it is prevented from hearing appeals from municipal planning strategies; the strategies appear to be like OPs in Ontario. Its decisions are based on planning principles. The grounds of appeal are restricted to conformity with the municipal planning strategy. The NSURB is bound to the contents of a municipal OP. Due to a recent amendment, the OMB cannot modify an OP that is not properly before it for review; however, unlike the Nova Scotis board, it can modify an OP or amendment on an appeal regarding that OP or amendment.**62**

> "The essential point is there is nothing unaccountable, or anti-democratic in a democracy in establishing a tribunal to deal with certain disputes and constitute it as an appointed body."

The Saskatchewan Municipal Board has one branch called the Planning Appeals Commission (PAC). Its hearings are adversarial and its powers are limited. The PAC only hears the second round of appeals, the appeals from the Development Appeal Boards or DABS. Neither can hear appeals regarding OPs, nor can they amend zoning by-laws. The PAC is limited to hearing only the evidence presented at the DABS hearing.

The Manitoba Municipal Board (MMB) also hears appeals in an adversarial manner. Appeals or objections to a development plan, like Ontario's OPs, can proceed on filing a second objection on second reading of the by-law adopting the Plan and if the minister refers the Plan to the MMB. The MMB holds a hearing and remits a recommendation to the Minister. It is the Minister's decision to approve or not confirm the by-law, or to alter it or to reject it after considering the MMB's recommendation. On second reading of a zoning by-law or amendment and if an objection is filed, the MMB may hold a hearing and thereafter it may confirm or not confirm the by-law or the part objected to, or it can alter the by-law.**63**

The essential point is there is nothing unaccountable, or anti-democratic in a democracy in establishing a tribunal to deal with certain disputes and constitute it as an appointed body.

In addition, a land use review tribunal, as a specialized tribunal, requires a variety of skill sets; appointment is the only way that a new appointment can be found to continue that diverse set of experience and skill set that can be lost through departure of retiring members. Election is by its nature a blunt instrument; it could not ensure that that kind of diversity of experience would continue.

We began this chapter by conceding two points made by less informed critics: one was that the OMB had power to render its own decisions on appeals. The critics speak of the Board as "powerful" because it retains this decision-making authority.

The charges of being unelected, powerful and anti-democratic contain a polemic appeal for people if not much substance. I will deal with all of these criticisms some to correct and others to agree with. At this point, what about the allegation that there is a pro-developer bias on the OMB? We will deal now with the alleged bias, in light of the evidence and literature that we have.

THE ONTARIO MUNICIPAL BOARD FAVOURS DEVELOPERS – OR – IS THIS A MANTRA FOR A MORE SERIOUS PROBLEM?

The word "development" is not necessarily a bad word. The person called a "developer" may be a property owner who is arranging for a house of his own to be built, or he or she could be funding a large mixed use proposal like a regional shopping and commercial centre, or she could be putting together an affordable housing project at a density per unit that will allow her to make money and assist in housing families who badly need places of their own. In other words, "development" is an active word that implies creation as well as making money, doing something worthwhile as well as pocketing a profit. By themselves, they are words with several meanings but they all come down to one common element wherever these projects are proposed: that is, change, and that is an unsettling word to established neighbourhoods.

The first thing that has to be said about the charge against the OMB – that it is pro-developer – is that it takes a point of view. It assumes that building proposals have a negative value and that a person or group with power to stop them should do just that. It says, "Leave us alone. We don't need another house or another shopping centre/condominium next door or anywhere near us." Yet the community that does not develop and attract new investment is a community on the way out – like all those towns and motels on the old two-lane highways that refused to change or move, and lost their livelihood and then their existence, to the new freeways with ramps directing drivers to the new grassy avenues and inns for the travelling public.

The media "have erected a picture of developers as a threatening force toward established neighbourhoods and all development as having little or no redeeming social value …"

To make things crystal clear here, I do not imply anything evil or necessarily good about development generally except some is better than none, if it fits within planning principles for the type of area it is, or is becoming. This charge comes out of the media who have erected a picture of developers as a threatening force toward established neighbourhoods and all development as having little or no redeeming social value, and municipal councils as democratic judges of the development that should not proceed.

In my view, this charge against the Board encapsulates an allegedly obvious tendency to decide in favour of appeals proposing new construction proposals and against appeals that aim to stop new construction proposals. It also amounts to a charge of outright bias in favour of development as a systemic characteristic built into the OMB's training of members and their performance in the field.

In two recent publications, two researchers with different methodologies and assumptions and from different fields of expertise have looked at this issue along with others pertaining to the Board. Aaron Moore's book *Planning Politics in Toronto: The OMB and Urban Development* focuses on the relationship of the power centres in development politics, developers, neighbourhood groups, and local politicians – what he calls the triad of players who dominate the politics of urban development. He is a political scientist interested in urban power relationships, using a politico-economic model of what should be expected. His objective was to determine the effect on the relationships between these groups of a powerful tribunal like the OMB that holds hearings on planning appeals and acts judicially.

Moore was not studying pro-developer bias; rather, he looked at whether the presence of the OMB altered the usual triad relationships one sees in U.S. cities, which share a fairly common history with Toronto in trends of urban development since the 1960s. Although bias toward one member of the triad was not the purpose of his work, he does have an interesting conclusion regarding a bias of the Board, and it is not a bias in favour of developers.

Moore found that regardless of institutional and cultural differences between the U.S. and Canada, residents in both countries who oppose development, and the developers who want to develop their lands, share a common interest from differing sides: they are both interested in local politicians. The politicians in turn are torn between the monetary resources of the developers and the electoral support of neighbourhood groups. They are also limited by their political horizons: every four years they reach their horizon line and need a new political affirmation from the voters whose collective memory can be very short. Developers have become very aware of the influence on OMB decisions that articulate planning experts have, particularly because they are masters of the "language of planning", as Moore describes it.

To cut out any leverage the neighbourhood groups may want, developers try very hard to obtain a positive report on their proposal from the city planning staff. This then gives them an advantage in the passage of the proposal from municipality to the OMB. Whether the city council decides for or against them becomes less of a problem, although they will of course court the city councillor for the ward where the development site is located. Should the council oppose the development on appeal to the Board, the developers' lawyer subpoenas the city planner to oppose the city's case and that evidence is often the decisive evidence in the case. The OMB is, after all, a planning review board, not a court of public opinion, and so evidence from the staff planner in charge of area planning for the proposed site is obviously important.

Now if this were always the case, one could rightly ask whether we need either the municipal council or the OMB. It becomes almost a caricature where the public, sitting between the developer and the planner in front of the desk of the OMB panel, is asking, "Who is going to look out for me? Where is the guardian of the guardians?" However, Moore's point is that the developer has a number of strategic options and obtaining a positive staff planning report is regarded by most developers and their lawyers as a first priority.

Moore views the Board's general acceptance of planning evidence, particularly the city planners, as the Board's "bias" in favour of municipal planning staff; this increases the importance of planning experts as against that of political players. He also finds that the presence of the OMB gives the developers more options: they can decide to work with and obtain the support of the city and planning staff, or they can court city council alone, absent a positive planning report, because the city will not send anyone to the hearing to oppose the developer's appeal if council supports it. But more common is the effort by the developer's legal team to get a positive report from City planning. Amid a constant sea of changing OP and zoning by-laws in Toronto, he writes, at page 163:

> [The] process of constant amendment (by the city of its own by-laws and official plan) erodes any significance the City's planning laws may have. As a result, the OMB bases its decisions on its own perception of good planning. The ... Board effectively removes actual planning decisions from the realm of the entirely political by exalting the role of planning experts. Although local politicians in Toronto use political calculations when deciding when to support or oppose a development in many cases, their calculations are often based on the planning rationale behind a specific proposal. The Board, thus, is a means to curb the decision-making authority of local politicians in Ontario.

Moore, therefore, finds that there is a marked tendency of the Board to accept the planning opinion of municipal planners. He calls it a bias; I disagree. He has shown no grounds for either his view that the Board is "exalting" the role of planning experts or for his view that by accepting the opinion more often than not of a person qualified by special training and education to express such opinions, the Board is biased in favour of planners generally. I prefer the word "tendency" as being more accurate simply because he at no time shows any evidence that the OMB possesses a systemic partiality for development per se or for the development industry.

"It is no bias to rule in favour of evidence that establishes good planning principles where that is your role."

More importantly, his description of a tribunal's interest in planning evidence as a bias is ludicrous in view of the law that this tribunal operates within: the present role of the tribunal is to rule in accordance with principles of good planning; they include the OP policies (regional and lower tier) in force, the zoning by-laws and provincial planning statements, in addition to the generally accepted tenets of good planning within the planning profession. It is no bias to rule in favour of evidence that establishes good planning principles where that is your role. There usually are several planners who provide evidence at these hearings in most contested cases, being the developer's own retained planner, the planner retained by the neighbourhood residents' group, and the municipality's staff planner for the concerned area. The evidence of each is scrutinized, it may be accepted, accepted in part or not accepted by the tribunal, depending on the factual context of the case and the degree to which the planners' evidence accords with the facts found by the tribunal.

What the Board's decision may equally show, as I am relatively sure it does, is the real problem lurking below this discussion, a problem that eats away at people and causes a sense of helplessness and vulnerability. That is, the inequality of resources at the disposal of developers as opposed to what ratepayers' groups and even municipalities can put together. Most home-owners these days are simply trying to maintain their homes and families. They do not have the thousands of dollars it takes to round up a team of professionals. And often, the municipality cannot mount an effective case where there are other hearings coming up that other planning staff must prepare for, as well as doing their required planning work for the municipality.

The development team would consist of a successful planning lawyer, one or sometimes two land use planners to cover different sub-specialties relevant to the case, a traffic engineer, an environmental planner and engineer, particularly where contamination and remediation of a site is an issue, and other expert assistance as needed. The cost of running such a case can be huge. In my interviews with many lawyers active in the planning field, mid-six figure costs are common on moderately sized development proposals without a major hot button issue and, for a development with serious issues with the province, as well as the municipality, over a million dollars is in the ballpark. The inequality in most development scenarios at the OMB is obvious.

This kind of inequality erodes any sense of justice. It is not assuaged by the lesser knowledge and experience of most members presently presiding at hearings on the present Board. Often in the court system a knowledgeable judge will try to balance the case where he or she sees inequality of resources causing a serious imbalance and will try to assist within the bounds of fairness to both sides by ensuring the right questions are asked of the claimant's expert witnesses to ensure some testing occurs. I know that Board members listen intently to self-represented persons from the neighbourhood. I am not aware of more than a handful of Board members who should try to actively assist in this way and whether that handful would see it as their prerogative to do it is doubtful. Even if a member tried, that member is acting in ignorance of the full case and may very well end up injuring the side that is outgunned more than helping it.

One member stands out in my memory due to her innate instinct for knowing how to deal with a situation like this. She was a former senior planner with Municipal Affairs whose initials on subdivision approvals became well known, Diana L. Santo. She was well known for using a hearing to educate unrepresented people and sometimes the legal profession and junior planners on what she knew well to be the areas where different types of development could be vulnerable, or how a home could be sited on a lot affected by an environmental protection zoning. Her ability to bring to the fore weaknesses in the proponents' case through their own witnesses, if there were any, was legendary. I know because I was there to watch her in many hearings at a time when members used to sit in panels of two or three to bring a diversity of experience to a complex file.

So to some extent the Board could help with this problem of inequality of resources where a matter is at its hearing stage. Often the issue can be an EP-type zoning based on larger scale maps used as a base for the zoning maps. A topographic survey on a microscale of the lot involved may well show the existence of a sufficiently high plateau of land on the person's lot that may not be in the flood plain. This would be done, of course, in consultation with a planner with the local conservation authority responsible for flood plain mapping. Some members are already good at this and from what I hear, virtually all members are quite solicitous of self-represented people and try to make sure they are understood. But it may not, and probably never will, significantly narrow the gap in resources available to each side. As one practitioner at the Board put it, this gap fundamentally is an expression of an inequality in the distribution of wealth in society.

One obvious solution, barring the development industry and the legal and planning professions and government finally acting to provide for assistance to cases of some merit, is to give the OMB power and fair criteria to order intervener funding to be paid by a proponent, in stages as the case progresses toward a hearing.

Apart from the limited amount the Board can do, a Barrie municipal lawyer of long experience, expressed his own unhappiness with "the fact that ordinary people who feel aggrieved by a development project cannot afford the kind of expert evidence that developers can, and, often get short shrift." He suggested that a fund similar to CELA – Canadian Environmental Law Association, a funding mechanism established for environmental hearings, should be established, which could contribute to the cost of hiring experts for meritorious cases.[64] Others also expressed a similar concern over the disparity of resources. Some development lawyers noted that at times the imbalance was so palpable that they felt something more was required of government in the interests of fundamental justice. I will return to this aspect in the final chapter on recommendations.

This is the soft underbelly of the problem people sense at Board hearings sometimes. Too often, the hearings engender a sense of powerlessness rather than justice among those who may not have been able to afford, or did not know or understand how to retain, the one or two expert witnesses that might have helped their case. The Board can assist in narrowing the resource imbalance by short careful questioning of a planning witness. But this is by no means an invitation to tribunal members to question a witness for lengthy periods of time to little or no purpose or unwittingly to the prejudice of the party they are trying to assist. As the character played by Paul Newman said in the film *The Verdict*: "If you are going to try my case for me, your Honour, I'd appreciate it if you didn't lose it."

Ultimately, there is one other direction that would ameliorate the inequality of resources. A mediation process conducted by a trained mediator-planner, bringing all interested parties into the 'tent', so to speak, will also be the most satisfactory way to deal with it, if it can resolve the important issues on a file.

John Chipman's work entitled *A Law Unto Itself: How the OMB Has Developed and Applied Land Use Planning Policy* looked in a more direct way at the record of the Board and the notion that the Board has a bias toward developers in exercising its land use planning review jurisdiction. I will concentrate on this work in a more systematic and comprehensive way in the next chapter. Briefly, the author of *A Law Unto Itself* looked at three periods of OMB decisions: 1971–1978, 1987–1994, and 1995–2000. His charts showing the results of his studies indicate that in the first study period, he looked at 344 decisions and in the period 1987–1994, some 320 decisions. The third period, added by the author to bring the publication almost to the date of publication, took in the period of the Harris Conservative government, which began with what could be commonly described as a minor housecleaning of those with less than apparent agreement with the new government's policies.

As one of the subjects examined, applications supported by developers were more likely to be approved than not. In overall terms, 51 per cent of applications supported by developers were approved. The overall approval rate for all applications was 44 per cent in 1971–78. In the period 1987–94, some 57 per cent of developer-supported applications were approved, above the overall approval rate of 47 per cent. Where the municipality and developer were opposed to each other, the approval rate was 50 per cent in 1971–78 and 40 per cent in 1987–94. Where applications were supported by both the developer and the municipality, the approval rate rose to 80 per cent. The author concluded that the results were mixed. However, they did not indicate that the Board had been captured by any interest group. The results do indicate an increasing rate of approval of owner-developer supported applications from 44 per cent in 1971–78 up to 59 per cent in 1995–2000.

"What Moore and Chipman's works indicate is that no actual bias toward developers or any one interest group is at work on the Board."

The increase in development approvals during the latter period is interesting and corresponds to a shift from more approvals to more refusals of interim control by-laws after 1995. This was the time when the Conservative government led by Mr. Harris, a severely right wing, private property-oriented party – a party well removed from the prior Progressive Conservative party of Frost, Robarts and Davis – took power in Ontario. The Board members by this time were subject to a term contract, usually three years, with no assurance of renewal. I was informed by lawyers active before the Board in those years that there was what can only be described as a clearing out of certain members perceived to have views of development that differed from those of the new government. The message was pretty clear to those remaining. There was no thought paid to the needs of the Board of the time for continuity and experience. The result of this period and of the next period of loss of members when the McGuinty government took over is still being felt.

What Moore and Chipman's works indicate is that no actual bias toward developers or any one interest group is at work on the Board. There is certainly evidence of a slightly higher approval than refusal rate for developer-supported applications but there are other explanations including that developers have the greater means to put together a compelling case in terms of expert witnesses and visual props to illustrate their points.

There is one other study published relatively recently.[65] However, it is, at best, a thesis that is subject to proof. The author uses the Chipman and Moore work, which indicates increasing success of owner-developers from 1987–2006. However, Moore's calculations from decisions in 2000–2006 indicate that the City won 57 per cent of appeals when city planning staff supported the City and the City opposed the developer. Finally, in Chipman's book, the author found that the municipality was successful in 60 per cent of cases when it opposed developers during the 1987–94 period and 50 per cent in 1971–78.

The evidence from both Moore and Chipman indicated that the case analysis and files they reviewed showed no actual bias in favour of developers, nor did it show a reasonable appearance of bias in the period from 1987–2000 and 2000–2006. The increasing rate of success through 1994–2000 and to 2006 by developers indicates a more likely target of the public anger toward the OMB was its reduced independence from government during the Harris Conservative years up to 2003 and thereafter for another three years. Eight of the eleven years from 1995–2006 were years of Conservative rule and appointments. The perception was that the Harris government was more favourable to development and less inclined toward regulation and controls; there is no reason to believe that members of the OMB, some appointed by the Harris regime, were not subject to the same perception as the public generally. That perception is very troubling and it is directly related to the present lack of tenure of members.

There is an argument that what was happening was the marked improvement in the evidence presented and in overall case development by counsel arising from the greater resources that developers were willing to devote to OMB hearings. Several counsel told me that the difference in costs incurred by development clients increased markedly since the 1980s. The expenditure of one million dollars or more on a case for the OMB was becoming, if not common, no longer unheard of.[66] As one author conceded and the other did not conclude, there was no breach of the doctrine that parties were entitled to an impartial hearing by a tribunal open to being persuaded and no case of bias or apprehension of bias by informed observers established by the record of decisions to 2006.

In summary, there is no case made out in the current literature or elsewhere to support a presumption against the Ontario Municipal Board that its members as a group or individually make decisions on grounds of bias in favour of, or against, a particular group, or anti-democratic characteristics. Like all decision-making tribunals put in charge of a certain area of disputes and controversies on a state or provincial level, it is appointed, not elected, and it is accountable both internally in job discipline and externally to the Attorney General for its overall work product. And finally, there is nothing anti-democratic in carrying out its responsibility to hear and decide land use and policy conflicts regarding land use. But the fact of lack of tenure remains critical – as long as single-member panels are allowed, and the member's next renewal period is close, there remains an educated perception that that member could be inclined toward the range of decisions of least friction with the government.

The major problems being masked by these uninformed polemic attacks are a sense of powerlessness caused at times by the inequality of resources available to the parties, the growing complexity of planning issues in light of the Provincial Policy Statement and a Growth Plan where it applies, the intimacy people feel about their neighbourhoods, which is disrupted by a planning tribunal they know little about, a perception of the OMB as using its discretion unfairly and lacking independence, as well as a very human dislike of change where the market for development in Toronto has been unceasing and relentless for over twenty years.

It must, however, be remembered that throughout all these years the OMB has continued to do its job, and often did its job well. The following case account is about the aspect of the Board that a number of persons mentioned during my interviews. That is the OMB as a place that was accessible to the ordinary person. The following expresses it well, from a former counsel:

> I first appeared before the OMB in 1962 or 1963. The Board's value was always that it fulfilled a democratic function. The citizen had a right to be there, it was their chance to have a say about something that might affect them. They had a say whether we liked it or not, and somebody listened, really listened to them.[67]

The following case is not a remarkable case in the development of planning law. However, it is an example of what too often is forgotten. City Hall can be a very intimidating place for many people and when things do not work justly, the OMB is still the place people feel they can come to make it right. This case is about a small church without influence, which the City committee decided not to help in their quest to locate a site for their church. Mr. Jackson was the presiding member, a man of stern habits in the hearing room but who saw that the City was not dealing with a full deck in opposing the church. He has since retired, leaving a large gap not easily filled.

BEING THERE 4: THE 'CHURCH ON NUGGET' HEARING

(Friends of Jesus Christ Canada v Toronto (City), (2010),68 OMBR 149)

The church of the Friends of Jesus Christ Canada commenced its mission to serve the spiritual, emotional and financial needs of new immigrants to Canada in 1991 in Toronto. The congregation grew yearly by an average of fourteen persons and as of 2010, the church membership numbered 270 persons. Three times the church has had to move, until in 2009 they found and purchased a property with an old industrial building at 181 Nugget Avenue, formerly in Scarborough, but by 2010 part of the city of Toronto. The congregation planned to convert the old building on this property to a place of worship. They closed the purchase and immediately applied for a zoning amendment from the City of Toronto in order to accommodate the new church. The day before the rezoning was to go before Council, someone with the City rethought its position and the next day the rezoning was turned down. The Friends appealed to the Ontario Municipal Board.

The City of Toronto did not go lightly into this; its legal counsel told the Friends' representative he intended to raise everything he possibly could to defeat the church's appeal: the location offended the City's OP; it would mean other churches may locate nearby, prejudicing the City's ability to meet its employment and job targets and so was inconsistent with the Provincial Policy Statement and the Growth Plan; the noise, dust and odour from the industrial and other related establishments would impact the church members, and complaints will make industry less welcome in an industrial type area; plus parking and transportation issues. It seems that the City saw this as the start of other institutions relocating there as well, causing significant problems for the employment and job growth expected.

Yet it was just this small church wanting to relocate to Nugget Avenue, its principal interest being to help people from the Philippines, as well as others, to adapt to life in Canada. Jason Park, lawyer for the church, could not believe the lengths the City seemed determined to go to oppose this church's attempt to build on Nugget Avenue. In fact, he wondered if he could act on this file at all; the client was not well financially endowed, but he could not stand by and not help them.

The presiding member of the Board was a bright, tough-minded former municipal lawyer from Kingston who did not suffer fools or non-fact-based arguments gladly, from either side. He heard evidence from the City line-up of experts – a well-regarded planner not on the City staff, an economic development official, traffic engineer, and ecological planner, as well as a city councillor and a local business owner who opposed the church relocation. Mr. Park lined up a planner, land economist, traffic expert, and a city councillor who supported the proposal. The battle lines were drawn and the evidence was heard. Decision was reserved by the presiding member, having heard thirteen witnesses, most of an expert character and competent in their fields. The fate of the congregation's plan had to wait longer to be fully known.

One day in early December 2010, not long after the hearing concluded, the decision appeared on Park's desk. He hesitated a moment before opening it knowing how much of the church's resources had gone into this hearing. Once into it, it was a short snappy read by an obviously highly competent member.

The City insisted, through its counsel, that the issue of conformity with the city's OP and provincial policies was their main issue. First up was the City insistence that a conversion from the land use designation of Employment Lands was necessary. The staff person from the economic development department stressed the importance of the Employment-designated land to the City. There was one major problem with the City position. No conversion from Employment Lands was necessary. Both the Provincial Policy Statement and the Growth Plan policies stated clearly that places of worship are regarded as institutional land uses and, like commercial and industrial, are recognized within the Employment Lands policy. The church has three employees; the prior business had five, so there is very little difference in that regard. The conversion issue is deemed a non-issue so we move on.

Next come the two key issues – compatibility and conformity. The city-led expert planning evidence that a "sensitive land use", if allowed to locate in an area of industry necessitating deliveries in and out daily by large transport trucks, might endanger the viability of those heavier noisier uses by creating a situation where, due to the church's presence, the Environment Ministry may require a certification approving noise, dust and odour discharges. It is not simply a one-way consideration of the impacts caused by the heavier noisier operations, which are in an area where the Plan says they should be. So this raises the OP issue of Planning Function in the designated area. The city's position is that this appeal does not meet the Planned Function policies for the Employment Lands section. The church's team was ready for this attack. They called the only expert evidence on air quality and noise and that evidence successfully addressed the city's concerns on those two environmental issues head on by suggesting that the Planned Function standards were in no peril because of the church on Nugget Avenue. The city could not produce any evidence to counter it.

What had happened is that when this area was still in the former Borough of Scarborough, there was a map showing in broad terms that churches were to locate on major streets on the edge of employment areas. Nugget Avenue was not even mentioned as a possible location. However, when Scarborough merged into and became part of the City of Toronto, the Toronto OP came into effect in old Scarborough. The Toronto Plan continued the mapping but now, Nugget Avenue is shown as a street on which places of worship may locate. The OMB found that Policy 2 of the Employment Lands section of the Plan specifically allows churches and some specific commercial to locate on major streets "on Map 3". That is the map showing Nugget Avenue as one of those streets. Policy 6 provides criteria such as support for the economic function of the employment areas, key clusters of economic activity to be encouraged, limit excessive traffic, adequacy of parking, and mitigating for impacts like dust, noise and odour. The Board found that the evidence Mr. Park called and elicited from City witnesses satisfied at least five of the six criteria including the presence of business synergy. The sixth – "supporting the economic function of Employment Areas" – is not met because churches do not have much economic benefit; however, they are within the classes of establishments planned for on streets on Map

3. An amendment to the Plan to limit uses like churches only to peripheral streets was far from being in effect; it was only in the early stages of public consideration and so no such limitation existed in the city OP at that time.

Reading the Plan and all the Employment Area policies as a whole and as context for the specific references complied with in Policies 2, 3 and 6, the Board found that the proposed zoning amendment put forward by the church conformed to the City OP as it read at the time of the hearing. What is particularly interesting, and confirms the Board's finding, is that at no time did the City suggest that an OPA was required to authorize the rezoning.

The Board concluded that, being satisfied that there is to be no incompatibility that cannot be mitigated by measures the proponent will have to carry out, the Friends' desire and plan to use the Nugget Avenue site for their new church met the Provincial Policy Statement, the Growth Plan and the City OP, represented good planning and was in the public interest. Mr. Jackson, the Board member presiding, found that this application would not tend to destabilize this Employment Area when considered with the other churches already established in the area.

Jason Park could hardly believe the completeness of the Friends' success. He held the decision in his hand for some time, sensing in that decision its importance to a small group like this whose faith that a tribunal would hear their cause and act with justice, received affirmation. As he explained:

> That case was the most challenging case I had ... It concerned a very small church that wanted to develop a property to serve its congregation and its neighbours opposed it ... The church was given some assurance that the City would support its application. At the last minute, the City decided against it, even though there were other churches in the area. What interested me was that, at the OMB, the City did everything it could to oppose this application, including providing not only their staff planner but a planner hired from outside City staff and a land economist to testify that permitting churches in the (Employment Area) would prevent the city from meeting its job goals.[68]

This was a strange case. All the city had to do was move its proposed OPA regarding location of churches forward to approval, let this one go ahead as it affected only one church and was decided before the change in policy and pass a zoning amendment to limit them to peripheral streets. The OP amendment had started through the process.

Instead, the city picked the wrong time and the wrong case to challenge, for reasons that seem to have little to do with planning considerations. Cases like this one may assist in developing a raison d'être for the OMB or a tribunal for land use and compensation cases – tribunals that decide on the merits of the case and not on grounds of power, money, fear or influence – as do the other ones for which you are there, through the pages of this book. This was one of many cases never covered on the front pages or the regional or national media where the system worked quietly and well.

CHAPTER V

THE PURPOSE AND MANDATE OF THE ONTARIO MUNICIPAL BOARD

If the doors of perception were cleansed
everything would appear to man as it is, infinite.
from The Marriage of Heaven and Hell
—William Blake (1790)

CHANGING TIMES, CHANGING PURPOSE

The Ontario Municipal Board began with the middle industrial period of railways before taking a giant leap into municipal corporations and the cave paintings of early planners. The Canadian Institute of Planners came into existence in 1919. This was a primitive time when by-law attacks had more to do with traditional ultra vires, constitutional and illegality arguments than any coherent planning theory. By 1983, the OMB was just completing its tour as the chief municipal regulator when the Province merged responsibility for expropriation and development charge appeals with the Board's other work and, on the planning side, by 2005, the Province introduced two integrated layers of planning policy. Fundamentally, the purpose of the provincial tribunal in these legislative schemes was always the same – to resolve conflicts in land use, expropriation claims and municipal service cost recovery in a fair, expeditious and less costly manner by a tribunal of expertise specialized to match the subject matters it deals with. At present and over the last two decades, its score on this basic yardstick is about 40 per cent. Its timelines have slowed, its reputation for fairness and consistency has slipped, and expedition and matching expertise have been luxuries it could not always bring to the table.

I think the purpose of the tribunal on the planning side became a check on the political and economic power of ward-based town and city councils and large development companies by use of planning grounds and principles as the measure of success in planning. Principles of land use planning in Ontario did not appear to develop into a coherent body of work until the 1940s to '50s. It is clear from the case law that some coherence in principle had been reached and applied to zoning issues by then. *Scarborough (Township) v Bondi*[69] dealt with an amendment passed in 1956 to a zoning by-law enacted originally before the *Planning Act* existed. The by-law was passed in 1938 pursuant to authority in the 1937 *Municipal Act*. By 1958, the OMB was enunciating planning principles that later were the subject of the decisions in *Hopedale Investments Ltd. v Oakville (Town)*[70] relying on *Re Mississauga Golf & Country Club.*[71] Those principles were derived from two OMB decisions in 1958.[72] The OMB in *Hopedale* alluded to the following concepts taken from those cases as live ideas and issues then:

- conformity with the OP
- stability and character of an area
- effect on single family residential zoned land of high density development as a precedent for more such development and potential de-stabilizing of area
- no change in land use or in OP to warrant introduction of high density proposal
- destabilizing of area by premature zoning change
- land use compatibility.

Since 1983, the OMB was handed an oversight function: to have regard for matters of provincial interest and consistency in the interpretation and application of provincial policy in light of the facts of each case. In this evolution of purpose, therefore, the aim of the retention of a provincial tribunal for planning, compensation and development charges now included both procedural and substantive goals: (i) meeting the duty of procedural fairness, founded on "the principle that the individuals affected should have the opportunity to present their case fully and fairly, and have decisions affecting their rights, interests, or privileges made using a fair, impartial, and open process, appropriate to the statutory, institutional, and social context of the decision;"[73] and (ii) specialized adjudication on coherent principled grounds, acting in the public interest and with reasonable consistency in the application of provincial and local policy then in effect. As the leaders of Stop Spadina found out, due to the accretion of power and a wide area of discretion by 1970, the OMB had a great deal of authority over the whole planning, financial and financing approval processes including all projects requiring municipal financing measures.

The expanse of authority is less now but no less important: a key area of planning focus now is that of resource preservation and reduction of urban sprawl for financial, transportation and energy conservation reasons. The research on urban sprawl has not produced high marks for the OMB from those who work in this field, at least in the areas surrounding Toronto. As S. Tandon concluded in 2014 (we will return to this subject later in more detail spotlighting the municipal performance):

> While Ontario's municipalities have had to deal with the consequences of urban sprawl, they face immense difficulties challenging aggressive land development, despite being the primary locus of land-use decisions. Sprawl has continued

in Ontario under the auspices of the Ontario Municipal Board (OMB), a provincial body with oversight on municipal land use decisions. Many opponents of sprawl argue the present state of Ontario's sprawling built environment has been the result of the cumulative pro-developer decisions at the OMB. This, among other factors, spurred calls for an overhaul of this institution, with the issue culminating in 2003 in the face of residential developments on Southern Ontario's ecologically critical Oak Ridges Moraine. It was in these circumstances that Dalton McGuinty's liberal party was first elected, with a platform committing to reform of the OMB. The evolution and effectiveness of such reform, as it relates to urban sprawl, will be a key theme of this paper.

She concluded later in the same paper:

> Drawing conclusions as to the degree of success of Ontario's new and often complex policies are both difficult and contentious. Burda hesitates to make such a conclusion, instead stating that "the effects of this legislation will need to be understood over time." (Burda, 2008, p. 39)

Conclusion
Although the Ontario government committed to a reform of the OMB, the additional legislation and policies that were meant to bring about this reform have clearly not been realized in practice. This is especially true in municipalities which fall outside both planning areas of Ontario's *Greenbelt Act* and *Places to Grow Act*. This implies that a partial remedy can be found by deploying additional growth plans under the *Places to Grow Act* to cover the remaining regions of the province. While the Minister of Municipal Affairs has the authority to intervene in the OMB appeals process if it is deemed a matter of provincial interest, this power has yet to be exercised in preventing an urban sprawl development.

The OMB, as a historic institution, may just be experiencing bureaucratic inertia. With time, board members should eventually be replaced by competent planners familiar with sustainable land-use policies and the problems associated with urban sprawl. With eight-year board member terms, such institutional change will be slow, and in that time, the natural lands will continue to be lost to concrete and pavement.[74]

As we have seen, the so-called eight or nine year terms are rhetoric; the actual renewals for members still occur every one, two or three years. Be that as it may, there is a planning consensus that tough policies are required, starting with the increase proposed in the 2016 Growth

Plan for the Greater Golden Horseshoe to an intensification target of 60 per cent. That is, 60 per cent of all residential development shall occur annually in the built-up area of each upper tier and lower tier municipality by the next municipal comprehensive review, an increase of 50 per cent from the previous target. This increase remains in place now that the proposed plan has been reviewed by the Province and the deadline for feedback on changes is now October 31, 2016.

A POLICY-LED PROCESS COROLLARY: A DECISION-MAKER TO TRANSLATE POLICY IN DIFFERING CONTEXTS

From this conclusion implying the OMB's failure to perform the oversight function consistently, and the top-down nature of the present planning process in Ontario, the Ontario government's aggressive moves into comprehensive provincial planning to guide municipalities have made the presence of a provincial appeal and compensation claims tribunal essential to the process in Ontario. The presence of a tribunal operating on planning grounds and, for compensation claims, on proper legal and appraisal principles should offer qualities of consistency, predictability, and mediation capabilities that seek consensus and positive contributions from all parties to resolution of community planning and compensation claims. The fact that it has not performed at times as some informed writers believe it should have does not change the conclusion on the need for an oversight tribunal with a mandate to provide policy leadership and a duty to provide fair and impartial justice within the provincial policy framework.

There is a corollary of importance and assistance to the future tribunal. As a senior counsel[75] with insight into both the planning and compensation spheres told me, there is a tension that the administrative tribunal in the municipal field has to live with: how it maintains its position as an independent adjudicator while respecting the role of elected officials. In dealing with that tension, the tribunal has to act effectively as an independent adjudicator while still respecting the role of elected officials. Provincial policy is the easiest route through that tension because it is the factor with which both the tribunal and municipal officials are directed by the *Planning Act* to act consistently. Therefore, in each case, the tribunal should not be reluctant to find, in provincial, growth and OP policy, relevant principles to guide the member through the findings of fact to an appropriate conclusion that gives due respect to the decisions of the municipalities' elected representatives. This has been a route that few decisions have found so far with consistency.

Whichever route is chosen for the planning and compensation tribunal of the future, the independence of judgment, inseparability of environmental from planning concerns, and sense of fairness to minority interests within a real sense of the wider public interest, espoused by the Kennedy and Stewart Boards at their best, must be reborn in a new conception suited to its pivotal role of leadership in the policy-led planning system of 2015–2050 Ontario. The history and laurels and jurisprudence, even the baggage, from 1906–2015 will remain a constant benefit and warning to the tribunal that the past must not dictate process or substantive decision-making where there are better, less costly and more expeditious approaches.

There is another more dramatic, hopefully theoretical, but most serious ground for retaining an appeal tribunal. That is, the huge amounts of money that many of the projects entail including cost of servicing debt for lengthy appeal processes. The Board, and its insistence on deciding cases on planning merit, or on reasonableness related to OP policy and the PPS, serves to keep everyone honest. There is a certain desperation that can set in which, without the public hearing process, can lead too easily to corrupt practices and illicit payments in exchange for something as simple as fixing a planning report. The fictional statement in some films – "Here, take care of this, will you?" – with the passage of an envelope from one hand to another, may become reality, given the huge profits at stake in some of these larger proposals and the risk of very large losses where the time of the planning process extends on into the future.

A former president of the Canadian Bar Association and one of the most senior counsel in administrative law testified in 1972 before the Select Committee on the OMB. The first point he made was this: that the OMB has played a role in preventing bribery and corruption in the Province and should be encouraged and structured to continue the role. The Committee noted this testimony but seemed to dismiss it. Yet, he was right in my view. The greatest value provided by the OMB and the planning process was the insistence that the success of a development proposal depends on proving the case before the Board on planning principles or, as one could rephrase it, in terms of whether a decision of a municipal council reasonably carries out the intent of the OP and provincial policy as they apply to the site in question. Once one gets away from this kind of principled approach, a place is provided for the matter being determined in ways that are criminal but may be hard to detect; it only takes a split second to transfer cash to those who will not be able to resist the lure of so much money.[76]

> "... the OMB has played a role in preventing bribery and corruption in the Province and should be encouraged and structured to continue the role."

That same senior counsel had a taste of this very behaviour one day. I was told by a partner of his about an event that happened one day. He and a client entered a local clerk's office to find a senior official of the municipality present. They wanted to locate a document that would assist the client's case. After they had found what they were looking for and they were waiting to make a presentation to council, the official told the counsel that if he would just give him a certain object that he wanted, they would get the approval they sought. The counsel replied: "We are going to the Ontario Municipal Board and the first question that you are going to be asked is what you just said and what you meant." The matter was resolved forthwith, to everyone's satisfaction.[77]

Another instance that crossed ethical if not fraudulent lines was discovered during the OMB hearing on the Minto Yonge-Eglinton development in Toronto. It came out as counsel for the developer was cross-examining a city staff planner.[78] The planner had been called by the opponents of the large proposed development who were very concerned with its height and density. This planner identified for the objectors' counsel a report he had done. After setting out the planner's findings regarding the density and the number of traffic movements calculated daily to be generated by the development and identifying the report, the opposition lawyer handed him over for cross-examination. The lawyer had interviewed him earlier; however, she was not sure how frank he was prepared to be. Gradually, she worked through the report to the conclusion, a summing up of why the development's density was inappropriate for the area, which included a single family neighbourhood to the south and east. She asked him whether the report seemed to contain reasoning that should have led to a completely different conclusion, i.e. that there was no serious incompatibility from the viewpoint of building density. He agreed. She asked: "Well, how can this be? You wrote the report?

A.   Yes.
Q.   And you wrote the conclusion?
A.   I wrote a conclusion but not this one.
Q.   I don't understand. Do you mean that this is not your conclusion?
A.   That's right.
Q.   Did you actually conclude that the density was appropriate to the area?
A.   Yes.
Q.   So how did this other conclusion come to be on your report?
A.   Someone wrote their own conclusion, this one, and replaced mine with this.
      This was not what I had written.

There have been other instances where a criminal line was in jeopardy of being crossed. In a case where Alan Patton of London was acting for a developer, the mayor and several councillors all swore affidavits about an 'in camera' meeting, what had been discussed, and perhaps what was voted on.[79] Patton was representing R.S.J. Holdings Inc., which wanted to demolish a heritage building and build a four-plex, a project that had raised objections from neighbours who said they were already overrun by university students. The council spent more than two hours in closed session, then emerged and immediately passed an interim control by-law freezing development in an area including Patton's client's land. They had carried out an illegal vote in camera, came back to the public session and without one word of discussion, passed the by-law without a word of debate in public.[80] They later swore that no such vote had occurred.

These instances and others demonstrate what can happen when people come under severe pressure due to the high stakes involved in the planning process and what otherwise respectable people will do to get themselves or someone else out of a jam. To all counsel whom I interviewed and who have practiced on both sides of cases, all agree that the OMB has helped to keep people honest because they all know that the hearing at the end will be public and fair, omitting for now the present decision-making difficulties. Therefore, no illegal motives can take hold. Several stated their view that, given the large amounts of money involved, and absent the OMB, there is little doubt that envelopes of money would change hands to seal a deal and any idea of principled planning would yield to the largest wallet.

When asked whether the OMB still performed a useful role in the planning process, the planners and municipal law practitioners that I interviewed were unanimous. That position is not unpredictable since they make their living before the OMB but their reasons were evidence of the sincerity of their comments and were certainly not always complimentary to the present OMB though they remain understanding of the Board's dilemma. The following are some examples:

- The Board continues to be useful although in a way that is unfortunately not as positive as it used to be. It used to be, when I started some forty years ago, that you could look at a Municipal Board decision from any member and have a general understanding of the kind of evidence required to test a particular principle and have some general understanding of consistent results from that: issue 1. Issue 2 – the members were around long enough and had enough interaction with the bar ... that you understood the individual member ... I think the usefulness of the Board today is reduced, at least from the perspective of having some predictability or certainty or understanding of the issues from which you would expect a decision more or less to follow along from the principles applied. Its usefulness in the broader planning process is almost a negative one ... to the point that people bend over backwards to avoid being taken to the Municipal Board."

  A Municipal Board hearing will eat up ten per cent of the budget for the entire year of a small municipality. So its usefulness remains in this weird and tortured expression as the overseer of the planning process but it's getting badly warped ...

  Here is my bias. What the Board is doing now is not the task that the Board has been asked to do ... The Board was always alive to the changes to the legislation and to public policy. It is because they haven't been given the tools any longer to do the job in a way that is predictable, reliable, respected, and at the moment the Board does not get the respect and support that it requires to do a job that means not only deciding the matters in front of it, which it has always done, but also shaping the thinking around policy and what is in the public interest. That is what it used to do. Just the way the Supreme Court shaped the law, the Municipal Board shaped planning in this province.[81]

- There are two reasons for requiring the OMB to exist. First, the planning process in Ontario is policy-led and a provincial tribunal is required to interpret and apply those policies to real situations. Second, it also prevents the abuses which could occur if it did not exist. It prevents graft at the municipal level. There is so much money involved in some of these projects that, without the OMB, it would be too easy for someone to slip some money to a councillor and say, 'Take care of this.'

  In addition it is the way we have done things here. It is not B.C. where they never had a system like this and therefore the dialogue is different and the process is different there ... One idea for different parameters is to allow appeals from changes in the OP policies but do not allow appeals where a by-law implements the OP I do not agree with that limitation ...[82]

- The Board has a primary role to play of interpreting provincial policy but it goes further than that. It provides what council cannot provide, a full hearing of all the evidence ... More importantly, hot button issues like a gravel pit, low rental housing, highways, none of these would get approved without the OMB. If it were up to the local council, they would simply think of their own wards and their own electoral security and vote the way that parochial view would require ...When we met earlier and I referred to areas of planning where the Board's role was essential to the oversight and implementation of provincial policy, I am not sure I mentioned "intensification". If the Board did not exist, there is little chance in my view that the MMAH intensification targets in York or any other regions or cities would be realized. The presence of the Board acts as a much needed 'pressure tower' to ensure the issue of intensification is properly implemented by the local councils.[83]

- I believe the Board is still necessary for part of the process. They criticize it for favouring developers, and that is simply not correct. The OMB most of the time ends up agreeing with the council or the city's planning report, not necessarily with the developer. The Board is still the place you go to for a fair shake.[84]

I am not in the habit of making or giving much weight to *in terrorem* arguments and these conclusions are not meant in that vein. However, it is clear to me from the above that with the OMB in place, practitioners know there is no point to a bribe since ultimately the tribunal will decide on planning grounds. No payment to anyone will decide the case. This is an important reason for a provincial land use planning and compensation tribunal to continue the work under the mandate in the *Planning Act*, performed to this year by the Ontario Municipal Board.

In fact, what this analysis has demonstrated, and will continue to demonstrate in different contexts as we go on, is that there are multiple reasons for a tribunal like the OMB to exist on different terms. Several were provided by a Toronto planner in describing the usefulness of the OMB today:

1. It hears appeals on land use planning grounds – those would go to the courts where planning would not necessarily be understood;
2. It ensures planners will give honest and accurate opinions knowing they will be weighed and tested at a hearing later; and
3. It helps to give public sector planners a certain level of protection, when they are put under pressure to write a planning report in a certain way.[85]

Other reflections of its mandate come from the Planning Act and the duty of procedural fairness, informed by the values enunciated by Justice L'Heureux-Dubé for a unanimous Supreme Court of Canada as being the content of that duty:

> I emphasize that underlying all these factors is the notion that the purpose of the participatory rights contained within the duty of procedural fairness is to ensure that administrative decisions are made using a fair and open procedure, appropriate to the decision being made and its statutory, institutional, and social context, with an opportunity for those affected by the decision to put forward their views and evidence fully and have them considered by the decision-maker.[86]

THE MANDATE OF THE LAND USE PLANNING AND EXPROPRIATION CLAIMS TRIBUNAL

The mandate of the Board within its *Planning Act* jurisdiction, from all accounts, remains important to the planning process. That mandate includes the following duties, in my view:

1. to hear matters and appeals brought under and within the terms of the *Planning Act*, *Expropriations Act* and *Development Charges Act* taking into account grounds and principles of land use planning, appraisal and service cost recovery;

2. to require high standards of professionalism and impartiality from land use planners, appraisers and other witnesses qualified to give opinion evidence;

3. to provide a standard of fairness to the process and hearing of all appeals;

4. to direct the process of, and make decisions on, all appeals properly before it taking into account the public interest, provincial planning policy issued under section 3, provincial plans, and municipal official plans and on all claims before it, to act with fairness, impartiality and competence and within the statutory framework;

5. to have regard to the decisions of municipal councils appealed to the Board and to any supporting material and information that were before the said councils when the decisions appealed from were made;

6. to shape the interpretation and application of planning law and policy in Ontario in accordance with the purposes and directions in sections 2 and 3 of the *Planning Act* and the principles of the Rule of Law; and

7. to provide an opportunity during the hearing of appeals for all those having an interest and/or standing within the *Planning Act* to express their views on planning issues affecting them and their communities.

The mandate is what the tribunal is authorized to do. It is not an automatic conversion to the quality and effectiveness of the performance of that mandate. We will explore that aspect shortly.

The importance of decisions about land use and the consequences are illuminated more darkly by the following case. It arose out of a simple error – the premature issue of a building permit and the commencement of work before the error was corrected – on a significantly sized apartment building, which for years loomed over the extension south of Bayview Avenue near Moore Avenue in Toronto. The structure was completed but no more – a constant reminder that the planning process deals with things that last, including errors, a fact that should weigh heavily on any decision-maker in this field. The huge costs that were run up on this account ensured that no one could afford to do anything about it for over twenty years.

BEING THERE 5: THE 'BAYVIEW GHOST' HEARING

(Ranch Home Builders Ltd. v East York (Borough),11 OMBR 466)

On a plateau of land well above the Bayview Extension, open to the view of motorists proceeding north or south below Moore Avenue, there was constructed an apartment building all in white. It was August 1959 when Bayview Avenue was extended south from Moore Avenue in Leaside to River Street parallel to the Don Valley Parkway, hence the name Bayview Extension.

As you rounded the curve down into the valley, the white building was far up the hill on your left. It was an eerie sight, year after year, this white building looking down over the extension through open windows like so many eyes, where you never saw anyone enter or leave. I never saw a road giving access to it. But there it was, the haunted empty shell known to everyone as the Ghost of Bayview.

Finally, by 1980 someone must have obtained the rights to the property because a company named Ranch Home Builders Ltd. brought forward to the local council a development proposal. This brought out another application sponsored by the Borough of East York and supported by the local ratepayers group. Both involved changes to the OP of East York and the site zoning; the East York proposal would designate the place for park use or a subdivision of one detached home per lot on sixty-six lots. The first proposal would see a high density apartment and townhouse complex with a total of 880 units combined together with a recreational complex, a commercial establishment to serve the residents only, a gatehouse for security people and parking. Needless to say, the apartment/townhouse project was not the one supported by the local neighbourhood association.

The problems with this unusual but wonderful site were several. The lot is crescent-shaped on a height of land overlooking the Don Valley, with the Bayview Avenue Extension on one side and the Toronto Brickyard and a CPR railway right of way on the others. It was strategically positioned as one of the last sizeable pieces of vacant land within minutes of downtown Toronto. The downsides literally were eroded, steeply sloped to the valley, no vehicular access existed, and servicing issues for water and sewer were problematic, all of which isolated it from the remaining community. An access road and servicing would cost over $1.5 million due to the awkward manner in which the road must connect in a kind of cloverleaf to the Bayview Extension. The servicing is the most expensive item. It cannot utilize the existing sewer, which overflows in storms. Any development would require slope stabilization.

Impacts were severe from several sources: noise from the trains on two nearby lines, noise from the Don Valley Parkway and the Bayview Extension, and blasting from quarry operations in the brickyards.

Both proposals came before the Board for approval in the late fall of 1980. The Board looked at compatibility issues and concluded, not surprisingly, that the OP for the East York Planning Area required any development on this site to be compatible with the North West Community, the nearest to it. That community had developed to include a shopping area and mostly single family housing with some smaller apartments. Sixty per cent of it is owner-occupied.

The problem was that the East York proposal before the Board was for 4000 sq. ft. homes behind a fortress-like concrete structured embankment to deflect the noise. The Board ruled that this did not fit with the nearby community, which was a traditional residential, mostly owner-occupied homes with families and children who enjoyed playing in the parks and yards. The ratepayer/borough-sponsored proposal was not approved.

In reviewing the 880-unit proposal, the Board found the projected population to be about two thousand; in traffic it would generate up to six thousand car movements per day, and generally it was found too intensive to be integrated into the North West Community. The Board reduced the density by over 50 per cent, from 185–220 units/hectare to no more than 75 units/hectare. It was recognized that the servicing would be costly and so some degree of higher density was permitted but not the 880 units.

The case was appealed to the Cabinet. This appeal to Cabinet from the OMB was held over from the 1946 *Planning Act*. The decision on the record is simply marked "Reversed." The Cabinet found in favour of East York on the argument that the OMB-approved project displayed a density far too high for the area. The old shell of the Ghost was demolished that same year. It took another twenty years to develop the site due to legal difficulties and the costs of battle for over forty years. The single family houses have been built but it is said that some of them remain uninhabited ... well, empty. The ghost may be alive and well in another form.[87]

> "...this site could have been a prime candidate for a mediated solution."

Counsel for the development company that succeeded at the OMB, Robert Doumani, told me those years later, when the Board had begun mediation efforts, this site could have been a prime candidate for a mediated solution. He described it in the following terms:

> There is a flat area of land like a mesa up on the hillside and somebody began to build an apartment [under a building permit issued in error, later revoked; road access was denied]. The plan was a ring building around the central area where there would be more apartments. It meant very high density and would have required a new road from Bayview. The road was too expensive and so the building remained unfinished and uninhabited for years.

Now, why is this case worth mentioning? It has no ringing passages about the continuing controversies surrounding the OMB. Nor does it say anything about improvements to the selection process to recruit new OMB members for this challenging job.

No, this case is here for two purposes: (i) to illustrate the kind of case that would have been ripe for mediation had it been available due to the smothering effect of costs; and (ii) to blow some embers bright enough to see if there are more case types than minor variance appeals, which may not require an appeal to a provincial tribunal because the only interests in the case are local.

These neighbourhood issues, one lawyer told me, are the very issues that affect people most in the planning process. It is one reason some say that minor variance appeals should remain to the OMB because there is too much variability available to local committees deciding those appeals, and because they need reminding by an objective tribunal of some legal or planning ability what the test of the zoning and OP intent means in analytical terms. As to variability of local committees, the comment of the authors of *Planning in the USA* was:

Various studies have shown convincingly that boards of adjustment commonly operate according to their own sense of what is right, with little regard for the law or even their own planning department ... It has also been suggested that variances should be subject to review by a higher authority such as a state review board... (Their) popularity at the local level assures (their) continuance as a major feature of the zoning system. There is more to planning than law.[88]

I understand the point and there may be another solution using provincial policy or interest as a way to rationalize why a land use tribunal appointed provincially as a lead tribunal in applying policy is supposed to deal with purely local concerns where there are so many time-consuming issues of consequence competing for the tribunal's time.

CHAPTER VI

SHAKE-UP

Whether 'tis nobler in the mind to suffer
The slings and arrows of outrageous fortune
Or to take arms against a sea of troubles.....
from Hamlet, Act III, Scene 1

THE POSITION OF THE PROVINCE

One party to all of the handwringing and criticism over the OMB and its mandate had been remarkably silent on the subject in recent years. That is the provincial government. In her first mandate letter to her ministers of September 25, 2014, the Premier hints neither of burial nor acclamation for the OMB. Under the heading "Improving Land Use Planning," there are three initiatives listed: first, a fuzzy direction to the minister to undertake initiatives to support growth, protect the environment and improve the social well-being of the province; second, a kind of wish to improve land use planning, and, among other things, to reduce applications to the OMB; and finally, a more specific direction to lead a review of "the scope and effectiveness" of the OMB and recommend "possible reforms ... to improve the OMB's role within the broader land use planning system." That was it. And that was September 25, 2014.

As of June 2016, no review had started. The mandate letter seemed to have led to silence and inaction from the lead minister of the time. One comment of note emanated from Ted McMeekin during this period. Following negative reaction to the Waterloo first phase hearing in January 2013, he was heard to remark on the OMB being too adversarial. That bore little meaning for the Waterloo hearing where positions had hardened so as to make mediation impossible at that time. He then explained: "We would like to see more conciliation, negotiation and less of an adversarial approach." He added, "We'd like to see more negotiated settlements and conversations about what the issue is and how we can get it resolved without ... a very expensive hearing."[89]Yes, Minister. He had added nothing and brought nothing forward in response to the mandate letter of the Premier.

From the Attorney General of the province, in whose ministry the OMB is placed for administrative purposes, there was more silence. Madeleine Meilleur of Ottawa-Vanier was the Attorney General in 2014. She was tasked to work with Mr. McMeekin on the review. To early June, 2016, there was no public evidence of the OMB review beginning from her either.

Suddenly, in the middle of June,2016, a mild but definite earthquake in politics occurred at Queens Park. Both the Minister of Municipal Affairs and Housing and the Attorney General retired. New minds were set to work in both ministries. This had exciting implications for the planning sector.

It is hard to explain the stasis that reigned in these ministries despite the call to action in the planning field by the Premier in September 2014. As the Minister of Municipal Affairs and Housing and the Attorney General should know, the government could have used the past several years to bring the OMB's full-time complement of members up to where it long had been, at twenty-seven to twenty-eight members plus perhaps two to four part-time members. It could have done so by selective recruiting of mediation-trained lawyers and planners to enable a real push to mediation. It would have capitalized on the great success achieved by a very small group of members. It could also have chosen persons of distinction from other related careers, and it could have assisted the selection process by remedying the tenure/remuneration situation. If the desire was to have more mediation and conciliation, as the Minister had stated, that had been well within the government's power all this time since 2009. I know the leadership of the OMB would have very much liked to widen the mediation effort but it was hamstrung by the paucity of members available to do it.

Another facet of governmental power that is not talked about and relatively unused, is the power of the Minister of Municipal Affairs and Housing to take action where the Minister wants to ensure that the development industry and the public get it about certain policy initiatives. If the government were not satisfied, for instance, with the municipal and/or OMB response to its policies for controlling urban sprawl, intensifying development within developed areas and/or protecting sensitive ecological areas of public importance, there are very specific powers open to the Minister. When the researchers into the reasons for urban sprawl were concerned over the related issues of intensification not being addressed in or about 2003–2007, and if the OMB or municipal council decision-making was responsible for not promoting those policies, the government had open to it the following weapons for use in selected hearings and pre-hearing processes:

1. The Minister's power to zone land as the ministry sees fit; section 47 of the *Planning Act* allows the Minister to take urgent action in place of the municipal councils with jurisdiction in the areas of concern to prohibit land from being developed by use of the zoning power without notice. Notice must be given after the power is exercised and where any person requests, the Minister must

request the Board to hold a hearing. The Ministry of Municipal Affairs and Housing through legal counsel could take a leadership role in organizing all the evidence from the relevant ministries to underline the importance of these issues to the public interest. Any decision must be subject to confirmation or variance by cabinet, also known as the Lieutenant Governor in Council, under section 47(13.5).

2. The Minister can request a municipality to amend the OP of a municipality where the minister is of the opinion that a matter of provincial interest set out in a Provincial Policy Statement is, or is likely to be affected. Section 23 of the *Planning Act* requires that if the municipality will or will not enact the requested amendment, provision is made for an OMB hearing from which any decision is subject to confirmation or variance or rescission by the cabinet.

3. There is also section 17(5) of the *Planning Act,* which allows the Minister to intervene in the planning process where any part of an official plan may, in his opinion, prejudice a matter of provincial interest. Again, this gives the Minister real leverage at the hearing to bring a matter of urgency to the OMB and to lead evidence to show the basis for its concern at a hearing open to the public. The Minister would command attention to an interest of importance and any decision would again be subject to final confirmation or variance or dismissal by cabinet. Where several of such plans in several municipalities must be the subject of the same concerns, in that case, the OMB could consolidate the matters and deal with them by mandatory mediation and one hearing if necessary.

There was no lack of authority where the Minister had a genuine problem with a decision or decisions of the OMB or with particular development proposals before the Board. The Minister had not seen fit to take any action as of early June 2016. The Attorney General, who is responsible for the Board's administrative needs, as well as the Premier through the appointments secretariat, had done nothing toward bringing the OMB to full complement or to fix the tenure/remuneration package that stands in the way of persons of unusual ability in the private sector accepting an appointment to the OMB.

I understand that the provincial deficit is real, that is understood, but it has not stopped governmental initiatives in other areas where there has been some commitment. I wondered at one point if this silence and the delayed review process was not a preliminary to a continuing failure to fund its operations, leading to an eventual capitulation to those who want that to happen but have no answers for any right of appeal at the municipal level that is unbiased or competent.

I finally wrote both ministries through the website services in March 2016, not expecting an early answer. However, I did receive a reply from Premier Kathleen Wynne. For those who may have thought the review was only a bad memory, the letter was more forthcoming than I expected. The Premier's April 6, 2016 letter stated, in part:

> During our government's review of the land use planning and appeal system, we heard concerns about the OMB and its process, including that it is too long. We all have a stake in how our communities are shaped and it is important that land use planning appeals are dealt with in an appropriate manner.
>
> In response to feedback from citizens, municipalities and stakeholders, our government has committed to undertake review of the scope and effectiveness of the OMB. The Minister of Municipal Affairs and Housing will work with the Ministry of the Attorney General and key stakeholders in undertaking the review, and will recommend possible reforms to improve the OMB's role within the broader land use planning system. This will begin shortly.

She concluded by indicating that a copy of her letter would go to the Minister of Municipal Affairs and Housing. While this letter is very broadly worded, it does say clearly that the OMB review is still to occur and she appeared to be nudging the Minister by sending a copy of her letter to him with this clear statement of the Premier's desire to see the review occur under his leadership. This at least indicates from the provincial leader her commitment to this review happening and her expectation that recommendations will come forward to improve the OMB's role in the planning system.

The Premier indicated that the intent was to focus on improving the OMB's role in the *Planning Act* process. This seemed to be a commitment on her part to maintain a provincial land use appeals tribunal in place. The period of the hands-off attitude toward the tribunal was ending.

The review would come under section 21(1) and (2) of the ATAGA legislation, which states that the following would be some of the topics to be considered:
- the tribunal's mandate and whether it continues to be relevant;
- the functions performed by the tribunal, and whether they are best performed by the tribunal or whether they would be better performed by another entity;
- whether the tribunal is effective in achieving its mandate and serving the public; and
- whether changes should be made to the tribunal or whether the tribunal should be discontinued.

In other words, the review cannot examine scope and effectiveness without considering the question of whether the OMB should continue at all. On the latter subject, the government's silence had ended. One reason for this book was that,

... the government has to decide fundamentally if it really wants to lead the planning process by maintaining a high quality planning and compensation review tribunal, which can have a chance to fulfil the mandate that... all stakeholders, including the municipalities of Ontario, would support.

In mid-June, with the announcements of the Cabinet appointments, a new Minister of Municipal Affairs, Bill Mauro of Thunder Bay, and a new Attorney General, Yasir Naqvi took their places. They replaced, respectively, Mr. McMeekin and Ms. Meilleur who elected to retire.

On the heels of these announcements, on June 23, 2016, a joint declaration was issued from the two new Ministers that the review of the OMB was to begin. A preliminary discussion paper issued setting out several questions for which the government wanted the public's response. They included: the jurisdiction and powers of the OMB, citizen participation, clear and predictable decision-making, hearing procedures and practices, alternate dispute resolution, and timely processes and decisions. Submissions on the OMB within these themes were invited from the public and a consultation paper was expected in the fall to further define the issues to be considered.

On October 5, 2016, that consultation paper was released. A date is set in that document for final submissions from the public.

The central focus of the review, continuation or termination of a provincial land use and compensation review, seems to be a matter of some consensus now within the government. The OMB has had a great deal to do with the continuing orderly development and economic expansion of the province. It has been under severe criticism in recent years for a perceived environmental irresponsibility and inconsistency. The major principle that the consultation paper stressed without equivocation was this:

*PRINCIPLES: IT IS IMPORTANT THAT ONTARIO CONTINUE
TO HAVE AN INDEPENDENT APPEAL TRIBUNAL THAT
CAN RESOLVE SOME LAND USE DISPUTES.*

This statement marked a definite milestone for this government. On retention of a land use appeals tribunal would rest the remainder of the review study and submissions. The OMB itself is not necessarily to be the vessel to carry the planning process forward; the idea of an OMB-like provincial tribunal as a cornerstone of that process would continue but in what form and with what powers? It is upon those remaining issues that the consultation paper called for further submissions.

Some twenty-four questions were put to the public, each group of three to five devoted to one theme. Theme 1 is the OMB's Jurisdiction and Powers. I will deal with it in some detail to give a flavour of the whole paper and to show the directions being contemplated by the Province in the important areas of fundamental jurisdiction and power.

The Theme 1 section starts with a recitation of the main arguments heard by the review. They point to a desire for change but the direction is not clear. Some want the Board's power to be reduced and its ability to overturn municipal decisions limited, whereas others see the need for a tribunal that has sufficient power to make decisions where municipal councils cannot decide, or where councils have failed to take into account broad provincial concerns. These are somewhat contradictory positions as power is required to make effective decisions. The kind of issues that can go to the Board can certainly be limited. The paper sets out the *Planning Act* limitations on the OMB including the directive to have regard to council's decisions. The changes being considered now are set out:

- limits on appeals to the tribunal to allow the Province to specify which parts of an O.P. would not be subject to appeal in the interest of farmland preservation and orderly community development , no doubt meaning in part intensification;

- where municipalities are required to implement new OPs or OPAs in order to implement Provincial planning policies or decisions, the Province's decision would not be subject to appeal; and

- where a Minister's zoning order is in effect to protect public interests, the Minister and not the OMB would have the authority to make the final decision.

The Province is exploring changes that could allow more decisions to be made locally. Those possibilities could include no right of appeal from a municipal interim control by-law (which is limited in time to two years usually for a planning study to be made) and restricting site plan issues to being resolved by local appeal bodies

One of the more interesting changes, and definitely one that would swing more of the power to make effective decisions and policy to municipalities, would be to change the standard of review used by the OMB to one of reasonableness: this would mean that the question for the Board on most appeals would be: does the decision of council reasonably carry out the intent of the OP and the PPS? This would produce a range of acceptable outcomes and as long as the council's decision can be seen to fall within that range of reasonable connection to the planning intent of the OP and provincial policy, it cannot be overturned by the OMB. Adoption of this standard would build into the standard of review deference to the decisions of local councils instead of the present situation where the OMB can come to its decision under section 17 and then have regard to the council's decision under a different section, section 2.1, having largely decided the case.

Other themes are citizen participation (exploring funding for citizen appeals and increasing assistance to citizens to make the process more accessible and more balanced); clear and predictable decision-making (return of multi-member panels with complementary skill sets for complex hearings and increasing the membership of the Board using selection criteria to ensure the necessary skills are met); modern procedures and faster decisions (considering such measures as hearings in writing and issue- and time-focussed hearings with timelines for decisions); and alternate dispute resolution or mediation (perhaps mandatory mediation, perhaps mediator availability throughout the appeal process, and most of all, greater promotion by the Province of mediation to resolve land use matters).

The final deadline for submissions to the Province is set at December 19, 2016.

The review process, once started, has met its timelines so far and is being carried out in a well-organized and open process. The matters under consideration include most of the themes I explore in this book. What is important to understand is, after all the alternatives that the Province says it is considering are listed and discussed, there is nothing as yet that it is committed to doing other than retaining a provincial land use appeal tribunal to deal with land use appeals.

Municipal government is now a recognized independent and accountable level of government within its jurisdiction, under the new *Municipal Act 2001*. It seems clear that the Province wants to reduce appeals to the provincial tribunal by having the municipalities provide the process for appeal. The problems with that are threefold: how the municipalities will fund this further cost at the local level, how they will address the problem of conflicting interests and taking account of broad provincial interests at the local level, and how they will find time to hear even abbreviated planning matters in the midst of governing the municipality. The council will be appointing both the local committee to hear minor variances and consent applications as they do now, as well as deciding zoning and OP issues, but the same council will be appointing the appeal body locally. For many appeals, they will be heard and decided by appointees of the same body (municipal council) that made the original decision, or by appointees beholden to council for their jobs. Without a great degree of care in mounting the local appeal structure, conflicts of interest will be numerous and intercessions by councilors on behalf of constituents before their own appeal body, as they do now, create another level of conflicting interests. These process issues will be a challenge to meet. On the other hand, many decisions largely revolve around local issues and require decisions from people who know the community.

As we proceed further, I will deal with many if not all of these themes and concerns and present at the end some ideas for change, which will be submitted to the review. It would be a help, I think, to anyone who wants to make an informed contribution to the review to read on. It is hoped that this recent activity promises a cessation of governmental neglect and disapproval, and a real intention to reform the system. Real reform would include a respected place for the OMB or a new tribunal with a renewed provincial mandate of mediation and high quality decision-making for the vital land use concerns that continue to confront municipalities and the Province and each one of those reading this book.

The Province needs to find a defined plan for the appeals tribunal to carry out its mandate within the planning process and commit to that plan as the purposes and provincial policy set within the *Planning Act* held promise for. One set of ideas for the future are in the final chapter of this book. A serious consideration in all of this is the ability, the credibility, of the appeals process and of the tribunal to act fairly and firmly, reserving to council its proper sphere of decision-making in order to govern effectively but also considering the parties who propose or oppose developmental ideas or policies, and the Province with the burden of leadership concerning significant public interests at stake.

For now, though, we have the present OMB to study with a view to an uncertain but now a somewhat hopeful future. Almost everything remains on the table for decision in the near future. It will depend on how activist or conservative a route the Province will opt for. The status quo is unacceptable. The following section and chapters 9 to 11 tell why.

COMPETENCE, SELECTION, REMUNERATION: HOW THEY ARE RELATED TO THE POST-2000 OMB

In section 14 of the *Adjudicative Tribunals Accountability Governance and Appointments Act, 2009*, the legislation that authorized the reorganization of tribunals into groupings called clusters, there is a direction that certain tribunals may require a specific selection procedure as an exception to the uniform cluster selection process. Subsections 14(2) and (3) require that where specific qualifications are required, the minister responsible shall declare publicly the attributes that are sought and the steps to be taken in the recruitment process; the members appointed must then possess those qualifications. It is one of the aims of this book to provide a basis for a selection procedure geared to the unique needs of this tribunal to meet its future mandate. This type of targeted selection process is necessary if the Board's level of competence and stature is to justify the exercise of discretion entrusted to this Board.

The grounds for such a targeted selection process are found in the powers granted this Board under the *Planning Act*, the *Development Charges Act*, and the *Expropriations Act*. Annexed to those powers is the authority under the *Ontario Municipal Board Act*. Those powers indicate the need for individuals capable of acting with a measured discretion and integrity, having the knowledge and experience required for the job within the fields embraced by the statutory jurisdiction granted to the OMB.

The *Ontario Municipal Board Act* authorizes the Board, in any inquiry assigned to it, wide and intrusive powers including the power to order production of documents, entry onto property, and attendance of anyone required as a witness, and by sections 27(2), 34, 37 and 39 the Board has all the powers of a Superior Court judge and a court of record to enforce all authorized orders and may instigate a procedure to appoint any specially qualified person to be appointed as an acting member. By section 48, the Board may order and require "any person, corporation or municipality to do forthwith, and in any manner prescribed by the Board so far as it is not inconsistent with this Act, any act, matter or thing that such person, company, corporation or municipality is or may be required to do under this Act, or under any other general or special Act, or under any regulation, order, direction, agreement or by-law." The breadth and implications of these powers granted this Board by the Legislature indicate that members must have the intelligence, character, knowledge, and stature similar to the attributes of a Superior Court judge within the fields of endeavour encompassed by the *Planning Act* and the other statutory authority bestowed on this Board. These are not powers to be entrusted to anyone who lacks the judgment, specialized knowledge and wisdom to know how to use them and when not to use them.

My reading of recent Board decisions and the comments of a number of senior and younger planning law practitioners who are concerned over the present situation on the Board discloses disturbing discrepancies between panels of the Board. Those discrepancies affect not only consistency but competence as well.

One younger lawyer said he had to deal with a Board member who did not know what a site specific by-law was.[90] I have referred in Chapter II to the views and concerns of practitioners' representative of much of the municipal bar and planning profession regarding the independence of the Board. In Chapters III and IV, the strong concerns of a number of experienced planning and law practitioners before the Board on its recent competence, usefulness and decision-making record are set out.

At a hearing relatively recently, the following situation developed, instigated totally by the Board members involved. A senior development lawyer attended for the beginning of a hearing in which his client was the responding party and proponent of the development under appeal. He and the self-represented appellant rose as the panel came in to open the hearing. He introduced himself as counsel for the respondent on the appeal and the owner-proponent of the development proposal. He was met by a statement he had never encountered before in over thirty years of practice. The chair noted that he had not filed a motion for party status. The lawyer replied that as his client was the proponent of the matter before the Board, the owner of the property in question, and the identified respondent to the appeal, it was not his practice to do that nor had he heard of such a requirement before. The chair replied that it was this panel's practice to require a motion in writing. Immediately, the appellant, a self-represented gentleman, smelled the faint acrid odour of blood in the water, as it were, and rose to protest that the proponent should not be recognized as a party. An adjournment was requested, and mercifully was granted.[91]

On the panel's return, the chair announced that an oral motion for party status could be entertained. Some fast advice had obviously been given and received but the chair's foot was not yet fully disengaged and it went right back into the chair's mouth. For almost two hours, the Board's hearing time was allowed to be occupied by the stupid charade of a property owner-proponent, respondent on the appeal, having to argue for party status on appeal of his own development proposal. And just why did the panel think they were there, simply to hear from an appellant who had not filed such a motion himself?

"Everyone needs to know at the start how each will fit into the process and be heard."

Other experienced counsel told me of their frustrations with poorly explained procedures and rulings at hearings. Several suggested that the Board should always use a hearing to tell the parties and the public how the Board sees the matter proceeding and allowing a chance, briefly, for any special requests dealing with witnesses' attendance or other procedural requests. Everyone needs to know at the start how each will fit into the process and be heard. The top priority for several counsels was a well written decision at the end. They pointed out that people pay a lot of money to develop and present their cases to the Board. They read the decisions carefully as do their lawyers, but the quality has been very uneven. It is particularly frustrating not to be able to tell the client why he or she lost, why someone else's evidence was chosen over theirs. "The loser is, at least, entitled to know honestly that much from the tribunal."[92]

With some decisions, there is not even a coherent thread of reasoning. Others disclose a clear appreciation of the evidence, applicable policy and a result, which is explained and understandable. The decisions, which aim at a level of excellence, however, are few in comparison with the majority, which leave the reader unsure that the member appreciated all the implications of the difficult issues raised.

An internationally respected planner specializing in urban design and a person experienced in big city planning administration in the United States and Toronto, Ken Greenberg, wrote of his experience with the Ontario Municipal Board both as expert witness, former city staff planner, and as a member of a revitalizing neighbourhood. His comments bring a non-lawyer's professional perspective to the table. Mr. Greenberg took in both his view of the level of competence and the effect of the Board on the City's planning program.

> My submission is that the OMB is a deeply flawed institution and poorly suited for the role it has come to play in a large city like Toronto. A judicial tribunal is fundamentally the wrong model:
> - it is loosely modelled on a court but without trained judges
> - the adversarial form of interrogation allowed by it is binary, reductive
> - it looks at each development proposal on a one-off basis in an adversarial environment; therefore, it cannot consider the cumulative effects of multiple developments, of how different developments might impact each other.

In anticipating and preparing for OMB hearings, the city's scarce planning resources are diverted from creative design and problem solving, severely diminishing resources for integrated long-range planning, social policy or neighbourhood and community planning, and impacts motivation for planning staff to do their jobs. This system frustrates productive conflict resolution and has produced great uncertainty, cynicism and alienation in local communities.[93]

THE IMPORTANCE OF FAIR REMUNERATION

While some may regard the raising of remuneration as a mistake, I believe it canot be avoided. It is very much part of any attempt to target people of the level in their professions required by the planning appeals and compensation tribunal. This Board's pay level has been virtually frozen for the last thirty years. The income level has risen from approximately $89,000 in 1990 to approximately $113,000 in 2014. This is far from fair compensation for members dealing with the huge value of development rights that they deal with every year. This state of affairs results from another fundamental misunderstanding by the government of the OMB's mandate and how to best meet it.

The latest freeze has been in place since 2009. The OMB has been doubly victimized: its responsibilities in law and practice equate to an assistant deputy to deputy minister's salary level, well above their present classification as senior management. I say that bearing in mind these factors: the range of discretionary powers; the long lasting consequences of the OMB's decisions, measured from multiple decades to a century and beyond, not just lifetimes; its duty to weigh the public interest in its decisions as a deputy minister and minister must; its day-to-day interface with the public as the provincial planning appeals tribunal with educational , adjudicative, quasi-judicial and administrative functions; its jurisdiction over OP, OPA and rezoning appeals as a continuing exercise of ministerial jurisdiction and discretion;[94] and the Board's function as a shield against financial influence and power being determinative where the monetary value of the subjects of its decisions is huge. Its presence is a strong check on the abuses of the ward system, and on any reason to resort to undue influence or bribery or other forms of abuse of monetary power.

> "The latest freeze has been in place since 2009. The OMB has been doubly victimized: its responsibilities in law and practice equate to an assistant deputy to deputy minister's level, well above their present senior management classification, arbitrarily set and unfairly maintained, in addition to enduring with others the long salary freeze. Its continuation threatens the targeted selection process that is so necessary. "

There is another approach to the OMB salary and low-membership dilemma. That is, to reduce the full-time membership to thirteen to fifteen, and increase the remuneration to the proper level, that is, an assistant deputy to deputy minister's level. In appointing new members to replace some of the many retiring members within the next year, six must be trained mediators with a planning or municipal-related career background. There is reason to believe that, with those mediation imports, the six (perhaps aided by a valuable hold-over from the present Board like James McKenzie and/or Susan Schiller to assist with introducing the new members to their tasks and as a repository of needed corporate memory), could handle all mediations and the remaining members could deal with the lesser number of difficult hearings that could not resolve. I am not recommending this but it does indicate a way to reduce cost by putting all the eggs intothe mediation basket

Years ago, the benchmark for members was the provincial court bench. Their rank and deserved recognition as badly underpaid for years was borne out to be correct by the increases in judges' remuneration since then. The present members' annual salary is $110,000 to $113,000. To put this in perspective, a first year lawyer in Toronto is paid $95,000 to $105,000 per year; a justice of the peace is paid more than an OMB member, and he or she is frankly not a person who would be desirable as a candidate for the OMB.

The Province has to decide to embrace or to reject the idea of a provincial planning and compensation tribunal. Between underpaying and underfunding the OMB, placing it in a cluster involving a thought process that has resulted in a loss of its core complement and use of an untargeted appointments system lacking relevance to the needs of the Board, the Province almost appears to be whistling on the way to a wake.

I am very aware of the response of government to any criticism along the lines of salary level and job security. It is, and was twenty-five years go: well, we have no shortage of applicants when the jobs are posted. It is important to note now the sort of Board that the present hiring policies have produced. I regret having to open this door but the point is an important one. I apologize for any unfairness anyone may feel because of characterizations or conclusions that I have to draw. There is no doubt that a core of members has outstanding ability and more than competence.

The following table indicates the respective career backgrounds of present members as of the end of 2015:

Municipal law background:	6	(of whom 2 are cross-appointed to the ERT)
Planning background:	3	
Related professional:	3	(1 cross-appointed to ERT)
Mediation:	2	(1 is cross-appointed to ERT)
Law:	3	(1 is unrelated to municipal law and 1 is cross-appointed to ERT)
Unrelated professional background:	4	(1 is cross-appointed to ERT)
Total	21 members	
Part-time:	4 (all former planners)	

On reviewing the biographical information and having recently attended before the Board members in 2015, I would estimate that at least twelve of the twenty-one are in a post-career situation where the remuneration supplements other income. Apart from perhaps two or three, they are not known beyond their immediate career placements; they are not people of publicly recognized stature. Of the twenty-one full-time members who have to carry the principal burden of the caseload, the availability of the six cross-appointed members cannot be assured in any given week. And the four new members are all cross-appointed to the ERT. They cannot be depended on for longer hearings unless they are without an assignment to the other Board when a particular hearing is scheduled. I would count them, for caseload purposes, as the equivalent of two full-time members. The part-time members, from information from the present Associate Chair, are not available for hearings beyond a day or two in length, nor does their part-time experience allow them the authority and edge to do weeklong and longer hearings.

Therefore, we had a Board of the equivalent of seventeen full-time members to cope with 1,500–2,000 hearing events of varying lengths yearly, from hours to months, less some that the part-time members can do alone, possibly 100–200. And of those seventeen, it is clear from the information provided by a large sample of career users of the Board process whom I have interviewed and the Associate Chair that for any major hearings (including large compensation claims of over one million dollars), the actual choice is really among six to seven members in terms of those with sufficient gravitas, authority and ability to meet the demands of presiding and decision.

> "There is still opportunity for the Executive Chair to take advantage of the vacancies still to happen in the coming year and the Province's commitment to make the Board more effective by taking the initiative in creating a board with real mediation capability and to build up more varied skill sets for panels on a correspondingly reduced number of complex hearings."

I appreciate that by the final edit of this manuscript in November 2016, some changes have been made to the membership of the Board. Executive Chair Bruce Krushelnicki expressed to me enthusiasm for the members he has recently recommended and are now approved by the government. The table of full-time members now appears in the following, using the biographical information made public by the Public Appointments Secretariat:

Municipal law background	4
Law	4
Environmental or planning law	4
Planning/ Land econ. background	4
Related careers	4
Mediation-planning	2
Total	21

In addition, the OMB now has six part-time members. Four of them are cross-appointed to other boards; one of those is cross-appointed to two boards; he is vice-chair of the Environmental Review Tribunal (ERT). The part time members are comprised of two municipal lawyers and four from the environmental law field. The four part-time environmental lawyers are cross-appointees to the Environmental Review Tribunal.

Unlike the membership as it was in 2015, there is now at least one member who practiced as a municipal lawyer for several municipalities; the other members with a municipal law background practiced as part of their work, or they were in the corporate sector. They may not have had the concentrated day-to-day enrichment of practical experience one gets as a lawyer for a municipality.

There is still a remarkable lack of diversity in skill sets on this Board: eleven of the twenty-one full timers are lawyers, though seven of them bring a considerable amount of experience in environmental and planning law, a valuable background for this Board and an improvement from before. Unfortunately, two of the four environmental lawyers are cross-appointed to the ERT so it is problematic how available they will be for continuing OMB work. There is still no municipal engineer to assist with municipal servicing and building knowledge. There are no former architects, urban design people, or municipal accountants. There is no former large-city municipal engineer. One member, though not a municipal engineer, has valuable experience as commissioner of development services with responsibility for building permit/inspection services and municipal civil engineering. The two persons from a related background (not law or planning), apart from two former long-serving and knowledgeable mayors and the ex-commissioner, are a hydrogeologist and a land economist. However the hydrogeologist is shown on both the ERT and the OMB as a full time member, and therefore her availability to the OMB on a continuing basis is questionable. How she will perform in two full time positions will be remarkable. The land economist is, I suggest, a most valuable addition in view of the growth plan demands for skills in that area.

There is still opportunity for the Executive Chair to take advantage of the vacancies still to happen in the coming year and the Province's commitment to make the Board more effective by taking the initiative in creating a board with real mediation capability and to build up more varied skill sets for panels on complex hearings. He has made a good start on the latter. But it may not be the most effective direction to place all the assets in one area, the most time-consuming one of long difficult adversarial hearings.

One important aspect of successful mediation is timing and having a force of trained planner-mediators who can take up a new mediation, or a formerly unsuccessful one, on short notice when the parties express their readiness to cut to the chase. Having a one day mediation available two to three months from now is no real answer if a commitment to mediation is to be made. Speaking to some who have done successful mediation in the municipal field with multiple players in play, the sense is that land use cases are ripe for this kind of commitment. The planners and lawyers to whom I have spoken all expressed strong support for mediation as the wave of the future in this field, where parties are, or want to be, members of a community where all stand to benefit from good development or from preserving areas where development can be a detriment or a threat to communal stability.

There is tremendous good will and desire to cooperate in a strong mediation effort among many of the leading lawyers and planners in the field and some residents' associations as well as the educated part of the development community. That is an asset to take advantage of, but it must be soon while there is a window of full time vacancies on the Board. Timing and availability of a mediator when the parties need help to make the last step to resolution is a vital part of any new commitment of this tribunal. That means a sufficient number on the team of trained people with some flexibility built into their schedules to answer the bell close to when it is rung. Regrettably the new Chair appeared not to agree with the timing that I speak of; I think that mediation will continue but not as the priority I see -- only after it is proven to have the capability of success that, I believe, the small media- tion triad already proved was possible on a much larger scale, will a move in that direction perhaps happen. That in turn means a continuing reliance on adversarial hearings for most cases in the coming years.

> "It remains close to unthinkable that one person should be in a position to overrule the decision of an elected municipal council."

Due to the workload pressures in recent years, most hearings have only one member assigned to them. It remains close to unthinkable that one person should be in a position to overrule the decision of an entire elected municipal council. This was the finding of the legislative committee in 1972 and it remains true now. In the past, as with the *Spadina* hearing or any one of dozens of major hearings since then, a three-member panel was the rule on a major case so that the Board and the public could be assured of a range of related skill sets being brought to bear on the issues and the decision could be divided for writing purposes and delivered in less time. In addition, the 1972 Select Committee on the OMB recommended strongly that no panel of less than two members should ever be assigned to a hearing where the panel may have to overturn a decision of the municipal council. Because of the shortage of members and ability and the depth of the hearing load, that cannot happen now. With the government's commitment to a provincial land use tribunal during the present Review, it should become the norm again soon.

SHOULD THE PROVINCE GO FORWARD WITH MUNICIPAL CONTROL OF MINOR VARIANCE APPEALS?

There are two jurisdictional matters that may inform part of the shake-up that faces the OMB and so should be dealt with here. The first is the move made by the Province in 2006 to add section 8.1 to the *Planning Act*. Section 8.1 of the *Planning Act* not only makes possible the establishment of a local appeal body to hear minor variance appeals. Its accompanying section,

section 8, also retains the idea from years ago of the local planning board to advise council on important planning matters. It provides:

> 8(1) The council of a municipality may appoint a planning advisory committee (PAC) composed of such persons as the council may determine.
>
> (3) Persons appointed to a committee under this section may be paid such remuneration and expenses as the council or councils may determine, and where a joint committee is appointed, the councils may by agreement provide for apportioning to their respective municipalities the costs of the payments. (R.S.O. 1990, c. P.13, s. 8)

Section 8 has produced an interesting idea for an in-Toronto solution to most appeals and not only minor variance appeals. The Province has put in place, not yet enacted, a new provision making the appointment of a PAC mandatory. The Planning Advisory Committee in section 8 of the *Planning Act* could be an avenue to a kind of in-house appeal system that a municipality could set up, with cooperation from the Province and the OMB. If it could show that the PAC was appointed without any political considerations and based on merit and having a diverse mix of people from planning-related careers or experience, such as municipal planning or engineering, architecture, urban design, ecology, or municipal law, it could go a long way toward a homemade solution to long OMB hearings; the framework for it probably would require a minor amendment to the *City of Toronto Act*.

Without an amendment, if the Board is convinced of the above factors (merit-based appointment and diversity of experience on the PAC and no more councillor communication with committee members (failing which the offending person would be disciplined by, e.g., loss of their appointment), it could develop a policy to the effect that where a proposal was accepted by council, staff and an independent PAC, the appeal would be based only on the record before council, the committee and the staff planners, and a report from the chief planner that the PAC, planning staff and council all support it subject to the conditions set out.[95] More effectively, the *City of Toronto Act* amendments would simply remove any right of appeal where the PAC, staff and council either approve or reject a proposed development. However, neither a politically independent PAC nor a local appeal body independent from the council, would be easy to achieve.

Minor variance appeals form the most frequent chance for interface between members of the Ontario Municipal Board and the ordinary homeowner, and so may be the most frequently encountered Board hearings by ordinary people opposing or wanting a particular relaxation from zoning strictures. They could include anything from a request to allow five feet off a front yard setback of 40 feet or a 100 square foot add-on to a maximum gross floor area to allow a new solarium to project out from the living area front wall, or to allow a 20-unit townhouse project in a residential area.

Locally, the group to whom the homeowner applies for a variance from the zoning laws is called the Committee of Adjustment. The committee is appointed by the municipal council and most members of such committees receive their positions with the municipality through the help of certain councillors. If a party is not satisfied with the rightness of the decision there, the appeal is to the OMB at this time.

That may change soon. Section 8.1 was added to the *Planning Act* in 2006 to provide municipal councils with the power to appoint what is called a local appeal body. No municipality has fulfilled the conditions as yet to allow appeals to go to the local appeal body but I understand that Toronto is considering doing so. This is a first step toward removing minor variance and consent appeals from the Ontario Municipal Board. Instead, the unsuccessful party at the hearing before the committee of adjustment would appeal to the local appeal body.

This is a serious policy and budgetary decision that municipal and provincial governments face. On one hand, why not allow section 8.1 to be utilized to accomplish this because by definition minor variances are supposed to be so minor that they do not offend the intent of the zoning by-law or the OP? These would appear to be merely local matters of no real importance beyond the immediate neighbours. The problem, on the other hand, is that "minor" can be quite subjective and abuses can easily happen, especially where the application and the appeal both go before committees made up of people beholden to the same council as decision-maker for their jobs, and councillors are not shy about appearing now at committee of adjustment hearings or submitting a letter to make clear which side the councillor favours.

If this occurs, it will mean that no impartial provincial tribunal (like the OMB) will be available as a specialized tribunal knowing what the statutory requirements for constituting a minor variance are and how to apply them. Section 45(1) of the *Planning Act* embraces all four of those requirements:

> Section 45(1) The committee of adjustment ... may, despite any other Act, authorize (i) such minor variance from the provisions of the by-law, in respect of the land, building or structure or the use thereof, as in its opinion is (ii) desirable for the appropriate development or use of the land, building or structure, if in the opinion of the committee (iii) the general intent and purpose of the by-law and of (iv) the official plan, if any, are maintained.

From section 45, the case law pulled out the four tests that define a minor variance:
1. Is the variance applied for desirable for the appropriate development or use of the land, building or structure?
2. Does it maintain the general intent and purpose of the official plan?
3. Does it maintain the general intent and purpose of the zoning by-law?
4. In all the circumstances, is it minor?

Yet even knowing these tests, does it lead everyone automatically to the same conclusion? In each case, you must have some understanding of scale, number of buildings affected, and how to determine the intent and purpose of a Plan or by-law.

That knowledge, that a tribunal of competence can be appealed to, is useful to keep in the minds of local committees when they face implied political pressure from the ward councillor. And if they don't, the unsuccessful party who may have received merely a perfunctory decision without any reasoned justification can seek relief from the provincial tribunal, which can give a fully reasoned decision to bring impartial justice to the situation.

The same argument could be made for purely local site-specific zoning amendments, which on their face seem to impact only a block in the immediate neighbourhood. There is no legislation as yet, like the local appeal body in section 8.1 of the *Planning Act* that would allow a similar process for site-specific zoning by-laws having no impact on provincially significant features, like a recharge area or a wetland or a watercourse linking different provincially significant systems. It may have no impact on provincial interests so why not allow a similar local appeal body to deal with them too?

In both cases, the variance and the zoning amendment is the one thing needed for a project to proceed. The variance could be to allow a whole townhouse development to proceed because only a seemingly minor change to the permitted uses in that zone, or to the maximum gross floor area, or to a height restriction on that one project site is in the way. Such seemingly local decisions can build on each other over time and each one will have some impact on growth plans and the job targets in municipalities' OPs, even if there are no natural features of provincial interest threatened by them. I do not see how a requirement can be framed in legislative form to differentiate successfully in order to carve out a purely local sphere of zoning activity.

The only recourse after a purely local appeal process through committees appointed by the same body of councillors would be to the courts. And no one can be assured that the judge will have any depth of knowledge of the *Planning Act*, if the parties can afford to access the court process with the threat of high cost awards at the end of the day. None of this is meant as anything more than to appreciate the change that can occur, which will affect anyone aggrieved by a local decision who may find that the Superior Court is the only recourse.

I am of two minds at this stage on the leaving of minor variance appeals to local appeal committees. It certainly allows that whole process to be more accessible locally. If people are not happy with the process council provides, they can make that clear to council very easily, because it is local. And as the Supreme Court has said in *Spraytech,* local matters can perhaps be best dealt with by the government that is closest to the citizen.[96]

Another subject to be considered in this regard is the restriction of appeals from municipalities' adoption of their .O.P.s. A possible alternative is to adopt the legislative policy in most other provinces that have a provincial planning appeal board (there are six in all; Ontario is not the only one, as some seem to believe), which is to restrict or remove the right of appeal from adoption of either a municipal OP or OPA. I will consider that idea in the next section of this chapter.

All that this discussion is intended to do is to make the point that if planning law and planning issues are important, and I believe most planning cases require the kind of serious consideration on a long range and distanced basis that a specialized provincial tribunal, properly funded and appointed, can give them, then we should be careful what we ask for. We might get it, and then it is too late to bemoan the loss.

Both the Ottawa hearing in Chapter II and the Bayview Ghost hearing in Chapter V can take our thinking either way where major issues of provincial importance are involved or, as in the next case, local issues are involved but maybe more. In the "Church on Nugget" case, there was the spectre of the provincial interest in employment lands perhaps being affected. And are they just local issues, where people's fundamental rights to enjoy their piece of this earth as they want and the right of others to oppose where the former's rights may impact the latter's enjoyment, are involved? And where rights to procedural fairness and natural justice are also involved?

> "...the fundamental conflict of interest in every municipality that elects to go this route: the appeal is to a body appointed by the same body that appointed the committee appealed from."

Where it comes to minor variance and consent appeals only, the passage of section 8.1 is the Province's answer. That answer is to ignore the fundamental conflict of interest in every municipality that elects to go this route: the appeal is to a body appointed by the same body that appointed the committee appealed from. And there are no statutorily enforceable provisions to prevent the same kind of interference with the local appeal body, which councillors routinely exercise, by letter and by appearance, with the committees of adjustment. A strong course of education in due process will be required in every municipality in order to avoid the unfair interventions into each committee's process by councillors trying to assist their voters and not seeing that they are converting a proper process into a political one where influence and power have too much to do with the results.

AN OFFICIAL PLAN IS THE MUNICIPALITY'S PLAN: RESTRICTIONS ON APPEALS

Official Plans are expressions of the municipality's hopes and fears, plans and constraints expressed in policies and goals for future land use within its borders. The OP and any amendment to it come after a lengthy process of notice, public meetings, and comments sought from all municipal and provincial agencies having an interest in the municipality's land use plans.

Among the provinces and states with a land use review tribunal or commission, the only ones that allow appeals as of right from municipal OPs or OPAs to the tribunal are Florida and Ontario. In Manitoba, an appeal hearing on a plan can occur only if the Minister refers it to the Board. Nova Scotia and New Brunswick have municipal plans prepared following a public process. Neither sees any need to allow appeals from the OP to which the local or regional council, duly elected, has sealed its approval.

The basic philosophy behind what is a longstanding status quo in Nova Scotia law is that the Municipal Planning Strategy, the document very similar to Ontario's OP, has been adopted as that municipality's expression for land use in that community for the future. It is a uniquely local document for which full transparency and several opportunities for public comment are provided. That would include comment from all development companies or individuals interested in development in that municipality, all local residents and businesses and nonprofit undertakings. The Ontario Court of Appeal wrote of an OP:

> To determine what may be included in an official plan, as distinct from what must be included by virtue of s. 16(1) (a), reference must be had to the *Planning Act* as a whole. In this regard, it is important to bear in mind that the purpose of an official plan is to set out a framework of "goals, objectives and policies" to shape and discipline specific operative planning decisions. An official plan rises above the level of detailed regulation and establishes the broad principles that are to govern the municipality's land use planning generally.[97]

Why is an appeal necessary to a provincial tribunal on planning merits from an OP that the council has already dealt with as its own considered plan, after receiving advice? The Board has the same power council has, and it can add or substitute its modifications to what the responsible council has adopted. And it can do so after hearing evidence that could have been put to council at any time in written form or as an oral overview before it made its decision. If the concern is that council may insert policies limiting height, size and density of future development on individual, tracts of land, that right can be removed. OPs would be more general and criteria- and process-oriented, leaving actual density control to the zoning by-law.

Why should the provincial planning tribunal have the power to alter the municipal OP where it complies with the *Planning Act* and is consistent with the provincial planning policy statement and the growth policy? Somebody has to set policy, and municipal councils were elected to represent the local community, part of their duty every ten years being to review the OP and decide whether to adopt a new OP or not. To assist, most councils have planners on staff. A few rely on an upper tier level of government's staff planners for advice. All have planning advice in one form or another to guide the council.

If municipal councils are to act in a responsible way, it is more likely that they will do so where their votes really count because there is no other body above them to appeal to. If councils act in a way that the local community disapproves of, then they can vote them out of office in the next election. And if they act so as to breach the duty of fairness or rules of natural justice, the court is well-equipped to deal with those kinds of issues.

This is all true enough where one is talking of policies in OPs and OPAs. However OPs do more than set policies; they apply them to areas of the municipality which are composed of privately owned land and these applications to lands can have serious effects on value and on the owners and the prospects for those lands in the future. To allow this to happen and then to remove their right of appeal to the one body equipped to deal with land use issues and remedies is to act arbitrarily and to forget that the reason for a land use tribunal was to provide a fair process with a degree of finality and a tribunal with sufficient expertise to make final decisions in such matters more expeditiously and more authoritatively than the court.

A response to this issue came forward from the Regional Planning Commissioners of Ontario (RPCO). In a report entitled Reforming the Ontario Municipal Board: Five Actions for Change, they advocate that the right of appeal from OP or OPA policies be removed but landowners would retain the right to appeal the application of policy or policies to particular lands. In addition, appeals would also be retained where the grounds for the appeal of an OP or OPA are the failure to come within the intent and meaning of the Planning Act standards and/or lack of consistency with the Provincial Policy Statement. In other words the municipality would have the right to set policy and an OP, or a new OPA such as a secondary plan, was adopted that the policies would remain in place subject only to consistency with the PPS and compliance with the OP land could not be altered or removed The RPCO make the following telling points:

> The intention of this recommendation is to limit appeals of entire official plan policies and while allowing appeals of how those policies impact development rights on particular pieces of land. Those disputes would still proceed through a reformed OMB process but the overall OP policies would be in force for the remainder of the Municipality.

> The Planning Act should be further amended to make all municipally-initiated comprehensive and area-wide official plans and OPAs as they apply to the full geographic area of the municipality ...or to a substantial part. People would, however, retain the right to appeal policies as they apply to particular lands without compromising the implementation and application of the overall policy.

> The Province would retain its right of appeal to ensure that municipal policies are in keeping with provincial policy. In addition, municipalities would retain their right of appeal to provide a check on the provincial power to alter municipal policy.

I recognize that in Ontario, consideration of a proposition that would restrict appeals to the OMB is a controversial one. It is also fundamental to the rule of law that a person may own property and not be deprived of it arbitrarily. The OP is a uniquely communal document, albeit its content is controlled by the parameters of the *Planning Act* and section 16 in particular, and its language is that of planners. It must be consistent with provincial policy and any area plans in the planning hierarchy above it such as the Greenbelt Plan or the Golden Horseshoe Growth Plan. The issue of whether any provision in the OP is properly in an OP, as meant by the *Planning Act*, should of course be subject to appeal to the provincial land use tribunal. That is an issue it is uniquely qualified to deal with.

> "In one move, the government and the Legislature would be acting creatively to deal with a longstanding problem that has damaged the Board considerably."

The Ontario Court of Appeal resolved the issue regarding the OMB's jurisdiction under section 16 of the Planning Act in the *Goldlist* case, mentioned above. The Board had found a by-law adopting an OPA to be invalid because its contents did not come within section 16. The Court of Appeal majority ruled that the Board had no jurisdiction to declare a by-law invalid. However, it could consider and decide whether the amendment was an "official plan" within the meaning of the term in the *Planning Act* before it considered the document on its planning merits.

A provincial land use review tribunal (like the OMB) is also qualified by its own statutory mandate to find whether policies or land use designations in an OP or a plan amendment are consistent with provincial policy.[98] I will give serious consideration for inclusion in Chapter XII Recommendations that the *Planning Act* be amended to restrict the right of appeal to the provincial review tribunal from an OP (and possibly an OPA), to issues of compliance with the *Planning Act* and consistency with provincial policy and legislation. The same will apply to zoning by-laws enacted solely to bring the by-law into conformity with the Plan and municipal refusal or failure to enact a zoning by-law that would not be in conformity with the Plan; in neither case should there be an appeal to the tribunal. However, while the content of policies in official plans and OPAs can be left to the final decision of the municipal council, the application of a particular policy or policies to specifically described lands within the municipality in the ownership of an entity or entities other than the municipality must continue to be subject to appeal. As a procedural requirement relating to this recommendation, and in addition to the present notice requirements, there should be another public notice of when the draft OP is going before council followed by representations to council, and review of all comments by the planning staff, redrafting of the Plan or amendment for council consideration and final adoption by council.

MUNICIPALITIES AS RESPONSIBLE AND ACCOUNTABLE GOVERNMENTS

Section 2 of the *Municipal Act,* 2001 gives full recognition and credit to municipalities as a level of government created to provide responsible and accountable government regarding matters within their jurisdiction. This part of Chapter VI asks the question: having recognized municipalities in this fulsome sense, is it not consistent and responsible to grant jurisdiction to allow them to act as responsible and accountable governments for purposes of the *Planning Act*?

The ward system in Toronto and councils' actions in smaller centres confirm that too often, there is more of local politics than planning principles in some council decisions on planning and development applications. In my view, the Board provides the necessary check and balance to the parochialism of ward-elected politicians. But in allowing full hearings on all issues well beyond the OP or provincial planning policy, has the OMB allowed councils to simply avoid difficult decisions by voting against worthwhile or socially desirable projects knowing that the Board will hear all of the issues and provide a decision?

Council-appointed planning appeal bodies may do little more than act as the councils that appointed them require but this is curable. Either council can accept an independent slate within certain criteria or agree to the local bar and the Ontario Planning Institute selecting the members to ensure the members all are properly qualified.

As one example of councils' reaction to difficult policy issues, research in the 905 area regarding intensification policy and reducing the amount of green field development shows that, save for Markham and, possibly, Vaughan, the other municipalities have scored poorly on the issue of meeting and exceeding the weak provincial intensification target. A policy changer it is not. Markham remained virtually alone (and may still be – the research took in a period prior to 2015) in its willingness to carry out and improve on the performance required to meet provincial policy. I will return to this issue when I provide my recommendation for changes. There is little evidence that municipalities are willing to take on their own constituents opposing change on matters of urban sprawl and energy and transportation efficienc. The present provincial intensification target is to require at least 40% of all new residential development to occur in already built areas. That target is likely to be raised substantially in the proposed growth plan now under consideration, but it is still in its formative stage. Thus far, most municipalities are trying to meet the present target. The new one may be more problematic but the withdrawal of the OMB from such local decisions will mean that councils will have to vote for real on such matters and not simply to send a difficult problem to the land use appeal tribunal.

Having said this, the area where the Board has been vulnerable to attack has always been the standard the Board uses in reviewing a land use decision of a municipal council. It is a standard that contains within itself a subjective consideration. The maintenance of planning merit as the principle or standard used to decide the fate of planning and development matters contains several different approaches to the same conclusion. In other words, the standard contains within itself a question: what is good planning on the facts of each case? This test has been used for at least the last 20 to 30 year, having morphed from a somewhat different principle in the early case law. The original test directed by the Court of Appeal was more objective. The Court of Appeal articulated it in 1965 in these terms:

The function of the Board is to deal objectively with any acts of the council with respect to any change of zoning, whether council has granted a request which some of the parties affected thereto think results in an abuse of their rights to continue to enjoy the protection of the restrictions placed by the by-law on the subject lands, or has refused an amendment which the owner of the subject lands considers perpetuates restrictions which prevent the desirable development of his lands. In either event the responsibility of the municipal council is to see in the result that changes are made or refused to the end that <u>the proper principles of community planning</u> as applied to the subject lands in the light of the prevailing circumstances, are maintained.[99](Emphasis added).

The test in 1965 looked at planning and planning law as the repository of objective principles and it was the job of the Board to ensure that municipal planning decisions were decisions made on objective planning principles rather than for reasons of expediency or political influence or other improper grounds.

The more recent progression of the phrase "proper principles of community planning" is what is referred to now as "good planning." As a standard on which to review decisions of an elected council, it seems to me now that "good planning" carries within it a number or range of solutions that all have some planning merit and that what is happening is that the member of a tribunal is making a decision within the standard the member is using that really the municipal council should be making, that is: among a number of acceptable solutions in line with principles of community planning or, perhaps, good planning, which should be approved? In making a decision like this where there were perhaps two other solutions that are within the words 'good planning' but which the member felt contained one the member preferred, in stating that it was good planning and the others were not because that member preferred the rationale of the planner who espoused it, is not the member making a choice that the elected council should be allowed to make?

Is that member not deciding that the council's choice should give way because the member preferred the planning rationale of the planner opposed to the municipality? What authority does that member have for overruling the decision of an elected council because the member decided only one rationale was good planning? That type of decision is the one where the Board, it strikes me, is vulnerable to not paying deference to the elected council, which was, after all, elected to make that choice between legitimate planning alternatives. And the member would of course cite section 2.1(1) of the *Planning Act* in quite rightly concluding that the council decision had received the respect it was due. Section 2.1(1) reads:

When an approval authority or the Municipal Board makes a decision under this Act that relates to a planning matter, it shall have regard to,
   a) any decision that is made under this Act by a municipal council or by an approval authority and relates to the same planning matter.

What appears to have happened is something that was very common in Canada since Victorian days, and that continued through the pre-World War II years and thereafter until the 1980s and the defeat of the Charlottetown Accord. It is a traditional way of thinking that tends to accept elite or authoritative opinion or more properly, a sober second thought on the substance, and the process, of decisions by electors and their local representatives. The unexpectedly close result in the Quebec Referendum, and the results of the two national elections in Canada and the United States and the "Brexit" vote in the United Kingdom have shown a continuation and international character of the trend of voters going their own way and eschewing the advice and opinions of previously accepted authorities. Another problem that I now recognize is that section 2.1(1) does not become part of the planning analysis that the Board must make. It comes in from outside that set of concerns.

A recently published and most interesting examination of the issue of standard of review concludes that the OMB should be required to consider municipal decisions on a standard of reasonableness. This is a more accessible approach, which courts are familiar with, as is anyone who must attend the Divisional Court on an appeal or a judicial review application. It also gives more deference to municipal councils and would require them, the ward system remaining present, to act responsibly as most matters would no longer reach the tribunal. This is so because, as an appellate tribunal, albeit one that must hear evidence on appeal, the first stage of an appeal to the tribunal should include an assessment by the OMB as to whether there are viable grounds in the particular case to believe that the Council did not reach a decision that reasonably carried out the intent of the municipality's OP and the Provincial Policy Statement (2014).[100]

To accomplish this standard of review, the Legislature could amend or repeal sections 2.1(1) and 3(5) and introduce a new section applying to all types of decisions that the OMB must make following a similar provision in Nova Scotia's *Municipal Government Act*. That section can be paraphrased to read:

> The tribunal shall not allow an appeal (from an OP, zoning by-law or amendment proposed or refused by the municipal council) unless it determines that the decision of council or the local committee, as the case may be, does not reasonably carry out the intent of the official plan and the provincial policy statement in effect in compliance with section 3(1) to (4).

This suggestion is a constructive one and, I think, one that should be closely scrutinized during the governmental OMB Review for possible use in Ontario. In one move, the government and the Legislature would be acting creatively to deal with a longstanding problem that has damaged the Board considerably. It has too often paid the unnecessary price for taking on its back the burden of deciding questions better decided locally by those accountable to their municipal voters and population at large. This change would probably also reduce the number of appeals and provide to would-be appellants knowledge that is more certain as to how the Board will look at the matter under appeal. It would not mean that there would be no more concern for procedural fairness. *Baker v Canada* remains the law on the content of the procedural duty of fairness and problems of that kind could be taken to the court on a judicial review application. This change would complement the *Baker* principles quite nicely. I will return to this idea in my recommendations in Chapter XII.

CHAPTER VII

REMOVAL

There's nothing either good or bad,
but thinking makes it so.
from Hamlet, Act II, Scene 2

There is one book now on the market, published in 2002, that actively supports the removal of the Ontario Municipal Board from its role under the *Planning Act* as the adjudicator of land use appeals. *A Law Unto Itself: How The Ontario Municipal Board Has Developed and Applied Land Use Planning Policy* by John G. Chipman puts forward the view that the OMB's jurisdiction under the *Planning Act* as the planning appeal tribunal should be terminated. I recall in 1976 that Mr. Chipman assisted James McCallum Q.C. who was legal counsel for the City of Barrie during the notorious Barrie Annexation case. It was notorious for two reasons: it stood for the uncompromising right of the objector-appellant before the Board to meet by cross-examination the case being put against the appellant's position even where the government announced as government policy the answer to one of the principal issues; and after all the appeals had ended, the panel who had heard much of it before the appeals began ended it 5 years later with a ruling approving the annexation without a hearing. The objector Townships appealed again. The annexation finally occurred through negotiation and legislation.

According to the author's note, he is, or he was at the time of publication in 2002, "an independent scholar who practices municipal and planning law in Toronto ... and is an editor of the Ontario Municipal Board Reports." Mr. Chipman was therefore in a good position to write on the Board's decisions and its treatment of government policy.

The thesis in *A Law Unto Itself* goes beyond the Board's decisions, however, and concludes that termination of the OMB's planning jurisdiction is required basically for three reasons: (i) most large municipalities have sophisticated planning staffs to assist council decision-making sufficiently to run their own planning process; (ii) the OMB has failed to control its own processes to overcome the long delays and high cost hearings its process entails; and (iii) it has not carried out, with any consistency, the application and implementation of provincial policy.

A paper by Aaron Moore entitled *Passing The Buck: The Ontario Municipal Board and Local Politicians in Toronto, 2000–2006*, does not take a judgmental stand on the OMB's role. The author, as a political scientist, is more interested in the effect of an institution like the OMB that has the final power of decision on the power relationships of groups in the planning process. He therefore does not purport to advocate either continuance or termination of the OMB. His conclusion in his 2009 paper was:

> I hypothesize that the OMB erodes a vital resource for local politicians by removing their power of final decision-making on planning issues, but in so doing, actually allows local politicians more flexibility in tackling what Kantor so ominously calls the "explosive dilemma." The OMB allows local politicians in the city to avoid making a decision between the wealth of developers and the support of the electorate.[101]

In the end, he adds that this finding (that the OMB removes the "power of final decision-making" from Toronto councillors' shoulders and provides them with "significant flexibility") has importance beyond Toronto. In other jurisdictions in North America – he mentions Los Angeles and San Francisco – politicians must consistently support the side that got them elected, the anti-growth or the pro-growth perspective, or as he puts it, they must court the side that keeps them in office, "either through campaign contributions or through votes."[102]

In fact, he seems to unwittingly indicate a distinctly and powerfully positive role that the OMB provides to Ontario's planning process at least as it operates in Toronto. He concluded at one point that in both San Francisco and Los Angeles, due to the fragility of anti- and pro-growth coalitions, when those coalitions did not hold, local government devolved to a level of parochialism and obstruction that frustrated any consistent exercise of power. Moore observes: "I believe that, absent the Ontario Municipal Board, the politics of urban development in the City of Toronto would be much as it is in Los Angeles and San Francisco."[103] As he agrees, it is not.

In approaching a discussion of the much more negative thesis in the book *A Law Unto Itself*, I think it is best to look critically at what is being suggested there and what the evidence actually is before anyone accepts the author's conclusion to remove the Ontario Municipal Board as the original tribunal for land use planning in Ontario from that area of jurisdiction.

This work is helpful in understanding why the OMB came into existence in the days of the steam railway and at a time when government found the regulatory commission as a solution for managing a rapidly growing sector or activity. But as for his central theme that the OMB continually, or in a majority of relevant cases, ignored the public interest in favour of private property rights, I think we have to look at the author's narrative and the evidence used to support it.

The evidence consists of reported decisions during three study periods. A total of 348 decisions are used from his 1971–78 study period, 320 from 1989–94 and 201 in 1995–2000.[104] These totals represent most of the decisions reported in the report series devoted to selected cases from the OMB's work during those years. There are many cases decided by the OMB each year, well more than the totals set out here. The cases that are reported are selected by the editors of the report series based on factors that are not made known. Their selection had nothing to do with being part of a representative sample from which conclusions should properly be drawn on trends or dispositions applicable to the Board as a whole. However, I do not want to belabour the point. It is a small one, for I think we can assume that the reported decisions represented in a general sense the work of the Board that was significant in any year.

ROLE OF A LAND USE PLANNING APPEALS TRIBUNAL: PUBLIC POLICY AND PRIVATE INTEREST

Let us start with the author's assertion that the OMB did not follow its own professed policy of ascertaining and deciding matters in the public interest. The author put it this way:

> The Board has endorsed this view (that the Board decides cases in the public interest and in light of public policy) by regularly stating that it bases its decisions on whether or not applications are in the public interest. Yet matters are not that simple and our analyses show that the board has accorded less importance to the public interest than its stated policy would suggest.[105]

It becomes clear as the text continues that he is not speaking of the public interest as an all-encompassing value or characteristic but of three varieties of what commentators have discussed as the public interest. He refers to these three iterations of the public interest and how it is identified. One is the objective public interest, meaning the entire "body politic"; a second is the group public interest, meaning that the public interest is identified with the parties or different groups having an interest in a land use planning matter. And he refers to a third view described by a *Planning Act* Review Committee (perhaps the one in 1972, but no citation is provided) as a public interest that no longer exists: "There is equally little doubt that there is today a wide disparity in views held by different groups in the community, and by different public agencies dealing with common situations."[106]

The latter two views of the public interest seem to assume that the term "public interest" is simply a consensus of views of certain interested public and private groups and agencies. It is obvious that none of these writers have adjudicated a case on a major public project or a lower or upper tier comprehensive municipal OP or zoning by-law. The text concludes that there is little doubt that the Board "has espoused the group public interest theory. It has not always been clear, however, which groups it has had in mind ... In doing this (treating as the public the 'municipal council' and at times 'local restricted groups'), it has often blurred the distinction between public and private interests."[107].

Eight pages later, the author concludes that the use by the Board of the analysis of adverse impact has resulted in the Board "lean(ing) heavily towards one element of planning – the protection of private property interests."[108] The adverse impact analysis is usually used by the Board in the context of a site-specific re-zoning or minor variance where there is disagreement about how the proposal will affect other properties, property values, and the way of life in that community. Most of these cases are disputes between groups of private property owners. They are localized issues between a determinate numbers of neighbouring properties. The element of public interest does not come into the analysis because it is limited to testing the evidence of individuals regarding how their properties may be affected by a proposal that is not in place. It is an analysis that does not decide the case; it only goes to compatibility arguments, one aspect of a decision only. And in some neighbourhood cases, impact evidence can be decisive where only neighbourhood interests are involved. But those cases say nothing about the Board's attitude toward the public interest, as there are only the owners' interests and evidence involved in the decision.

From these limited cases of individual owner versus neighbourhood owners, the author makes a somewhat surprising leap to the conclusion that the Board has devoted itself largely to a private-law oriented approach "by giving precedence to the property protection aspect of planning, even in the face of express statements of public policy."[109] Yet he concedes that his conclusion comes from planning appeals where the issues only concern "limited groups of property owners."[110]

It is difficult to see how this limited sample of disputes between individual property owners, without the involvement of any wider issue of municipal or provincial interest, would call for a discussion by the Board of the public interest in any of those cases. They are an extremely odd base from which to draw the inference that private rights are given precedence repeatedly over an attempt to find a reasonable balance with public policy interests.[111] It seems to be suggested that the Board became acclimated from dealing with so many private law disputes that this carried over into other cases where public policy interests were very much involved. However, to this point, there is no evidence presented to support it.

Before we leave this section on the public interest, during the second period studied by the author, there is a decision by the OMB that is very much to the point. It found no place in the author's thesis on the OMB and the public interest perhaps because it does not fit within his relativist limits. In that case, the Ministry of Municipal Affairs took an active part with the City of Etobicoke, Metro Toronto, the Toronto and Region Conservation Authority. The Ministries of the Environment, and Natural Resources also presented evidence in this case. In that decision on the Secondary Plan for the Motel Strip and OPA C6586, the planning document for a prominent waterfront and revitalization area, the Board gave some articulation to its concept of the public interest:

> Any consideration of the public interest in a democratic society desiring high standards of government and justice must be all-encompassing. It must then involve the difficult task of distilling from the array of detail to the essence of all the evidence to achieve a real and sound sense of the public interest. Any planning consideration of this nature requires judgment. The process ensures the complementing of difficult and controversial decisions of locally elected officials by the right to request referral to this Board and by the awareness that that right exists. For its part, the Board must look at all the factors including the decision of the Council and local imperatives, but in a widened context without any local axe to grind.[112]

To move to another related point in *A Law Unto Itself*, the author criticized strongly the line of cases in the Board's jurisprudence that address what are called downzonings, i.e. where a municipal zoning by-law amends the prior zoning by reducing the permitted use of the land to a park or other open space use, thereby removing any development potential the owner thought he had when he bought the property. The classic statement of the Board's policy when this happens is:

> This Board has always maintained that if lands in private ownership are to be zoned for conservation or recreational purposes for the benefit of the public as a whole, then the appropriate authority must be prepared to acquire the lands within a reasonable time otherwise the zoning will not be approved.[113]

The author describes this as the elevation of one element of a balance to the status of a policy. As a result, he says that there has been little evidence in Ontario of any taking or radical diminution of development rights in the public interest. The threshold for getting over this hurdle to allow downzoning without compensation being required was expressed as a high one: "where the health and safety of existing and future inhabitants are involved, where there are patent and imminent hazards to the well-being, of the community, the municipality should have the unfettered discretion" to remove development rights without the burden of paying compensation.

The Board described this policy as a balance of public and private interests. The Board's explanation was set out in the following excerpt from a decision in 1999:

> 8. .... the Board's long standing tendency (is) to ensure that privately owned lands will not be transformed to public purposes such as open space or park by zoning instruments unless there is a concomitant commitment on behalf of the

municipality to expropriate or to acquire the lands in question. This rule, like many traditional rules of the Board, must be subject to a number of exceptions. We will deal with the exceptions later.

9. It is important to reiterate that this principle stems from a strongly held belief of the Board that planning decisions must allow neither the concerns of the public good nor the private interests to become the exclusive and singular goal. It is motivated by a time honoured experience of the Board that planning is often a delicate balancing act between these two noble and sometimes competing objectives. Both are important and none should become the sole pampered darling of the decision makers. Above all, these words are a sober reminder that planning decisions, regardless of how benevolent their intent, how farsighted their vision and how friendly to the public interest, can easily become an unwitting and unquestioning tool to extinguish or debilitate the proprietary interests of an owner. No decision maker should gloss over this obvious but awesome power in planning.[114]

THE OMB RECORD: SOCIAL HOUSING, FARM LAND POLICY AND INTERIM PLANNING CONTROL

There are three other points which, I think, bear mentioning before we consider the overall thesis.

First, the author observes that "the most revealing examples" of the Board's favouritism directed towards private rights over the public interest are its decisions on affordable/social housing. He states:

> The most revealing example of this policy of leaning towards the protection of private rather than public interests is found in the decisions dealing with applications to build affordable housing ... and social housing for persons having specific needs such as group homes for the disabled. During the 1987–94 review period the board continued to subordinate the provision of social housing to its primary concern of ensuring that proposed developments did not have an adverse impact on their neighbours. [115]

The Chart 4.4 titled Social Housing – Decision Data is the chart of social housing decision numbers. It does not support the statement that the Board was protecting private interests over the need for social housing. This type of development proposal – it could be a form of housing for families with disabilities or a type of group home for persons with developmental challenges – never failed to rouse opposition in the intended residential neighbourhood due to fear of the people not being properly supervised or from prejudice. The opposition is couched in terms of an apprehension, almost always unproven, of devaluation of their properties. The author's research represented in the chart shows that of eight total decisions in the period 1971–78, seven were approved, or eighty-seven per cent. In all eight cases, the neighbourhood owners opposed the building of social housing in their area and the Board approved all but one. In three cases, the local municipality also opposed the proposal and in at least two of those, the Board approved the rezoning to permit social housing.

In the period 1987–94, there were a total of thirty-one appeals involving social housing proposals. Of those, twenty were approved. In twenty-one of the thirty-one, the opposition was by neighbours and in ten, the municipality opposed it. In sixty-five per cent of the cases, the Board decided in favour of the proposed social housing project. In all three periods, the evidence presented was that the Board approved well over a mere majority of them despite neighbourhood and at times municipal resistance.[116] Chart 4.4 shows thirty-seven proposals of fifty-three over the three review periods, or seventy per cent, were approved.

I fail to see how one can pass over the statistics in asserting, as the author did, that this was a clear area where the Board had disregarded the public interest. The need for housing in the community for persons with challenging issues but who are found to be ready to live in the community in a controlled situation is a kind of development that the Province had shown to be in the public interest. The Board did take into account impacts to the neighbourhood but that may or may not have played a part in the decisions not to approve the proposal. It must be remembered that, since 1983, matters came to

> "There simply may have been no evidence to show the appeal should be allowed or there may have been no reason not to accept the council's decision where it had planning reasons for rejection."

the Board as appeals, sometimes by the developer and sometimes by the municipality or the neighbours. There simply may have been no evidence to show the appeal should be allowed or there may have been no reason not to accept the council's decision where it had planning reasons for rejection. The Board has to consider the council's decision as one factor and that was so well before the amendments in 2006 to express this in the *Planning Act*. In some cases, there was simply no reason shown for rejecting council's decision not to approve.

The fact is that the author's own evidence did not support his theory that the Board was refusing to approve social housing proposals against the public interest and in fact it approved most of those proposals even over strong private owner resistance. Where I think there is a point to be made in regard to the OMB's record in the 1980s and early '90s regarding the public interest lies in two facts: (i) at least one-third of social housing cases resulted in the proposed housing project being refused despite public policy, and (ii) a reading of many of the decisions indicated a uniformity of reasoning whether the project was social housing or a private development proposal. The Board failed to pronounce on matters of public interest too many times and simply dealt with them as adverse impact cases where a neighbourhood's fear of change was translated into incompatibility issues. Compatibility is not uniformity, as one member used to emphasize, and yet sometimes the Board did fall into that error. In the lack of consistency in the treatment of public interest issues, the OMB could be faulted as too often favouring private homeowners.

A Toronto advocate in development and planning law has been counsel on many affordable or social housing proposals. She is deeply committed to that cause and has been during her more than thirty year career. She told me in no uncertain terms that the principal factor about the Board's usefulness to the planning process was that it did act in the public interest in these cases and without it, many such housing proposals for disadvantaged persons would not have occurred.[117] Part of the analysis has to include public attitudes towards such projects. It was a time when NIMBY ("Not in My Back Yard") attitudes gained strength among even liberal-minded persons. In the abstract, affordable or social housing is a wonderful idea ... but not near me. This is why the moderately favourable record of the Board toward these projects marked a remarkable achievement, as the housing advocate suggests. Without the OMB, there would likely have been none.

Second, another public policy aspect of the Board's work was cited by the author of *A Law Unto Itself*: the policy statement on agricultural planning issued in the late 1970s, named the *Food Land Guidelines* (FLG).[118] It was the reigning agricultural policy during his second study period from 1987–94, together with the Agricultural Code of Practice for minimum separation distances between residential and various farm uses. The Guidelines were framed as a resource for rural municipalities drawing up OP policies for agricultural areas. However, it became used by agricultural planners and land use planners as a guideline or policy statement to assess various applications involving severances, plans of subdivision, zoning by-law amendments as well as for drafting of OPs.

It was accepted by the author that the OMB actually took the FLG beyond what they were intended for, applying them in many cases that did not include OP policy referrals. He also notes that the Guidelines themselves stated that they were not to be applied independently of OPs. This limitation was never insisted on by Ministry officials who gave evidence or by counsel who were retained by the Ministry.

In the final comment on the OMB and the FLG, however, the surprising view was expressed that, despite the Board's recognition and general over-application of the FLG, it has never considered itself bound to accept the interpretations by Ministry officials and the Board has even approved development proposals opposed by the Ministry. It is difficult to understand these comments. The OMB was never directed by law or even by the province to consider itself bound by every line in the FLG, no matter what the facts are found to be and it has never been suggested that Ministry officials have a right to dictate to the Board as if everything they say is Ministry or Government policy. It is not. Chairman Kennedy wrote in this regard:

To say that the Board follows government policy is certainly not to say that it would or should seek to ascertain the wishes of the government, the executive branch, in a particular case and then decide as the executive council may request, or as any member of that council may request or suggest. No...

The Government states its policy as of general application and this Board interprets and decides how that policy applies to the facts of the particular case without assistance from the Government or any member ...[119]

Third, the subject of interim control by-laws comes into this story in part regarding the thesis in *A Law Unto Itself* and in part regarding the Board's present independence issues. Interim control by-laws are by-laws that freeze development in a planning area to allow the municipality time (up to two years) to consider if a different strategy of land use restrictions should apply.

The problem with interim control by-laws is that the power to use them can be abused. They are sometimes used more as a quick way to stop a certain development that complies with the by-laws in place, usually after a visitation to council by irate citizens from the neighbourhood who simply do not like the project and want it stopped despite the fact that the law in place, which they did not object to, allows it. Then the municipality does a planning study, which starts from the presumption that the project must not be allowed to go ahead permanently, instead of a neutral study based only on fact and professional planning opinions.

The chart on interim control by-laws during the 1987–94 study period shows that most were approved. If the Board were once again indulging in its so-called tendency to protect private rights over the public interest in developing proper planning controls, one would expect a record of refusal to approve. However, as the author himself points out, in the 1987–94 study period, the Board "came to treat the public interest in imposing interim control by-laws as paramount."[120]

The next part of the story veers into the shifting political winds of the mid-1990s. The discussion of cases in the author's third review period [1995–2000] demonstrate a marked swing away from the earlier trend; out of nine decisions, only two interim control by-laws were approved. The remainder (seven) were refused. The author's conclusion was that this change in direction was in line with what he considered as the OMB's usual stance of promoting private rights at the expense of the public interest. This time, he equated the public interest with decisions by councils. Yet, as I have explained, the interim control power can easily be used as a quick way to get what amounts to an injunction restraining work on a project. Another way of looking at this shift in trend relates to the change that occurred in government in 1995 from the NDP to the Conservatives, whose stance on development tended to be much more favourable. I have nothing more than the convergence of the two during the period 1995–2000. It could well be that more of the hearings on interim control by-laws in the late '90s produced evidence of either decisions made without any planning merit by councils and/or the Board's maturing jurisprudence, which became more systematic and strict with more rigid policy requirements as the decade wore on. However, I suspect that the change in government affected the degree of the shift in interim control decision-making.

In brief, I found *A Law Unto Itself* too ready to justify a pre-existing disposition of the author towards the OMB as a tribunal that he sees as catering to private interests and tending to either ignore or downplay the public interest expressed in OPs, provincial policy statements and municipal council decisions. The author's own statistics simply do not support his thesis, in my view, that the Board has failed to achieve a balance between public policy goals and protection of private property interests. Whether the balance in particular decisions was appropriate or not is not the issue; I think the place of the public interest and public policy, which was far less comprehensively expressed before 2005 varied greatly in decisions because some did not have any other interest involved than those of the individual property owners who each wanted their way, or the municipality in trying to uphold its by-laws.

> "The author's own statistics simply do not support his thesis, in my view, that the Board has failed to achieve a balance between public policy goals and protection of private property interests."

Using an imagined trend line over the years since 1971, the balance has wavered somewhat across a line between the rights of property owners to control their own usage or their neighbourhood's character and the rights of the community or the province generally in matters of public interest. It perhaps sometimes went too far one way and at other times the other way but over the years to the 1990s at least, a reasonable balance has been achieved by independent decision-making of this tribunal. But it is that reasonable balance that the author of *A Law Unto Itself* enunciated as the path that decision-making in Ontario planning law must search for and keep to. When decisions are being deliberated, the conclusions, tentative at first, must be tested by ascertaining the degree to which they promote the public interest as expressed in government policy and in all the evidence and submissions. At the same time, decision-making must take into account the reasonableness of the impact on private rights. One must not be sacrificed to the other unless the strength of the case and public interest combine to make it compelling. It is often possible to achieve the public benefit by use of regulatory zoning standards and use restrictions to lessen adverse impact acceptably.

The proposition that was not demonstrated was the need for removal of the Ontario Municipal Board from its *Planning Act* jurisdiction up to 2000, when it was written.

PLANNING POLITICS AND PLANNING POLICY: WHEN WORLDS COLLIDE

The book *Planning Politics in Toronto*, referred to in Chapter IV, raised the interesting situation produced by the ward system in the largest city in Ontario. Because a removal of the OMB from the planning process would leave councils, or their delegated appeal bodies, as the final decision-makers on land use issues, the way councils proceed to do their business under the *Planning Act* becomes important. From my interviews with non-political observers and participants in the planning process, Moore is correct that the presence of the OMB may detract somewhat from the otherwise commanding position a successful ward councillor in Toronto would have if council were the last decision-maker. However, in Toronto, there is a frequently repeated understanding that most councillors will defer in voting on development proposals to the wishes of the ward councillor on what is good development for that councillor's ward. There is another body of opinion among observers that the politically smart local councillor has not lost much of his or her power in land use decisions. As Stanley Makuch wrote in his essay *The Disappearance of Planning Law in Ontario*, a survey of the voting patterns on City Councils in the former East York and City of Toronto was carried out during a particular period recently. The survey showed that 103 of 115 decisions on the subject at that time, sign variances, were determined by the councillor for the ward where the sign was located. In other meetings where similar surveys were carried out, one hundred per cent were determined by the ward councillor. As this author states:

> It is not surprising, therefore, that in Toronto, councillors have been accused of acting like kings or queens in their own wards. On the other hand, an applicant, who had significant interest in approval of his or her application had no greater rights than anyone who wished to appear before the committee, was generally restricted to speak for only five minutes ...[121]

So if Moore is correct that the presence of the OMB as the review tribunal for planning matters lessens the authority of ward councillors, at least in Toronto that diminution of authority starts from a very high perch and is not as marked as Moore seems to imply. I find his description of the OMB as eroding local politicians' authority to be an overstatement; perhaps it would be better to say that the OMB acts as a check on the power of ward councillors as ward politics are played in Toronto and some other large city councils in Ontario.

Aaron Moore's other recent work was his 2009 paper *Passing The Buck*. The OMB, according to Moore, is the reason why Toronto's city government, the body of forty-four "fiefdoms" or ward councillors, has not reached the level of paralysis that some councils have in the United States.[122] The conflicts between neighbourhood associations and developers cannot dominate urban politics.

In *Passing the Buck*, Moore studied in detail two very different development applications and their fate. Both tend to confirm the preeminent role of ward councillors in development decision-making and they downgrade the notion that councillors' authority has been eroded at all in planning matters. The practice in Toronto is not suggested as the practice in other municipalities in Ontario. It is Toronto council's practice in council after council as its collective reaction to the ward-based structure of Ontario municipalities.

First, a site plan application by North American Development Group for the former Lowe's paint property was defeated by passage of an interim control by-law covering the area of and around the site. The council majority voted with the ward councillor, Howard Moscoe, against this redevelopment proposal and to confirm an interim control by-law freezing development for a limited time. On appeal to the OMB and during the waiting period for a hearing, the proponent brought forward a settlement proposal. The developer suggested that construction be delayed until the interim control period expired; if the city agreed to process the application by the same date, the proponent would reciprocate by waiting until then to go ahead. The ward councillor, Mr. Moscoe, looked into his political tea leaves and changed not only his vote. He moved adoption of the proposed settlement. Council approved it.

The second, known as One Sherway to the author, ended at City Council with a split vote. The residents in two different wards were both interested in this proposal. They perceived the effects on each ward group as quite different. One ward group liked the idea; the other ward's residents did not. One councillor entered the fray at council pitted against the other, each supporting the view of that councillor's ward voters. The project lost narrowly. City planning staff had recommended in favour but this had no traction with the council, given the involvement on different sides of two ward councillors. This was atypical; normally, a development proposal affects only one ward. In the end, One Sherway went to the OMB where the appeal was allowed over the objection of the City; the City's planners supported it before the Board.

Earlier, Moore wrote that one source interviewed by him, a Toronto land use planner, told him that each ward represented by one councillor is "a fiefdom", and therefore the council was really forty-four separate fiefdoms. Moore said he took this to mean that "there was little consistency between each ward concerning the councillors' views on planning and development."[123] That is one limited inference one could take from the interviewee's use of "fiefdom." But what he was referring to was, I believe, much more. He was talking about ward politics and what most experienced counsel in the development and planning law field observed – that it represents the power of each ward councillor in his or her ward and the resulting deference by other councillors in votes on ward development issues. The developer must therefore come to the ward councillor if council support is to be had. In that case, if the ward councillor either

> "I see the OMB as more a check on political power."

divines that planning staff don't like it and he does not get what he wants or strong neighbourhood groups in his ward are against it, the only check on the power of the ward councillor is the appeal to the OMB where the full case will be heard and decided on planning merit. This is why, in the case Moore studied where the interest of one ward was involved, council voted twice, each time in an opposing direction and both times it was in line with the motion by the ward councillor.

In making the above observation, I do not totally disagree with Aaron Moore who is obviously an accurate and careful researcher. But I see the OMB as more a check on political power which may or may not be consonant with the merit of the proposal and less the "culprit" or the party eroding ward councillor's power, as Moore describes the OMB.

The question remains, however, whether the Board as it now exists is doing the job that the legislators and government intended it to do within the reconstituted *Planning Act* where the former vacuum of leadership has been filled by the Province and the lack of policy guidance of years gone by, is replaced by the Provincial Policy Statements. This, for the OMB as I knew it, is a whole new world. And in that new world, the Moore effect – councillors avoiding difficult choices by voting to provoke an appeal and allowance by the OMB of a well planned proposal or a sound but unpopular policy-- may be more frequent.

To me, of the critics' arguments the three that have the most resonance are:

1. Local and Regional Alternative – the improved administrative capabilities of municipal governments today have reached a mature level making possible the subsuming of an appeal process into the municipal planning process;

2. OMB's Costly Uncertainties – the failure to control its own processes resulting in continuing costly and time-consuming hearings and uncertain results provide a double whammy to the continuance of the Ontario Municipal Board; and

3. The public sense is that Board members have an unfettered discretion to do whatever they want on an appeal before them, that they lack the discipline of a court not to act without knowing all the facts, and that this sense, this frustration, is what the criticism alleging lack of accountability really is coming from.

CHAPTER VIII

ELTO

> [*Even if it all goes bad*]
> *It's all good*
> —G. Burr, 2011

The Ontario Municipal Board attracted power and authority to it from the time it was formed in 1906 as a financial and railway overseer and thereafter until 1932 when it became the regulatory tribunal for municipal financing and urban and regional planning. By 2006, the same government of Ontario that had entrusted the OMB with preeminent authority as the provincial land use, expropriation compensation and development charges adjudicator with oversight power over elected municipal councils, decided to merge its administration and location with four other boards and encourage cross-appointment of their members among the tribunals as a way of sharing best practices and enriching the experience of all in the cluster. The roster of OMB members began to contract, no doubt on the assumption that sharing of members could bring new efficiencies in use and number of members. It was now part of an undefined, vaguely delineated entity called a cluster, and the cluster was called the Environment and Land Tribunals Ontario – ELTO.

ELTO as a cluster was supposed to protect the independence and specialized expertise of each constituent tribunal. When support services for an adjudicative tribunal are integrated with others without commonality of subject matter, without similarity of full-time job requirements, workload and complexity of decision-making, and the larger and busier tribunal already incorporates aspects of each of the others in the cluster that they cannot reciprocate, it is difficult to understand how the independence and operating capability of the broader-based tribunal will not be compromised. Why did this happen to the OMB, as it did not with other powerful tribunals with which it used to share preeminence, like the Ontario Labour Relations Board and the hearing division of the Workplace Safety and Insurance Tribunal? And would this bring an opportunity for the OMB to operate more effectively in delivering hearing services and its mediating expertise than it could alone?

The origins and hopes for ELTO and the concept of clustering had their roots some time before 2006 but it was in or about 2006 when the Ontario government decided to act. It needed some way of putting adjudicative tribunals, both those with members from the civil service and those with appointees, under one standard or code of conduct. And there were also the tribunals that bought into the desired organizational common base of mission statement, code of conduct, strategic plan, and other accountability and transparency measures, and those tribunals that did not. Each tribunal had a home statute granting it certain powers within a defined area but there was no administrative coherence to their governance, accountability, and governmental expectations of their members.

> "Twenty-five years ago, the OMB had twice as many members as it has now ... and was considerably healthier in terms of related career experience and diversity on the Board."

What I have not, to this point, conceded was that the OMB was a powerful entity in the political structure. Twenty-five years ago, the OMB had twice as many members as it has now, suffered no loss for days and weeks to cross-appointment to another board or commission, and was considerably healthier in terms of related career experience and diversity on the Board. At the present time, its best interests do not appear to be high in the collective minds of the Wynne government. It is not the powerful tribunal some may think it is within the pantheon of administrative tribunals. For instance, there has been no indication to me from current or past Chairs or the Associate Chair that the OMB was provided with the opportunity to contribute its own input into the decision to cluster it in ELTO, either to set terms for doing so or expressing any opposition. The Province decided to proceed and it did so, after a trial run of ELTO as a pilot project.

Not even after the swinging metronome of change represented by the Harris government taking power in 1995 and the McGuinty Liberal regime in 2003 has the OMB become so diminished. With the coming of Dr. Krushelnicki as Executive Chair, the government has made some part time and full time appointments as we discussed in Chapter VI. (It still remains well below its historic strength and diversity of experience. It is ironic that at the very time this Board is accused of being one of the most powerful bodies in its subject area, it is probably at its most deprived level internally. It is looked to as a model by tribunals in other provinces and its process for expropriation mediation and hearings on compensation is admired by expropriation counsel in the United States. I had assumed that this reduction had occurred years ago, perhaps when either the Harris or the McGuinty people took over but no, in 2000, the Board was still at thirty members. However, it was shaken by the changes in personnel during the Harris years and after the McGuinty government took over.

THE ATAGA LEGISLATION: ADMINISTRATIVE CLUSTERING

According to the OMB Annual Reports, the number of members began to fall significantly in 2010 and 2011. It had declined somewhat over twenty-two years from thirty-eight (after the absorption of the land compensation members in the mid-1980s) to twenty-seven or twenty-eight, which it maintained until 2008. The one substantive change that affected the Board in and about 2008–2009 was the passage of the *Adjudicative Tribunals Accountability, Governance and Appointments Act, 2009* (ATAGA).[124] ATAGA is the Act that authorized administrative clustering of adjudicative tribunals, and in particular, the formation of the cluster of land tribunals called ELTO. It was in or about 2010 or 2011 that Board officials recall the beginning of the cluster idea and ELTO. That is their memory. Actually, the pilot project for clustering using the ELTO tribunals began in 2006, as we will see shortly from the project's facilitator.

Was the confluence between the enactment of ATAGA and the initial reduction in OMB membership a coincidence? Or is there a causal connection? This called for a closer look at ATAGA and the segue of the OMB into ELTO. One scenario has it that this initiative toward more effective coordination of public resources and maximizing the usefulness of "the pool of resources currently committed to the tribunals," as the cluster facilitator for ELTO reported, may have been used by the ELTO bureaucracy or their superiors for unexpected and perhaps improper ends.

That is one scenario.

But there is another happier scenario provided by those who appreciate and admire the concept of clustering for what it has brought to staff in new possibilities, a wider scope for new ideas and to administrators, more choices for efficient use of tribunal members in the cluster.

A recent study of clustering in Ontario, using comparative models in the United Kingdom and Australia, produced an optimistic ambivalence.[125] It credited Ontario with a novel strategy to organize the many administrative agencies and boards. The vehicle of that strategy is the law passed in 2009. The study described the aim of the strategy as the formation of tribunal clusters "to capture intersections in tribunals' logistical, procedural and substantive adjudicatory features and to reinforce links between constituencies of tribunal users." The Ontario strategy is to group together related tribunals while maintaining their statutory mandates and memberships intact. The authors describe it as a unique strategy for reform, for which the long-term vision is not clear.

According to one source, the former Chair of ELTO, the concept of clustering emanated from two matters of concern. One was the gap between the standards to be applied to two groups: (i) the professional civil service who worked in tribunals and (ii) the staff who worked with appointees. Those in group (i) had uniform standards of conduct and conflict of interest provisions; group (ii) did not have similar standards or if they did, they were not uniform across the sector. In addition, there were tribunals that had practiced the common governance base of mission statement, code of conduct, strategic plan and other governance and accountability measures, and those tribunals that refused to do so. To some in government, the inequality of treatment was inappropriate and was neither good governance nor a satisfactory perception of the sector. The first step was the passage of the *Public Service of Ontario Act, 2006*; the second step equalized the statutory standards for good governance of tribunals with the enactment of the ATAGA legislation in 2009.[126]

Since 2006, the Board itself was part of the pilot project, to be reconfigured into a larger structure, a "cluster" according to the *Adjudicative Tribunals Accountability, Governance and Appointments Act*. It has become known by its acronym, ATAGA, a name hauntingly reminiscent of a prison in upstate New York. The purpose of ATAGA in section 1 is:

> to ensure that adjudicative tribunals are accountable, transparent and efficient
> in their operations while remaining independent in their decision-making.

The mechanism was to empower the Executive Committee of Cabinet through the Lieutenant Governor in Council's authority to enact regulations to designate two or more tribunals to form a cluster, "if the matters that the tribunals deal with are such that they can operate more effectively and efficiently as part of a cluster than alone."[127] By section 2 of regulation 126 of 2010, the following adjudicative tribunals are designated as a cluster of environment and land-related tribunals:

1. Assessment Review Board (ARB)
2. Board of Negotiation continued under subsection 27(1) of the Expropriations Act. (B of N)
3. Conservation Review Board (CRB)
4. Environmental Review Tribunal (ERT)
5. Ontario Municipal Board.

By succeeding sections of the same regulation, two other clusters were formed, one consisting of eight social justice tribunals and the other of five tribunals in the fields of safety, standards and licensing.

The remainder of ATAGA consists of requirements to be met by each adjudicative tribunal for seven types of public accountability documents and governance documents. Public Accountability documents include a mission statement, code of conduct, and public consultation documents. Governance documents included a memorandum of understanding with the minister responsible, a business plan, and an annual report complete with the yearly deadline. There was no doubt great satisfaction felt by the formalists in government for having achieved this documentary uniformity that occupies over half of the Act. There is nothing in ATAGA that suggests more than forming business combinations to handle the work more efficiently and effectively. ATAGA certainly expresses no intention in any way of becoming an impediment to performance, nor is there any suggestion that this was being done as a

> "... its whole aim is to promote more effective and, yes, efficient performance."

cost-cutting exercise. On the contrary, its whole aim is to promote more effective and, yes, efficient performance.

The word "cluster" was not defined, its meaning left open to be filled in whatever way the ATAGA bureaucracy decided. The Sossin/Baxter study also noted this strange gap; there are no criteria describing when formation of a cluster is appropriate, and no rationale to clarify the concept of a cluster. Despite this rather central lacuna in the ATAGA legislation, the facilitator of the ELTO cluster had no difficulty providing a definition. The facilitator was the chair of the Labour Relations Board, appointed to assist the process using the ELTO cluster as the pilot project in 2006. He described clustering as, "the grouping together of different tribunals that work in related areas and deal with related subject matter." According to him, the goal is to improve the quality of services offered to the public by sharing resources, expertise and administrative and professional support. The essence of clustering is to safeguard the present standards and promote development of the unique expertise within each tribunal while sharing best practices within the cluster without prejudicing the specialized resource and tribunal independence.[128]

The idea of clustering makes absolute sense from the government's point of view: it provides room for the efficient management of the civil service and maximizes the resources of its appointees to meet the growing demands of the public for more services, transparency and accountability. This is the view expressed to me by the immediate past Executive Chair of ELTO.[129] The governmental goals were clear: space is shared, staff of tribunals are restructured and integrated, mutual goals are set, the system is more transparent, and the base documents are standardized and in place for all tribunals. Within the office group in ELTO many new ideas have been shared, the staff have merged and undergone restructuring, and by December 2013 the strategic plan for the cluster as a whole including the OMB, was finalized. To her, clustering has improved governance and, as one staff member told her, being part of a larger organization had stirred him and his manager to think in new ways and on a bigger scale; it was exciting. When discussing how appointee members seemed to respond to clustering, she said that they were not in the office much. They rarely see each other or the office staff, and how most of them feel, working in their home offices alone, she did not know.[130]

> "The view that the OMB can operate more effectively in a cluster with the other tribunals ... remains subject to proof."

The view that the OMB can operate more effectively in a cluster with the other tribunals, none of which have the range or the caseload of the OMB, is an interesting one and one that remains subject to proof. As the past chair told me, clustering is a long-term project but she felt they had met the goals so far when her term ended in May 2015.[131] The goals she was referring to were those for the cluster. The goals of the OMB as an independent "specialized resource," now that it was embedded within another organization, were not clear and probably no longer existed separately from the aspirations for ELTO.

There is the question that is posed by section 15 of the ATAGA law, for which I see that no answer was ever sought. Are the work and the requirements of the tribunals such that they can operate more effectively and efficiently as part of a cluster than alone? That question does not appear to have received any attention amid the enthusiastic reception given the cluster policy as a given for the ELTO tribunals.

The actual wording of the section refers to the decisive factor for the content of the cluster as the common subject dealt with by all the tribunals – "tribunals that work in related areas and… related subject matter." If shared experience and cross-cultural learning are important benefits to be expected from a cluster arrangement, as the cluster literature maintains, then operational and user-benefit considerations could be two factors together with other factors that allow for some diversity of experience. For instance, it might have been more helpful from the point of view of shared experience and benefits from cross-appointments, to remove the ARB, and add to the cluster with the OMB, tribunals like the Building Code Commission and the Fire Safety Commission as safety and building-related boards, and the Criminal Injuries Compensation Board as another claims evaluation body but quite different in the source of the claims from the *Expropriations Act* claims. The B of N, CRB, the OMB and the ERT would also be part of it. This kind of cluster would provide boards that deal with building safety issues and mediation, land use appeals, expropriation and injury claims evaluation with opportunities for sharing of best practices among tribunals with some similarity and within discrete legal contexts, as well as to share and learn reciprocally together and to break down the cultural boundaries between them. There would be a great deal more opportunity for inter-agency 'best practices' discussions, mediation techniques from differing sources that could provide beneficial exchanges in other areas. At the same time, it would provide real debate and a realization that subject-related is wider than merely dealing with land and use issues.

ELTO's rationale is that the mutual subject and core jurisdiction is grounded in land – land use conflicts, land use policy and employment targets, compensation for loss of land, service cost recovery charges, and the democratic-administrative interface of appeals from elected bodies (OMB); environmental aspects of land use, applying ecology, the biological sciences, and environmental engineering techniques and remediation (ERT); negotiation, mediation, valuation and assessment of land (B of N and ARB); and land-related heritage and conservation issues (CRB). The common element of land is a rather benign and not terribly significant rationale for a claimed new flexibility and group cultural dynamics that clustering should open up. It is a focus that misses the point – how do their operations work well together and how does this grouping assist their stakeholders, as well as how do the much less busy and focused boards provide anything to the experience of the wide range and experience of the OMB? Yet, given the commonality of user-practitioners and environmental-conservation-planning concepts and the determination of the government to use the cluster paradigm, where else would the OMB rationally fit? The fundamental question remains unasked because the OMB's continuation as before appears never to have been an option. Yet other major boards like the Ontario Labour Relations Board (OLRB) and the Workplace Safety and Insurance Appeals Tribunal have continued either on their own or by being assigned the responsibilities of certain other related boards in an amalgamation-type reorganization like the Ontario Labour Relations Board. In recent years, it has taken in the Pay Equity Hearings Board, the employment standard appeals administration and adjudication, the Education Relations Commission and the College Relations Commission; the OLRB Chair is the chairperson of both. Though the language of clustering is used in its Annual Report, the OLRB remains unclustered in the ATAGA cluster regulation as an adjudicative tribunal unallied with any of the three existing clusters.

For the ARB and the CRB, both primarily part-time operations, their client base is not the same as that of the OMB though often the advocates are. In fact, the CRB can only recommend as part of an unrelated process and it is questionable how the ARB's assessment focus is of assistance to stakeholders of the OMB. On the other hand, two tribunals fit almost too well with the OMB's mandate. Instead of the B of N and the ERT retaining their identity and, in the case of the ERT, sharing cross-appoint-ments, which reduce the OMB's capability of coping with a busy schedule, does it not make more sense to merge them fully with the OMB's operations? Planning and environmen-

"... it is questionable how the ARB's assessment focus is of assistance to stakeholders of the OMB."

tal review mandates should have always been united because one cannot have sustainable planning and development without environmental imperatives being addressed. The B of N is an arm of the OMB's mediation service in compensation matters, which can join operationally while keeping a separate identity as a branch or division if some degree of separateness was the problem when they were joined years ago.

Nowhere in the Facilitator's Final Report is there a hint that this initiative was to be used to seriously reduce the size and capability of a tribunal or to reduce cost. The purpose seemed to be the reverse – what the facilitator called "making the most of the pool of resources currently committed to the Tribunals." That statement implies no cuts from "the pool of resources currently committed ..."[132] In fact, the facilitator expressly denied that this was an exercise to cut costs. Yet if clustering is to create new efficiencies and the saving of money, the key question as Sossin/Baxter ask is, who benefits? If the savings are directed to general revenue and expenditures, the cluster strategy would be subject to some cynicism over the real purpose of the exercise. The suspicion from the sudden growth of the bureaucracy in ELTO to virtually double the number of office personnel on the former OMB organizational chart is that the latter is occurring, or is being devoted to the larger ELTO bureaucracy.

What it has produced, from the information internal sources have provided, is a parallel organization that has developed to staff ELTO's requirements. More than half of the three row, full page width organizational chart for the pre-ELTO, OMB is now duplicated by ELTO positions. It has also meant cross-appointment of certain members to the Environmental Review Tribunal, so that each tribunal has the full use of that member when he/she is not scheduled in the other.

At the end, the Facilitator's Report refers to physical and Internet co-location as having been achieved. About "sharing operational units," the Report stated that pooling of operational and professional areas were to be agreed and costs apportioned. That appears to have occurred by 2013. Next steps were to include standardized core competencies, written protocols for recruitment and assessment of members, a training program (OMB and ARB were to work toward such a program), harmonizing of some general rules, and resourcing early mediation practices. Of this list, the one element that would have helped certain members of the OMB – the training program – has not come about as a co-produced program with the ARB; the OMB's Associate Chair, Mr. Lee, took it upon himself to do this at the regular monthly OMB meetings, complete with imposing case books to be read ahead of time. The same trios of mediation specialists at the OMB have continued their excellent work with little assistance from new appointments or training of other members.

In his final conclusions, the Facilitator writes:

i.   The range of mostly administrative and some professional practices will all "culminate in continuous service improvement and adjudicative excellence."

ii.   The initiatives set out in this report represent an action plan that, once fully realized, will ... position these tribunals at the forefront of a modernized administrative justice system in Ontario.[133]

The OMB members, with up to two thousand new files and hearings spread throughout the year, were expected to share areas of expertise and specialization with tribunal members whose hearings simply do not have the same complexity and multi-issue content spread across many fields of law, the sciences, planning, architecture or urban design, policy issues, and issues of the OMB's own jurisprudence. Most of these components are simply not common to the B of N, the CRB, which makes recommendations, not decisions, and the ERT where hearings are somewhat more confined in subject matter and whose members reportedly have some difficulty when they sit in a multifaceted OMB case.[134] These are tribunals facing, respectively, annual hearing events in the order of thirty-five, 12–18, and 150.

The ARB presents a different category. It opened 58,000 new files and resolved about the same number but many of them are different files under different roll numbers for the same property so the total is misleading. The intake is seasonal, and it is primarily a part-time operation for that reason, with a core of full time vice-chairs and members. The proportion is 3.5:1 part-time to full-time. The appeals are similar to property valuation disputes except the values have to be calibrated to the same standard used for other properties of the same type. Most are residential appeals with one or two issues or simply a homeowner who wants to question the assessment but has no real evidence to do so. There are some complex commercial appeals with difficult issues, there is no doubt of that, but it is a one theme tribunal, assessment review.

The ARB work at one time was all done by the OMB. It is ironic that it returns as part of the first cluster with the OMB.

Of the other tribunals in the cluster, the Board of Negotiation supplements the OMB on the front end of the expropriation mediation process and the ERT operates and deals within a framework of environmental issues that the OMB faces in some planning hearings. One of the most experienced lawyers in the field, also an authoritative writer on planning law, when asked about clustering, commented that he saw good reason to go beyond clustering as a half measure and explore merging at least the ERT and the OMB.[135] Several other legal and planning practitioners saw the ERT and the OMB in the same way. Merger would address the problem of non-availability of cross-appointed members for more than two week increments with the OMB. While cross-appointment can enrich both tribunals and the members involved, and they are useful to cover long joint board hearings, the OMB constantly loses those members to the other boards because it is the one with the majority of hearings and experience to share and it has far fewer members to cover them now.

EFFECTS OF CLUSTERING ON A LAND USE PLANNING AND COMPENSATION TRIBUNAL

Whether the "more effective operation" part of ATAGA has come about for the OMB is a question that requires more of an answer than the preliminary conclusions that documentary governance and accountability standards have been set and met, and that staff integration has occurred. The degree to which clustering has added to overall costs by the parallel office organization imported for ELTO personnel is beyond the scope of my study; however, the suspicion remains from the sheer numbers and positions added to the previous organizational chart for the OMB alone that this is so. It is also confirmed by the observations of a lawyer who attended regularly at meetings of the advisory committee held by the former Executive Chair of ELTO; each time there appeared to be a number of different OMB lawyers added to the roster.[136] This was a tribunal that had one unofficial Board counsel from about the late 1980s and before that, none. The senior Vice-Chair, Mr. Arrell, who was a lawyer, acted in that capacity as part of his regular duties. The addition of a Board counsel was a step forward as it meant the Board would have representation at Divisional Court hearings on appeals from the OMB to assist the judges with the Board's jurisprudence. But having the budget for a number of lawyers was indeed something profoundly new and costly.

The thinking behind the cluster ideology appears to be that the OMB fits because the OMB's hearings are mostly minor variance matters or are one day or less. I wondered why, concerning only one of the tribunals, the facilitator made this comment about so much of the OMB's intake in raw numbers being under one-day hearings. That factor weighed heavily in his estimation of the fit of the ELTO tribunals together. What is not appreciated is that the remaining twenty per cent in numbers of cases take by far the most time to hear, consider, research, and write, and they are the fulcrum on which the main mandate of the OMB pivots.

It appears that the cluster idea has many good things to recommend it for dealing with and integrating certain administrative functions – such things as flexibility, mutual improvement, enriching expertise, and greater consistency throughout the cluster. But there appeared to be, behind the rhetoric of the Facilitator, a thought process that was keen on moving beyond the administrative, toward the coordinated use of cluster appointees from a pool of mostly cross-appointed members to feed all the various cluster tribunals. The former Executive Chair stated: "When I was at the Board, I was able to increase the cluster's use and skills at alternate dispute resolution by cross-appointing members with high skill levels to other tribunals in the cluster. The second concept was increasing the adjudicative skill levels by cross-appointing full-time adjudicators to tribunals in the cluster where part-time members were used so that the full-timers could assist the part-timers both in hearings and in training."

> "… the sharing of best practices and of experience in ELTO is all one way, away from the OMB and moving toward the part-time tribunals."

The flexibility that cross-appointments give the Executive Chair would be considerable. The problem comes from the fact that the sharing of best practices and of experience in ELTO is all one way, away from the OMB and moving toward the part-time tribunals. And where the full-time contingent reduces in numbers on the busiest tribunals because of the increasing use of part-time members on the OMB, the further reduction by cross-appointing other members to the remaining cluster tribunals means that on any given day or week, the tribunal with the heaviest use and need of competent members would always lose in this pool kind of scenario.

If the policy became one of bringing together most or all of the cluster membership through cross-appointments and shared assignments into one common pool of adjudicators as a source for all the cluster tribunals interchangeably, that policy would seem to undermine the intent of the Legislature to provide and protect the services of each specialized expert board or tribunal to the public to match its own subject matter. The result would homogenize the membership of tribunal into more generalist members whose specialized knowledge individual to particular boards will slowly be lost through disuse. It is not yet clear that that kind of pooling of tribunal membership is what may be intended in the long term. At this point, there seems to be a reluctance to go beyond a limited number of cross appointments and a will to retain the independent identity of the member tribunals.

This kind of possible scenario points up the importance of setting out in the ATAGA law a clear definition and purpose of the cluster. There is none now; it is a tabula rasa, open to be used in a multitude of ways.

A further clue to what has happened to reduce the number of full-time members of the OMB came from the past Executive Chair of ELTO, Ms. Tanaka. I asked her about the decline in full-time members since 2010. She could not answer for what had happened before she assumed the Executive Chair position in 2012. However, since her appointment, she began to push for more part-time members in place of hiring only full-time members. She saw the use of part-time members as the key to the sudden fluctuations in workload and consequent lack of availability of full-time members for the shorter hearings; some full-time appointments were made to replace retiring members during Ms. Tanaka's term to prevent a potentially disastrous decline but the pre-2000 full-time complement of members was never rebuilt.

As she said quite rightly, the key to managing the workload in the case of adjudicative tribunals is to realize you do not know ahead of time what it will be. She was very excited by the use she could make of cross-appointed members and part-time members to deal with those fluctuations. In the case of two long joint board hearings with members of the ERT, she said,

> the consumption of Board resources was enormous with three members on each. There was one member of the OMB who was cross-appointed to the ERT since 2011 whom I was able to assign to joint board hearings. That meant that cases that normally could have taken three members of the OMB and ERT only took up one member's time. And I used the part-time members on the one-, two-, and five-day hearings while the full-time members were used on longer hearings.

Use of part-time members became the answer to the unknowns of the scheduling problem and assisted with the Executive Chair's budget. She described her efforts to cope with these facts: "The demographic of the Board was aging. I arranged before I left for hiring competitions and recommended appointment of more part-time members." To her, they were the reason for the resilience of the organization.

Significantly, she explained that they were also cheaper to use as they got only a *per diem* payment, no benefits and did not receive a Blackberry, laptop and health, dental and pension coverage that the full-time appointees receive. The budget saving and the flexibility she saw as being provided by part-time members explains the increased number of part-time members by 2015 and no increase in the full-time group. Full-time appointees to the OMB (excluding cross-appointed) had fallen to fifteen as of June 2015 plus use of three of the six cross-appointed members each week. However, those cross-appointed members had responsibilities with other tribunals and so were not often available for the longer OMB hearings. And part-time members could really only be available for, and were suited to, the shorter hearings.

The reliance on part-time members to cope with the uncertainties of scheduling certainly became an initiative of the ELTO Chair at an early stage of the cluster. The corresponding reduced reliance on full-time members appears to have been accepted by Chairs of the Board since 2009. The reduction of the full-time complement had begun in or about the 2009–10 period.

The policy of not replacing full-time members appears to have come from upper management within the Ministry of the Attorney General or the Public Appointments Secretariat, and that decision was not actively opposed by Board or ELTO management. The Public Appointments Secretariat administers the public appointment process for the Ontario Cabinet but it is a support service reporting to the Premier for its administration of the public appointments process. It has not acted to counter the continuing loss of full-time members since 2010. Appointments have been made but no more than to keep the Board at less than two-thirds of its former full-time level of twenty-eight to thirty members before 2000.

The decision to reduce the full-time complement is somewhat anomalous within the cluster concept. It is the full-time element of tribunals that tends to attract high quality members to tribunal work, as the Sossin/Baxter study illustrated. The Facilitator stated in the conclusions to his report that the OMB contained only full-time members (this would be in 2006–2007 when it still had some twenty-seven members). He viewed part-time members as useful for fluctuations in workload; however, he stated, as does the Sossin/Baxter study, that full-time membership provides more efficient and effective deployment, more attraction to able people to join the Board, and a higher level of corporate memory and knowledge. These are not advantages shared by adding only part-time members.

The Final Report of the Facilitator stated that the cluster concept proceeded in order to answer the question: how can tribunals, by working together, use their existing pool of resources to provide the highest levels of public service and at the same time strengthen individual tribunal mandates? The principles meant to guide the ELTO cluster project included the following seven values:

a) Protection of the independence of tribunal mandate-centred work and decision-making
2. Respect for legislative mandates
3. Changes where necessary to achieve cluster objectives
4. Easier navigation of tribunals by users
5. Accountable outcomes for transparent innovations
6. Resources focused on high quality adjudicative service
7. No compromise in protecting the public interest and access to justice.[137]

In my view, from what I have seen and learned from inside and practitioners outside the OMB, the OMB can no longer meet at least five of these principles. As for (4), I do not know, though I doubt if too many users of the OMB need to use the CRB or the ERT except in the odd case of coincidence by two separate problems converging and the common practice of some planning lawyers. And (5) in the OMB's case would not be met from the responses of most OMB practitioners.

The next steps, according to the facilitator, should have included increasing the full-time complement targets and recruitment plans. This applied to all the ELTO tribunals, most of which had part-time members. It certainly did not mean increasing the part-time contingent on the OMB without increasing the full-time group. Contrary to the facilitator's suggestion, the opposite trend has occurred within the OMB; part-time members are now close to one-third of the net Board membership (21 less four for the loss of, or impaired ability to use, the six cross-appointees = 17 net membership – there were four part-time members as of December 2015, 6 in December 2016, none in 2006–7). The problem here is not the addition of the latter, but the allowance of the full-time membership to decline so far without proper recruitment. What was lost sight of was that the cluster literature reported full time membership as facilitating the objectives of sharing knowledge and development of a corporate knowledge and memory. "The increased physical presence of full time members also makes it easier to organize member training and meetings, and ... greater opportunities for informal exchange between individuals."[138] Again, the emphasis of clustering should be on the collegiality and culture of consistency in principle that full-time membership entails.

It appears that the loss of up to four full-time members had occurred before the past Chair took up her position in May 2012, bringing it down to twenty-three. The reduction in full-time members continued from 2012 to twenty-one members and effectively to seventeen (because of the limited availability of the six cross-appointees).

The idea of clustering is still exciting to those who appreciate the challenges and the spur to new ways of doing things it represents and are in a fixed location with only limited travel demands. The OMB faces schedules requiring members to be on the road about two-thirds of the time. Some of the problems at the Board resulting from the reduced number of full-time members could be the difference in decisional style and strategy between the former Chair and the present Associate Chair's approach to it. But that accounts for only a small portion of the issues now.

The Board, as the past Chair pointed out, is aging and though she was in favour of greater diversity of experience and skill sets on the Board, the full-time contingents have not been continuously renewed. Thirteen members were either lawyers or planners. There are no other municipally-related careers represented other than two former municipal politicians. I do not see in the recent past the appointment of younger mid-career specialists from municipal careers and from planning consultants in the private sector in order to lessen the aging of the Board. From both the past Executive Chair of ELTO and the present Associate Chair who is now handling the scheduling, the small number of members whose skills and knowledge are sufficiently sharp, and whose experiential and moral authority require them to preside at major hearings, is reduced further by the need for them to be assigned for large blocks of time to major hearings.

I cannot escape the sense that the idea of clustering carries with it not just new ways of doing things and sharing of best practices but a sense that one earns recognition now for saving money, finding new ideas to save money, and expecting more from less. The comment of the former Executive Chair about the relative cheapness of part-time members is an indicator. The Facilitator's use of factors like reduced disposition time and reduced

"Part-time members ... cannot take the place of the nucleus of members whose abilities are hearing-ready and honed by continuing challenges."

decision-writing time as part of his model are stronger indicators.[139] The problem that gets lost in that kind of thinking is the totality of requirements of a cerebral and responsible job with a huge public dimension. For hearings of significance, only full-time members at the top of their game and kept that way by continuing work in the field and on decisions can take on those assignments. Part-time members can fill in when they can on less consequential hearings but they cannot take the place of the nucleus of members whose abilities are hearing-ready and honed by continuing challenges.

Nothing in what I have written is meant to detract from the clustering idea and principles. When there is a clear reason consistent with the aims of clustering beneficial to both tribunal and users, it is a welcome development. It simply may not be suited to a tribunal with a wide range of controversial responsibilities and a public interest component suffering from a shortage of members to meet its schedule. Yet, it is clustered with part-time, less busy and less complex tribunals. The dilution of the pool of members by cross-appointing and not recruiting, thus losing most of those members' time on the OMB, detracts from the specialized expertise the OMB is intended to provide. There is no doubt that the reduction of the membership from thirty full-time to a net seventeen effectively by 2015 was the principal factor causing difficulty for the OMB within the ELTO cluster.

All other things being equal, there is potential for a merger of the ERT and the B of N with the OMB to form a new OMB-like tribunal. Like the blending into the OMB's mandate of the Land Compensation Board, such an action could benefit all three tribunals and their stakeholders and increase the union of two critical areas that have been adjudicating apart too long. It would end the deprivation of one to the benefit of the others because the schedule for ERT and OMB members is often common in issues and difficulty.

THE SUPER-TRIBUNAL MODEL

The other tribunal reorganizing model is the super-tribunal. It is the one utilized by Quebec, New Brunswick and Nova Scotia. I understand that the Nova Scotia Utilities Review Board (NSURB) has incorporated into one tribunal containing groups of adjudicators who deal with particular sectors of activity, so that specialized expertise continues to be used and not lost. The various sectors the NSURB serves as regulator and/or adjudicator include the provincial electrical sector, gas and water utilities, auto insurance, liquor licence, petroleum pricing property assessment, expropriation, criminal injuries, municipal and school board boundaries, and municipal planning and development.

The NSURB is given high marks for its regulatory activity in the electrical sector over the last decade for its responsiveness in meeting the challenge of greening its electricity system in the aftermath of a recession and in the midst of growing anxiety about the province's long-term economic future. The Board is also said to have "demonstrated the mundane but core attributes of effective regulators, including fairness, responsiveness, practicality, judgment and accountability."[140]

My interviews with a lawyer who practices in the municipal planning area and a member of the group responsible for the planning hearings of the Nova Scotia board confirmed that the tribunal has married the needs of stakeholders in each area in which it has authority to maintaining the specialized expertise in that area. That practice includes the areas of planning litigation and mediation. The law practitioner stated that there is general satisfaction with the job being accomplished by the tribunal.[141]

With that direction in mind, there is potential for a possible merger of the Environmental Review Tribunal and the Board of Negotiation with the OMB to form a new tribunal with a mandate similar to the OMB. Like the blending into the OMB of the Land Compensation Board in the mid-1980s, such an action could benefit all three tribunals, their stakeholders and the public interest in the adjudication of planning issues with environmental issues, concerns, and remediation measures. It would end the problem of scheduling cross-appointed members on the OMB as most if not all the cross-appointments were between the ERT and the OMB.

The cluster initiative is a serious effort to organize and put disparate groups of adjudicative tribunals on a standard footing of mission, conduct and governance. There is no reason to suppose it will blow over or suddenly disappear like a victim in *Forensic Files*, and there is reason not to act precipitously by supporting without question merger of the ERT and the Board of Negotiation with the OMB. Sossin and Baxter remind us that the academic literature, though not yet large, contained some cautionary examples regarding amalgamation.

The Australian experience was taken from the effort of two states in Australia to put several tribunals on a proper administrative footing, each with a statutory base and structure in two different ways. Victoria formed the Court of Administrative Tribunals (VCAT) from those tribunals and divided the organization into three sections: Civil, Administrative, and Human Rights, each further subdivided into subject lists. Each section and subgroup had some degree of freedom and identity. New South Wales brought its group of tribunals into a more unified grouping, the Administrative Decisions Tribunal (ADT). Due to a committed hands on leadership and encouragement of a culture of exchanges and sharing of experience between sections, the VCAT was found to be the more vibrant and happier organization, open to the different sections and subgroups learning from each other's best practices and promoting that kind of sharing through the use of cross-appointments. The ADT has become less innovative and seems to have failed to break down the barriers between the former tribunal groupings. The Australian experience reports that the cluster-like organization has benefitted by developing greater consistency of decision-making due to greater interaction and exchanges, common values, and improvement in the public repute of each section, hence a stronger sense of independence from government. Strong leadership was the key factor with VCAT's success, not so much the form it took.

THE IMPORTANCE OF STRONG LEADERSHIP

It is clear from what has happened and reported in the literature on clusters, particularly the importance of effective leadership, that the Australian experience is not alone. The flexibility and the lack of mandate embodied by the failure to give any particular meaning or purpose to the "cluster" in the founding ATAGA legislation underlines more than the Australian examples of tribunal governance in Victoria and New South Wales the supreme importance of strong leadership. That was a key to the resurrection of the tribunals in a more disciplined form. That is why the key to a renewed ELTO may be the recent appointment of a former OMB member and vice-chair as Executive Chair of ELTO, Dr. Bruce Krushelnicki. He is an imposing figure of ability and charisma, and an example of someone who has done it all and can lead by example and by strength of will in most areas of the cluster.

> "The OMB is not a tribunal for part-time members except for occasional help with one or two-day hearings."

Meanwhile, Dr. Krushelnicki will have to deal in the short term with the hand he is dealt. The flaws in the timing and inclusion of the OMB in the cluster continue, unabated. I think two fundamental misjudgements were made in bringing the OMB into the cluster at this time. One was the decision that a specialized Board with a wide range of legal, planning, servicing, design, urban and rural growth distinctions, heritage, ecological, appraisal, and mediatory knowledge involved and a full year-round work schedule could be brought productively into a cluster with the largely part-time, smaller workload, or narrow issue tribunals. The operations are different as are the tradeoffs to deal with constant schedule changes and the deliberation/writing demands are substantially different. The OMB is not a tribunal for part-time members except for occasional help with one or two-day hearings. And, as said before, the sharing of experience and best practices tends to flow only one way, and that is away from the OMB towards the more part-time boards. Second, the selection process for a Board like the OMB must be targeted toward the professions relevant to the workload, and to able energetic persons within those professions with communications skills and mediating ability. It must contain a pay/benefit package that is enough to attract people. Selection cannot be handled in the same way as other tribunals with a lesser range of discretion to exercise in the public interest using a generalized set of qualifications. The price to be paid by not understanding these things is the continued progressively worsening public cynicism and the record over the past ten years of insufficient deliberation and writing time, inconsistency in policy and outcomes, reliance on part-time members continuously to fill scheduling gaps and uneven quality of decisions.

No matter how good those who preside over the major hearings are, in order to produce reasonably capable work that deserves attention from others in the planning process, they need time to do their jobs. What was not factored into the case of the OMB was that these reductions would be made possible by maximizing use of mediation and of alternatives to traditional civil trial-type hearings. The OMB was given none of the benefits of clustering in the form of increased mediation-trained members to carry out the increased use of mediation, or the strategy to increase, or at least maintain, full-time member levels. In both cases, resources were reduced. The results that the Board has been able to achieve came largely because of the efforts of the three-member mediation group who have each been on the Board for at least eight years: Mr. McKenzie, Mr. Lee, and Ms. Schiller.

There has to be time allowed to deliberate on decisions, understand the full nuances of the evidence and the submissions and get the research done, in order to avoid the pitfalls of short-sighted hurried decision-making. Those pitfalls can result in taking a tribunal on a detour of conflict, final synthesis, and potential rehearing that was totally unnecessary if time had been taken in the first place. In that kind of case, and there are more than a few of them every year, much of the research, organizing, and deliberating could not be done fully until the final submissions were made. Those in charge simply don't see the need for anyone to require time for deliberation and writing decisions of a high calibre because that is not visible work done out there in public that gets the schedule done. And yet it is and it does. And it gets the workload done while allowing for those doing it to produce work of excellence from which municipalities can take guidance and assistance in implementing policy and new planning initiatives.

I think of the recent Waterloo Region Plan decision and the time and embarrassment undergone before it was resolved. For an important decision, it reads as a very light, basic listing or outline of short factual resumes and findings on decisive points, supported by only conclusory reasons: *Waterloo (Reg. Mun.) Official Plan and 1541179 Ontario Ltd., Re* (OMB File No. PL110080). We discussed it in Chapter III and will be more specific about it in Chapter X. Others may include *Miller Paving Ltd. v McNab/Braeside (Township)*, the *James Dick and Jennison* decisions and the cases discussed in Chapters X and XI, as a small sample.

The ATAGA legislation contains a six-year review clause and, in subsection (3) the threat of a review by the responsible minister at any time. Section 21 reads:

> (1) An adjudicative tribunal's responsible minister shall direct a public servant employed under Part III of the *Public Service of Ontario Act, 2006* or any other person to conduct a review of the adjudicative tribunal at least once every six years.

[Subsection (2) lists the factors and performance elements to be reviewed.]

> (3) An adjudicative tribunal's responsible minister may at any time direct a public servant employed under Part III of the *Public Service of Ontario Act, 2006* or any other person to conduct a review of the adjudicative tribunal in respect of any of the matters listed in subsection (2).

The coming 2016 review of the OMB can be seen, in this provision, as including not simply operational and goal-measured progress or recession; it can include consideration of the tribunal's continued relevance and /or discontinuance.

As I have found from material provided to me by the Board, by late 2015, the Ontario Municipal Board was down to fourteen full-time members (not including the Associate Chair or cross-appointees). At the time of the Facilitator's Final report in 2007, it listed the OMB as having twenty-seven and before that its membership was maintained at twenty-eight to thirty. There are six members now who are cross-appointed to other tribunals in the ELTO cluster; only three are actually available for a week at a time.

The more troubling aspect of this time spread is that, after the delay getting to the hearing, apart from minor hearings, the Board cannot produce a timely decision with reasons. Often, even for expropriation cases that were scheduled within six months of filing and the hearing completed, the parties are unlikely to see a decision with reasons for at least ten months to a year and more. Compensation hearings are ever more complex, they approach art in the most abstract when, for instance, the land rights to be evaluated are strata of material some twenty feet or more underground. They are the hearings that are most like a trial in Superior Court where the amount in question is often $700–900 thousand or well over one million dollars. And the law and detailed facts are not simple.

For a two-week planning law appeal, the member presiding at the hearing will probably not be able to produce a decision for five months or more from most users I have spoken with. A recent decision, which was keenly awaited by many involved in the development and subdivision field, was the park levy decision in Richmond Hill. It was a time-sensitive case and yet the decision did not appear until almost seven months following the hearing.[142]

The problem is that unlike a court where judges have non-sitting weeks during which they have time to research and write decisions, the Board members have no scheduled off-hearing weeks, none. Only if a hearing suddenly settles early, or for some other reason a hearing has to be postponed at the last minute, may the member have a day or two to try to take care of the several reserved decisions that have built up. Unless one has written, or seriously contemplated the time for writing, judgments or tribunal decisions, especially in hard fought cases on issues of the moment that require a measured and considered examination and a carefully reasoned decision, it is hard to appreciate that time is required in members' schedules for that purpose. The cluster facilitator's assumption that writing time should be cut may address a concern on some other less busy tribunals but, in my view, that was an extraordinarily ignorant standard to use. It was made worse by the failure to increase the number of trained mediators in order to reduce the hearing caseload.

The Board's weakened condition is showing very clearly in the way decisions are written. They are organized more in the way the hearing unfolded instead of starting from the position that the hearing is over, here

"The Board's weakened condition is showing very clearly in the way decisions are written."

is the context of the decision, here are the common threads if several matters are dealt with together, the issues and here is how we deal with each issue, culminating with a conclusion that pulls the whole together and is consistent with Board and government policy or is an exception that must follow a different road of principle and policy.

The conditions and the strain under which members are working are evident. And this has not yet taken into account recent OP hearings to start soon for the City of Toronto and an ongoing one in York Region. A five-year duration is being discussed as probable for those large municipality OP hearings. They are conducted as bifurcated phased hearings where appeals from the most urgently required portions of the new OPs are heard first, the partial decisions are given effect to and then the next most urgent portion will be scheduled; the numerous site specific appeals are left to the end. It is probable that as a Plan hearing is finishing in five to six years' time, the next OP review hearing will be coming on. That kind of delay for sophisticated and busy congested municipalities requiring regional strategies gives real truth to the old saying, paraphrased for the subject matter, justice delayed is planning denied.

The saving feature to all this is the success that OMB-sponsored mediation has had, both through the related B of N early in the expropriation process and the OMB later in that process, and in planning law cases even more so. There would be substantially longer delays to every stage of the Board's lists but for the results that mediation has achieved. What this effort has proven is that the most holistic and multidimensional approach that mediation can bring to planning problems, even the most intractable ones, carries the seeds of great promise for both process and resolution in the future.

> "... the most holistic and multidimensional approach that mediation can bring to planning problems, even the most intractable ones, carries the seeds of great promise."

For instance, I am told that a war of attrition went on in Guelph over the hierarchy and scale of commercial in the city for ten years. It was about to head into the court system. The Board brought it into its mediation process and through extended sessions, all were resolved except one, and the objections in that one case were substantially narrowed. This was a turning point for the mediation program at the Board and for the member involved. If this could be done for such a difficult set of issues in Guelph, many if not all of the planning cases with parties having an interest in resolving issues have a realistic chance of successful and principled results. This is the added, unique key to success of mediation in planning matters, and why only those knowledgeable of planning principles and planning law as well as having mediation training can do Board-sponsored mediation: any resolution must meet the test of good planning and policy consistency or it cannot be ratified by the Board.

If this Board had a full-time complement of twenty-eight members, eight to ten of whom were mediation-trained *and* competent planning lawyers, professional planners or from other related professions, the hearing process could shift to a process that can properly bring all interested parties into the tent. It could focus the issues, enforce those choices consistently and ensure that all must accept solutions that meet good planning standards using the hearing process as the lever to keep the parties focused on a mediated solution to each issue in turn. Where mediation does not work, those issues go immediately to hearing.

Another important aspect is that the OMB is the only tribunal that deals through the Board of Negotiation process with mediation of loss claims after an expropriation occurred, and later through its own process, for claims not settled. It is the hearing tribunal to consider and decide on due compensation for lands taken and for damage to the retained land of the claimant. The importance and unique quality of these claims lie in the sensitive fact that they are the only type of claim before any court or tribunal where the claimants have done absolutely nothing to put themselves in the way of what has happened to them. As the tribunal directed by the *Expropriations Act* of Ontario to determine these claims, the OMB plays the central adjudicative role for the whole Province of Ontario.

Despite the inherent delays in the Board's undernourished process, a well-known expropriation compensation lawyer sees the mediation process as having kept the pace of cases moving toward hearing relatively well.[143] The court process is much slower. It is important for this type of claimant to be able to navigate through the process in an expeditious way and compensation mediation has allowed this to happen. The delay in rendering decisions in this field of ten to twelve months and sometimes more is not acceptable.

Some practitioners provided their concern about the cluster concept that included the OMB. I refer to only a few because this aspect of the ELTO reorganization is not well known. It is not my intent to include comments that are based on less than knowledge of the situation as it exists. In most cases, it is only the product of the ELTO period, the decline in full-time Board members that most are familiar with, and I have dealt with that aspect.

> I would go further than the idea of clustering. I think there are several tribunals that need to be more integrated with each other. For instance, the Conservation Appeal Board regarding heritage matters could be integrated with OMB, also the Assessment Review Board which deals with very similar issues to those in expropriation work which the OMB does. The Environmental Review Board could be aligned more with the OMB because both deal with environmental issues. As well, it is important that the Environmental Assessment Act work with the *Planning Act*. Having more integration of the two Boards would create a greater understanding of how the various policies can work together and not in isolation.[144]

> The one issue that really bothers me is related to the clustering idea. It is the issue of cross-appointments between Boards. When you have a specialized tribunal, you have people on it, specially chosen for it, and who will understand and apply the jurisprudence with some consistency. But when you

cross-appoint people between tribunals, you interfere with the whole concept of what a specialized tribunal is and the benefits that it brings. I have no problem with clustering as an administrative tool, for instance, in order to save money; two tribunals can share hearing space or two offices can share computer facilities. Where clustering crosses the line is where it affects the expertise of the tribunal. I am not so concerned about the cross-appointment between, say, the ERT and the OMB. What I am concerned about is the idea of pulling members of several tribunals into one common pond from which you can select anyone for a particular hearing.[145]

Clustering is a failed initiative. If you had a number of tribunals, each of which does not have full-time work, then it would make some sense to cluster those tribunals but when you cluster a tribunal as busy as the OMB with other less busy tribunals, then it only adds to the OMB's problems and that initiative should end.[146]

Meanwhile, this Board faces its expropriation, development charges and planning jurisdictions with vastly reduced numbers and competence; due to the ten-year window for tenure set by this government, it is about to lose all three of its trained mediators and in total, ten of its twenty-one members – almost fifty per cent – by July 2017 unless some exception is made to that policy. Its work in the new world of provincial policy leadership, with the new demands of growth plans, is greater and more detailed than ever before. That was a theme that all participants in the planning law and compensation sides agreed, as was the theme that mediation carried the best hope for the future. For this tribunal to be trying to run planning law, development charge and expropriation compensation cases of large significance with half its former complement and maintain a high level of product output seems almost futile in the long run. And still the question remains in the air, kicked around without response: how can this reduced tribunal with a busy agenda and stretched membership possibly meet the high standards of adjudication the ATAGA Facilitator reported was the goal of the cluster concept?

The answer at present is that it cannot.

CHAPTER IX

CHOICES

Two roads diverged
In a wood and I –
I took the one...
—R. Frost
from Mountain Interval, 1916

The 1972 Select Committee of the Legislature on the Ontario Municipal Board, of which I have written earlier, was an experienced group of legislators – eleven in all – and eight of the eleven were former municipal councillors. In fact, four had been mayor or reeve of their town or city. The Chair was John Macbeth, a former reeve of Etobicoke and the membership included Philip Givens, a former longtime city councillor and mayor of Toronto; Dennis Timbrell, a former North York councillor and well-known minister in the Davis government between 1975 and 1985; Frank Miller, once a Bracebridge councillor who became premier of Ontario briefly in 1985; and Donald MacDonald, longtime leader of the CCF and NDP between 1953 and 1970 as well as representatives from the extreme south in Niagara, from eastern Ontario, and from central and northern Ontario. It was one of the more talented and competent legislative committees formed on one defined subject: municipal law and process centred on the OMB. It was that committee that made the important recommendation that the Board be kept in its independent state and not folded into one of the line ministries.

This committee made the other important recommendation that was not acted upon until 1994 and 2005, two to three decades after it was made. That is, the recommendation that the government should establish a clear-cut method of stating government policy and that it should clearly state the policies it expects the OMB to follow, such declarations to be issued to all municipalities and to the public at large. Before doing so, however, the Committee almost became mired in one of those mysteries buried in legislative archives over the years since 1906. No one I have read has ever discovered the complete inventory of statutes that, over the decades, gave more and more authority to the OMB of one kind or another. The range extended, years ago, from the *Cemeteries Act* to Acts dealing with the regulation of bull and stallion semen. One estimate placed the number at well over a hundred. It is amusing to read the section of the report where this comes up; it is early in its general observations section.

Clearly, the committee had started out thinking that they would solve this minor problem in short order. It bravely directed that all functions of the OMB be set out for its consideration. Various lists were consulted and perhaps an assortment of tea leaves because the next note is to the effect that the *McRuer Report* on the Royal Commission into Civil rights had made the most extensive list. It could not say that their list was exhaustive. The Committee next noted that there were representatives from the larger municipalities who, when asked, could not recall their town or city ever using any of the powers additional to those in the planning, capital expenditure/municipal organization, and assessment appeals section of the Planning and OMB Acts. The immediate former Chair and authority himself for years on the work of the OMB, J.A. Kennedy, was asked. He was unsure what the Board's complete catalogue of authority really was. The Committee report states almost thankfully: "His uncertainty is understandable." They then recorded their finding on those statutes known to contain problems and those with no problems. The final words of the report on this subject are:

> Many inconsistencies are to be found in the *Ontario Municipal Board Act* and other relevant statutes ... the result is a considerable lack of uniformity and clarity. For instance, section 182(11) of the *Municipality of Metropolitan Toronto Act,* which purports to give certain powers to the OMB has been held ultra vires by the courts (i.e. unconstitutional). Some of the OMB's powers and functions (e.g. under the *Drainage Act*) are being reviewed ... Such a piecemeal approach, however, will not solve the whole problem.

> Committee Recommendation 1A:
> "All functions of the OMB and all legislation relating to its role should be catalogued."

> Committee recommendation 1B:
> "All functions not dealt with specifically in this Report should be reviewed in detail [to determine] whether each power and function should be left with the OMB, transferred to some other body, or abolished."[147]

These were far cries from that brave world in which the Committee started where it was going to slay the dragon of the Board's powers and leave a clear thread out there for all to find their complete and final location.

Now, years later, we have a *Planning Act* that is purposive, and those purposes flow through the matters of provincial interest to the PPS (2014), the comprehensive provincial planning policy and a supplementary policy process. From these, filtered through the local conditions and land use policies of each municipal OP, the more immediate controls over zoning, site plans and lot creation take hold. Yet, at the time when the Province most needs some central leadership in adjudicating the application of this policy in concrete situations, cuts are maintained to Board personnel, remuneration is frozen at an anomalous level, and decision-writing time is reduced to virtually nothing during working hours to keep up with the schedule. It seems a strange way to prepare and encourage the recruitment of qualified, competent mediator-planners and lawyers of stature to supplement the small membership on the Board in order to meet what is required.

PROVINCIAL POLICY

The concept of a comprehensive statement of government policy was first recommended in 1972 by the Select Committee of the Legislature. The idea received its first thrust of interest during the NDP's term in power in 1994. Sections 1 and 2 listing the purposes of the planning process in Ontario and the many aspects of the provincial interest were passed by the Legislature and enacted as part of the *Planning Act*. Then in 1996 and 1997, the first policy statement under section 3 was put forward as a result of a policy initiative begun before and completed during the Harris Conservative government. It was made up of excerpts from the existing policy statements on agriculture, aggregate resource and housing existence merged with some other broad goals into one statement. By 2005, the first integrated provincial policy statement (PPS) was issued, superseded in 2014 by the current one.

The leadership displayed by the Province since 2003 has been impressive in the preparation of plans and policy as one comprehensive document that has objectives and directives on virtually all aspects of the planning process. The 2005 statement explained its direction in this way:

> The Provincial Policy Statement supports a comprehensive, integrated and long-term approach to planning, and recognizes linkages among policy areas.

> The Provincial Policy Statement is more than a set of individual policies. It is intended to be read in its entirety and the relevant policies are to be applied to each situation. ...

> Part IV, Vision for Ontario's Land Use Planning System, provides the context for applying the Provincial Policy Statement. Implementation issues are addressed in the Implementation and Interpretation section."[148]

The Statement covers objectives, priorities and means of setting priorities and implementation policies for land use in urban areas as growth centres; it sets out rural and agricultural land use and waste management priorities, and includes policies for infrastructure, transportation, energy efficiency and air and water quality issues. Section 2 deals with protection of the natural and cultural heritage areas and sites, including agricultural lands and farming areas, aggregate and water resource policies, wetlands, recharge areas, and water resources. Sections 3 and 4 are aimed at directing development away from certain natural and manmade hazard areas like floodplain areas and water courses with implementation policies.

The hierarchy of layers of plans is set out in section 4. Provincial area plans take precedence over policies in the Provincial Policy Statement to the extent of any conflict. Those include plans created under the *Niagara Escarpment Planning and Development Act* and the *Oak Ridges Moraine Conservation Act, 2001*.[149] The Provincial Planning Statements are to be implemented by the regional and local OPs, meaning that in case of conflict with an OP, go with the Provincial Statement.

> "Policy Statements do not necessarily give you an answer to a land use problem ..."

The problem comes when the municipal council and its planning staff, or the Municipal Board on appeal to it, must read and apply sections of the policy statement in relation to one planning area or development site. Policy Statements do not necessarily give you an answer to a land use problem; often there are several objectives in play for differing land use configurations and policy directives aiming toward different objectives and coming from a variety of subject areas that converge and choices have to be made. These differing objectives and policy directions come about because the reason for the conflict between parties that brought the case to the Board is that the area or site involved is at a crossroads or on the cusp of two or three developmental patterns or of a significant natural feature and differing land usage nearby. But there are clues to the balance of future land use in the policy and in the site and area patterns that help the planner, land owner and council to achieve. To me, one essential part that helps to pull it all together is what the PPS refers to as Part IV, providing the context for applying the policy statement.

PART IV EXCERPT: VISION FOR ONTARIO'S LAND USE PLANNING SYSTEM

The long-term prosperity and social well-being of Ontario depends upon planning for strong, sustainable and resilient communities for people of all ages, a clean and healthy environment, and a strong and competitive economy.

Ontario is a vast province with diverse urban, rural and northern communities, which may face different challenges related to diversity in population, economic activity, pace of growth and physical and natural conditions...

The Provincial Policy Statement focuses growth and development within urban and rural settlement areas while supporting the viability of rural areas. It recognizes that the wise management of land use change may involve directing, promoting or sustaining development. Land use must be carefully managed to accommodate appropriate development to meet the full range of current and future needs, while achieving efficient development patterns and avoiding significant or sensitive resources and areas which may pose a risk to public health and safety.

Efficient development patterns optimize the use of land, resources and public investment in infrastructure and public service facilities. These land use patterns promote a mix of housing, including affordable housing, employment, recreation, parks and open spaces, and transportation choices that increase the use of active transportation and transit before other modes of travel. They also support the financial wellbeing of the Province and municipalities over the long term, and minimize the undesirable effects of development, including impacts on air, water and other resources. Strong, liveable and healthy communities promote and enhance human health and social well-being, are economically and environmentally sound, and are resilient to climate change.

The Province's natural heritage resources, water resources, including the Great Lakes, agricultural resources, mineral resources, and cultural heritage and archaeological resources provide important environmental, economic and social benefits. The wise use and management of these resources over the long term is a key provincial interest.[150]

-oooooo-

This straightforward short passage certainly makes clear that the PPS is meant to be read as a coherent set of policies and goals that are to work together in assisting planners and councils to properly weigh proposals for land use by citing what are significant values, less significant and what are not. The staff planning report would provide a framework of planning policies and some ordering of priorities based on the PPS and the OP due to the site location in an urban or rural area and any sensitive natural features near or across it.[151]

Like any policy document, when it is read in relation to one site, there are overlaps and some sections may apply that may seem to conflict. For instance, the PPS favours intensification but also a mix and range of housing types, objectives which, in some centres with large residential lots, would definitely conflict if the planning principle of something new being sensitive to the scale and height of built forms and the character of the area applied. In any urban residential area, intensification and range of housing will conflict where more single family residential is desirable for a stable area but multiple projects are being proposed near the commercial street intersection. Another example is the promotion of economic opportunities and affordable housing while at the same time meet sometimes costly design, density and compatibility concerns wanted by existing communities.

It is always an interesting challenge to try to find the right, the appropriate, balance in design and built form and scale, that meets the PPS, as well as the right direction and intuitive sense of the site. At least one Board member suggests that the policies are to be read as a whole 'purposively,' and are not in conflict.[152] There is no balancing required because a purposive sense of the whole would give the answer. Others suggest that the role of the Board (and other decision makers) is in fact to identify and 'balance' apparently competing objectives, without finding them in classic 'conflict'. I can only say that my earlier remark about balance gives me away.

> "… the local decision must always be recognized as important as a self-endorsed solution by those elected from the community. But that does not save a project that goes against the tenor of the policy statement …"

An in-depth read of the policies most directly related to the site, studying the design work and the photographic and plan perspectives will provide insights to a possible resolution of the evidence and the policy that one only perceives dimly at first and then more clearly. That balancing of the choices to meet policy objectives is another reason the local decision must always be recognized as important as a self-endorsed solution by those elected from the community. But that does not save a project that goes against the tenor of the policy statement such as estate lots in a growth centre or a large commercial mall in a manufacturing area with needs for transport accessibility continuously and use impacts that would be unacceptable. Nor would it save the rejection of a proposal because a crowd of angry citizens from the ward involved demanded that it be defeated and the council voted to do so against a staff planning report of solid merit.

In *Kelvingrove*, the case cited above regarding balance and conflict resolution in land use planning, the Board summed up its conclusions early in the decision. They included the member's reflection on the approach to the PPS in the context of a proposal to redevelop a site in Toronto with a building higher and of more dense massing than the rest of the area and considerably more rental and condominium units than the present development, which had been approved by the OMB, with heritage features supporting a CRB recommendation to designate under the *Ontario Heritage Act*:

5. This is not a matter of "balancing" Provincial policies for heritage against other Provincial priorities; one starts from the premise that Provincial goals are complementary, not conflicting. As for the "fit" between the proposed apartment block and what the OP calls "the physical character of the area," that apartment "face print" along Bayview exceeds the *next* largest building by a

factor of four, and that of recent nearby buildings by much more. It meets no City volumetric guidelines.

6. The Applicant's experts nonetheless insisted on its "planning merits", notably intensification. The *Growth Plan for the Greater Golden Horseshoe* (GP) and the OP forecast a City population, by 2031, of 3 million plus; the Applicant's experts said the City was "falling behind"... Furthermore, the Provincial Policy Statement (PPS) instructs that intensification be "directed", according to "policies" – which, in this case, the City has already done in its prioritization of areas to intensify (its "Urban Structure").

Later in the case, the member returned to this theme of reciprocal complementarity within the PPS (2005). He wrote:

40. That analysis, said the Applicant, means "balancing" the "planning merits" of the project against allegedly feeble heritage aspects. *The word "balance" often appears in Board Decisions – usually in weighing public interests against private rights. But does one presume that within the realm of public interests, Provincial instructions are mutually contradictory and similarly need "balancing"? Does one presume that PPS Policy 2.6 on "heritage" conflicts with other policies (e.g., intensification, or about "efficient development"), thus necessitating enquiry on "which policy direction is the stronger one"?* [Emphasis added]

And again later:

63. The Board was not persuaded that this is the thrust of Provincial policy. In Ontario, land use planning is not normally about quotas for growth, but locations for growth. The very name of the GP's statute, the *Places to Grow Act*, announces that its subject-matter is not whether there is growth, or how much, but rather its *place*.

64. That is quintessentially what "planning" is about. It also reflects declared public policy. Although intensification is crucial, the PPS specifies at Policy 1.1.3.3 that it shall be *"directed"*, in accordance with *"policies"*. As one would expect in "planning", it is "arranged beforehand"; it is about change being "managed". It is not haphazard; it is not *ad hoc*; it is not a matter of a municipality randomly "doing the best it can". Indeed, although the PPS refers to intensification targets (not population targets), the task of establishing those targets is vested in planning authorities at the local or Provincial level. Nowhere do these documents say that intensification preempts the rest of the planning process;

on the contrary, they contain a roadmap of how intensification is to be *incorporated* in the planning process."

I simply want to clarify a couple of things here that are, I think, important. First, the Board must write about matters of policy with some care. These excerpts do not sound as if the Board as a whole had considered these matters so that there has been some care taken in expressing a policy or a well-considered partial consensus of the Board. They read as if they had simply been put together by the member without any collegial and collective thought.

> "It is simply not correct to use a statute that has effect only in certain parts of the province – the *Places to Grow Act, 2005* – as providing what planning is about throughout the province."

Whether or not these statements about the PPS are the subject of a Board consensus on their meaning, thoughts like these should be treated with care in order to ensure their factual correctness. When one writes that, "In Ontario, land use planning is not normally about quotas for growth, but locations for growth" – one is expressing a characteristic of the planning process throughout the province and about one aspect of planning, being growth. It is simply not correct to use a statute that has effect only in certain parts of the province – the *Places to Grow Act, 2005* – as providing what planning is about throughout the province. In any event, neither the PPS nor the *Planning Act*, which express the content of the planning process across the province, provide that land use planning is normally about locations for growth, though part of the process certainly is. As for the growth targets or goals, they must be given meaning in the sense that they were inserted to provide the population, which the OP was designed to provide for and accommodate.. The goal of the whole exercise is to increase residential capacity where it is acceptable in the built-up area in order to reduce urban sprawl from the GTA primarily and to control the huge expenditures in transportation infrastructure that it entails, to say nothing of the protection of some prime agricultural land closer to markets than California and Florida.

Finally, when one talks of "balance" in a land use planning sense, it is again incorrect to start a consideration of the PPS with some inbred assumption that this is a document that is complementary in nature or that it is replete with conflicts. The assumption in the member's thinking seems to be that if one speaks of balance in approaching the PPS, one is speaking of offsetting one provincial priority against another and that they are in conflict. That again is not correct. The word "balance" is a somewhat complex word that includes the meaning "to offset against another (*must offset the advantages [against or] with the disadvantages*)." However, it also means "to compare with", which carries no necessary implication that you are comparing things that conflict. When one thinks judiciously on a policy document of this sort, the meaning that I would be using would be, "bring into or keep in equilibrium", or "establish equal or appropriate proportions of elements in (a balanced opinion)."[153] The application of complex policy documents requires a deep knowledge of the document and a sense of the whole, with the parts having a meaning within that whole, and relating that to achieve an acceptable balance in land use terms in and around the site in question.

I think it would be a much better use of members' time to try to talk these matters of policy out as a body and try to find a sense of the document on which all or most can agree; then you have a much firmer base to start from and you may be able to bring predictability and consistency to "similar circumstance" cases. Your many stakeholders would thank the Board for this. They do not thank the Board for overlong dissertations of members' personal thinking on subjects requiring great care in interpreting.

The balance that the PPS seeks in any particular case is a matter the Board must rule on after making the necessary findings of fact in the case. I cannot see the Province having erected this edifice of policy and not finding the land use review and compensation tribunal a useful body between the policy-maker on a macro scale and the adjudicators who can adapt and interpret that policy on a micro scale to one site or area. As one counsel told me, the PPS and the OP contain the policies with which both the municipalities and the Board must find consistency. It is the Board's ever inventive and fact-based role to find how to make those policies practical and apply them in the real world in which the stakeholders are living. It is through policy that the tension between municipalities and the Province and the Board can best be worked through by the adjudicator and reduced. All have their place in a democracy that values resolution, decision-making and fairness in land use and compensation matters.

THE FINAL CHOICES

As I see it, there are four choices regarding the OMB and the future planning process:
1. maintain the status quo with some statutory and executive directives to fix the problems;
2. dissolve the Ontario Municipal Board;
3. dissolve the OMB and during a transition phase move toward establishing a new tribunal with a new name, new mandate, new jurisdiction, new role, and some statutory and regulatory fixes of prior problems; and
4. remove the planning jurisdiction under the *Planning Act* from the OMB.

If the OMB is dissolved, this would leave the local and regional councils or their delegated appeal bodies, as the final decision-makers on all matters within the *Planning Act* and related legislation. They would, of course, be subject to judicial review by the courts in cases of denial of the rules of natural justice and/or breach of the rules of procedural fairness.

Some critics and other interested parties advocate dissolution of the OMB. This would cause major structural changes to legislation and the need to fill the holes left in several statutory regimes that no one wants to disturb. They include the need for groups of administrative adjudicators to replace the OMB as the lead tribunal under the *Aggregate Resources Act,* dealing with new or extended pit and quarry licences, in company with amended zoning to permit new site gravel operations. The same is true for the *Development Charges Act* for appeals of development charge by-laws and the way hard and soft costs are accounted for. The *Expropriations Act* would also lose its tribunal for deciding compensation claims. It would mean major amendments to the *Planning Act* as well. Decisions would have to be made about the use and appointment of local appeal bodies and the breadth of delegation to them of planning-related appeals.

> "... there are no grounds put forward by anyone for dissolving the OMB. All of the issues relate to its planning jurisdiction only."

From what I have seen of the criticism and allegations against the Board that are recent and public, there are no grounds put forward by anyone for dissolving the OMB. All of the issues relate to its planning jurisdiction only. Are there hard reasons now for removing and terminating the planning law jurisdiction of the OMB, leaving the local and regional councils or their delegated appeal bodies, as the final decision-makers on all matters within the *Planning Act* and related legislation? They would be subject, of course, to judicial review by the courts in cases of denial of the rules of natural justice and/or breach of the rules of procedural fairness.

Or, should a new tribunal be formed with a revamped jurisdiction and a recognized role as the lead agency for interpreting and applying provincial policy? Or should the OMB continue subject to recommended changes to improve its deficiencies? Either of these alternatives would mean that expropriation and development charge cases would continue to have a tribunal and a hearing process.

As we have found, there are principally four credible grounds for removing the *Planning Act* jurisdiction from the Board. They are:

1. Municipal governments now have the administrative capability, experience and planning advice necessary to make final decisions in land use planning without the need for appeals to a provincial tribunal; as they are elected in part to make decisions within this parameters of provincial policy, their decisions should be final, subject to judicial review only.

2. Any positives that the OMB brings to the process are negated by long-delayed and uneven decision-making, official plan appeals that are literally to take three to five years to complete, and cost heavy hearings, which sometimes sink the whole enterprise that they are about.

3. The public perception of unaccountability of the OMB and its members for decisions made without judicial discipline or control, using a discretion that

appears unlimited, allowing decisions made by whim rather than by principled reasoning has damaged the Ontario Municipal Bard irreparably.

4. There is also the suggestion that the efficacy of strict public notice and meeting requirements as in British Columbia resolves the concern over the civil rights of property owners asking for a zoning change and/or an amendment to an official plan.

WARD-BASED MUNICIPAL COUNCILS AND LAND USE PLANNING

The research of Aaron Moore in *Planning Politics* confirmed the parochialism of a ward-based council as in Toronto, but to me, he missed the full story. And his research may or may not be relevant to other councils in smaller municipalities.

On councils of the larger cities, the presence of the OMB in the process allows councillors to vote the way their ward constituents want, knowing that the OMB would make the decision they would not. That is true. But the *Planning Politics* author did not fully see that in Toronto the ward system produces a systemic tendency of council to vote with the councillor in whose ward is located the project in question. The OMB provides a shield behind which councillors can protect their positions with their supporters by opposing proposals objected to by neighbourhood groups and others. They can vote against proposals knowing that if they do not pass, the proponent will appeal to the OMB, which will probably allow the appeal if the planning merits are as good as the city or town staff see them.

But the problem with this use of the Board is that it produces a two-edged sword – (a) probable support for the ward councillor by council, at least in the larger centres, and (b) it creates more appeals, more administrative litigation before the provincial tribunal. Appeals caused by councils, who act to protect themselves in this way, take up hearing resources that may not be necessary if the council voted in a responsible way on the merits of the proposal. This in turn means a further load on the OMB process.

But could this penchant for using the Board to avoid an unsavoury vote against one's political interests be resolved by the options being considered here? Dissolving the Board or removal of its *Planning Act* jurisdiction would mean council would no longer have that way out. But would that mean they would not still act for political reasons and simply reject proposals that are required in the public interest, like a pit or quarry or a housing project to assist challenged people who need to live in the community? The objections by neighbourhood groups and other voters would still occur, and they always involve the short-term political interests of councillors in re-election.

1. One approach could involve mounting a new tribunal with a reduced jurisdiction geared to problem issues in zoning, subdivision and site plan and

development permits (if DPs are introduced, as appears likely), and perhaps OP adoption or amendments only.

2. Another approach could be to delete all appeals from municipal adoption of OPs, leaving the municipal council in each case as the final authority on future planning, subject to appeals only in cases where the OP or OPA includes material not properly part of an OP according to the *Planning Act* standards and consistency with provincial policy statements, growth plans and other provincial plans with statutory authority over specific geographic features and areas. Most other jurisdictions having regional or provincial/state OPs do not recognize appeals from them, leaving future policy to each municipality, its planning staff recommendations, and council. Or one could exclude all OPA appeals.

3. When one comes down to basics, do you leave the basic land use rules and policies to an elected council that has accountability locally subject to regional supervision or to appointed members of a tribunal, which will hear the evidence and make decisions on all appeals on the merits of each? Perhaps it is time to allow municipalities to set their own development strategies, subject to provincial policy; appeals can be heard by the council on strict terms in the form of written reports, which are to be read and full submissions by the parties' representatives before a quorum of council. These are some of the alternatives and choices as we head toward the conclusion.

On the positive side, an experienced applicant for planning relief will know with whom that applicant must deal, the one person he/she must convince if the support of the city, in addition to planning staff, is sought. So let us look at the municipal process option seriously.

1. As for smaller cities, towns and townships, I have heard little similar criticism. Most lawyers and planners whom I interviewed seemed to point to Toronto as the municipality where a proponent or an opponent of a proposal before council never actually appears before council. They appear before a district committee of council. Most times in other municipalities, the councillors appear to listen to the parties and often vote as the planning staff recommends. When it comes to a vote, most times in Toronto, council votes as the ward councillor does.

2. One lawyer from a smaller Ontario city said that his local council and most other rural councils he has appeared before tend to be political in their votes. Others say that they tend to vote as the planning report suggests. But these reports are based on what someone else, i.e. a municipal clerk, told the person.

Over all, I received the impression that most councils took their duties seriously, but simply do not have the time to hear each person concerned about a development proposal for more than five minutes as an ongoing process throughout the year. It seems to me that, given the professional planning advice most municipalities have from their own staff or from the upper tier level of their county or region, the OP is a document to which they could devote necessary time every five to ten years, provided a clear step by step process was provided.

3. If municipalities are to start being more responsible for their own planning as locally inspired proper policy documents setting out their future, it should be to produce, with professional assistance, the municipal OP. This would help to meet the cynicism and frustration of people who see their work in aid of their municipality's future sometimes interfered with by a board member without any sense of that community, its strengths and its growing or ebbing weaknesses and its hopes for the next twenty to thirty years.

4. This is a case that has validity to it – the proposition that local government should be responsible for their own OP provided that matters of height and built density not establish limits. General policy trends can be dealt with and decided by the local council on an OP review but height, built density and lot limits are to be left to the zoning by-law. For the ongoing succession of zoning and OPAs, the provincial review tribunal has a role to play as the appellate body charged with the fair and full hearing of these matters, their consistency with provincial and local policy set by the Province and by the local council. The standard of review can be looked at in relation to the local OP and provincial policy on a more objective standard than good planning, as we will discuss further.

5. Regarding the process for the stream of OPAs and zoning amendments requiring council's attention on an ongoing basis, if you are not a major player, where are you left in the system? Makuch's research showed that it means at the community planning committee in Toronto (you have to go to a community committee for development matters – you never get before the full council) or council outside Toronto, you are just one applicant with no greater rights than anyone else who chooses to speak. You get your five minutes to speak. And you get no more than that later; even if the opposition to your proposal takes two or three hours (you were not informed that there would be opposition). You only get five minutes to reply. You receive no reasons for the decision that turns you down. And as the ward councillor whom you did not know agrees

with the negative recommendation, the staff report may not be well reasoned or even make sense. Makuch concluded:

> In these situations, the characteristics of a 'standard of justice' referred to by Mr. Justice McRuer have been cast aside.[154]

There is no reason, however, why municipalities could not take control of the OP process. This would only occur at infrequent intervals, probably every ten to twenty years. There would be no ongoing demand for hearing time as there would be with OPAs and zoning amendments. And the OP is peculiarly a municipal expression of its future. But producing land use policy is one thing; applying those policies to all the properties in the municipality which can have the effect of adding potential development rights or decreasing them on individual properties, is not just the business of the municipality as a whole. It then becomes an issue between individual ratepayers and the municipality and perhaps the province, with issues someone must adjudicate or mediate knowledgeably for there to be any credibility to the planning process. Who will win, who will come out even, and who will lose in the long term? The differences can amount to millions of dollars in one case. Will the council be able to not only set policy, and also apply it in individual cases, and hear appeals themselves (or their delegates would), from the councils' decisions, and be seen to be acting justly and without undue influence being exerted through possible under-the-table payments or pressures of one kind or another? That is the dilemma of ridding the OP policy process of a land use review tribunal in order to provide more responsibility to municipalities in the planning field.

THE DILEMMA OF HEIGHT/DENSITY BONUSES

There has been too little attention paid to the bonus concept, the trading of additional height and density for social, aesthetic or environmental benefits. Too much of this process is left to off-the-record bidding for the local councillor's support. That councillor in turn will affect council's attitude by the kind of section 37 benefits that the developer is willing to make. Section 37 is quite simple to read and has virtually no criteria to limit council regarding the nature and amount of benefits to be sought. Section 37(1) to (4) read:

> 37(1) The council of a local municipality may, in a by-law passed under section 34, authorize increases in the height and density of development otherwise permitted by the by-law that will be permitted in return for the provision of such facilities, services or matters as are set out in the by-law.

> (2) A by-law shall not contain the provisions mentioned in subsection (1) unless there is an official plan in effect in the local municipality that contains

provisions relating to the authorization of increases in height and density of development.

(3) Where an owner of land elects to provide facilities, services or matters in return for an increase in the height or density of development, the municipality may require the owner to enter into one or more agreements with the municipality dealing with the facilities, services or matters.

(4) Any agreement entered into under subsection (3) may be registered against the land to which it applies and the municipality is entitled to enforce the provisions thereof against the owner and, subject to the provisions of the *Registry Act* and the *Land Titles Act*, any and all subsequent owners of the land.

For additional height and density benefits, the developer must pay or provide facilities or services limited only by policies that the municipality is not necessarily specific about in the OP. The virtually unbridled power this gives the ward councillor is wide open to abuse by use of the planning system to obtain campaign funds or for other illegal purposes. A Toronto planning and development lawyer describes the problem, using this example.

On this one occasion, since the developer (client) was not familiar with the City of Toronto process, I attended an initial meeting ... I questioned the City Councillor as to his or her thoughts as to the most appropriate use of the section 37 funds in this case. The Councillor's face lit up when I posed the question, and I was advised that, just the previous weekend, the Councillor had run into someone heavily involved in working on upgrading the grounds of a local library. According to this Councillor, this person advised the Councillor that this particular library was in need of funds for a special garden to be located adjacent to the library, where patrons could read their books when the weather permitted.

The final project was approved, and $500,000 was allocated to section 37 benefits for the library mentioned by the Councillor. The problem is that no other official with accountability to more than one ward, such as the Mayor, has any oversight as to what would be appropriate for the city or even the district in which the development site is located.

A solution has been proposed, which does not involve any fundamental change by which half the council, or twenty-two councillors, would be elected for each two wards (or for each federal riding). This would mean the election of twenty-two or half the present number. The other twenty-two would be elected by district, using the present community council districts. This would mean election of the following number of candidates as District Councillors:

North District	6
South District	6
West District	5
East District	5
Total	**22**

The District Councillors would be responsible for overseeing actions and decisions made in individual wards. In this way, District Councillors would have the right to scrutinize a decision like the one involving funds for the library from the perspective of a broader accountability and understanding of the city than one ward. The district councilor would determine whether the ward councillor's sudden inspiration from a chance meeting or some other purpose would be the most appropriate use of the funds. That question is not even asked beyond the ward level today.

This is one way of having at least half the council elected by, and accountable for decisions to, voters in an area beyond the ward level. In utilizing current political ward and district boundaries, this is the type of solution to the problem, left open by the legislation where no criteria of any definition are provided in the OP that could work and improve decision-making to the benefit of the district and the City as a whole.[155]

APPROACH TO THE PLANNING PROCESS FOR REGIONAL AND VARIOUSLY SIZED MUNICIPALITIES

Of the experience in London, Ontario, a moderate-sized city with some big-city issues, a counsel of long experience with council there said:

> I see the OMB as very useful to the planning process because, without it, there would be even more politics involved in planning decisions. Most of my work is with the council in London and there is a lot of politics on the floor of council and sometimes it even gets into the city planning reports. In the hundreds of OMB hearings that I have done, I have never had a member whom I felt that his/her mind was on some political objective. It is a necessary check on city council's political motivations ... Without the OMB, a strong mayor and strong councillor can dominate a council. A few years ago, there were a number of councillors who did not like some decisions on matters where there was really no adverse impact. They joined together to create a bloc on council.

> (About the Toronto ward councillor dominance) I am familiar with this kind of practice, not on the present council, but on the two prior councils in London.

In those days, one councillor would be trading a vote with another in order to get support for a particular proposal. And, of course, there was the bloc who always voted together. I have been told by various municipal clerks that the same kind of things occurs on smaller councils as well, and I think that is true of much of Ontario."[156]

In the case of development applications in larger cities like Toronto, the ward system has produced a situation of almost unbridled power in the ward councillor which, without any check to balance it, skews the vote to go as the ward councillor wants it for his or her own political reasons. To development and community planning lawyers and to a neighbourhood group who doesn't have the ear of the ward councillor or to a property owner without connection to that councillor, who simply needs a zoning amendment to, say, open a business in a mixed use area, the Ontario Municipal Board, at its best and as it should be, provides that necessary check and balance to the parochialism of ward politicians.

For the appellant who has lost at council for reasons that have little to do with planning merit and whether the proposal represents a potential asset to the community or a planning disaster, the ability to present the entire case, to know ahead what the case against that appellant would be, to have the right to reply and to have it heard in public is priceless – the tribunal provides to that appellant and to all interested parties a correction, a chance to be heard on the merits and to have a decision made on the merits, not on short-term political goals or entanglements that have nothing to do with the land use proposal before them.

> "… the Ontario Municipal Board, at its best and as it should be, provides that necessary check and balance to the parochialism of ward politicians."

For smaller municipalities and the regional councils, other rules may apply. Parties do get to appear before council and often are listened to. However, I am not aware of any council in Ontario that has the time to hear the evidence on an ongoing list of planning proposals with all their issues and also to successfully run the municipality with all the problems that must be attended to day to day – frost-heaved roads, sink-hole suddenly opens, the police commission asking for more money for community policing, the fire department needing new or refurbished equipment, several organizations demanding time before council on miscellaneous local issues, the local theatre needing an emergency infusion of cash or they will have to close in a week, several persons needing to be recognized for special citizenship efforts to help others, and the list goes on. Nor are councils trained to adjudicate such issues. In the case of most councils, statements from persons interested in development proposals are heard for a very short time, probably only five minutes, and so they lack the full knowledge of the shape and impact of what they are voting on unless they read the reports provided to them by staff. Do they read them? That is an unknown.

Smaller councils have their habits born of political necessity in the form of individual deals to trade votes without regard to the merits of the issue, or informal alliances develop behind a particularly charismatic or a particularly strong councillor or several councillors to prevent development in certain areas or town or township-wide. As a general comment, these councils listen to submissions, read the staff planning report and usually vote the way it recommends.

Finally, for the smaller municipalities without the best planning advice, a tribunal that comes in and hears all the evidence on development proposals that the local council was not sure how to respond to is greatly appreciated locally. Such issues as a water deficiency, or pollution developing and leaching into wetlands or a river system from septic systems where wells are the water supply, or a rezoning proposal to all year residential on a private right of way can be difficult ones where planning advice may not always be sufficient. A provincial tribunal can relieve this major burden and provide, or should provide, a reasoned decision, which will assist the council in their consideration of the next development issue. Those councils of smaller municipalities need and benefit greatly from the Board process and the local hearing in public, in my own experience confirmed by that of the tribunal members and practitioners who act for them.

> "A provincial tribunal ... should provide, a reasoned decision, which will assist the council in their consideration of the next development issue."

For most of them, planning services are available, either through the upper tier municipality or by hiring a planner for, say, advice and direction throughout the drafting, meetings, and processing of a new OP should municipalities have charge of their own OP process. That assistance can be made mandatory by the Province and small grants could be made available out of revenue for that purpose if necessary. This would be necessary because appeals would be allowed if there was any question over conformity with the provincial policies.

As to the ability of municipalities to operate their own hearing and appeal systems within provincial policy limits, one counsel of forty years' experience in dealing with smaller rural as well as county and city councils said:

> What would the planning process be like if the Board is not there. Municipalities like to have the Board there because it is a useful way of deflecting difficult decisions. The politicians can say that they opposed something but it was the Board that approved it. I feel that there would be many more municipal decisions that do not conform to the provincial guidelines if the Board were not there.[157]

Another counsel of long experience with Toronto area and 905[158] councils said:

> (On the ward system and election at large) I think that if councils were filled with visionaries, you could do away with the OMB but that will never happen.

I agree that the ward system leads to shortsighted and parochial decisions but I do not see that a change to electing councils at large would alter the situation much. For example, I see regional councillors as acting very much in the same way as those who represent only one ward, and they are elected at large.[159]

From a different perspective, policy set by the Province could be subject to 444 views of the meaning, priority, and manner of implementing provincial policy.[160] There is no evidence that the discipline is there to provide any consistent approach to policy issues even within one municipality. However, each would have planning advice and most will not want to run the risk of an OMB hearing on provincial policy grounds. Their voters would no doubt see the cost of such appeals caused by the municipality proposing something not reasonably within the intent of provincial policy on a probable abstract point as a waste and irresponsible.

I see few reasons of merit for, and there are strong reasons against, making arbitrary differences in process between municipalities based on size. The issue over behaviours of different councils, each one elected locally and responsible locally, is not to be handled by arbitrary process distinctions.

MUNICIPALITIES UNDER DEVELOPMENT PRESSURE: THE RECORD OF MUNICIPAL DECISION-MAKING IN RELATION TO PROVINCIAL POLICY ON URBAN SPRAWL AND INTENSIFICATION

The more difficult challenge will be to the 905 municipalities. They face development pressures continuously and whether they will keep to the provincial policy of intensification or give in and allow too much green field development. The evidence for the ability of Ontario municipalities, especially those on the fringes of the Greater Toronto and Hamilton area, to buck development pressures and enforce provincial and growth plan targets, is far from convincing. One recent researcher on urban sprawl and sustainable development found that:

> At present, Ontario's municipalities are largely aware of the relationship between the aforementioned problems and urban sprawl.

> They further realize that in addition to the less tangible social and environmental costs, municipalities bear substantial cost burdens in building and maintaining infrastructure to sprawling suburbs, that the expanded property tax base will not cover (City of Ottawa, 2003, p. 73). While Ontario's municipalities have had to deal with the consequences of urban sprawl, they face immense difficulties challenging aggressive land development, despite being the primary locus of land use decisions.[161]

Another researcher on urban sprawl and green field development found that most of the municipalities in the 905 area, where the urban sprawl is acute, were scoring low results in their willingness to enforce higher intensification and density levels in the urban areas. The provincial target of forty per cent of new housing to occur in urban growth areas is little more than business as usual, compared to the target set by Vancouver of seventy per cent.[162]

Interestingly, one municipality showing leadership in this area is the city of Markham, in the south part of York region. It has not only selected sixty per cent of new development to be in developed areas as its target and put it in the 2013 OP but it is doing something about making that target a reality now. Its construction of high-density development in urban centres has grown from thirty-two per cent in 2004 to sixty-two per cent by 2014. Its density level is embedded in the OP at seventy jobs or twenty units per hectare, as is its intensification level.[163]

Even Markham has a soft underbelly vulnerable to criticism. One developer is quoted as saying of the impact of the Greenbelt Plan: "There's a ton of land left in the white belt, so the greenbelt is not really an issue." The whitebelt is a space between the growth boundary of municipalities in the Greater Toronto Area (GTA) and the Greenbelt. While these largely rural and agricultural lands are not currently designated for growth by the Growth Plan, they are also not covered in the Greenbelt Plan and so, are vulnerable to development. In Markham alone, there are two thousand hectares of white-belt land.[164] This is a large tract of land that presents a significant opportunity for development in Markham and elsewhere across the Greater Golden Horseshoe Area (GGH). It is no surprise then, that white-belt lands have been one of the major criticisms of the Greenbelt, which was reiterated by the developer who stated, "I don't believe the greenbelt plan has had any impact whatsoever on compact growth" (unidentified developer, 2014[165]). That is his view. It is not shared by other knowledgeable observers.

Markham proves that a municipality can make a difference using the current tools and it will require continued dedicated commitment to those targets. But most others had not yet followed Markham's example. This research work containing references to low scores for intensification acceptance and action relates back to conditions as they were from 2008 to 2011, some five to eight years ago. As the Province is working towards a new Growth Plan containing a 60 per cent intensification target based on work by the Crombie study group in 2015 that is some indication of greater acceptance happening at the 905 and other municipal level.

> "Clearly, if the Province wants to reduce the rate of urban sprawl, more has to be done at its end."

As cited above, municipalities face "immense difficulties" from aggressive land development enterprises. In Burda's assessments of Ontario's new policies (as of 2005 and 2006), she notes that, while they afford greater decision-making authority to municipalities, municipalities need not do anything more than to "conform to broad policy, which [presently] allows for 60% of development in green fields, resulting in sprawl." However, she also advocates for municipalities to have even greater decision-making authority, which although "democratic", could in many instances serve to aggravate the aforementioned problem. Clearly, if the Province wants to reduce the rate of urban sprawl, more has to be done at its end.[166]

Tandon notes the paradox in what organizations interested in the effort to stop urban sprawl advocate:

> Despite this possibility, many environmental organizations like The Pembina Institute and Sierra Club continue to advocate for these strengthened decision-making powers at the municipal level, while at the same time advocating stronger direction from the provincial government. This paradox is highly illustrative of the difficulty in provincial oversight mechanisms that attempt to further a particular policy direction.[167]

Apart from legislation, of course, there is the ministerial test case approach. This would require the Minister of Municipal Affairs and Housing to declare a provincial interest in a number of OMB hearings involving this issue, as he has had the power to do for years. This is a powerful tool as I recall when the Province decided to get tough about severances and subdivisions impinging on wetlands and river systems in Grey County in the 1980s. It focuses public attention as well as ministerial effort to produce the best evidence and give the OMB some ammunition on the non-development side of the cases. There is no stronger application of provincial force on a tribunal than making clear the strong policy interest the Province has in an issue and bringing evidence to bear that proves the case.

Without provincial strengthening of intensification goals in urban fringe areas, and the financial incentives to reinforce municipal action, it is probably a wasted effort at this point. The point here for my purpose is that it is not municipalities alone that were failing to meet this particular challenge where provincial policy itself does not initiate change.

To get municipalities to act in accordance with higher standards, those policies and the growth policies where they apply, must be enforceable either through financial disincentives for failing to meet the higher intensification standards, and by incentives to meet them. Both the province and municipalities must act in this regard to slow dramatically or stop the rate of loss of good agricultural land to development. Either way, a provincial tribunal will be required to oversee the transition to greater provincial requirements through implementation by most municipalities that have not yet signed on. As one writer found:

> Affording final say in land use decisions to municipalities is also no guaranteed solution to urban sprawl. As evidenced by statistics on developer campaign contributions to councillors, it may be the case where council pushes through a pro-development agenda. In comment submissions on the *Strong Communities Act*, the Ontario's Environmental Commissioner's Office concedes this point, stating that: 'the transfer of final decision-making powers from the OMB to municipal councils may be positive when municipalities are progressive in their

approaches to land use planning – but potentially problematic when they are not.' (Environmental Commissioner of Ontario, 2005, pp. 36–39).[168]

The above authors, with the exception of D. Adeola on Markham, were writing from a provincial perspective and tended to accept the argument that it was the OMB that had to take the blame for the continuing loss of agricultural land to development by its pro-development decisions. Yet why has not the Minister used his powers to intervene in the OMB process with strong evidence that the OMB can act on?

Be that as it may, I agree with the idea of one researcher that better, more targeted selection qualifications for members of the OMB must be put in place and the new Executive Chair believes that he has already achieved those stricter selection qualifications. I may not agree that all members must be planners but I suggest a diverse mix of experience, including mediator-planners and mediator-lawyers who understand the imperatives in Provincial policy but can look at each fact situation to ensure that the facts warrant the direct application of policy to the particular situation. Where the facts fit, then, with stronger growth plan and provincial policies in place that expect more of municipalities and the land use tribunal, that tribunal or the Board must do its duty and enforce the policy. Markham has been the focal point for some of the strongest urban pressures to be felt in the GTA. There, councillors seized the nettle of urban intensification and are enduring some of the pain of doing so already.[169]

> "… better, more targeted selection qualifications for members of the OMB must be put in place."

The Province must also act by bringing in more areas under the growth plan legislation because, as the Markham research shows, it was the growth plan that seemed to affect Markham's approach to raising its intensification sights. The description of the Board now by Tandon as "experiencing bureaucratic inertia" may be somewhat unfair and I hope my assessment of the internal issues being faced by the tribunal may have some useful understanding of the causes of the OMB's predicament and the remedies that are still required urgently.

This is the situation now. The ward system produces what it does in terms of short-term thinking largely because the ward councillors are not given the opportunity to make their votes count on the most important planning document for a municipality, its official plan.

One argument is that, in order to produce levels of government that have the maturity to look further ahead than the next election, they must be given the chance of doing so. The time is different now from years ago; municipalities must comply with provincial standards in adopting their OPs, including the provincial interest in providing housing for a diversity of need, such as affordability and social housing.

Until we grant responsibility, the current dependency of some politicians on the OMB to do what they should have done in the first place will continue. This is a Gordian knot from which municipalities should be allowed the right to break free. The example of Markham's acceptance and action on a more aggressive target than the PPS requires, is evidence that municipalities can choose to set their own course.

On the other hand, there is the record of municipal councils continuing to go with the path of least resistance, which is of course, with the voters if they make enough noise. As of November 2015, the council of York region rejected a target of forty-five per cent intensification, only slightly above the provincial target which allows sixty per cent of new development in green field areas. We will have to wait now in order to see what York council will accept this fall. I would not be surprised if it is the target they initially rejected. If not, that is a case where financial disincentives and incentives may have to be applied to the end of intensification acceptance, if the Province is to realize its goals.

The OMB as it is today has, according to those who have done the research on the ground, not been much keener on leading in a reasonable but firm path on provincial policy matters. But it is the one body that is most easily fixed by a new direction, a proper selection and recruitment process to find persons with planning and other municipally related experience and the stature required to gain back its lost respect, coupled with mediation expertise.

THE OMB'S RECORD: TIMELINESS IN DECISION-MAKING

The timeliness of the Board's hearing and mediation process has been a sore point for years and more so now that the Board's numbers are significantly reduced. As of December 2015, when a one-day mediation is requested, the wait time will be at least three to six months or more. For mediation to be effective, timing is important. For *Planning Act* mediation to be successful, it is best mandated and controlled by the tribunal responsible for seeing that planning principles are not ignored or squandered by parties in order to get a settlement, or by a reputable mediator recognized by the Board as producing solutions within the intent of provincial and OP policies. However, a half-day mediation should be available within seven days and a full-day mediation within fourteen days. Those targets are impossible now, at the OMB's present member level. A first hearing date should be within 120 days of the filing, and ninety days if the hearing is under one day. But these dates are not when the hearing will start. These would be pre-hearing conference dates.

This recalls another example of a difficulty that did not have to exist in the planning process. The times for review of the various plans required by planning legislation have not coincided and were confusing. This has been cleared up by making the review period the same. The review time for the Greenbelt Plan now is the same as the review time of the Niagara Escarpment Plan, being ten years after each came into force. Growth Plans have the same review deadline, ten years after taking effect.[170] OPs had a review time still of five years. However, a recent amendment has introduced a new section 26(1) to the *Planning Act*, replacing the five-year review by ten years as well.[171] The *Oak Ridges Moraine Conservation Act* does not require a review of the

Moraine Plan at any given time. This is an irritant the Province is acting on and shortly should resolve when the new ten-year OP review time comes into effect.

The Board's problems with timeliness can and will be in the Chapter XII recommendations. It will then be for the Province to decide if it will commit itself to fixing the appeal situation and to follow up with a continuing program of public awareness and respect for the planning process including the place a future planning appeal board may or may not occupy within it. Briefly, I have consulted many of the busiest and most experienced practitioners in planning, development and municipal law, as well as some of the bright younger advocates in the same areas of work. I have also spoken with the current Associate Chair of the OMB and the past Executive Chair of ELTO. Most differentiate between the mandate of the Board and the operation of the Board as it is now.

The mandate of the Board, from all accounts, remains important to the planning process. This is my version, taken from the relevant statutory laws, and it bears repeating here:

1. to hear appeals brought under and within the terms of the Planning Act taking into account grounds and principles of land use planning;

2. to require high standards of professionalism and impartiality from land use planners and other witnesses qualified to give opinion evidence;

3. to provide a standard of fairness to the process and hearing of all appeals;

4. to direct the process of, and make decisions on, all appeals properly before it taking into account the public interest, provincial planning policy issued under section 3, provincial plans, and municipal official plans;

5. to have regard to the decisions of municipal councils appealed to the Board and to any supporting material and information that were before the said councils when the decisions appealed from were made;

6. to shape the interpretation and application of planning law and policy in Ontario in accordance with the purposes and directions in sections 2 and 3 of the *Planning Act*, government policy, and the principles of the Rule of Law; and

7. to provide an opportunity during the hearing of appeals for all those having an interest and/or standing within the *Planning Act* to express their views on planning issues affecting them and their communities.

I see no significant problem in what I have stated above as the average wait times for hearing dates but I suspect that these are not the dates when the hearing begins; these are the times when a pre-hearing conference occurs and the hearings would not start for another period of several months. I have no doubt that the Board is doing what it can in its present state. But the delays generally are not acceptable, especially the delayed time for mediation dates. Hearing delays must be addressed by increasing the full-time membership to twenty-eight, four to six of whom should have mediation credentials coupled with a Board-related profession or career, by much tighter control over fixing of relevant issues, and by the Board being able to dismiss without a hearing where the appellant cannot satisfy the Board on request at the pre-hearing conference that there is a viable issue to be heard or mediated within the Board's jurisdiction.

The other problem is with the uneven quality and delay in writing and issuing a decision. That and the mediation timing delay mentioned earlier are correctable by the recommendations I will make in Chapter XII, if they are accepted and acted on.

This second ground dealing with the current state of the Board and its management can be addressed by legislative and regulatory changes and so, standing alone, it provides no sound reason for removing the board from its *Planning Act* duties.

STRICTER PUBLIC NOTICE AND DUTY OF FAIRNESS: THE BC PRECEDENT

Critics of the OMB say that British Columbia survives quite well and apparently without a rights revolution, with a planning system where the last word within the system is the decision of the local council. Individual rights are covered because public notice of meetings on development applications is stricter than Ontario's public meetings notices.

It seems to me that the stringency of notice requirements before a public meeting is only part of due process and the principles of fairness. It does not go even half way to meeting the standard of justice that the McRuer Report spoke of. The standard of justice that the McRuer *Commission Inquiry into Civil Rights in Ontario* recommended comprised seven points. They are summarized in Makuch's essay in *Public Interest, Private Property: Law and Planning Policy in Canada*:

a) Government interference with individual rights and activity only where, and to the extent necessary;

2. Elected representatives a citizen can turn to for help;

3. Information available informing individuals of their rights;

4. Fair procedure before government exercises authority;

5. Reasons to be given explaining government action;

6. Judicial supervision in the interest of legal and rational process; and

7. Administrative appeals to review decisions.[172]

I suggest that no more than one or two of these points are possibly met by the present procedures of ward-based councils in Ontario, at least in Toronto and some smaller municipalities throughout Ontario may provide for (4) and (5) as well as (3).

I would suggest that, unless a tribunal like the OMB was present as a check on the power of ward-based councils with parochial and short-term electability issues like Toronto, the planning system there would not meet more than two of these so-called standards – judicial supervision and review tribunal. Whether (1), (2), (3), (4) and (5) are accomplished in the working and actions of municipal government depends on the availability to the individual of (6) and (7) and the costs of access to the court system are well known. Municipalities can meet the time demands once in ten to fifteen years but not the continuous business of planning hearings throughout every year in busy municipalities.

More contemporaneously, the principles of fairness were given content by the Supreme Court of Canada in a case called *Baker v Canada* (*Min. of Citizenship and Immigration*). The case is a human rights case but Madame Justice L'Heureux-Dubé's brilliant summary of the principles of procedural fairness and their adaptability to all tribunals and councils empowered to make decisions that affect individuals' rights, bears on this discussion. Her analysis on the content of the duty of fairness was adopted unanimously by the court. The analysis shows how it can be applied to any decision-maker including a council empowered as decision-makers on matters with potential policy and user impacts on individuals' rights. Those principles are briefly summarized here:

- the nature of the decision being made and process followed in making it;
- the nature of the statutory scheme and the "terms of the statute pursuant to which the body operates";
- the importance of the decision to the individual or individuals affected;
- the legitimate expectations of the person challenging the decision; and
- the choices of procedure made by the agency itself.[173]

This list is not exhaustive.

Applying these factors to the process before most councils, the first factor tends toward a lower level of procedural protections; the process and decision-maker selected by the Legislature do not resemble a court. The second factor ensures that there is an appeal to the Ontario Municipal Board that provides for a fair hearing of the parties' cases as much as is relevant to a true administrative tribunal appeal; third, the decision can be of importance not simply to the parties but to public interest concerns as well, the result of the process involving construction of a structure with lasting impacts or benefits, or its non-approval and loss to the property owners and perhaps to the community; fourth, the legitimate expectation of the property owners potentially affected is that they would receive notice if new municipal legislation affects the use of their property, and would be heard by council. The choice of procedure is mostly dictated by precedent, the *Municipal Act 2001* and the *Planning Act*. It means a public town hall type of process and a vote by council after they have heard from all interested parties. And it is within council's jurisdiction to limit the time for any presentations before them.

Section 61 of the *Planning Act* declares that the intent of the Act is to treat what councils do, in passing or not passing a by-law to decide the proposal before it, as a legislative function, *not* as a judicial function. This is there to protect the council process against any claim of unfair treatment. And it is fine in the context of an Act that also provides as the prime procedural protection the fact of the potential of a hearing before the OMB if any party feels

> "It is the assurance of the administrative tribunal hearing on appeal that provides the prime safeguard to procedural fairness."

aggrieved by the council procedures and decision. It is the assurance of the administrative tribunal hearing on appeal that provides the prime safeguard to procedural fairness.

Again, notice of public meetings is only one factor in the process up to council's decision, in which procedural fairness takes second place to the legislative function of council. It is no answer in itself to the requirements of procedural fairness. The substance of the duty of fairness is only supplied by the right of appeal and a fair hearing before an independent tribunal. Use of a local appeal body in section 8 of the *Planning Act* to hear appeals within the municipal structure is problematic because those bodies are appointed by the council whose members show no hesitation in involving themselves before the Committee of Adjustment whether it is in Toronto or in Killaloe. If that problem is overcome, perhaps by councils accepting a slate named by the planning and legal societies or institutes, or by strict rules requiring a variety of qualified professionals, that could provide an answer that could meet fairness and independence tests. Use of a section 8 neutrally appointed PAC for OP hearings is an alternative to council hearing objections or appeals every ten years, or by default the courts would deal with disaffected parties after the municipal process.

In British Columbia, the process had developed as it has, focused on the municipality as decision maker, whereby the requirements of fairness may be built into the municipal process. The downside to that system is that the court, with a stricter approach to appellate and judicial review applications, is the only remedy for cases of a poorly functioning municipal process. The BC system comes out of the culture of the west coast, which has developed differently. The Ontario process of a specialized tribunal to review municipal decision-making in the planning field is the pragmatic Ontario answer to a specialized area of law where a longer term view is often required than the view based on the next election.

In summary, a mediation or hearing hearing before an administrative tribunal, which can take in all relevant grounds of the party who is aggrieved, remains the basis for concluding that the duty and standard of fairness can be said to be met. That right of appeal and hearing is not simply a luxury, a bonbon added after the main event. In Ontario, it still provides, in my view, the process that addresses the requirements of the duty of fairness and rules of natural justice in a way no municipal council can do on an ongoing basis.

The final case report concerns two hearings, one in Oakville and the other in Toronto. They share one major attribute. Both are cases where provincial policy became important. Both were handled with efficiency and justice and both acted on policy, both local and provincial, as they found it. Intensification policy is central to one and indirectly involved in the other. It is an interesting intertwine of two accounts that were well decided and with consistency of principle. For professional planners, one case involves a planning director who was subpoenaed to testify against her employer-municipality. It says much about the dignified and courageous way in which the planner involved acted even under intense and unnecessary cross-examination. The same can be said of several other members of the planning profession who have been placed in the same difficult position. These cases are representative, one of the independence of mind that a professional planner must have in doing her job well, and both, of cases where the municipality aligned itself with parochial short-term interests to try to manipulate the system to get its way.

In both cases, the municipality was acting on short-term motives, backing local residents either to get an advantage for itself and with them, or acting in the face of policies the Town had adopted but they were not convenient to follow. Both are cautionary tales, which should be of special interest to both law practitioners and planners.

BEING THERE 6: TWO VARIATIONS ON A THEME FROM THE PROVINCE

Someone said that while Coleman Hawkins gave the jazz saxophone a voice, Lester Young taught it to tell a story. It's a narrative out of black tradition and the player's complex life as an African American.[174] For me, a Canadian, a white middle-class person coming from different roots yet in a slight sense sharing the roots of desperation, the music of Lizst and Mahler speak to me; but not alone – the simpler melodies of Burns came with my immigrant ancestors from Scotland and Ireland, only two generations ago struggling across the ocean to find something they could hold on to. Like music, good writing finds a theme, introduces variations, develops it into something of meaning, and leads to an end through a recapitulation and a coda.

This is the story of two OMB hearings that have a similar theme. Both hearings occurred in 2015 and both, in their development and recapitulation, illustrate the great contribution this Board can make to provincial planning and principled consistency of policy.

The first comes from the Town of Oakville, a stable, sublime community on the edge of the throbbing metropolis of the GTA. The site is just inside the Town's Central Business District (CBD) on the major thoroughfare that leads east through the Town's old and still attractive centre toward Toronto. This site is not in that attractive core. It's near the western edge of the extended CBD. There are three residential lots now in one ownership across from a row of low-rise commercial – a market and shops – along Lakeshore Road, as well as condominiums, row housing and two-storey townhomes, all bookmarked by areas of single family residential homes in stable areas to the north and south of the fringes of Lakeshore Road development. The proposal is to develop a four-storey mixed use condominium with residences over street commercial in one building on this corner site.

On Lakeshore Road, next to the proposed site, townhomes immediately adjoin the site in three blocks at a lower elevation and in the next block to the west sits a four-storey condominium building erected recently – in overview, a mix of low-rise multiple residential and commercial shops common along Ontario main streets as they lead out of the central core towards the outer edges of their communities. In the 1930s and probably as late as 1959–60, this was an area of open fields and largely agricultural uses,[175] north of the elegant old residences along the shore – now it's an area that throws out variations of old-style plazas and row housing in the midst of which a whisper of a new motif condominium residential.

The second hearing centres on a piece of land in the City of Toronto next to a small private school. The vacant part of the lot had been slated for use by the school board but now it is no longer needed. The application by the Toronto District School Board for consent to sever the vacant lot from the rest came to the OMB as an appeal from the refusal of the school board's application by the Toronto planning committee. The severed lot would have an area of about two acres (0.8 hectare). It is zoned for residential or institutional use. The lot the school board is retaining will continue to be leased to a private school. The location is in a primarily residential area in traditional north Toronto, south of Highway 401 running east from Bathurst St. toward Avenue Road.

The Town of Oakville nestles on the shore of Lake Ontario, its grand old residences on the shore giving way to homes that are less grand as you move away from the lake; it's Wagner's Tannhauser theme yielding to the pleasantries of Garfunkel's version of Barbara Allen. About one to two kilometres to the north of the lake is Lakeshore Rd. West, one of the main roads through Oakville. The site is at the southeast corner of Lakeshore Rd. West and a primarily residential street running north from the lake, Brookfield Road, with a generous frontage on Lakeshore Rd. of 130 feet (40m) and 230 feet (70m) on Brookfield. About a block to the east along Lakeshore Rd.,A Harvey's anchors a small commercial plaza. Across Brookfield are the two-storey row houses, which turn at Brookfield to take up the south side of Lakeshore to the west ending at a cemetery

The tension that darkens both is the threat of the new, change, something that will break the rhythms of life in both neighbourhoods.

In the second, residents have enjoyed for years the open park setting on the school board's land. They have used it for their weekend ball games and, at other times, just for enjoyment of the openness it gives the area. What most neighbours have not appreciated is that that land is not parkland. It is owned by the school board, which now cannot use it for the one purpose the board exists – to provide schools. Just like any owner, its maintenance has been at the school board's expense and now the board must show on their books replacement for an asset that they have to sell to do that.

The city planning staff saw nothing inappropriate in demanding its transfer gratis to the city for parkland. Counsel for the school board told me that what the planners don't seem to get is that the school board has no mandate from its ratepayers to supply free parkland to Toronto or to give away an asset it has purchased.[176] It is complying with the existing zoning of residential and institutional and with provincial policy of intensifying residential use where it is acceptable, and this kind of change was foreseeable for years if anyone had bothered to look at the provincial policy and the zoning by-law, which allow residential and institutional uses.

Provincial policy and the provincial interest lead to the coda of the Montessori School, a familiar institution that will stay where it has been for some time to come on lease from the school board. There is no proposal as yet for the severed lot. It is available for sale for residential development. This is precisely the kind of underutilized pre-zoned land to which provincial policy speaks in requiring efficient development, especially intensified residential use to lessen urban sprawl and the costs it exacts in extra transportation and energy expense and loss of prime agricultural and resource lands.

There is a rival motif from the city and some residents expressed by a planner retained by them. He spoke eloquently to a shortage of parkland, which will be sharpened by the anticipated much heavier planned intensification in the Avenue Road corridor.

The city has money set aside to purchase this lot for parkland but refuses to do it in hopes that its strong-armed holdup of the school board's appeal will obtain an asset free at the cost of the school board. It's the sound of tight-assed Methodist Toronto trying to play hardball with a new jazz that says you can play but you have to pay. A serviced urban lot of two acres does not come cheaply.

In the first hearing in Oakville, the clash of transitional planning ideas in the Central Business District policy again leads the way. The Town and residents say the building should go no higher than three storeys, not the four the applicant wants. The Town's official plan deems this area on Lakeshore Road West part of the CBD – not only that, the Plan adopted by the Town Council contains policies which call for new mixed use residential-commercial development in this area up to four storeys in height, not three, provided that impacts to neighbouring uses are minimized. The looming problem is the lower grade or ground level of the townhouses next door, making the effect of height greater. The residents of the block of townhouses in the lowest block had a real concern for the loss of sunlight and greater shadows cast by a four- rather than a three-storey building.

The proposed building is designed to meet that problem. The building plans show the building set back sufficiently from the street and the tower stepped back as it rises to full height. With that step-backed tower and setback, the actual loss of sunlight in the summer was shown by professional shadow studies to be zero. The shadow studies use well-known measurements and trajectories of light from the sun throughout the year showing the effect of the new building as designed on the neighbouring lot. According to the studies, only in April and September would there be a short time of reduced sunlight, months when outdoor use is infrequent.

The Town's official plan policy for this area in the CBD calls for precisely this kind of development in this area. The four-storey height as designed would not be a hurdle; it was found to be acceptable for sound and tested reasons. An approved site plan or a design annexed to the zoning by-law with appropriate amendments can ensure that the approved design will happen if the project proceeds. The final coda written by the presiding Board member said it like it is, as a now dead famous American sportscaster would have said. This building site is:

> ...located on a main thoroughfare in the heart of a fast-growing, rapidly urbanizing and highly desirable lakefront community on the outer fringe of Toronto, a city that ... the *Economist* magazine found to be 'the most livable city' in the world. These lands play an important role in the Greater Toronto Area. In the Board's view, it makes good planning sense that they should be developed according to the land use planning policies developed by Oakville Council itself (and subsequently approved by the Board) to be consistent with Provincial Policy.

The important point behind all this was made by the Board's decision where it stressed that Ontario's planning system is now led by policy and that means a planning system that values predictability. Land use decisions must achieve consistency with provincial policy and with the growth plan of the Golden Horseshoe region, a region encircling and including all the urban lands from the west end of Lake Ontario east to Oshawa. And, it must be added, Oakville council is bound by these same policies. What is more, the same policies approved by the Oakville council designate this area as a growth area where more intensified residential uses are to be welcomed provided they meet the provincial and local policies. Part of the problem was the misunderstanding by the residents who thought the CBD's westerly boundary ended at Harvey's. In fact the council had approved its extension to the west of and including this site.

The fact that this council, for a difference of one-storey in height, which to the neighbouring townhomes will signify no change from what could be built there within the current policies, would flout provincial policy and their own planning intentions, to court votes at the next election is a reminder of the discordance of democracy and the short term thinking it produces. And this position was taken by a council knowing that within 125 metres, there was a new condominium development four storeys in height in place.

When we return to the second hearing, a similar position is being taken by a council siding with neighbours who want their park to remain at the expense of public school taxpayers rather than the City, which will receive the benefit of the park. The City could still buy this land. As the city's own parks witness conceded, the city does have the funds to acquire the new lot as part of its parks acquisition program. The school board has been open throughout to any offer by the city but it never came. This site was not a park then. It was land owned by a publicly funded body. Not until the City acquires it, pays for it, and designates it as open space for park use is it a park.

Again, a municipality, looking to short term gain by playing to the desires of the area voters and refusing to see that their position was against provincial policy and the public interest (realized by the continuance of the Montessori school on school board land), produced a position it well knew was against public policy adopted by the OMB years ago on acquisition for open space purposes. The Board's policy considers both private rights of individual homeowners and other owners of land in the manner that the Board's Associate Chair described rather elegantly in *Dickinson*:

> It is motivated by a time honoured experience of the Board that planning is often a delicate balancing act between these two noble and sometimes competing objectives ... Above all, these words are a sober reminder that planning decisions, regardless of how benevolent their intent, how farsighted their vision and how friendly to the public interest, can easily become an unwitting and unquestioning tool to extinguish or debilitate the proprietary interests of an owner. No decision maker should gloss over this obvious but awesome power in planning."[177]

The Oakville council had one last card to play. It happened after this hearing. The council disliked intensely that its planning director would not support council's stance on this mixed use four-storey proposal. In this case, the planning director studied the proposal and advised council she would have to testify in support of it and against the Town's position if she was subpoenaed. She saw that she could not compromise her professional principles as a planner by prostituting her reputation for the sake of pleasing her employer. She was subpoenaed by the applicant school board. She acted impeccably, professionally and with dignity throughout. Afterward, the council failed to act as impressively. They fired her as planning director.

The provincial interest and the public interest were both front and centre in these two decisions of the Ontario Municipal Board, as they should be. I am not aware that either of them was covered by Toronto media. The *Planning Act* states, as two of the purposes of the Act, to provide for a land use planning system led by provincial policy and to integrate matters of provincial interest in provincial and municipal planning decisions. For the two councils involved – one opposing a severance of one lot in an attempt to pressure a school board to turn over land free of charge that the City could pay for, and the other opposing a zoning amendment for one storey in height to placate a few voters – I can only remind them they have a duty to the public and to the law. To adopt the words of Thomas More, in these two appeals, one could rightly ask the municipal decision-makers, in different words:

> *Why Richard, it profits a man nothing to give his soul for the whole world ... but for Wales?*
>
> —Robert Bolt, A Man for All Seasons, Act 2, Scene 9

CHAPTER X

BAGGAGE

Anyone whose goal is 'something higher' must expect to someday suffer vertigo. What is vertigo? Fear of falling? No ... It is the voice of the emptiness below us.
from The Unbearable Lightness of Being
—M. Kundera, Harper's, 2004

For fifty years, the *Planning Act* had no purpose. During that time, how was it that that omission never failed to stop some judges from providing "purposive" interpretations of that Act? A strict constructionist or a fundamentalist would definitely agree; how can a statute be construed as having a purpose that was not expressed in the Act, Elmer Driedger and statutory rules of construction aside?

It brings to mind the story of President Ulysses Grant being shown how to play golf. An old friend, an Englishman, was invited to visit the President. After dinner, the two found themselves outside on the White House lawn. The Eng- lishman asked the secret service guard, for a golf club, or what passed for it in the nineteenth century, for a tee and a ball. They were produced and the Englishman set about placing the ball carefully on the small tee. (Now you are about to see why it could not have been a Scotsman doing this.) The Englishman positioned himself in front of the ball and took a great swing. The club hit the turf. It splattered soil and grass up as far as the President's beard and beyond. The ball continued to sit benignly on the tee. Again the Englishman swung, and again he missed. The President waited patiently through six tries. He then drew the man aside and quietly stated, "There seems to be a fair amount of exercise in the game, but I fail to see the purpose of the ball."

THE SECTION 3 FORMATION PROCESS: OMB AND PROVINCIAL RESPONSIBILITY FOR URBAN BOUNDARY PROBLEMS

Apparently to assist those judges, while making up for the empty baggage of those fifty purposeless years, the Legislature in 1994 produced in section 1.1 not one but six purposes to the *Planning Act*. Those that popped out included the worthy goals of sustainable development, province-led policy development, integrated intergovernmental decision-making, open accessible and timely process, coordinated planning, and recognition of the decision-making authority and accountability of municipal councils.

Section 3 of the *Planning Act* provides the process for preparing and issuing Provincial Policy Statements. One academic, commenting on this process, noted a gap, something missing, between the goal of an open accessible process and policy formation within the ministry responsible. The academic, who is also a practicing lawyer and an author of a textbook on planning law, wrote of this gap as part of a theme of denial of appeal rights:

> The denial of appeals and hearing rights is imposed not only by these Acts and the plans approved under them (i.e. *Greenbelt Act 2005, Places to Grow Act, 2005* and the *Oak Ridges Moraine Conservation Act, 2001*) but also by the Provincial Policy Statement, 2005 (PPS) adopted under section 3 of the *Planning Act*. The province once again imposes policies without first having them tested or holding a hearing, for there is no right of appeal of any nature with respect to the policy itself.[178]

Section 3(2) contains the only process that precedes issuance of the provincial policy statement; it leaves the consultative discretion completely to the Minister of Municipal Affairs to confer with whomever he deems to have an interest in the policy to be announced. There is no right of appeal because the issuance of a Provincial Policy Statement is not a decision after an adjudicative process. It is the announcement of government policy. This section has to do with policy formation, not with its application to the detriment of anyone and so the duty of fairness does not require an adversarial hearing.

The planning process does provide an owner whose land is affected by provincial policy and a related planning decision with a right of appeal. The landowner can appeal to the OMB and the hearing in turn provides an opportunity to challenge the provincial policy behind the decision to apply it to a particular property by leading evidence and by cross-examining any official or expert witness who testifies on the application of the policy to that case. The opportunity can go as far as challenging the policy's relevance, its analytic basis and framework and the methodology used, in addition to the way in which it is applied to the property in question. This kind of attack is not unusual. The decision and appeal process provide what is lacking if an appeal were somehow allowed from the policy itself: it provides a necessary factual and environmental context rooted in reality and not mere hypothesis.[179]

The objection above, however, is to the lack of any opportunity to test or provide input prior to a policy coming into effect. At that stage, there is no duty to allow a testing mechanism, nor do I see a particular value in providing one. However, there is value to owners potentially affected by a new policy, and to the government, of granting a right to owners with a legitimate interest to notice of the new policy being considered and a right to file submissions within a certain period of time. An amended process allowing such limited rights would improve the Act in the interest of transparency and good governance. I will revisit this issue in my recommendations in Chapter XII.

The *Planning Act* now provides the general purposes and interests of the province, which in turn feeds into the provincial policy statements. This Board is being looked to as the lead provincial tribunal charged with the responsibility of interpreting and applying provincial and local planning policy to the various cases coming before it. The results have been mixed in terms of predictability and certainty of policy interpretation, application and outcome.

As a result, the Regional Planning Commissioners of Ontario (RPCO) took a position in December 2013 that a full systemic examination of the OMB's role in the planning process should occur. The RPCO made a submission to the Provincial Review of Land Use Planning and Appeal System in December 2013. In it, they urged that the focus should be on the following areas:

> The Review must focus on OMB accountability (a critical principle not enunciated in the stated purpose of the Review), especially in the following respects:
> * To municipalities when not upholding Council decisions, despite the direct language of Section 2.1 of the *Planning Act;*
> * To citizens, by making the process much less costly and time consuming, and thereby more accessible;
> * To investment interests, who require decisions on development proposals in a much more timely and cost efficient manner;
> * To all participants, by issuing consistent Board decisions based on clear planning rationale; and
> * To the Province, through more rigorous reporting requirements regarding its performance, legislative and/or policy ambiguity, and adequate Board resources to effectively and efficiently manage its caseload.

That organization also recognized timely decision-making and consistency in the way policy is applied as major concerns.

Two other sources of disillusionment with the OMB were the Sierra Club and two researchers on urban sprawl, Burda and Tandon, discussed in Chapter IV. They blamed the OMB for the unnecessary loss of agricultural land to urban development in and about 2000. They did not accuse the OMB of bias in favour of development, probably because they knew there was no case supporting such an accusation. Their suggestion was that the OMB had a tendency to support it and in and around the year 2000 green field development was triggered by certain OMB decisions. Yet, Tandon failed to cite the decisions they were referring to in her recent article.

Sierra did refer to the work of Moore and Hamilton to support its contention. The work referred to was from the publications we discussed in Chapter IV. Neither Hamilton nor Moore produced evidence of bias or even reasonable apprehension of bias. Hamilton simply used Chipman's basic research in *A Law Unto Itself* to which he applied a new methodology but he could go no further than Chipman as to what he could prove, that is, that the OMB decided cases on the evidence before them and the developers' could muster abundant funds and retain first rate expertise and in addition their sites were usually carefully chosen as close to existing urban approved designated and serviced land. No case authority was presented to demonstrate any bias or apprehended bias charge. There is no case to be made.

Having realized that, Sierra seemed to start saying something quite different – that in fact it was the learned lessons of experience before the OMB that taught the owner-developers and their counsel how to put together a convincing case there. Sierra called the developers' ability to devote huge resources including high quality expert testimony to their cases "leveraging" against cash-strapped citizen's groups and financially constrained municipalities. Sierra Club cited several instances where citizen's groups or a municipality had been ordered to pay costs of more than a token amount including a cost order against the Town of Collingwood for $500,000 in favour of a successful owner-developer and the community group "Save the Rouge River" was asked to pay $10,000 in developers' legal expenses after they lost their appeal, despite spending $20,000 on their own legal fees (Sierra Club, 2003, p. 21).

In this same period, neighbourhood associations participated in seventy-seven appeals, winning just five favourable decisions (6.5%). It is notable that Moore's findings were never cited fully. First, his findings deal only with Toronto so they have no application to the 905 area or beyond where the urban-rural interface is under the most pressure. Second, the real opposition in cases before the Ontario Municipal Board for a developer is the municipality, where it decides not to approve a development application. The neighbourhood groups usually add their pressure to the municipality's case as the appeal is against the municipality.

In Chapter IV, I showed that things are not quite the one-sided situation that this group would have us believe. I will repeat only two statistics, which are telling – there is no doubt that developer applications or appeals do better than the overall approval rate: forty-four per cent of all applications are approved in his study periods, whereas fifty-one per cent of all developer-supported applications were successful. Where the municipality and the developer opposed each other, the rate was virtually even, fifty per cent in 1971–78 and forty per cent in 1987–94. Moore's work only reflects Toronto practice; however, where the city and its chief planner were on the same page opposing the

> "The real problem behind the figures is not pro-developer bias on the OMB but more often, the lack of equality in resources."

developer, the City won fifty-seven per cent of the appeals in 2000–2006. For the proposition that, "Adjudication patterns at the OMB have effectively disrupted the efforts by other actors to prevent urban sprawl", no authority is presented, only Sierra's opinion. The real problem behind the figures is not pro-developer bias on the OMB but more often, the lack of equality in resources (e.g. legal representation, expert witnesses) that developers and lay persons can afford to make their cases before the Board and, at times, hubris on the part of the objectors who fail to settle for an acceptable solution, and proceed without the involvement of the municipality with no real case and lose. A group that does that will have placed themselves at risk for a cost order. One research analyst's suggestion: that intervenor funding should once again be on the table, or some other method of funding for cases with some merit in order to close the real gap and correct the real problem – the development side often has the resources that the other does not and this gap needs to be at least partly closed. Mediation should be a remedy for the rest if all parties are willing to think beyond their own doorstep.

The Sierra Club of Canada's 2003 report dismissed Harris's self-proclaimed Smart Growth policies as inherently pro-development. Municipalities no longer had to be "consistent with" solid policies, but only had to "have regard for" a general Provincial Policy Statement (PPS). This onus has now been shifted back to require "consistency with" the PPS. Sierra's recommendations were:

- Abolish the OMB, replacing it with a new appeals board
- Prevent the appeals board from overturning municipal urban boundary decisions
- Train board members around issues relating to urban sprawl
- Reinstate intervener funding to community groups
- Establish enforceable urban growth boundaries for all Ontario towns and cities.[180]

Burda made a number of suggestions for changing the trends of urban sprawl:
- Reforms to the OMB, paralleling recommendations made by the Sierra Club five years earlier
- The re-establishment of intervener funding for advocates of the public interest
- OMB appointment process should be modified such that new openings are subject to an open call for qualified candidates
- Review by a nonpartisan advisory committee selected by the Attorney General.[181]

But as Burda and the other researchers (Tandon and Adeola) on urban sprawl point out, the Province really has to increase the intensification rate to a target that would mean a real policy shift. The other moves open to the Province are to use the Growth Policy as Markham was able to take advantage of and provide financial incentives to municipalities for programs to educate their residents on this subject including local developers. There should be disincentives for municipalities that do not do so.

PURPOSE AND BETTER REASONS FOR DECISIONS: DIALOGUE WITH THE LOSING PARTY: BAKER V CANADA AND THE DUTY OF FAIRNESS

To some extent, the members of the OMB are their own worst enemies. The quality of too many of the decisions that I, and others who are involved in the system, have read is too often not at the standard to be expected of this Board. Quite apart from analytic insufficiency, too many do not encourage the reader to read and understand the subject matter. Instead they are written in a kind of prose that distances the reader to the point that the decisions become inaccessible and frustrating.

The Supreme Court of Canada, in *Baker v Canada* (*Min. of Cit. & Imm.*), accepted as recently as 1999 that it was now a part of the duty of fairness that a person or tribunal give reasons for a decision. The content of the duty varies with the circumstances of the case and the tribunal. It bears repeating:

> 22 ... I emphasize that underlying all these factors is the notion that the purpose of the participatory rights contained within the duty of procedural fairness is to ensure that administrative decisions are made using a fair and open procedure, appropriate to the decision being made and its statutory, institutional, and social context, with an opportunity for those affected by the decision to put forward their views and evidence fully and have them considered by the decision-maker.

Because this is so, and because fairness requires openness, an opportunity to present the affected persons' views and consideration of those views by the decision-maker, the law now can be said to include the duty to give reasons that demonstrate that those views and evidence have been considered. The decision-maker should at some point or throughout the decision direct the reasons and decision to the unsuccessful party. The reasons must tell the unsuccessful party in a cogent manner why that party lost or did not prevail.

In other words, the writer should think of the decision at this point as a dialogue with the side that lost to this extent. It is not sufficient to hope the unsuccessful party understands that the decision-maker's authority made him do it. The unspoken start of that dialogue is always the question any losing party would be asking – why? Coupled with that idea, in every hearing

"... the writer should think of the decision at this point as a dialogue with the side that lost ..."

there is an interesting story that gives life to the issues. The concept of a decision shaped by a story is helpful in bringing some form to the mélange of facts, law and science that confronts the decision-maker. There are other ways that can assist in bringing a sense of drive and meaning to the whole. One is a chronological or historical approach. Another is a thesis approach where you are clear on the outcome and how you will get there but you must have kept open other outcomes so that you can show clearly why they are not acceptable or appropriate and that they have been equally considered. I suggest the story is the most useful and adaptable to most cases because all people can relate to that form.

Within the particular contextual cast you choose, the writer should work and mould a straight answer to the unspoken question from the loser: why did you accept the evidence from the other side and not the evidence we produced? It is far from enough to merely say that X was a qualified land use planner and I accepted his evidence over yours.

Beyond the implied duty in *Baker* to show that the parties' concerns have been heard and considered, the Supreme Court of Canada has enlarged on the duty to give reasons in cases that invoke that duty. The court is still waffling somewhat on the range of cases where reasons are required. From *Baker* and later cases, I think one must assume that reasons are required in most cases under the *Planning Act* because of their importance to the public and to the landowner and others depending on that owner's and others' decisions following on allowance or dismissal of an appeal.

The Supreme Court has filled in the duty to give reasons by providing as the purpose of reasons the need to demonstrate "justification, transparency, and intelligibility." The Court was addressing itself to a court reviewing the decision of an administrative tribunal; however, from this list of guidelines pertaining to the standard of review of reasonableness, I am taking the following as some useful principles for tribunal members to remember when writing reasons for decision:

- Justification – a decision must indicate reasons that show how the result falls within a range of possible outcomes, which are acceptable and rational solutions defensible on the facts and the law

- Transparency – the reasons must indicate why the tribunal made the decision it did

- Intelligibility – the reasons must allow a reader to understand why the tribunal made its decision

- Reasons do not need to include all arguments, statutory provisions, jurisprudence or other details; the reasons must allow a reviewing court to understand why the tribunal made its decision and how the conclusion comes within the range of acceptable outcomes.[182]

One suggestion in the provincial review of the OMB is that there should be a set form for decisions and their reasons and the presiding member would simply fill this out. This is perhaps possible on a minor variance appeal, though it would end up merely encouraging use of generic terms and no one would know why it went the way it did if that were to be the trend. For other hearings, where the above principles must be addressed in each decision and each decision is a unique situation, with similarities of principle, no doubt, but requiring a straightforward intelligible explanation to the loser and a properly detailed explanation to the planning profession, municipalities and the public of how all evidentiary points were considered without being misapprehended, a form would be a disaster and could lead to more successful appeals and rehearings, in my view.

> "What comes now are not rules but some brief suggestions ... to improve the ability to relate to the public in ways that can be more easily understood and accepted."

The above points come from the *Planning Act* or appellate courts, which bind the tribunals. They encompass directions of law that are important and should be followed. What comes next are not rules but some brief suggestions for the Board, and for others who may find them useful, to improve the ability to relate to the public in ways that can be more easily understood and accepted.

As with any story, a decision should have a beginning that says something interesting about what is to come. It should invite the reader into the decision. It is important that a decision commences in a way that suggests a door opening, whether it be to a certain property with a certain character, or a group of people or an action taken. And through that door, the writer wants the parties to enter and read on. The operative word is "inviting"; the decision should invite readers in, not shut them out.

I want to be clear. In my comments, I mean to convey only the effect on readers of the particular opening or introduction. Nothing in what I write is to be taken as a rule. The comments only indicate reasons why most OMB decisions are not understood by ordinary readers; they push the reader away, instead of making the reader feel like entering and reading on. Most make it difficult for a lay reader to get into the decision if there is nothing in the opening to help them feel the decision is accessible to them.

I am providing some samples from a collection of decisions, which the registrar of the OMB provided to me. I will comment at the end of each excerpt. I should add that the final two show a vibrancy or insight that is welcomed; they are worth consideration by anyone interested in tribunal writing. The last one in particular represents something a tribunal should do sometimes, when the writer feels sufficiently in command of the material and one's authority – that is, to comment on something that happened during the hearing that promotes an understanding of a legal duty or a planning feature or principle of importance to the parties or to the development of the OMB jurisprudence or the public interest. The examples of the first four decision openings that follow are unfortunately repeated too often. Throughout, it must be kept in mind that the difficulties imposed on the Board writers due to lack of time for deliberating on their reasons and decisions are imposed on them by the shortage of members to meet the workload.

I am taking this aspect of decision writing because, other than the page where the decision appears, the opening page of a decision is probably the one most read; whether the parties continue with interest, or at least with a growing understanding, or reject it because it is not understandable to them, is determined by that first page. Without that, readers will thumb through until they find something of interest, disregarding how the writer intended that it be read and understood. And then a member may hear complaints because they could not see why they lost, and yet the member did explain that on pages 30 to 32, thinking they would come to it after reading pages 28 to 30. I apologize to anyone who will feel ill done by but it is better that people understand these things, including the Board and those who may read a decision again in the future.

> "... the opening page of a decision is probably the one most read ..."

Opening of the Decision by the OMB in *Sifton Properties Ltd. and Grandview Ravines Inc. v Brantford* **(City), Files PL 100472-3** et al., **released June 26, 2014**

[1]   This is the decision for multiple appeals against nine planning instruments related to properties at 277 Hardy Road and 125 Golf Road ("subject properties") in the City of Brantford ("City"). The matters that are under appeal and are dealt with in this decision are as follows:

1.   Applications by Sifton Properties Limited ("Sifton") for a residential Plan of Subdivision, an Amendment to the City's Official Plan, and a Zoning By-law Amendment for the property at 277 Hardy Road, originally filed on March 11, 2004 by the previous owner of the land and carried on by Sifton after acquiring the property in January of 2008. The applications were appealed by Sifton on March 17, 2010 on the statutory basis of the lack of a decision by the City.

This is the start of a list of five similar descriptions of applications. Missing from this kind of opening is any apparent interest by the writer in the subject matter. What I would have hoped to see here is an opening paragraph that captures the common thread that unites the whole and a sense of what this decision means for the natural and built features of this area and its future. Or the beginning of the story of what happened here and why those who testified saw this as important. There may be some unifying or common theme to explain why these files were heard together; instead the opening treats each file as separate, devoid of any commonality of issues or evidence.

The theme, which could have been set at the beginning is felt as being absent, somehow there but lost. The introduction or overview was the place to define the overarching themes and issues that bind these matters together and thereby provide understanding early to what is going to be a very detailed and challenging decision. Unfortunately, the decision never finds a form, a shape that makes the whole meaningful and that discourages the reader from trying to understand. It leaves no option but to go to the last pages to read the ultimate decision and react. As I know that the writer has done excellent work, I can only surmise that this decision is a victim of loss of writing and deliberation time by a person stretched to the limit.

Opening of the First Appeal heard by the OMB on City of Ottawa Official Plan Amendment 76: *Friends of the Greenspace Alliance v Ottawa (City)*, **File PL120109, released Dec. 22, 2010**

> This is the first Appeal hearing held into the 30 Appeals made to Ottawa Official Plan Amendment 76. Official Plan Amendment 76 is a comprehensive Official Plan Amendment made in a five year Official Plan review under the *Planning Act*. Following modifications made by Approval Authority and then the launching of Appeals, the Board held three Pre-hearing Conferences respecting process and procedure. Most Appeals were set down for Hearing in 2011. The Friends of the Greenspace Alliance (hereinafter Greenspace) sought an earlier hearing date for its appealed interest in section 4.7.4 Endangered Species. That request made on August 26, 2010 was opposed by the City, but granted by the Board with the hearing to commence on December 1, 2010 for a period up to two weeks in duration. Other environmental appeals were set down for hearings in 2011.
>
> The Greenspace Alliance is an incorporated nonprofit group that takes an active interest in planning in Ottawa. In addition to the present case respecting Endangered Species, the Alliance has been active in environmental planning on related matters in the past and has other appeals scheduled before this Board. Amy Kempster announced herself as the representative of the Alliance. When differences arose in the Hearing between Kempster as spokesperson and Cheryl Doran, a member of Greenspace and a witness in this hearing, the Board permitted both to question witnesses. As the divergence grew the Board asked that Ms. Kempster and Ms. Doran confer."

In one and a half paragraphs at the start of a decision, I would have thought we would hear something about the appeal. Instead, we are told a great deal of housekeeping about the procedure of the overall OP hearing, the fact that the hearing of the first appeal was moved up and the disagreement between the appellant's spokespersons. Again, it is a distancing kind of opening about what by then was old news about the pre-hearing conferences and the date of the hearing. The hearing is over. Hey, this is now the decision and should not something be said up front about what in fact the appeal was about? After all, the panel knows all there is to know about the appeal. Why do we have a 'secretary of the meeting' approach when the member could share with us the story of the appeal rather than discreditable facts about its presentation? There is nothing here to interest anyone other than Ms. Doran and Ms. Kempster and what they had to confer about.

Opening of the Decision of the OMB in *Uniform Urban Developments Inc v Ottawa (City)*, File PL120109, released Feb. 14, 2014

[1]   This dispute, over an Official Plan Amendment (OPA) and Council rezoning, was about the shape of a project in the City of Ottawa (the "City").

[2]   It was proposed by Uniform Urban Developments Inc. (the "developer"), in the Westboro district, where height has been analysed and debated for years, resulting in a number of changes to planning documents.

[3]   In this dispute, the issue was not the amount of density (undisputed), but about whether to deploy it mainly horizontally ("midrise") or mainly vertically ("highrise"). The developer proposed a vertical design – a pair of residential towers of 14 and 16 storeys, whereas the Official Plan ("OP") listed a "maximum" of "4–6 storeys". City planning staff was nonetheless supportive, and in 2011, Council rezoned, via By-law 2011463. The By-law would permit the new proposed height; it would also decrease the permissible footprint dramatically (except on the north side, where it was increased substantially)."

This is what I call the 'bracket' opening. In the first ten lines, there are seven brackets with short forms or information in them. It has the effect again of distancing a reader from the decision and a sense almost of futility about all this interrupting material.

It also speaks of the issue being several things – about the shape of a project first, then there is a reference to height being analyzed over years, and by the third paragraph, there is mention of density, that density was not the issue, but in the next two lines, the issue has metamorphosed again into density, in particular how density was to be deployed horizontally or vertically. The by-law passed by the city permitted the new height and decreased the building "footprint" dramatically, except it would be increased substantially on one side. This is an unnecessarily confusing amalgam of interrupted sentences and contradictory statements whereas what all of this was about was height – whether the height limit should be reduced to the plan's 4–6 storeys or allow 14–16 storeys on this one site with two towers of those heights. The obvious effect of greater height is contracted footprint, assuming no change in building density. The issue here was height and that became lost early on. The attempt at the start should be a series of strong statements to clarify the issue, not to hide it or obfuscate it. As it is, the decision again distances the reader and loses interest and the simplicity it needed. After the beginning setting the issue and its context clearly, then the detail can come within a framework that is easily understood.

Opening of the Decision of the OMB on an Application by Miller Paving Ltd. For Extension of the Licensed Area for Extraction and for an Official Plan Amendment to allow a permanent asphalt plant and for a Zoning Amendment for both

1. This dispute was about proposed quarry expansion – to unfold over a time span of 187 years, extending into the 23rd century.

2. The dispute originally involved three distinct positions – those of the quarry operator, the local municipality and neighbours – though some positions eventually converged. For reasons to be outlined, the Board finds mainly in favour of the municipality, with some exceptions.

3. Miller Paving Ltd. ("the applicant") operated a gravel quarry in the Township of McNab/Braeside ("the Township"), in the County of Renfrew ("the County"). The quarry had been in operation for half a century, near rural residential properties. For a few years recently, it also had a portable asphalt plant on site.

4. In 2007, the applicant proposed: to almost triple the footprint of the extraction zone, and to build a permanent asphalt plant.

5. Studies ensued, to satisfy what is now the Ministry of Natural Resources and Forestry ("MNRF", formerly "MNR") and the Ministry of Environment and Climate Change ("MOECC", formerly "MOE"), in order to meet the requirements of the Aggregate Resources Act, ("ARA") and obtain the desired ARA Licensing.

6. There would also need to be amendments to documents under the *Planning Act*. The Township's Official Plan ("OP") would not permit asphalt plant without an Official Plan Amendment ("OPA") and rezoning. Expansion of the quarry itself, and related measures, would also require rezoning. The applicant applied for an OPA and zoning accordingly.

7. The Township obtained advice from the County. In this County, planning advisory services are provided to local municipalities by County planning staff.

8. Neighbours objected to the project. They had obtained one Court Order about blasting, and another declaring the former portable asphalt plant a nuisance (for noise and odour).

9. However, after years of peer reviews, etc., the applicant's proposal (including a new permanent asphalt plant) was approved by Provincial Ministries and County planning staff. In 2013, the then Township Council adopted By-law No. 2013-31 ("the 2013 By-Law") permitting the quarry expansion. But it still turned down the OPA for the new permanent asphalt plant.

10. That prompted appeals to the Ontario Municipal Board ("the Board") from two directions. The applicant said Council had not gone far enough, when it failed to approve the new asphalt plant; the applicant appealed to the Board accordingly. Inversely, various neighbours argued that Council had gone too far, by increasing the quarry's extraction zone to the extent proposed..."

These opening paragraphs begin the history of the process in outline. They are acceptably written. However, they are out of place. What the reader needs to know at the start is what this is about now, after the hearing. In the second paragraph, the decision says the result is in favour of the Township without telling the reader what that result is. To do it this way seems to me to be almost trying to get some approval for deciding in the township's favour as it tells one nothing else.

To make this a more understandable and informative decision is not to open this decision with the part of the story that is not really in issue. The size or life of the enlarged extraction area in paragraph 1, while interesting, was not in itself the problem. If the decision is to be announced as early as the writer seems to want to do, it is best not to be this vague about it. What the decision is about are two things: setback from surrounding properties of the extraction area and the permanent asphalt plant. Tell the reader straight out what the decision is on each and save the detail for later. To launch immediately into the history after an unclear statement of the decision seems to put the cart before the horse.

This decision could have started with the two issues that the decision is about and gone on to tell the reader which way the decision went in brief, if it is to be announced this early. Or it should not announce the decision too early, vaguely or otherwise; instead, it could tell the story from the start in outline, which the writer does but not from the best perspective – one is to tell it from the opening of the pit fifty years ago or whenever it was. Another approach is to start with the parties now, how they relate to each other and what their relevant backgrounds are, showing how the issues developed in an overview and where they ended up on each of the two issues. Then tell the detailed history after that.

It is always best, whatever one decides to do, to keep in mind what the decision is about now currently, after the hearing, and to be straight with the loser about why it, she or he lost. This decision seems frankly to be written more to tell the Township that it succeeded and to justify it, rather than to act as an evenhanded presentation, which includes an overview, the decision in brief and a straight account of why the quarry owner did not succeed on either the setback or the asphalt plant, with the detail later. This decision is well written and has elements of what I am talking about but it seems unclear in its organization and what the fulcrum of the situation is.

I must repeat here that my remarks are directed to writing style and organization as well as direct comprehensible explanation for the findings in it. This decision was upheld recently by the court by refusal of leave to appeal. I had given an opinion to the contrary and still maintain that it is in error. A sitting judge disagreed and so I must acknowledge that.

Opening of the Decision of the OMB on a Site Plan referred by *Sentinel Broadway Holdings Inc. v Toronto* (*City*), **file MM 130048, released June 19, 2014**

> [1]   The Yonge-Eglinton Centre is a vibrant urban node in North Toronto. Bustling with verve and energy, it is endowed with a wide range of uses in its fabrics, including office, retail commercial, entertainment, residential and institutional uses. Within its midst, there are point towers coexisting in amity and close contact with buildings of wide-ranging vintages and architectural forms. There is no question that the area is undergoing a transformation of a sort as applications for development abound. There is also little doubt that such a transformation would not have been possible had it not been for the number of epoch-making and enabling policy instruments enacted and promulgated within the last decade by the Province and the City of Toronto.

This is an example of a vibrant exciting opening that makes the reader come in and want to stay to find out what the transformation is and from what. It shows how the Board can bring to life a dynamic scene without being inaccurate because it is describing a scene that is changing but the elements remain much the same in movement and life daily.

Excerpt from the OMB decision in *822403 Ontario Inc. v Oakville* (*Town*)**, released August 5, 2015**

> [33]   The Board qualified Dana Anderson, a registered professional planner employed as chief planner of the Town, to provide opinion evidence on land use planning. She appeared under summons initiated by counsel for the Applicant.

> [34]   Before reviewing the evidence of Ms. Anderson, it is incumbent on the Board to provide a few brief comments regarding the obligations of a municipal planner who testifies under summons before the Ontario Municipal Board. It is a well-established principle, that like any other witness who is qualified to present opinion evidence, a municipal planner who appears under summons has an obligation to provide her evidence in a fair, impartial, objective and unfettered manner on the matters on which she has expertise. To put it bluntly,

her evidence is not to be fettered by fear of her employer (municipal council) or by fear of contrary instructions from a person within the municipal hierarchy.

[35]   In order for the Board to carry out its function (which is to make decisions which reflect the public interest) the Board must rely on objective and impartial opinion evidence. That includes the evidence of a municipal planner who may have an opinion on matters at issue in the appeal that are contrary to the view or position of her employer. Many Board decisions have confirmed or emphasized this obligation, as the appearance of a municipal planner who appears under summons is not uncommon.

[36]   The Board observed at this hearing, primarily from the vigorous cross-examination of Ms. Anderson by Nancy Smith, counsel for the Town, that this well-established principle was unfortunately overlooked. The Board appreciates the challenge for a municipal planner who testifies under summons. That planner, typically a public servant, once qualified to provide opinion evidence has a duty to this Board to provide fair, impartial, objective and unfettered evidence.

This excerpt is not an opening but I have included it here because it did something not many OMB decisions do now. It was sent to me by an experienced planner from Toronto because it contains a very nice résumé of the duties of a professional witness. I don't see enough of this kind of public recognition. It shows the reader that the tribunal understands the situation and recognizes the importance of impartial expert evidence unaffected by uninformed direction and pressure from a municipal employer. The pressure on a planning witness in this type of situation can be intense. This decision, as I noted earlier, was identified by a number of experienced counsel as one of significance when it was released. It is from the decision on the Oakville case, one of the two cases combined and outlined at the end of Chapter IX.

But the problem remains. The narrow, overly technical language, the unpredictability and uneven quality of too many of the Board's decisions have damaged its reputation. It is not as if the majority of members are short-term – of the twenty-one full-time members in 2015, fifteen have been engaged in Board work for eight years or more. And the provincial initiatives to amend the *Planning Act* to adapt it to a more activist policy leadership, together with the *Places to Grow Act*, are no longer new to anyone in or outside the Board. The load faced by those few members who have been most productive and conscious of the need to struggle toward a more comprehensive and comprehensible jurisprudence has strained them to the limit, I am sure. All members are facing cases involving amounts far in excess of, and issues as complex or challenging as, cases faced by judges on the Ontario or the Superior Court. The respect due members of this Board should be the same respect shown an Ontario Court judge, something that was well understood three decades ago in the wake of J.A. Kennedy and later, Henry Stewart, each of whom worked differently but tirelessly to put this Board at the forefront of planning and municipal law.

It is true that the Board in those days was a pervasive presence throughout all phases of municipal work. Now the planning jurisdiction alone equals or surpasses past workloads. The administrative work of reviewing files and signing off on staff-prepared orders took much of the time in the days when the OMB was the municipal regulatory Board; and the hearings did not include the level of work and witnesses required by provincial policy and the Places to Grow threshold for changes from Employment to non-Employment designations in the OPs. Of course the present work no longer includes, as examples, financing and a sewer tax by-law in Belleville, or a new auditorium in Carlow/Mayo Township.

It is significant that even as the OMB had entered the modern world of tribunals with the 1971 Spadina hearing, the legislative committee in 1972 was also concerned with consistency and the tribunal's responsiveness to government policy. OMB independence was emphasized in that report while at the same time it stated that tribunals must understand that government sets policy and that policy is generally meant to be carried out. The committee understood well the task consistently before the Board and the depth and range of required knowledge. It found, as I have in differing circumstances and new jurisdictions, that the OMB may usefully interject its own views on the by-law before it but only if they have been tested by the wisdom of others and the member's own experience; the matters that it can shape and control are "of much greater... magnitude than those dealt with by the courts but unlike the courts, which are bound to strict accord with the law, the OMB decides within much broader terms of reference including government policy" as known. Where policy is very broadly stated or not known, the OMB must operate on its own interpretation of facts and the public interest as it sees it. But the Committee also stated its view that while the Board is free to act, it must do so within the broad framework of government policy and should try to follow a consistent policy of the Board.

It was for this reason that the Committee saw as unacceptable that one member would be in a position to reject a decision of a municipal council; there should be two members on any panel where matters of policy and contention over policy are concerned because "the frailties of human nature make it more likely that certain inconsistencies will creep into the Board's approach to matters that should, for fairness, be treated uniformly. Beyond that, it disturbs this Committee to know that one member of an appointed body is thus empowered to overrule the elected council on a matter of far-reaching and intense concern."[183]

> "Everyone I talked to ... all still active, all are well aware of the increased workload, the serious shortage in membership, of capability in decision-writing, and of time for members to deliberate. They also know of the dedicated mediation capability and consensus building efforts carried out by the reduced OMB of today."

Everyone I talked to in researching this work, all still active before the Board and some for three to four decades, others much less – all are well aware of the increased workload, the serious shortage in membership, of capability in decision-writing, and of time for members to deliberate. They also know of the dedicated mediation capability and consensus building efforts carried out by the reduced OMB of today. Respect and appreciation is seldom expressed by anyone in government or in the professions that are active before the Board. The Board knows of the negative comments made outside their hearing, which float through the air like viruses, expressions of cynicism and lack of confidence from certain senior officials in government as well as the shrill remarks in the press. It is a seriously damaged institution in these ways. Unfortunately, in matters of public trust and respect, perception becomes reality.

EXAMPLES OF POOR CHOICES IN DECISION-MAKING

Added to the frustrations for practitioners in planning and planning law, decisions that have incomprehensible reasoning and scant assessment of the evidence are continuing to occur. I do not argue whether the following are right or wrong in their bottom lines. Some examples of skewed reasoning, groundless conclusions, insufficient or no real explanations, and reaching beyond the record are set out in abbreviated fashion below.

  i.   *Johnston v Toronto (City)*, OMB File No. PL 070771, issued March 25, 2008 [deficient template reasons from a Committee, missed opportunity to set a policy standard that use of a generic form without reference to any evidence or legal precedent is simply unacceptable; Divisional Court authority improperly distinguished, it was on point];

  ii. *Kelvingrove Investment Corp. v Toronto (City)*, (2010) 65 OMBR 57, issued April 7, 2010 [the term "balancing" where the PPS is relevant was misunderstood as explained in Chapter IX; application of policy to the facts as found should reflect the balance in the PPS;[184] reasons indicate reaching beyond the record regarding several documents found on the Internet; reasons are written as if the member reacted personally to unsuccessful counsel's representations negatively; reasons skewed by these factors];

  iii. *Sorauren Developments Inc. v Toronto (City)*, OMB File No. PL 130568, issued January 6, 2014 [no explanation is provided in ordinary language to objectors why they lost, planning language used throughout; "heartfelt and sincere" re objectors' concerns telegraphs the result without showing an understanding of their position; message is: have planner, will win and that misses the point that planner's evidence is scrutinized as carefully or more so, than other witnesses because they are giving opinions that may or may not be based on evidence];

iv. *109 Ossington Ltd. v Toronto (City)*, [2014] O.M.B.D. No. 434, issued June 12, 2014 [proposal slightly reduced in height, provided greater step-backs as height increased and angular plane improved; neighbourhood association appears to have been abandoned by City expert witnesses who now support revision; whole issue is impact on streetscape and scale of neighbourhood, yet no detailed description of the neighbourhood scale and feel on the street; without that, no indication to unsuccessful parties that Board member grasped their point; repeated use of "Board finds" and "Board views" preceding general conclusions and no evidence of a witness or exhibit indicates a supposed talent that the Board does not possess of basing findings on some innate ability; no "dialogue" with unsuccessful parties in straight language relating to Board's role and how it reached its decision; technically this is a very competent decision but when dealing with people's neighbourhood, that is not enough];

v. *Miller Paving Ltd. v McNab/Braeside (Township)*, OMB File No. PL130785, issued October 27, 2015 [newly-elected council changed decision immediately after election despite application having been found acceptable by County planners with reduced setback; new council increased setback from neighbouring properties, rendered twenty-four additional acres in aggregate extraction zone immune from extraction to protect development rights of surrounding private owners in large rural rear yards; application of acoustic guidelines from rear lot lines imposed by Board contrary to uncontroverted expert evidence; one vague statement in local OP referring to no disturbance beyond the aggregate property contrary to other policies which qualified its meaning and a prior holding of the Board that silence is not the test; no reconciliation with rule that PPS having priority over local OP and PPS places a priority on availability of aggregate to markets; no explanation for upholding political decision of council without planning advice to support it];

vi. *Waterloo (Reg. Mun.) Official Plan and Lea Silvestri Investments Ltd., Re*: OMB File No. PL110080, phase 1 (land budget and urban boundary), decision released January 21, 2013 [conclusion was that neither budget methodology of landowners nor of the region perfect; flaw throughout the decision was using statutory interpretation rule of ordinary grammatical meaning modified by scheme and purpose to interpret policy whereas conformity with a policy document like an OP – and likewise a growth plan – is more properly judged by "giving to the plan a broad liberal interpretation with a view to furthering its policy objectives"; the Board treated the budgets as either right or wrong, flawed or correct, whereas the approach should have been to consider whether there was a reasonable basis for the region's determinations; effect of government policy to change past trends, for instance regarding the capability of intensification policy to lessen urban expansion into agricultural areas and municipality setting higher and stricter target for future urban density than the PPS is not prevented by the growth plan, section 2.2.7.2 – it is part of being "planned to be achieved"; presumption that council members do not understand what they voted for undercuts even the more relaxed requirement of "having regard to" decision of council.]

These are just a few of the decisions of the current OMB, which have demonstrated problems of communication, deference, and inconsistency in policy direction.

CHAPTER XI

RESOLUTION

> In my beginning is my end. In succession
> houses rise and fall, crumble, are extended,
> are removed, destroyed, restored, or in their place
> is an open field, or a factory, or a by-pass.
> houses live and die: there is a time for building
> and a time for living and for generation...
> from Four Quartets, East Coker
> —T.S. Eliot

TRIBUNAL CONSISTENCY AND COLLEGIALITY: SHOULD HOPEDALE DEVELOPMENT LTD V OAKVILLE (TOWN) BE REVISITED?

Uncertainty can be a useful quality in poetry or in a suspense novel. In works of adjudicative decision-making, it breeds inability to resolve cases and a sense of frustration in advising clients. The degree of uncertainty in and about OMB decisions, coupled with members not fully able or trained to do the job, is symptomatic of a lowered standard of selection and competence on the Board. It also speaks to a reduced level of collegiality. This combination cannot be acceptable.

Where members do not have time to come together to discuss policy or to work on decisions, as they often do not (barring something unusual happening to their full schedule of hearing time), the familiarity, the trust and the ability to share with each other important insights, as well as to get to know and trust each other's judgment, are no longer present.

Collegiality is of importance to the establishment of a culture of consistency and continuity of principles and outcomes. The picture I was given as recently as late 2015 – members working alone in their home offices or at hearings in various parts of the province, part-time assistance being used to fill gaps in scheduling, and members taxed for any time to deliberate fully on cases – is not a picture of a tribunal that could have much chance of consistency and a high quality of work. And yet, it is vital to the goal of hearings before any member of a tribunal that they be dealt with efficiently, with proper explanations to the public of their opportunity to be heard, and that they reach a result that is well and understandably reasoned, to the end that the process and result would have been the same had any other member presided.

I understand that the OMB meets monthly in a structured way. Preparation for a topic of the meeting is required by reading case books relating to that topic. The members are expected to know the cases and be able to discuss the issues on the chosen topic. However, I am told by an internal source that these meetings are happening despite some initial resistance from ELTO staff. The sense of their issues stems from the degree to which clustering favours the diverse, the creative, and the innovative. Meetings are seen as passé, not innovative. Telephone conferencing or contact via cells is preferred. Yet those distant means of communication do little to help erect a collegial home where all members of the Board are to gather at regular intervals to discuss their difficulties with one another or talk out differences, if possible, over policy issues.

As we have seen, the downturn in the Board's quality and timeliness of work since the 1990s relates, in part, to a misjudgment about the OMB as part of a cluster and mismanagement within the ELTO cluster – for thehe rest, neglect by the Province in allowing the full-time membership to drop so drastically. The reduction of full-time membership means less ability to attract capable members of some stature in their profession, less effectiveness in mediation and hearing sharpness, and a loss of institutional knowledge and memory.

> "Policy consistency does not bind a tribunal to a particular result but it must have meaning. It must be part of a tribunal's priorities for it to retain credibility with its stakeholders."

I am, of course, aware that in administrative law, one panel of a tribunal does not bind another to reach the same conclusion. However, the Board is now directed and obligated by statute to produce decisions that are consistent with provincial policy. Policy consistency does not bind a tribunal to a particular result but it must have meaning. It must be part of a tribunal's priorities for it to retain credibility with its stakeholders. It simply means that the Board is to be consistent in its application of policy so that similar fact situations are to be treated similarly in relation to the way provincial policy is interpreted and applied, and similar fact situations involving the same policy should produce similar results. This principle of equality of application of the law is a precondition of equality before the law and a principle of the Rule of Law.[185] It is that basic.

In stating that an important attribute of decision-making is principled consistency, there are those who argue that members of a discretionary tribunal like the OMB must not adopt certain rules or guidelines and use them in deciding the matters before it. They say that what I am suggesting when I talk about the Board adopting and applying policy or using a standard of proof consistently is that very sin. In the often referred to case of *Hopedale Developments Ltd. v Oakville (Town)*, (1965) 1 O.R. 259; 47 DLR (2d) 482, the Ontario Court of Appeal set out the issue as follows, in an appeal from the OMB where the Board, in addition to other reasons, issued an opinion that the appellant has not brought itself within the requirements of certain OMB decisions:

> 8.   The authority which was conferred upon the Board to hear the appeal in the present instance is to be found in s. 30(19) (now s.34 of *Planning Act*, R.S.O. 1960, c. 296, which provides:

> > 30(19) Where an application to the council for an amendment to a by-law ... is refused or the council refuses or neglects to make a decision thereon within one month after the receipt by the clerk of the application, the applicant may appeal to the Municipal Board and the Municipal Board shall hear the appeal and dismiss the same or direct that the by-law be amended in accordance with its order.

> 9.   The extent of the power thus given is wide and was delineated by Kelly, J.A., speaking for the Court in *Re Mississauga Golf & Country Club Ltd.*,[186] as follows:

> > In the circumstances prevailing, s. 30(19) [of the Planning Act, now section 34(26)(b)] gives the Board power to "direct that the by-law (the zoning by-law) be amended in accordance with its order". These words coupled with the very broad provisions of s. 87[now sections 37 and 88] of the *Ontario Municipal Board Act* leave no doubt that the Board in acting pursuant to s. 30(19) is not fettered as the appellant submits here. On the appeal to the Board, the Board is exercising an original jurisdiction and may direct the council to do anything a council could have done in dealing with the application to it, even if this departs from the strict terms of the relief requested in the application...

> 10.   The Board was thus required to exercise its independent judgment upon the merits of the appellant's application. It is the basis of the appellant's case before this Court that the Board, by its reference to decisions in the *Highway Developments Ltd.* and *Sutton Place Developments* cases and by its statement that the provisions quoted in these cases must apply before that Board will interfere indicated that the Board had, in so doing, closed its mind and had failed to consider the appellant's case on its merits as it was required to do."

And further, at paragraph 13, the Court continued along the same line:

> Although it is proper for the Board in an appeal under s. 30(19) of the *Planning Act* to consider certain principles in deciding an appeal, it is not proper for the Board to limit its consideration to the application of these principles. It is, of course, important to keep in mind, as the Board has done, that it is being asked to interfere with the discretion exercised by an elective body but that can be but one of all the considerations which must be taken under review. The hearing before the Board is a hearing *de novo* and must be conducted as such ... To lay them down as principles by which the Board would be guided may therefore be both reasonable and wise but to say that the appellant must comply with them before the Board will allow the application is clearly wrong and the Board, if it so fettered its jurisdiction, would be in error.

These well-known excerpts have been read and cited by many over the years to mean that the Board is not bound by the proponent's appeal or application and may grant any relief that the council could have done in the original hearing; but it may not set out guidelines or principles or policies that guide it in making its decision. This, of course, is a misreading of the case and disregards the actual holding in the case. In *Hopedale*, the Board had indeed set out principles from earlier cases by which it would be guided. And in fact the Court approved of what the Board seemed to be trying to do in the following passage at paragraph 11:

> 11.   The right of an administrative tribunal to formulate general principles by which it is to be guided is undoubted and has been considered upon many occasions in the Courts, particularly in cases dealing with the issuing of licenses. Numerous examples of this are referred to in Robson, *Justice and Administrative Law*, 2nd ed., p. 297; and in S.A. de Smith, *Judicial Review of Administrative Action* (1959), p. 184, the learned author, quoting authorities therefore, states:
>
>> It is obviously desirable that a tribunal should openly state any general principles by which it intends to be guided in the exercise of its discretion. The courts have encouraged licensing justices to follow this practice.

What happened in *Hopedale* is a very convincing delineation by the Court of the argument by the appellant's counsel. What did not happen was agreement or acceptance by the Court of Appeal of that argument. It made manifest its rejection of the proposition that the Board had fallen into the error of closing its mind or fettering its discretion. At paragraphs 13 and 14, the Court states the following, with an illustration of its meaning from the Board's reasons:

13.   To lay them down as principles by which the Board would be guided may therefore be both reasonable and wise but to say that the appellant must comply with them before the Board will allow the application is clearly wrong and the Board, if it so fettered its jurisdiction, would be in error.

14.   <u>In the present instance, however, notwithstanding what was said on this point in its reasons, the Board has shown that it did not so fetter itself and that all matters entitled to be considered were considered</u> and were weighed and were dealt with. The Board found:

(1) That there was no evidence to establish that the subject lands could not be developed economically within the existing land use;

(2) That a higher density land use might have an undesirable effect upon the adjacent undeveloped lands;

(3) That a change of zoning in this instance might readily stimulate and perhaps justify similar requests with respect to undeveloped land in the immediate vicinity;

(4) That the Board is not satisfied that the situation has changed sufficiently since the present zoning was imposed to merit the direction of an amendment to the by-law. (Emphasis added.)

I read *Hopedale* now, at a time when the Board has adopted certain policies and has acted on them without narrowing its consideration of the whole case before it, as in fact an affirmation that tribunals granted wide discretion to adjudicate matters, even those involving decisions by elected councils of municipalities, should set out the principles that guide it as part of its reasons. In fact without them, the decisions are incomplete because the tribunal, in omitting that part of its reasoning, has failed to provide open and transparent factors that would help the parties to understand what the tribunal has decided. All that *Hopedale* is cautioning tribunals against is failing to meet the duty cast on them by the Legislature to look at and consider the whole case before them. In the more recent judicial consideration of *Hopedale*, I think the courts are finding a more contemporary meaning, bringing it into the twenty-first century by emphasizing the values of transparency and openness that the *Hopedale* court was trying to articulate.

The following are the readings of *Hopedale* that are in tune with the modern need for tribunals to try to apply policies and principles on which they act. The penalty that parties must pay for tribunals failing to do so are more and more extreme in terms of costs, access to justice and a sense that they have not been justly dealt with.

In *E.A. Manning v Ontario Securities Commission*, [1995] O.J. No.1305, the Court of Appeal stated:

> 43.   In this context, Mr. Waitzer's comment about getting the penny stock dealers into the self-regulating system is clearly a reflection of what he sees as the ideal regulatory solution to the industry's problems. It is a solution he advocates for all players in the market, not just for the class of traders to which the appellants belong.

> 44.   With respect, I fail to see how what was said by Mr. Waitzer could form any basis for concluding that there was a reasonable apprehension of bias if he were to sit on either of the pending hearings, let alone disqualify the other Commissioners from conducting the hearings. In making the comments complained of here, Mr. Waitzer was fulfilling his mandate as Chair of the Commission.

> 45.   In this respect, what was stated by Doherty J.A. in *Ainsley Financial Corp. v. Ontario Securities Commission*, supra, at pp. 108–09, is apt:

>> The authority of a regulator, like the Commission, to issue nonbinding statements or guidelines intended to inform and guide those subject to regulation is well established in Canada. The jurisprudence clearly recognizes that regulators may, as a matter of sound administrative practice, and without any specific statutory authority for doing so, issue guidelines and other nonbinding instruments: *Hopedale Developments Ltd. v. Oakville (Town)*, [1965] 1 O.R. 259 at p. 263, 47 D.L.R. (2d) 482 (C.A.) ...
>>
>> Non-statutory instruments, like guidelines, are not necessarily issued pursuant to any statutory grant of the power to issue such instruments. Rather, they are an administrative tool available to the regulator so that it can exercise its statutory authority and fulfil its regulatory mandate in a fairer, more open and more efficient manner."

And in *Council of Canadians with Disabilities v. Via Rail Canada Inc.*, 2007 SCJ No. 15, the limitations on the authority of guidelines promulgated tribunal were explained, in part using *Hopedale*:

> 347.   As Doherty J.A. of the Ontario Court of Appeal held in *Ainsley Financial Corp. v. Ontario Securities Commission* (1994), 21 O.R. (3d) 104, at p. 109, a case dealing with a policy directive issued by the Ontario Securities Commission:

Having recognized the Commission's authority to use non-statutory instruments to fulfil its mandate, the limits on the use of those instruments must also be acknowledged. A non-statutory instrument can have no effect in the face of [a] contradictory statutory provision or regulation: *Capital Cities Communications Inc., supra*, at p. 629; H. Janisch, "Reregulating the Regulator: Administrative Structure of Securities Commissions and Ministerial Responsibility" in *Special Lectures of the Law Society of Upper Canada: Securities Law in the Modern Financial Marketplace* (1989), at p. 107. Nor can a non-statutory instrument pre-empt the exercise of a regulator's discretion in a particular case: *Hopedale Developments Ltd., supra*, at p. 263. Most importantly, for present purposes, a non-statutory instrument cannot impose mandatory requirements enforceable by sanction; that is, the regulator cannot issue *de facto* laws disguised as guidelines."

For all its warnings about a tribunal fettering its discretion, the decision of the Court of Appeal in *Hopedale* upheld the right of the OMB to announce guidelines and policies. In fact, it is considered part of the duty to give reasons, for a tribunal to which *Baker* applies, that the tribunal sets out any principles or guidelines on which it acted or that it considered. This would include, in my view, most decisions of the Ontario Municipal Board. However, such self-promulgated principles cannot be used to support actions prohibited by statute, nor can they be used to limit the discretion of the tribunal. There is no limitation in *Hopedale* on the tribunal's ability to declare and apply such principles and guidelines in a consistent and predictable manner provided that the tribunal cannot use such principles to restrict or limit the exercise of discretion so as to fail to consider the full case before the tribunal.

Hopedale has rarely been applied in support of a finding that a tribunal has actually fettered its discretion. Provided the OMB does not allow any principles or guidelines to restrict the hearing of the full case and the live issues, *Hopedale* does not go further than hold that it is good practice for a tribunal to set out the principles and policies by which it is guided. That effort does involve members confronting common issues like standard of proof and the provincial policy statement's direction that there be no negative impact on significant provincial environmental systems. If a consensus is arrived at, *Hopedale* stands for the proposition that a tribunal should express those relevant principles as they apply to cases before the Board. The caveat is that use of consistent principles is always subject to the facts of the case and must not restrict the tribunal from considering the whole case and exercising its discretion without restricting itself to arbitrary limits. It may, or it may not, come within the principles set out by the Board and if it in fact does not come within them, then the Board cannot fetter itself but recognize that fact and articulate it. In its present applications, Hopedale requires no re-visitation.

In a helpful and insightful article titled *Consistency in Tribunal Decision Making*,[187] the author writes of the culture to be built within a tribunal and how "the goal of consistency must be balanced against other prerequisites to the Rule of Law – the ideas that decisions be made on their own facts and be made by those who hear the dispute. Such balancing lies at the heart of administrative tribunal decision-making." He provides a path by which tribunals can achieve and enhance consistency while remaining responsive to the facts of individual cases. An excerpt from that article follows. I commend it to board members, though others may prefer to move on.

INSTITUTIONAL DECISION-MAKING PROCESS

A Tribunal may establish internal processes whereby a group of tribunal members – often all members – will consider and comment on the draft decisions of individual members or panels in advance of the release of those decisions. One of the purposes of such processes is to ensure that "lone-ranger" tribunal members, who "conceive of themselves as occupying islands of justice within a tribunal's office," are not able to create a situation where the outcome of an appeal or application is different depending on which tribunal member hears it.

An example of such a process is found in the case IWA v Consolidated Bathurst Packaging Ltd.[188] In this case, the Supreme Court of Canada examined the consideration by the full Board of the Ontario Labour Relations Board of a draft decision written by a panel of three, but did so before that draft decision was finalized and released. The Court held that this process did not create a reasonable apprehension of bias or lack of independence on the part of the panel. Such an institutional consultation process will not offend where it: (1) is not imposed by a superior level but is requested by the adjudicators themselves; (2) is limited to questions of policy and law, rather than fact or evidence; and (3) the panel members remain free to decide according to their consciences. Further, the possibility of new arguments being raised in the institutional consultation process will not offend the 'audi alteram partem' rule[189] where the parties have an opportunity to respond to any new arguments raised during that process.

Where there is such institutional review, adherence to the principle of deliberative secrecy will permit interaction between the members who have heard the case and those who have not.

CULTURE OF CONSISTENCY

The creation of a culture among tribunal members which values and seeks consistency is likely the most durable and difficult to create. Such a culture should both foster continuous improvement across the organization and lead tribunal members to share a common understanding of the range of acceptable views on significant issues of procedure, law and policy. In keeping with most of the other tools for enhancing consistency, methods to foster a culture of consistency are, as stated, generally more "practical" than "legal".

INTERACTION BETWEEN MEMBERS

Open office environments encourage casual interaction and exchange of ideas. Similarly, regular meetings for geographically disparate tribunal members help establish and reinforce best practices. Tribunal chairs might have regular and informal, but also private, discussions with tribunal members.

NEW MEMBER RECRUITMENT

The addition of new members is an important means to create a culture of consistency and tribunals should participate in the process of member recruitment. This enables tribunals to assess the candidate's ability to fit within the tribunal's internal culture, and to assess how the candidate understands the relevant issues of law and policy.

MEMBER TRAINING

Initial – and ongoing – member training is a valuable tool. A regular program of training members together will result in greater consistency. Tribunal managers may also consider designated training officers, combining classroom and practical teaching, and providing ongoing guidance and support.

MONITORING OF MEMBER PERFORMANCE

The flipside of training members is the monitoring of their performance. The quality of decisions made by tribunal members, including their consistency with other decisions, determines and may reflect those tribunal members' overall performance. Provisions which confer on the Chair of a tribunal responsibility for supervision of performance may permit the Chair to develop codes of conduct with professional and ethical responsibilities and with performance standards.

REVIEW BY TRIBUNAL COUNSEL OF DRAFT DECISIONS

Oversight of tribunal members as a means of enhancing consistency in decision-making may focus more directly on the decisions themselves rather than the members. As a tool of quality control, a tribunal may employ tribunal counsel to review draft decisions for consistency and for a proper assessment of the applicable law. However, care must be taken not to interfere improperly with the reasoning of non-legally trained members.

DECISION WRITING

The development of internal writing guidelines covering style, forms of expression, and the format of reasons will help members to consider consistency when drafting their reasons. Further, the circulation by members of draft decisions and commentary for discussion will encourage and develop a culture of consistency, as will the possibility of appeal through "reconsideration".

Consistency in policy is not dissimilar from the way courts view decisions of colleagues who are co-equals. In *R v Northern Electric Co.*,[190] McRuer J. stated that the decisions of a superior court are binding on all courts of inferior rank and, while not absolutely binding on courts of equal authority, they will be followed in the absence of "strong reason to the contrary." That phase "strong reason to the contrary" does not mean simply a reason appealing to the particular judge. It means something indicating that the prior decision failed to consider some authority that ought to have been followed. He added, "I do not think that 'strong reason to the contrary' is to be construed according to the flexibility of the particular judge's mind."[191]

A member of an administrative tribunal not only is not bound by decisions of other members. The behaviour of turning out decisions as if the member is "an island of justice" within the tribunal's river cannot continue without a continuing loss of respect for both.

My suggestion for the OMB to deal with consistency issues is this: when a difference between members occurs, or there is doubt, a member who is about to issue a decision that contains a conclusion about a provincial policy statement, a point of law, or OP policy, must check prior decisions on that point. If the member's opinion is at odds with prior decision(s) of the Board in a case with similar circumstances, the member should reexamine his or her own thinking. If the member cannot see a way to bring the approach into line with the prior reported approach to the same policy issue, he or she should bring the draft decision to the attention of the Board Chair who can discuss it as a policy issue with the member. The Chair could raise it as a reason for a meeting with the Board as a whole without any reference to the case facts, as in *IWA v Consolidated Bathurst Packaging Ltd.* If the member still is of the view that he or she is correct and the prior decision is wrong on the point, the draft should contain analysis to that effect. This is the way a responsible tribunal charged with the duty of policy consistency should deal with disagreements. Then all members and the stakeholders can know and can address the issue when it arises again.

This is the way jurisprudence is formed. Mistakes or lack of practicality with either approach can be identified and corrected. As long as some attention is paid to the issue and there are reasons set out for the difference in policy judgment, the issue can be faced and the error or impracticality of application in one of the decisions will eventually be found and corrected. It is important that there be a culture of consistency but no slavish adherence to error when it is found.

Examples of the kinds of inconsistency I am talking about are found in three cases where questions of level and standard of proof came into question. Two were cases regarding environmental-natural heritage features and mitigation measures to meet the "no negative impact" directive in section 2.1 of the PPS. In both instances, the proposal was a new aggregate extraction license. One is *Jennison Construction Ltd. v Ashfield-Colborne-Wawanosh (Township)*.[192] The other two are *James Dick Construction Ltd. v Caledon (Town)*,[193] and *Miller Paving Ltd. v McNab/Braeside (Township)*.[194]

Jennison was a case of appeals from the Township's refusal to adopt an OPA and zoning amendment and an application for a gravel pit license. There were water quality issues concerning groundwater that required attention by hydrogeological evidence and mitigation by continuing monitoring and works to be installed later under ministry supervision. In the course of its findings, the Board stated as follows:

> 44. The Board after considering the evidence is satisfied that the hydrogeology of the site is well understood and that appropriate mitigation techniques subject to the changes set out in this decision are in place to ensure that no negative impacts will occur to the groundwater and adjacent seeps and springs to the west. Nor did the Board hear any compelling testimony that the gravel pit in this location will negatively impact the hydrogeology of the Maitland River. Nor was there any testimony that the existing adjacent gravel pits have had any negative impact on the Maitland River Valley.

> 45. We do not live in a risk free world. The Board accepts the uncontradicted testimony that the "High" Intrinsic Susceptibility Index (ISI) for the groundwater water directly below the gravel pit floor would remain unchanged as a result of the gravel pit extraction and that the mitigation measures required to protect the groundwater from petroleum spills and equipment spills are appropriate.

> 46. The Board finds that the ARA application subject to the changes directed and set out in this decision to be consistent with the policy directions set out in Section 2.2 of the PPS, and the applicable sections of the County of Huron and the Township of Ashfield-Colborne-Wawanosh Official Plans dealing with the protection of groundwater matters and that the Site Plan Notes, as amended by Exhibit 51 and further amended by this Board, are satisfactory and require "Spills Contingency Plans" to be in place as a condition of the ARA licence. The Board is satisfied in this case that these prescribed Spills Contingency Plans are appropriate mitigation measures to protect the quality of the groundwater found in the area and are consistent with the Policy directions found in the

2005 PPS and the County and Township Official Plans and the ARA subject to the changes directed above.

71.   It is the Board's finding that the proper interpretation to be given the 2005 PPS definition of "negative impacts" for Significant Natural Heritage Features should take into consideration the directions found in the Natural Heritage Reference Manual with respect to "no negative impacts" as they may relate to the significant woodlands, their associated wildlife habitats, and the other identified Significant Natural Heritage Features found on the site.

72.   It is the Board's finding that a proper reading of 2005 PPS Policies 2.1.4.b and c is that mitigation may include replacement of the woodland components and wildlife habitat, and that such actions are appropriate tools to alleviate negative impacts resulting from the interim loss of a portion of significant woodland..."

By a decision dated December 16, 2011, the Board allowed the planning appeal and the aggregate extraction license application in part subject to compliance with the site plan and its conditions to include the reforestation plan, determination of its success on set criteria, and groundwater monitoring by two wells. What this amounts to is that a significant part of the aggregate area applied for could proceed on the basis that mitigation measures to protect and replace the significant natural features on which the order was conditioned would be carried out under the supervision of the Ministry of Natural Resources.

In a decision dated November 12, 2010, one year earlier, the OMB issued its decision in *James Dick Construction*. There were appeals from refusal of an OPA and a zoning amendment to allow an aggregate quarry to operate on rural land for which an application for licence was also before the Board. The environmental concerns in this case were over groundwater protection, creek and mountain systems, and a vernal pond for salamander breeding, a reptile within the *Endangered Species Act*. The Board had before it expert evidence from aquatic biologists and a hydrogeologist regarding the mitigation systems to be put in place to meet the PPS and the Town OP regarding no negative impact. The Board was highly complimentary to the expert witnesses retained by the appellant-applicant and their work, accepting what they found subject to the AMP proposal for mitigation. The mitigation system was called an Adaptive Management Plan, said to be a well-known method of managing continuing conditions using accepted scientific principles in order to protect the natural systems from negative impacts. The Board found as follows:

233.   The AMP and its significance to the protection of natural heritage features and functions are summarized in the Witness Statement of Ms. MacMillan and Mr. Goodban:

The AMP is a system of design, implementation, performance monitoring, evaluation and optimization/adjustment of mitigation measures. It provides a proactive, responsive and fully integrated system for implementing mitigation and monitoring measures to protect water dependent ecological features, based on a sound understanding of the underlying surface water and groundwater systems. Specific seasonal targets are based on sensitive cold water stream, fish refuge and wetland functions. The AMP also incorporates specific ecological mitigation and contingency response measures and supplementary aspects...

234. The conclusions of all of the work of Ms. MacMillan and Mr. Goodban are contained in Part 5 of their Witness Statement. The general conclusion may be summarized as follows:

"Study has led to a 'sound ecosystems-based understanding' of the water inter-relationship between the Rockfort Site and the natural features, on, adjacent to, or in the vicinity of the Site. The 'interrelationships of many of the ecological features with water and the inherent variability of the groundwater system in particular, were clearly realized from the outset.' The AMP 'was specifically developed and refined to address this variability. Therefore a decision to approve the project would be consistent with the Statement of Environmental values of the relevant ministries.'"

235. The following specific conclusions of the witnesses are based on a significant premise: "the recommended extraction envelope" would be adhered to and there would be "the implementation of the proposed mitigation measures outlined in the 2000 EIA and 2008 Addendum, and as specifically supported by the measures laid out in the May 4, 2009 AMP..."

236. The Board finds that the "bottom line" of the data collection, analysis and assessment work done by Ms. MacMillan and Mr. Goodban may be simplistically, but accurately summarized as follows: if the AMP works properly, the impact of the quarry on the natural heritage features and functions around the site will be acceptable."

The Board made the following significant statement regarding this method of countering adverse environmental impacts post-decision:

243. The Board finds that all of JDCL's consultants in the areas of geology, hydrogeology and engineering undeniably collected data, assessed data, and

modelled the behaviour of the hydrogeological system on and off site and arrived at countless supportable conclusions. However, demonstration of no unacceptable impact on the natural environment is the test established by the PPS and OP, and that test goes beyond supportable conclusions...

263. Further, the Board finds that JDCL has not met the requirements of Policy 5.11.2.4.2(d) of the OP. JDCL has not "completed all environmental investigations and studies as required by this Plan and by all relevant agencies and demonstrated that the proposal will not have any unacceptable impacts." Again, the completion of the Milestones might allow for such demonstration, but that would be post- not pre-Board approval.

264. The Board would be abdicating the responsibility assigned to it by the Planning Act, the ARA, the PPS and the OP, if it determined that proof that the mitigation measures will work as planned could be left to post-approval. Section 11 of the ARA specifically delegates to the Board the authority to consider issues with respect to an application that has been referred by the Minister to the Board. Section 12 sets out matters to which the Board must have regard in considering a referred application. The Board must make a determination on these matters, not leave them to be dealt with by another authority post-Board approval. With respect to the natural environment, section 12(1)(a) requires the Board to have regard to the effect of the operation of the quarry on the environment. As the AMP leaves so much demonstration work to be completed in a post-approval process, the Board cannot find that the operation of the quarry would have an acceptable effect on the environment. Until the work set out in the AMP is completed, the Board finds that the requisite degree of certainty about the efficacy of mitigation has not been demonstrated."

Jennison was decided eleven months after James Dick. In the latter case, a reference is made to an earlier OMB decision *Ron Forbes Enterprises Ltd. v Bruce (County)*, [2006] O.M.B.D. No. 1328 holding that failure to deal with compatibility and impacts was an error in law. In *Jennison*, the member did address the *James Dick* decision and the 2006 decision in the following:

83. ...in *James Dick Construction Ltd v. Caledon (Town)*, 66 O.M.B.R. 263 (the Vice-Chair) reiterates the findings in *Ron Forbes Enterprises Ltd v Bruce (County)*, [2006] O.M.B.D. No. 1328 which states:

The Board makes a manifest error of law or fact if it approves planning instruments but in effect put off the burdensome task of properly considering issues of compatibility and impact to some further date.

84.   Clearly in that case, Vice Chair Campbell was not satisfied that the Proponent had met their obligations under the policy regimes in place and was not prepared to defer the consideration of issues of compatibility and impacts to some further date through an Adaptive Management Plan (AMP) beyond the Board's jurisdiction and control in the first instance. In other words, the Proponent in the Board's judgement in *James Dick Construction Ltd v. Caledon (Town)*, 66 O.M.B.R. 263 had not met their onus to justify the change in land use and as such the Board should not defer these basic policy tests to a later date and different jurisdiction.

85.   In this case, the Board is satisfied for the reasons set out in this decision that the impacts associated with the gravel pit application have been properly addressed within the context of provincial and local planning policy regimes."

To deal with an issue of principle concerning the standard of proof used by the Board, you have to recognize it as such. This was an exercise of distinguishing one case from another where no real difference in principle existed. The principle involved is: what is the requirement of the Board in terms of standard of proof and credible expert evidence properly qualified to show *prima facie*, that mitigation measures in accordance with accepted science as opposed to installation and satisfactory operation are acceptable to the Board? In both cases, the science appears to be in accordance with known principles and in both the issue was proof of mitigation of adverse effects to meet provincial policy. An attempt to distinguish another case going the opposite way on the same point simply by saying the Board is satisfied in *Jennison* but not satisfied in *James Dick* does not cut it. It appears that little or nothing had been done by the Board after the 2006 case and the *James Dick* decision, and before *Jennison* was issued, to try to resolve the different approaches to the standard of proof, an issue fundamental to any tribunal.

So, in one the accepted evidence was that post-decision mitigation was acceptable for groundwater issues. In the other, not only was it not acceptable but the Board announced in paragraph 264 that,

> ... *a high degree of certainty,* which would be attendant upon demonstration by JDCL (the appellant-applicant), *is required* before the Board approves the applications. Such demonstration has not taken place. [Emphasis added]

By failing to treat this question as an important matter going to Board requirements generally in the area of environmental impacts and mitigation, the Board left future parties in similar cases in a quandary as to the degree of proof. As Ms. Pepino said, concerning the Board's unpredictability,

(The Board's) usefulness in the broader planning process is almost a negative one ... to the point that people bend over backwards to avoid being taken to the Municipal Board.

How are parties to prepare for cases like these where the decision-maker does not apply the same measure of proof to a similar issue? While the Board member can hide behind the old mantra that no panel binds another, it is irresponsible for this Board not to concern itself with this kind of fundamental disagreement. It may be that these cases are reconcilable in principle but the effort should have been made. Certainly after *James Dick* and before the issuance of the *Jennison* decision, consideration was required within the Board of this same issue. In *Jennison*, there is no evidence of an attempt at a consistent approach having been developed.

Another example of the failure of the Board to consider as a policy issue the standard expected by the Board of expert witnesses dealing with noise/vibration impacts on a quarry licence application. These applications are far from new. Until recently, I had thought the Board expected, *prima facie*, in the absence of some directive in a local OP or provincial policy statement, noise reception evidence to concentrate on the human activity area immediately around the house, not on the rear lot line of large deep rural lots next to an adjacent quarry application where no one normally would be expected to spend considerable time. And certainly, I had understood that what was acceptable in terms of impact was not complete silence but an ambient noise level as found by the Ministry of the Environment according to the applicable noise guideline.

In *Jennison*, the Board member stated his understanding of mitigation of noise impacts generally in the following terms:

> 34.   *The Board would note that with respect to the issue of noise, silence is not the test.* Instead, acceptable noise guidelines have been developed by the MOE. The Board accepts the uncontradicted testimony of Mr. Gastmeier that this pit can be operated within MOE guidelines for noise, and further finds that for the purpose of clarity Site Plan Notes 1.2.27 i), 1.2.27 ii), and 1.2.27 iii) should be amended to replace the word "should" with the word "shall" and further that the following sentence be added to clause 1.2.27 ii):

>> No crushed material shall be removed from the site until the stockpile berms have been constructed or the crushing equipment is situated a minimum of 8 metres below the western limit grade. [Emphasis added]

The mitigation measures were conditions to ensure that the equipment used met the sound emission standards set out in the Site Plan Notes, and that a ten metre high U-shaped stockpile berm be employed to screen crusher operations until such time as the crusher could be located on the pit floor.

In addition, in dealing with the noise mitigation issue, Jennison dealt with the PPS and the public interest in the exploitation of aggregate resources where impacts were acceptable. The Board concluded on this point that,

> 124. *It is the Board's conclusion that after a full reading of the PPS that this document, as with the local planning policy documents, requires a balancing of competing public interest objectives.* In this case the use of an aggregate resource in proximity to markets on an interim basis must be balanced with the protection of the natural heritage features and functions found in the area for the long term benefit of this area and society as a whole. This is the essence of the public interest test for this part of the municipality." [Emphasis added]

Another more recent decision of the Board, *Miller Paving Ltd. v McNab/Braeside (Township)*, referred to earlier, took a remarkably different view of the PPS and the priority it gives to aggregate extraction. The member in that case dealt with an issue that developed over the setback distance required from the extraction zone. In that case, a gravel licence application and rezoning appeal came down to two issues, one being the setback of extraction from the neighbouring lots. Council passed an amending by-law setting a 180 metre setback. The second issue had no relevance to this one. The election happened in late 2014 and the first action of the new council was to increase the setback to 300 metres. The applicant Miller Paving opposed the second by-law opposing the 300-metre setback, which prevents twenty-four acres of aggregate from being extracted.

The purpose of the greater setback was not due to some policy reason or to protect a rare natural feature; it was granted to protect the development rights of neighbouring owners over the rear 150 metres of their rural properties. They had not objected to a provision added to the 1999 zoning by-law whereby a separation distance from a neighbouring quarry was added. The quarry has now expanded and, the member stated at paragraph 155, the two neighbouring owners who were objecting raised a legitimate question but he did not have to rule on their sterilization argument because "this matter can be determined on other grounds." He then proceeded to use a provision in the OP stating any environmental disturbance to be limited to the site in question to mean that noise caused by the quarry must be limited to the site. This makes no sense first because other OP provisions showed that impacts were expected from industrial-type and aggregate uses and secondly that even with the 300-metre setback there was evidence of some increased noise. Yet, he used silence at the edge of the quarry site as the criterion. He later converted that to mean no noise impact that was over the guideline of 50 dB. He determined that if the setback were 180 metres, the noise level could be 4 dB above 50; the amount limited by the guideline, and that would remove any development rights the objecting owners would have in the rear of their properties. Throughout there was no planning evidence supporting the change from 180 to 300 metres or the proposition that the OP called for silence at the quarry's lot line.

The PPS recognized the importance of aggregate supply near market areas and required protection of the aggregate operations from development that would preclude expansion or continued use incompatible with the extraction operation (sections 2.5.2.1, 2.5.2.3, 2.5.2.4 and 2.5.2.5). Yet, the zero requirement for disturbance including noise at the quarry lot line was used to protect the alleged development rights of neighbouring rural residential lots on the rear portions of their lots. I saw no support in evidence for the alleged development rights of these private owners whose lots were already in use as rural residential lots.

To compound the errors in this decision, it should be added that the 300 metre distance separation was taken from a guideline of the Ministry of the Environment and Climate Change, which stated that the guideline had no application to pits and quarries. I can only say that the manipulation of evidence and supposed development requirements to reach a preordained result that the member determined he wanted to reach in order to assist the private interests of the neighbouring lot owners and the misapplication of the PPS make this a decision right in line with Mr. Chipman's criticism of the Board pre-2000 – that it favoured private interests over the public interest. [The court recently rejected the motion for leave to appeal on the grounds that it failed to raise an error in law and the setback was supported by other evidence, not specified.]

Again, the conflict between one panel manipulating an OP to mean a zero impact from noise of a quarry operation and the *Jennison* statement that silence was not the test show a Board that has not attempted to be consistent in principle on a point that is for the Board to set – what standard is an applicant to prepare the case for: a zero disturbance or increase in noise level, or a noise separation guideline not applicable to a quarry, or one that is not adverse or unacceptable, looking at applicable noise level guidelines. The Board should also try to be consistent about the receptor point for noise impacts in rural residential situations, the rear lot line or line closest to the development site in question on the one hand, or the human activity level near the home.

Standard of proof is an issue that the Board should at least be consistent about -- whether it is to be the civil standard of proof or something stricter for applications raising important environmental or species-threatening issues. It should also be demonstrated to Board members just what certain decibel levels sound like. The Board would require for *prima facie* proof, i.e. subject to hearing any opposing evidence, proof on a standard of probabilities, the normal civil standard, perhaps with a heightened standard closer to certainty where sensitive human or natural features are involved. It may be that tolerance for error has to be closer to zero in cases of sensitive natural features of provincial significance, though complete certainty at that level is virtually impossible. Whatever the Board practice may be, I hope there will be a consistent approach by all members on this and other areas where members are at odds on what are basic practice points. The amount of costs at risk makes this point imperative.

It would assist all parties and it would assist settlement discussions as well, giving less hope to those with low level cases to hope for a renegade finding. The Supreme Court provided the means:

However, the criteria for independence are not absence of influence but rather the freedom to decide according to one's own conscience and opinions ... The full board meeting was an important element of a legitimate consultation process and not a participation in the decision of persons who had not heard the parties.[195]

THE RULE OF PRECEDENT IN COURT AND TRIBUNAL PRACTICE: PREDICTABILITY V. RIGIDITY

There are those who say that the Board should instigate the use of the concept of legal precedent to its decisions in order to address the complaint common to many that there is little predictability about OMB decisions. According to one article by a prominent municipal lawyer and a member of a residents' association, this would mean the following:

> Implementing the concept of precedence will force Board members to become exceedingly careful when drafting their written reasons. The Board member must not only be cognizant of the facts and applicable law to the appeal before it, but the Board member must also be aware that all findings of law set out within the decision will be binding upon future Board members. A Board member will be less inclined to make a "one-off" decision in favour of a particular party based upon flawed thinking ...[196]

First, it is necessary to correct the view of the doctrine of legal precedent that is stated in this interesting article. The rule of precedence means, as it is commonly understood in modern terms, that every court is bound to follow any case decided by a court above it in the hierarchy.[197] Another way of putting it was articulated by Hogg J.:

> The doctrine of stare decisis is one long recognized as a principle of our law. Sir Frederick Pollock says, in his First Book of Jurisprudence, 6th ed., p. 321: *The decisions of an ordinary superior court are binding on all courts of inferior rank within the same jurisdiction, and, though not absolutely binding on courts of coordinate authority nor on that court itself will be followed in the absence of strong reasons to the contrary.*[198] [Emphasis added]

As between Board members, even the strictness of the stare decisis rule would not apply in the way suggested in the article above whereby "all findings of law set out within the decision will be binding upon future Board members."

The statement that findings of law by one member would be binding on other Board members according to the rule of precedence or stare decisis is almost correct. It would be fully correct if it involves a decision by a court higher in rank than the court bound by the decision. In fact, the rule can be more broadly stated that where the material facts are the same, the decision (not just a finding of law in it) of a higher court binds a lower court within the same judicial system. It is not true to say that a finding of law or a decision by one judge is binding on a judge of the same court level.

Mr. Justice Granger of the Ontario High Court, as it was called before court consolidation, produced a very good dissertation on the rule of legal precedent as it applies between members of the same court in *Holmes v Jarrett*.[199] That assessment was made known throughout the trial court in the mid-1990s. This analogy would be the equivalent to members of the same Board. According to Justice Granger, there have been at least three slightly different views expressed by courts. The three approaches he described as:

- The Authoritative View: A judge is to apply the law as it was applied in previous cases by judges of coordinate authority
- The Persuasive View: a judge is not bound to follow a ruling of a judge of the same court level; instead the judge will follow it as a matter of custom, and therefore where a judge finds another's ruling to be wrong, there is nothing requiring that judge to follow the prior ruling
- The Conformity View: a judge should feel bound to follow decisions of a judge of the same level in the same jurisdiction unless there are strong reasons to the contrary

> "... it has to be remembered that one of the reasons for resorting to adjudicative tribunals was to try to get away from the rigidity and formalism of the legal approach and allow tribunals with specialized expertise to use flexibility and common sense ..."

Mr. Justice Granger agreed that the object of all these statements of the doctrine of stare decisis is to provide for uniformity in the law and in particular to always have in mind the goal of maintaining predictability in the law. In considering how he should approach decisions of colleagues in the same court, he concluded that he was bound to follow them unless they had failed to consider a relevant statute or a relevant authority in the law, such as a decision on similar material facts of a court of higher rank in the same jurisdiction.

I am not of the view that the rule of precedent as articulated in the article referred to above should be implemented. The rule as articulated is stricter than most judges have articulated it where precedent is applied to judges at the same court level or members of the same board or tribunal. The policy of consistency that I favour is similar to, but not as rigid as that formulated by Granger J. I think that in contemplating this subject, it has to be remembered that one of the reasons for resorting to adjudicative tribunals was to try to get away from the rigidity and formalism of the legal approach and allow tribunals with specialized expertise to use flexibility and common sense and a less costly process in arriving at conclusions. Tribunals are dealing with policy as much as, and often more than the courts, and there should be room to come up with innovative solutions that do not necessarily follow to the ultimate degree prior decisions where the facts of the case require a somewhat different approach.

As I stated above, there is need for greater consistency in law and policy in Board decisions. Predictability plays a great part in the ability of parties to resolve issues and whole cases without a costly hearing. At the same time, there is good reason to resist any approach that forces members to follow rulings whose only virtue is they were made before the present one and should be followed despite error and despite there being a more equitable solution to a policy issue that would help cases in the future or achieve justice in a truly unique situation.

I have set out a practise in this chapter that the Board could implement without any change to the law. It would, I think, resolve most disagreements between a present proposed ruling and a prior ruling on similar facts and where it did not, the two approaches would be set out publicly, to be addressed by parties and counsel in a future case or motion on similar facts. In this way, correction of error and development of planning and expropriation compensation law can take place accompanied by an insistence on consistency and predictability as serious values that in most instances will be achieved once the culture of consistency I have spoken of is inculcated in all members.

Recently, the Supreme Court of Canada had reason to examine the rule of precedent or stare decisis in *Canada (Attorney General) v Bedford*,[2013] 3 SCR 1101. It involved constitutional issues surrounding prostitution-related laws dating back to the *"Prostitution Reference"*,[1990] *1 SCR 1123*, applying to workers in the sex trades and the Charter, and the threshold for a trial judge, when confronted with a case involving issues decided some years ago, to enter into a reconsideration of the rulings in the earlier case which are normally binding on her. The court held unanimously in *Bedford* that,

> the threshold for revisiting a matter is not an easy one to reach. In my view, as discussed above, this threshold is met when a new legal issue is raised, or if there is a significant change in the circumstances or evidence. This balances the need for finality and stability with the recognition that when an appropriate case arises for revisiting precedent, a lower court must be able to perform its full role.

If the Province decides that the OMB should be compelled to follow a stricter approach to the issues of consistency, then the rule should be applied correctly. The position adopted by the Supreme Court in *Bedford,* an approach not dissimilar to that of Justice Granger, would be the correct approach: that the tribunal was bound to follow prior Board decisions on similar questions of law and mixed fact and law unless a new legal issue is raised, or there is a significant change in circumstances or evidence.

CAUSES OF OMB PERFORMANCE DECLINE: ADVERSARIAL HEARINGS, DE NOVO JURISDICTION, AND THE GRADUAL MOVEMENT TOWARDS MEDIATION AND A HYBRID HEARING MODEL

The research that I have done in the planning literature, the interviews with the planning and law practitioners who work before the Board, the reading of decisions of the OMB from years ago and today, and the writing of this book leave me in no doubt about the essential truth of my thesis.

First, the Ontario Municipal Board since the mid-1990s has slowly declined from a senior respected and highly competent tribunal to a place where there is no tenure, a strong perception of the related loss of independence, and working conditions imposed by what is now a chronic state of under-resourced, underpaid, and time-deprived pressure to keep the schedule moving at the cost of excellence, quality, and timeliness in what is being produced. The fact that this Board is still productive to the degree it is, is a testament to the commitment of its members and staff and to the success, limited by lack of trained personnel and available time, of the mediation efforts of the trio led by Mr. McKenzie and other members who have helped in this effort.

The second point that I conclude has been demonstrated is that the decline of this tribunal resulted from management and governmental misjudgments and lack of reasonable care in not determining a properly reasoned basis for placing the OMB in a cluster with other tribunals related in subject but having little in common operationally or in service to clientele.

The principles in the ELTO facilitator's report of delivering high quality adjudicative services with no compromise in protecting the public interest and access to justice have been lost in the case of the OMB. This is one tribunal with a wide-ranging knowledge requirement and constant challenge to members' knowledge and imagination in the search for mediated resolution or post-hearing solutions that have planning justification. It needs to form and maintain its own pool of diverse talent and character and stature to meet its workload. It must maintain sufficient numbers and mediation training to run a busy list of land use, expropriation and development charge appeals at a high level of service in both resolution and adversarial tracks.

To sum up, this decline in overall competence, respect, and ability is at least partly due to these several factors, including:

    i.   some less than wise judgments within ELTO and the OMB administration over the suitability of the Board for clustering;

    ii.   the reasonable inference from evidence before me that clustering brings with it a new pooling of resources, which by judicious use will lower tribunal membership numbers, reduce time for writing decisions and for dispositions and lower costs; whereas the intent should have been as it was stated – to recognize and use the unique expertise and share the best practices of each tribunal to the extent possible, while protecting the public interest and the independent mandate of each;

iii.   the resulting use of part-time members to deal with scheduling fluctuations but also with up to five-day hearings, and at the same time failing to retain and to increase the complement of full-time members;

iv.   the loss of deliberation time to study, research, and consider the issues before writing decisions and loss of collegial time; plus

v.   ill-informed tenure arrangements and close to frozen remuneration for the past thirty years, stagnating recruitment of significant mediators who are significant people in their career fields to settle for people who cannot command a salary scale greater than senior management

Ultimately, the entity responsible is the one that has had control of the operation of the OMB, the selection process, and its ability to produce decisions of acceptable quality efficiently, since 2009 when the Board was submerged in a cluster organization to which it has given but from which its members cannot receive. That is, the provincial government. The ministers bearing the responsibility for the OMB review since June 2016 are the Minister of Municipal Affairs, now Mr. Bill Mauro of Thunder Bay, and the Attorney General, Mr. Yasir Naqvi of Ottawa. The decline of the OMB over the last two decades and especially since 2009 has occurred because some persons in power in one or both ministries decided that one size will have to fit all; they never asked nor answered a key question. Can the OMB and its powerful and demanding mandate operate more efficiently and effectively as part of a cluster than alone?

That question stared out at those responsible for the cluster decision, before Mr. Mauro and Mr. Naqvi took office, from section 15 of the ATAGA law.

There is still a process issue causing distress among many persons who otherwise find merit in this tribunal. It has been 111 years since the Ontario Railway and Municipal Board was formed and that grant of wide power and authority, wedded to the pervasive use of a formal court process, now grates on many people to whom cross-examination and court formality seems out of date and unsuited to the planning process. Don't misunderstand me, there may always be a place for cross-examination of a witness where the issue simply is intractable and someone must hear out the evidence, have it tested, and make a decision.

The OMB is by no means the only land use tribunal in North America that uses an adversarial procedure. The Saskatchewan Municipal Board, the Manitoba Municipal Board, the New Brunswick Assessment and Planning Appeal Board and the Nova Scotia Utility and Review Board all hear planning appeals and all use an adversarial approach or a modified or hybrid model. The Saskatchewan Board's website[200] describes its hearings in planning matters as following the hybrid model tending more toward the adversarial:

In its publication *"Practice Essentials for Administrative Tribunals"*, the office of Ombudsman Saskatchewan describes three hearing models:

ADVERSARIAL HEARING MODEL – The process used by courts in Canada is known as the adversarial hearing model. In an adversarial model, parties are set in opposition to one another. The decision-maker depends on this opposition between the parties to reveal information necessary to decide the case. The parties present evidence and argument to the decision-maker who uses it to decide what happened in the case and what the outcome should be.

INQUIRY-BASED HEARING MODEL – An inquiry-based hearing model is an alternative to an adversarial hearing model. In an inquiry-based model, the decision-maker actively seeks out the evidence to decide the case by questioning parties who may have relevant information. The decision-maker is responsible for leading the questioning and gathering the evidence.

HYBRID HEARING MODEL – The inquiry-based and adversarial hearing models are not completely separate. Many tribunals adopt a model with process steps that look more like the adversarial model, but with characteristics of an inquiry-based model such as the tribunal leading the questioning process. This model is known as a hybrid hearing model.

There are those who see the adversarial approach as fundamentally unsuited to planning issues. Issues in land use planning are often polymorphic, multi-dimensional, with many inter-related variables and cumulative effects of developments to consider on the existing and future developmental landscape and among each other.[201] Others see cross-examination as not only necessary but as "the greatest legal engine ... for the discovery of truth." As an aside, this may be true but legal counsel who do not know the rest of this quotation may suffer a reverse effect. The quote comes from John Henry Wigmore and here is the rest: "You can do anything with a bayonet except sit on it. A lawyer can do anything with cross-examination if he is skillful enough not to impale his own cause upon it."[202]

Compounding the situation, some practitioners say that the Board retains what is referred to in law as a jurisdiction *de novo*. That means, every appeal that comes to the Board brings with it the duty of the Board to hear all of the evidence and make findings on, not only the issues arising from the decision of the council under appeal, but all issues arising from the development application as it was then and with amendments made to it since it was filed with the municipality. According to one law dictionary, *de novo* means "anew; afresh." A trial *de novo* is "a new trial before a different judge or in a different court. A trial that is held on appeal as if the prior trial didn't exist."[203] An authority in administrative law describes a trial *de novo* as "a hearing in which the decision-making authority deals completely afresh with a matter that has already been heard before either by that or another authority."[204] The tension between a hearing *de novo* and an appellate review hearing where the decision-maker must have regard to the decision of the prior authority, i.e. a municipal council, is palpable. If the adjudicator is to have a true hearing *de novo*, then no deference is paid to the first decision-maker because that would mean the matter was not receiving attention afresh. It is my view, expressed in the final chapter regarding the nature of the present appeal process, that the jurisdiction of the Board should no longer be regarded as a *de novo* jurisdiction. The Board's appeal jurisdiction is now as an appellate review Board, which hears evidence on appeal issues that arise from the application that was considered by municipal council and on grounds that existed then and since that decision, recognizing that that decision is one that the council had the right to make.

As for the adversarial process and cross-examination, two well-respected land use planners, one of whom has managed a planning program for a major city on the northeastern seaboard, have a very different opinion of the use of the adversarial method of examining witnesses. One sees mediation as the avenue of the future for the OMB, and, less and less, the adversarial approach:

> I think the thing that can bring everyone together – proponent, the city, the neighbourhood associations – is the use of mediation of land use conflicts ... There should be a rule that no case goes to a hearing until it goes through mediation ... There should be more emphasis in appointing members on their having been trained in mediation and able to resolve conflicts. I think the days of adversarial battle are over and mediation will be the stronger emphasis in the future.[205]

The other sees the adversarial process as counterproductive for planning issues. He sees such issues as properly the subject of a more consultative, more consensus-building process rather than the "binary", "reductive" form of examinations and divisiveness that the adversarial system forces on parties in conflict over planning matters.[206] He uses "binary" to mean, limited to one of two alternatives.

From my own observation of hearing rooms and courtrooms, the use of cross-examination as it is meant in criminal or civil litigation is seldom necessary in tribunal hearings involving land use. And frankly, for every one or two cases where it was successful, there is another where it did nothing but take up time.

The most effective examination in planning law cases is simply direct questioning of witnesses using data in unexpected or contextually altered ways. It should mean confronting a witness that counsel has reason to believe is less than credible with short sharp questions requiring only yes or no answers to the disputed facts in a slowly enclosing web that exposes the person who has lied or was loose with the truth. It does not include endless pointless questioning nor does it include demeaning and insulting questions with editorial comments in between, often used to belittle a self-represented party when nothing else worked.

It is interesting how even a discussion of alternatives to cross-examination stirs up some sort of base fear in lawyers active in litigation. It happened with me as I wrote this. The lawyer inside me started nattering, warning me:

> Remember, it is a material aide to probing the truth, credibility, veracity of a person, proposition or facts. It is but one important element of an inquiry system and deserves a seat at the table ... Can't it be used as a sword or as a necessary and available shield where circumstances warrant?

The next internal reminders are even more pointed, nervous that I had forgotten sitting for twenty-three years on all types of trials from homicide to a family estate dispute. The lawyer in me was feeling his deepest insecurities. There is a sense in all this of something lost, of fear and change that may leave the old forms behind. Yet all that may be happening is a slowly growing sense of community replacing the individualist, the old gunslinger with the 32-calibre questions and sharpened skills. The approach must be suited to the occasion and one occasion may be the issue that can only be dealt with using the verbal scalpel of cross-examination. The lawyer inside me needs to be heard:

> You have seen cross-examinations that were remarkable – remember – exposing unsupported opinion; correcting inadequate information; eliciting origins of opinions; evidence coerced; achieving admissions against interest and elucidating a myriad of relevant (and irrelevant) considerations beyond mere hypothetical reconstructions. Again, it is a component of an adversarial system which, once engaged, deserves a part.[207]

[And then finally a ray of comprehension breaks through my defences.] One issue being tracked is whether, ultimately, all land use planning instruments and circumstances warrant access to an adversarial system.

And, like a snap of his fingers, that inner voice is gone.

"Good planning depends on consultation, creativity, sound judgment, and openness ... rather than a fortress mentality around one set of absolutes from which all other ideas must be protected and defeated. ."

What I am searching for is an idea – perhaps that in land use planning, the best answer is not necessarily to be found by unmasking a liar or destroying an expert's hypothetical. Each of those adversarial victories probably had little to do with deciding what is the best policy for a region with water supply issues affecting part of it or with whether a mixed affordable housing project of townhouses should proceed next to stable older neighbourhoods fearing a fictional loss in property value. I agree without more at this stage of my work, that of course there will always be a need for adversarial examinations in circumstances that demand them but only after a mediation-centred alternate dispute discussion seeking consensus has been really tried and failed.

Good planning depends on consultation, creativity, sound judgment, and openness to all possible solutions to a problem when good sense and honesty are allowed to shine forth, rather than a fortress mentality around one set of absolutes from which all other ideas must be protected and defeated. But sometimes opposing sides, or just people with different ideas, come to that point of complete conflict. Each sees the relevant facts and law as being in full and complete opposition to each other. This type of collision of ideas and interpretation of facts and policy require serious testing by pointed questioning by trained legal counsel to lay bare the factual misunderstanding that several planning witnesses and perhaps a specialized fish or plant biologist have fallen into, perhaps due to insufficient testing or a difference of water temperature undetected by one team of scientists. Or the error could be the reading into policy of an idea that a full reading of the policy documents shows to be untenable.

The resulting clash, the challenge to perceptions to find their root cause, can sometimes be the only way to bring light to a fundamental misinterpretation or inadequacy in soil or acoustic testing or some other issue of importance to the decision – procedural or substantive. The consequence of not finding that error could have meant long-lasting consequences to an entire ecological system and eventually to people. Cases like this are not frequent. But they require a hearing and sufficient time to build an evidentiary base for the lengthy submissions that can change minds. And that is how law is made.

One example of this kind of case was the hearing some thirty years ago concerning the site of the Rosedale subway station.208 At this point, a large frontage on Yonge St. opened across the Yonge corridor in both directions into expanses of open space parkland. The park sites across from each other mark one of two locations where the incessant development on Yonge St. is broken in order to allow a place in the centre core of the greatest urban area in Canada for people to breathe and walk and picnic or play in an openness and green space that helps to preserve humanity in the city.

The case came down to two visions of the city's main street: one of a corporate uniformity where every site, no matter the surroundings, must become part of a wall of office or street commercial or concrete mixed use development with larger walls near every subway station; the other view seeing the main street corridor as one of variation in density of development and in development itself at two places where low density and open space passive parkland should be maintained. This second view would break the developmental monotony, which would hide neighbouring lower density residential areas from the street and the street from the public investment that the city has made in parks and open space at both Lawrence Park and at Rosedale. Each of these sites are next to older residential areas still alive and well within the city. The City proposed to have the site remain in use for the subway tracks and station and that it should be allowed to keep to the second vision of the main street corridor by turning down the commercial office proposal.

The Board deferred to the City's vision as a defensible planning vision of interest and variation that it should be allowed to maintain and that this subway station site should not provide the site for more office commercial development. The caveat was that a residential building with proper planning to preserve the open vista across Yonge St. could be contemplated there because Metro transportation planning encouraged higher density residential development at station sites to use infrastructure efficiently. That kind of proposal was not what was before the Board.

This was a case that could not have settled and the Board was assisted by the cross-examination from both sides. There must be continued accommodation at the OMB for such cases.

We have looked at the OMB as it is now and the importance it has been to the Province in 1971 and the difficulties it has been facing since 1996. We have considered its history, its mandate, alternatives or not to the adversarial system at hearings, change in the policy framework, municipal takeover of minor variance and site specific zoning appeals, its expropriation jurisdiction over compensation hearings, and various issues over the Board's performance of the recent past and present, its selection process, the impact of clustering, the questions over its ability to give independent decisions, and the recent decrease in its personnel and funding.

As I set out earlier, there are four choices:

1. Dissolve the Ontario Municipal Board.
2. Maintain the Ontario Municipal Board with a few statutory fixes and directives to correct the most serious problems.
3. Remove the planning jurisdiction under the *Planning Act* from the OMB.
4. Dissolve the OMB and move toward establishing a new tribunal with a new name, new mandate, new jurisdiction, new role, and some statutory and regulatory fixes of prior problems.

The fundamental question that underlies all four options is: should there be a provincial tribunal for all appeals under the *Planning Act* as well as for all hearings required under the *Expropriations Act* and the *Development Charges Act* and all other statutory jurisdictions now dealt with by the Ontario Municipal Board? The Province appears to have answered that one in the affirmative.

Apart from the *Planning Act* jurisdiction, the issues that are live ones are municipal control of the planning process, the failure of the OMB to promote a timely process for planning and compensation claims, and the lack of accountability of a tribunal with the power to overturn decisions of the elected municipal councils on planning appeals.

ANALYSIS: PURPOSE, STAKEHOLDER EXPECTATIONS, AND NEEDS AND BENEFITS OF AN APPELLATE PLANNING/ EXPROPRIATION COMPENSATION TRIBUNAL

In considering in principle the continuation of the OMB or something else like it, we should undergo one last analysis. We must get down to first principles and consider the purpose of this tribunal, the expectations of it, and, if these factors are still relevant, how both are to be met:

Why was a provincial tribunal maintained in the planning process?

What are the expectations of stakeholders for this tribunal?

How can a tribunal maintain the purposes and expectations for the process as a whole?

The purpose of the OMB and its evolution was discussed in Chapter V. By the 1990s, the Board had acquired a seven-point mandate, which is set out here, with one addition: the duty to produce an annual report to the government and the interested public of the Board's work. They include:

i.   to hear appeals brought under and within the terms of the *Planning Act, Expropriations Act* and *Development Charges Act* taking into account grounds and principles of land use planning, appraisal and service cost recovery;

ii.   to require high standards of professionalism and impartiality from land use planners, appraisers and other witnesses qualified to give opinion evidence;

iii.   to provide a standard of fairness to the process and hearing of all appeals;

iv.   to direct the process of, and make decisions on, all appeals properly before it taking into account the public interest, provincial planning policy issued under section 3, provincial plans, and municipal official plans and on all claims before it with fairness, impartiality and competence and within the statutory framework;

v.   to have regard to the decisions of municipal councils appealed to the Board and to any supporting material and information that were before the said councils when the decisions appealed from were made;

vi.   to shape the interpretation and application of planning law and policy in Ontario in accordance with the purposes and directions in sections 2 and 3 of the *Planning Act* and the principles of the Rule of Law;

vii.   to provide an opportunity during the hearing of appeals for all those having an interest and/or standing within the *Planning Act* to express their views on planning issues affecting them and their communities; and

viii.   to produce to the Legislature and the public a report of the Board's work and of the resources it needs to provide its services and render decisions efficiently and effectively and in a timely fashion, in accordance with the accountability and good governance principles espoused by the ELTO cluster facilitator and the ATAGA legislation.

A good measure of the need for a body with a certain mandate, as in the above example of the OMB, is the legitimate expectations of its stakeholders. The stakeholders in a system or process comprise anyone who is affected by the process. In this context, they include the parties to the appeals, proponents and opponents, and the claimants for compensation. They include the municipalities as they become involved, whether as parties or affected entities, and the Province as its interests and policy become affected. They also include the public, both those who attend and more distantly but nevertheless affected, the larger public.

The legitimate expectations of all these stakeholders can vary with each group. However, they have a common and legitimate set of expectations, in my view. They should be able to expect a fair and expeditious and less costly process than a court. They can legitimately expect to attempt to resolve cases by mediation or to be heard where they have a particular interest in the matter before the tribunal and relevant evidence to provide at the time of the hearing. They must be able to expect that their evidence and position in relation to the proposal or issue in question will be duly considered. There is no further need for a *de novo* approach that simply ploughs furrows already deeply ploughed. They can also expect the appellant to be able to advise the Board at the commencement exactly and succinctly why and on what type of evidence the decision of the municipal council is in error or does not come within the range of reasonable outcomes. And they all legitimately can expect timely mediation by a trained and knowledgeable mediator, or an independent decision from a tribunal with specialized expertise providing reasons that are coherent, cogent and communicate effectively to the party or parties, and to the public at large, why the conclusions necessary to the decision were reached.

Each group of stakeholders no doubt has their own expectations, such as the desire to prevail, or at least not to lose, but those are their individual expectations, not necessarily legitimate. On the planning side, the municipalities have a legitimate expectation that the council's decision will be recognized and respected as that of the elected representatives and local government of the inhabitants. And the Province has a legitimate expectation that Provincial policy will be treated according to law and with reasonable consistency where the case contexts are similar, and that the balance intended by the Provincial Policy Statement and, where applicable, the Growth Plan is maintained.

There is no evidence that the voting tendencies of ward politicians are going to change, if there were no tribunal to appeal to. They may, or may not, and that is why I prefer to start incrementally. The politics of development proposals is done differently from Toronto by councils of smaller municipalities but whether the result will be the same where local political pressures are expressed on controversial proposals is the question. They can include matters of provincial interest like maintaining the supply of aggregate for development and roads by opening pits or extending older ones, and housing to assist disadvantaged groups in the community. If the tribunal is not present in the planning process, pressures by local residents will occur and sometimes they may have a defensible case on planning grounds, sometimes not.

There is no reason to simply assume that councils will react to pressure without a defensible case, absent the Board, where the document is as important to the municipality's future as its OP. And if they do, the municipality will eventually feel the effects in time. It will be for the inhabitants who vote to hold the council to account. I sense that when there is no "out" position for the council to take, most will act responsibly after a transition period. Where the use involved is the kind of unwelcome proposal like a gravel pit locating to mine the aggregate that is on site, provincial policy will activate a right to appeal and the tribunal can deal with that case even where it is an OP designation involved.

Secondly, there would continue to be no time for most councils to hear them out, both the evidence for and against, and deal with all the other problems of running a municipality, if they were to handle all ongoing planning files.

Thirdly, there is no evidence that municipalities would appoint a fair selection of qualified people from a diversity of planning related fields to hear appeals from the decisions of those who appointed them. As with committees of adjustment, councillors will continue to intervene on behalf of influential persons to try to tip the result on political grounds of decisions by a local appeal body or planning advisory committee as they try to do with the existing committees.

Councillors have intervened on behalf of one side often in local committee of adjustment proceedings by letter or in person or by telephone. It is visible and I have seen it done on several occasions, as have all lawyers in this field. This would represent a direct influence on the committee whose members are beholden to the council or certain councillors for their positions. There is no evidence that any educating to discourage such practices or more direct action to that end is being taken by any municipality. However, if the Province inserted definite criteria in the *Planning Act* for the makeup of the Planning Advisory Committee or the local appeal body, to

"... there is no evidence that municipalities would appoint a fair selection of qualified people from a diversity of planning related fields to hear appeals from the decisions of those who appointed them."

whom people could appeal from the council, municipalities would follow them, especially if there were financial incentives and disincentives involved for decision-making in conformity with provincial policy.

Finally, quite apart from denial of fair process, if the provincial tribunal appeal hearing was removed, there is simply no evidence that 444 municipalities can act with any degree of consistency on matters of provincial policy and interest. The research to date on the continuation of urban sprawl and the somewhat relaxed provincial intensification target indicate to the contrary.

The OMB decision on the Waterloo Official Plan land inventory did not respect the decision of an elected council to set a higher intensification target of forty-five per cent and its urban boundary, using a study method with some pedigree to it that did not simply repeat the past by using historic trends as the developers' statistics did. Other reasons that were not easily comprehensible were given, technical ones related to methodology, but in the end, the above statement represents what happened.

The Waterloo plan was settled but not before the OMB's allowance of an added 1,000 hectares of agricultural land for development was cut back severely. These are moments that pass by all too quickly when a message could have been sent that was more consistent with the intent of the *Planning Act* and provincial and regional policy. The intent of a document is not one number that is used but the overall objects that the plan is aiming to achieve. And the intent of the Act is that elected council decisions are not to be treated lightly by tribunal members who have no accountability to the region involved – a regional municipality that had taken the time and the trouble to make the commitment to restraint regarding the urban boundary that it did. Their loyalty must always be to the public interest, not simply in forming opinions about what steps in a land inventory they agree with and in favouring use of historic figures where a government is trying to take steps to change historic trends by implementing policy. Anyone who remembers how far off reality the Board's history-based population projection of less than 75,000 by 2010 in Barrie, where government was saying that its policy of creating regional growth centres would change that, must acknowledge the force that effective implementation of policy can have. By 2010, Barrie had actually grown to over 135,000.[209]

Yes, there are problems with the perception of compromised independence with its relation to short tenure and no assurance of reappointment. Yes, there have been problems with timeliness of process and with taking the lead on provincial policy consistency with, as Sylvia Sutherland said in a recent decision about intensification, a degree of reasonableness. These can be addressed by different approaches to tenure, remuneration and selection process, as will the concerns over the hearing model employed by the OMB and inequality of resources, but there must be the will of the government and the public and the tribunal itself to bring about these changes. The examples of Markham and some other municipalities such

"… there must be the will by the government and the public and the tribunal itself to bring about these changes."

as Waterloo with their acceptance of the higher than policy-required target for intensification and concrete steps already taken to achieve that target on the ground – examples like these demonstrate that governments can act against popular opinion where there is a will, where there is effective public education and where it is addressed in the spirit of community. But is that enough to build a new jurisdiction based on municipal control of the planning process? In my view, if taken alone, it is not. However, the new recognition of municipalities as a government level of its own requires to be dealt with. The continued need for a provincial tribunal to review and oversee land use policy implementation and adjudicate and mediate cases of conflict is clear. But it cannot be on the same terms and working conditions.

I will provide in Chapter XII my thoughts on the process and new focus of a new or renewed tribunal. The driver of change will be the standard of excellence that must be maintained in future by a specialized tribunal with the range of interest, authority, and discretion that this one has; it is one of the few instances of direct intersection of administrative and municipal law with democracy. The tribunal should have the opportunity to take the initiative to control its workload better. The preconditions to this happening must be a full complement of mediator-planners and mediator-lawyers and other members with a range of job-related experience on the tribunal.

I would prefer that the name this Board has carried since 1932, and substantively since 1906, be changed. The name of the tribunal should be suited to the times we live in and must incorporate all the facets of the tribunal's work, from land use planning, municipal law, land compensation and public policy, planning education, principles of evidence and a large hearing/mediation presence and coordination. One idea is the Planning Appeals and Compensation Tribunal using the acronym PACT to underline its future and greater emphasis on mediation. However, the question whether there is a need for a name change or not, I leave to others to assess. No doubt if there is such a need, the public and those who are its stakeholders will sense it and act on it.

CHAPTER XII

PLANNING AND COMPENSATION TRIBUNAL:
A CENTRE FOR MEDIATION AND ADJUDICATION ("PACT")

Maria: Between the brain that plans and the hands that build there must be a mediator. It is the heart that must bring about an understanding between them.
A worker: But where is our mediator, Maria?
Maria: Be patient, he will surely come.
from Metropolis
—T. von Harbou and F. Lang, 1927

The following recommendations are mine and mine alone. They encapsulate the changes in statutory conditions, appointment conditions, and other factors which, in my opinion, are necessary to allow the land use planning review and compensation tribunal to provide the service that the public of Ontario is entitled to.

It is also my view that, given the deficiency in numbers, quality of service and of decisions, lack of deliberation and decision-writing time, and lack of skills diversity on the OMB, if the present conditions are to be the norm in the future , the government should terminate the tribunal now.

There should be either an effective provincial appeals and compensation tribunal (whether the decision is to retain the title "Ontario Municipal Board (OMB)" or not) capable of providing the consistent leadership in applying provincial, growth and other planning policies, or leave the planning implementation and land use conflicts to the municipalities with appeal to the Superior Court of Justice. The equivalent of the Commercial List could be put in place by that court for planning and expropriation appeals. The continuance of the present slow decay of this once respected tribunal, the OMB, should be unacceptable to the public and the planning and municipal professions.

The recommendations include the important commitment that the Province will elect to fund, and use selection procedures to form, a competent tribunal adequate to the leadership duties in policy application and adjudication to carry on its appellate and oversight functions with consistency in a sustainable planning process, and in the development charge and expropriation compensation areas.

THE RECOMMENDATIONS

1. MEDIATION AND PARTICIPATORY PLANNING

The main thrust of all my recommendations must be to turn this new appeals/adjudicative tribunal from its primary purpose as a quasi-judicial hearing body to one having the predominant purpose of mediation and consensus-building. A hearing will follow only if mediation fails. The tribunal will still provide hearings as the ultimate and final stage of its work; at the start, it must be so, until the selection process as reformed can recruit and put in place sufficient and necessary mediation-trained professionals and other municipal and planning-related careerists of stature. For some planning matters and for unresolved land compensation matters, a hearing using a hybrid hearing model will be required where all mediation attempts have failed.

Ultimately, hearings on the planning side will no longer be the central core and raison d'être of the tribunal. The central spark that will provide the dynamism for the tribunal will be its role as a mediation and conflict resolution centre for those persons, municipalities, corporations, governments, farming organizations and co-ops, interest organizations and neighbourhood groups, and individuals in conflict over land use planning, land use policy, zoning regulation, development permits, development charge principles and calculation issues, and expropriation compensation matters.

This direction has already been started under the leadership of prior Executive Chairs, Marie Hubbard, Michael Gottheil and Lynda Tanaka, and the insistent determination of the recently retired Associate Chair of the Ontario Municipal Board, Wilson Lee. I am sure it will reach new heights under Executive Chair Dr. Bruce Krushelnicki who is well aware of the unique requirements and responsibilities capable of being delivered by this tribunal. I am less sure of his commitment to the kind of change in overall focus to mediation, and the energizing potential and meaning of that change. His first recommended appointments are all people with qualifications in environmental planning and law, not mediation or conflict resolution. Land use planning matters raise issues beyond the limits of a purely adversarial approach and comprise the polycentric realities of modern planning required for our communities of today. Every recommendation of mine must be understood as being inspired by and infused within this purpose of a mediation centre aimed at resolving, through discussion and expert mediatory guidance and planning realism, our disagreements and conflicts and being freed to come together in order to construct more creative and healthy communities with a human scale and diversity.

I have heard loud and clear that the bar, land use planners and other participants in the Board process all see mediation as the major requirement for this tribunal as it heads to the future. It is clearly time that this Board becomes a major land use planning and compensation mediation centre. New appointments must include, as a priority, at least six to eight persons who are mediation trained, have a related career field, and can go through the new member review successfully.

> "Appreciative Inquiry (AI) is a method for studying and changing social systems (groups, organizations, communities) that advocates collective inquiry into the best of what is in order to imagine what could be, followed by collective design of a desired future state that is compelling and thus, does not require the use of incentives, coercion or persuasion for planned change to occur." —E. H. Kessler, *Encyclopedia of Management Theory (2013)*

> "It is beyond time that the language and the mindset become open to ideas, ready to discuss new ideas ... and look at what the concepts are that can help to make our communities and province even more vibrant."

The cases will still be called for hearing from the main hearing list. The difference will be that at the pre-hearing conference, the counsel and the parties are to be ready for mandatory mediation sessions. Parties and counsel will either agree on a focused list of issues; or the Board will set the list of the issues in the case, i.e. not all the subsidiary issues but the ones that would determine the hearing. All parties and the tribunal will attempt to resolve the issues one by one, through discussion and expert mediatory guidance and planning realism but always within the range of reasonable planning principles. Any issues left outstanding after all reasonable steps to resolve them have been taken will then be determined by the hearing process. It is beyond time that the language and the mindset become open to ideas, ready to discuss new ideas, stop talking about density and height in the abstract, and look at what the concepts are that can help to make our communities and province even more vibrant than they are. Protection must be afforded to what is vital in the rural/agricultural areas, special geographic regions, and places of importance to Indigenous peoples and to all of us. The first essential must be to change the entire dynamic of communication away from the adversarial 'they and us' approach and try to see what all interested parties can achieve if all are open to the appreciative inquiry process, and all are listening and engaged. I am hoping that as experience builds, at least 97–98 per cent will be settled through mediation.

The adversarial process will be the alternative for the cases that will always be intractable, requiring evidence tested by cross-examination and where a decision between two irreconcilable planning directions must be made.

It is time for another culture change.

2. A POLICY OF MANDATORY MEDIATION BEFORE AND DURING A HEARING

The tribunal is first and foremost an instrument to build consensus, to ensure that parties and the interested members of the public understand the limitations and the remedies that the tribunal can properly provide, and then to begin to talk. It must be understood that any mediated settlement must meet the test of reasonable proximity to the intent of the OP and consistency with the Provincial Policy Statement (2014). Subject to that condition, the presumptive process to resolve matters shall be mediation for any case that comes on for hearing. All parties must come to the hearing or pre-hearing ready to find a solution through mediation and prepared to consider all options and to make final decisions with assistance from professional assistants and legal counsel who must be available at all times during the hearing time for consultation. Any unreasonable delay or bad faith conduct shall be considered, as with any conduct that prolongs matters unnecessarily, in an award of costs if requested.

With regard to the adversarial nature of tribunal hearings, there continues to be a place for a structured hearing where each witness is examined, cross-examined and reexamined, but not until all attempts to successfully mediate the matter have been unsuccessful.

The following guidelines are recommended to apply when the tribunal is settling the directions for the hearing at a pre-hearing conference. They are a suggested first step, subject to refinement or modification as required.

i. All cases except for short minor variance and severance appeals shall undergo at least one mediation process within the Board before it is scheduled for hearing.

ii. If the first session did not produce a final resolution, the panel assigned to the case shall determine if the case will benefit from another attempt or attempts at mediation, and in each case it shall be left to the assigned panel alone to determine the next step, after hearing submissions from interested parties or their legal counsel. Only when the panel finds that further positive results will not be achieved through mediation shall the case be sent to the hearing room for a pre-hearing conference.

iii.　At the pre-hearing conference, where a final issues list has not been arrived at, the Panel shall determine the essential issues to be focused on after consulting counsel for the parties. There may be many sub-issues, but this list should include the principal issues. This determination would be those issues, disposition of which would conclude the hearing, and any sub-issues arising from them, which should take more than 2.5 hours to hear. If the parties cannot agree, the panel shall make the determination of the issues after consultations with counsel and unrepresented parties in the tribunal's sole discretion and it shall bind all parties at the hearing. The tribunal, with the assistance of counsel will determine which issues could benefit from further mediation and which require a hearing. A date will be set for further mediation, provided the panel can find no attempt to delay. A date will be set for the filing of all witness statements, the earlier date for the appellants' witnesses and the later date for the respondents' witnesses. "Witnesses" include the parties themselves. A witness may not be heard unless the witness statement is filed for that witness within the time ordered.

iv.　The chair of the pre-hearing conference shall check on each case held under his or her presidency to ensure that all filings are carried out in accordance with the order. Failing compliance, the case shall be called up before the same presiding member where, after hearing briefly from all counsel and the party in default, if necessary, the member shall determine if the appeal shall be dismissed, or the terms on which it proceeds further.

v.　The witness statement shall be filed as evidence and shall be the party's direct examination of the witness. For expert witnesses, compliance with rule 53.03 of the Rules of Civil Procedure is required and the filing dates shall be established at the pre-hearing conference.

vi.　Total wait time from mediation to hearing shall not exceed 120 days. Notice shall be given to the Attorney General if this condition is not able to be met so that the government can take action to ensure that it will be met in short order. This is now an appellate tribunal. The tribunal has the right and the duty to require the appellant to demonstrate the merits of the appeal, failing which the tribunal shall dismiss the appeal.

vii.　At the hearing, the list of issues with their detailed resolution terms settled in mediation shall be filed by the party having carriage and confirmed by all parties. The panel must first determine whether the agreed terms of these settled issues are sufficient for an order and if not, order the parties and counsel to arrive at an effective set of settled terms forthwith.

viii. After the opening addresses by the parties, the appellant's or appellants' evidence shall be heard first. The panel shall have read the complete record and all late expert reports and council's return remarks completed prior to the opening of the hearing. The presiding member will have the right and duty to call upon the appellant to show grounds for the appeal and, if necessary, to hear from the respondent in reply, following which the panel may dismiss the appeal for lack of planning grounds.

ix. Where possible, counsel shall organize their witnesses in panels by subject matter or by process or by such other factor as the panel is advised by counsel The counsel shall have the witness identify the statement and have it marked as evidence, and may question the witness first to cover any updating since the filing of the witness statement.

x. The questioning will proceed with the appellant or counsel having the witness identify the witness statement and entering it in evidence. Opposing counsel and self-represented parties only may then cross-examine the witness.

xi. In every instance during a hearing, the panel shall direct the most expedient and fair way to proceed, including use of witness panels whenever there is a common connector between witnesses and questioning by the panel.

xii. The panel or the member designated to write, shall be given time to deliberate and write the decision. The decision should be ready for release within two months of the end of the hearing.

3. PLANNING RECOMMENDATIONS

A.   Appeal Limitations on Official Plan and Zoning Amendments

The appeal provisions shall remain as in the present *Planning Act* with the following exceptions:

1.   Appeals from a municipal adoption of a new OP will be limited to the following grounds:

a. that the OP or part of it does not come within the description in section 16 of the *Planning Act* or within the said Act read as a whole;

b. the proposed OP fails reasonably to carry out the intent of the Provincial Policy Statement (PPS) (2014) or other statutory planning document in the policy hierarchy that applies to the land (See clause 3.A (6) below); or

c. the application of a policy or policies of the OP or the OPA identified in the notice of appeal to particular lands described in the notice is not appropriate or necessary to the accomplishment of the goals and objectives of the OP and the PPS.

2. The following are also recommended for statutory and rule change authorization:

a. No appeal shall be allowed from a by-law that brings the site or area zoning into conformity with the PPS (2014) and/or the OP, or to comply with an order of the provincial appeals tribunal;

b. No appeal shall be allowed from a refusal or failure of council to act within the statutory time where the proposed OP or zoning amendment is not in conformity with the PPS or the criteria for OPs;

c. Any question as to whether a matter is one for which no appeal is permitted shall be decided summarily by the tribunal on motion brought and returnable within 25 days of the decision or termination of the refusal period for leave to appeal: on a close case, the onus of showing that the appeal does not come within clause 1.a,b,or c is to be on the party opposing the right to appeal on the civil standard of proof; and

d. The tribunal should have sufficient numbers to have the capacity to assist municipalities who request special assistance from the tribunal to obtain that assistance and enable the tribunal chair to appoint a panel to enquire into and investigate a planning issue with which the municipality requires assistance and has not the staff sufficient to carry out the enquiry itself. The Chair shall provide written reasons within one week of the request why such a request was refused.

COMMENT

Regarding the OP, I have seen that in several jurisdictions that provide appeal from planning decisions, no appeals are allowed as of right from the OP or the municipal strategy as it is referred to in Nova Scotia. OPs are described in the *Planning Act,* section 16:

16. (1) An official plan shall contain,

(a) goals, objectives and policies established primarily to manage and direct physical change and the effects on the social, economic, built and natural environment of the municipality or part of it, or an area that is without municipal organization;

(b) a description of the measures and procedures for informing and obtaining the views of the public in respect of,

(i) proposed amendments to the official plan or proposed revisions of the plan,

(ii) proposed zoning by-laws,

(iii) proposed plans of subdivision, and

(iv) proposed consents under section 53; and

(c) such other matters as may be prescribed. 2015, c. 26, s. 17.

(2) An official plan may contain,

(a) a description of the measures and procedures proposed to attain the objectives of the plan;

(b) a description of the measures and procedures for informing and obtaining the views of the public in respect of planning matters not mentioned in clause (1) (b); and

(c) such other matters as may be prescribed. 2015, c. 26, s. 17.

The recommendations in paragraphs 3.A.1 and 2 attempt to recognize the OP as an important expression of the municipality through its elected officials within the parameters set by section 16 of the Planning Act. The OP expresses the municipality's planning goals, objectives and policies for dealing in the future with the matters in subsection (1): to manage and direct physical change; and to manage and direct the effects on the environment, human, economic and natural.

It is time that the right of appeal from OPs should no longer be unrestricted. It is always the right of a property owner affected by the OP to oppose part of an OP as it affects his or her property . Parties do not require a tribunal to do so. The corollary to this change is that the process provision in the *Planning Act* shall be revisited to require definite steps that municipalities are to take before adopting an OP that are transparent, open, and accessible by the inhabitants.

If amendments to an OP are desired, any affected owner or resident can make a presentation to the council following two years from adoption of the new OP. The council can dispense with this delay in any case it chooses under the provisions that came into effect following the passing of Bill 73 on December 3, 2015 – the *Smart Growth for our Communities Act, 2015*. It is the council's right to deal with such requests, subject to appeal to the provincial tribunal within the policy framework put in place by the municipality and the Province and to the appropriate application of policy to particular lands within the municipality. This restriction of appellate rights is subject to the use of common sense approaches by the tribunal and consistent application of policy by the tribunal where a planning case in principle is similar to other planning cases previously decided, unless the tribunal finds an error in law in the prior ruling.

A right of appeal is to be left in place for any landowner to appeal the application of the OP to that owner's property and to instigate a hearing where grounds exist to require a hearing to deal with the issue, in addition to the rights of appeal under clauses A.1.a or b. The intent of this restriction is to allow the policies of the OP to come into force across the whole municipal area, subject only to consistency with provincial policy and the requirements of the Planning Act and to the appropriateness of their application to the specific lots or areas under appeal. This would still allow a land-specific attack on the policy itself as it applies to the tract under appeal.

Regarding the limited changes in paragraphs A.2. a and b above, I see them as necessary to allow councils to rezone or redesignate land in order to bring their planning laws and strategies into line with the PPS without having to undergo an expensive tribunal hearing where the result should be pretty obvious. In each case, the plan adoption and any amendment would have resulted in notice and an appeal hearing if any change in planning for the area were in the works.

Subparagraph 2.d is proposed to assist smaller municipalities where they require such assistance, and also to provide a resource to any municipality facing a serious problem requiring investigation. The tribunal should be available to assist through its investigative powers in The OMB Act issues of importance to the municipality or to the development of planning and municipal law in Ontario.

The following is a suggested program to ensure as full input as possible into the OP process:
- There should be an open meeting at the start;

- A first draft done of the OP, and notice provided
- Hold a second meeting open to the public or series of meetings by area
- Minutes must be taken of each.
- Planning staff should then do a final draft of it and take it to council and follow council's instructions for further work if they agree with provincial policy.
- The meeting to adopt the plan should again be on public notice and all who wish to be heard, should be.
- The planning staff should complete its final report to council at least two weeks prior to the council meeting to consider adoption. That report should recommend adoption or ask for direction if further work is required with a schedule to complete to adoption.

B.   Standard of Review by the Provincial Tribunal of Councils' Decisions

I recommend that the *Planning Act* be amended to allow appeals from a planning decision of council only if the appellant can show that the decision of council does not reasonably carry out the intent of the OP or the PPS then in force under the Planning Act

COMMENT

The above recommendation amounts to a suggested course of action. I only ask that it be considered because I cannot give it the full study and testing from different points of view that it requires; however, it is based on a thoughtful paper by a Masters student released in 2012 by Ryerson University.[211] It appears to be a common sense answer to a troubled area of the OMB's jurisdiction. Because the standard of review would probably result in a lower number of tribunal hearings, it should provide motivation to councillors to vote on the merits of proposals. The alternative would mean losing the benefits that some proposals may offer the municipality as an appeal hearing will be less likely to succeed.

The present standard of review used by the Ontario Municipal Board is derived from the Court of Appeal decision in *Hopedale*.[212] It has become somewhat subjective, produces variable results, and is prone to public criticism and cynicism because the decision often appears to come out of an unlimited discretion without accountability for it. It also makes the whole process that the appellant went through seem pointless when citizens do not understand how and why the decision was made. The suggestion that appeals should be limited to those from council decisions that fail to reasonably carry out the intent of the OP and provincial policy statement puts in place an objective examination of the path of reasoning to the decision. Coupled with the principles of procedural fairness, they would produce an analysis of substance and procedure that grants deference to council for choices made between acceptable alternatives while still allowing appeals to succeed that represent poor planning within the policy framework in place, without a reasonably proximate relation to the intent of the OP, stated provincial policy and the growth plan.

The reasonableness standard is well known to lawyers and the court as the formative factor in a review of a tribunal's decision. The question for the Board in each case would become:

> Does the decision of the council reasonably carry out the intent of the official plan and of provincial policy in the PPS (and any other provincial plan that applies to the subject area)?

This change merely brings the planning appeals tribunal into line with the appeal court's standard of review and should expedite the system; at the same time it should produce timely results where attempted justification by lengthy coverage of expert opinion evidence to attempt to shore up what is really a value choice, will be in vain. It should produce results that, if not in council's favour, will let the appeal result rest on the shoulders of the council for making a choice that was not reasonably open to it.

C. Site-specific Zoning By-law Appeals

Where a site-specific zoning amendment with no issues of provincial or extra-municipal interest is involved, I was prepared to recommend that there was no need to involve a provincial appeals tribunal in the decision-making process regarding that by-law. However, I cannot make such a recommendation because it is still this tribunal, on appeal by persons dissatisfied with the decision of the council, that provides on an ongoing basis for the application of the rule of law, rules of procedural fairness referred to by the Supreme Court of Canada in *Baker v Canada*, and a reasonable standard of justice. Decisions of municipal councils are sometimes politicized and that comment applies as much, if not as often, to other local councils as it does to the City of Toronto. A land use review tribunal is particularly important for zoning by-laws and amendments because their affect in law is immediate.

As W.D. "Rusty" Russell said, from his long experience with smaller town and township councils (echoed by Alan Patton whose practice takes him through much of southwestern Ontario and other counsel who have collectively had dealings with councils from the smallest to the largest):

> You know, without the OMB, councils do strange things about votes. You get one councillor voting for a rezoning because he owes a vote to another councillor; they made a deal and he did not know at the time what he would be voting on ... I believe the OMB is the accountability factor – it brings matters out in the open. You have to prove your case."[213]

I am therefore not recommending any further changes in zoning appeal rights.

I see the need, in the interests of fundamental justice, for the right of appeal to the OMB to continue in zoning and other planning matters, except where the by-law's purpose is solely to bring the zoning into line with provincial policy or the municipal OP or where the local council's refusal or failure to respond to a development application concerns an application that lacks any consistency with provincial policy.

D.   Minor Variance and Consent Appeals

Section 8.1 of the *Planning Act* allows municipalities to appoint a local appeal body if it meets certain conditions. By subsection (6), the council may by by-law empower the local appeal body to hear appeals under subsection 45(12)(a). Section 45(12)(a) permits appeals from decisions on minor variances by the committee of adjustment.

By enacting section 8.1, the Legislature has stated its intention that minor variance appeals are to be handled locally in due course. I see no need to add anything beyond this acknowledgement of the legislative intent.

The appeal to Divisional Court under section 8.1 is at present only with leave on a question of law. This is the same as appeals from the OMB. That provision is too narrow. I do not think that that is wise, at least for the first five years. Appeals from the local appeal body should be on a wider basis than from the Board, especially at the beginning when such appeal bodies will need direction on individual appeals and the application of the factors from section 45(1). This is not as necessary if the appeals remained with the Board, which is well aware of the tests for variances and what is minor in the circumstances. I wrote in Chapter VI the following in discussing minor variance appeals:

> All that this is intended to do is to make the point that if planning law and planning issues are important, and I believe they are, they require the kind of serious consideration on a long range and distanced basis that a specialized provincial tribunal (can provide).

This excerpt was part of a discussion of zoning by-laws appeals as well as variance appeals. It seems to me that the minor variance is one place where the expense of an OMB hearing, and the fact that the applications should affect matters that the community will be well aware of and can bring their own local perspective to the matter, outweigh my concern. If some decision occurs that seems to be out of line, perhaps a favour being paid, the appeal to the Divisional Court should exercise a preventive function. The municipality should have a right of appeal whether or not it appeared on the original application because the intent of the local OP is one test of a variance and the municipality has an interest in that interpretation.

I am not recommending that appeals from severance decisions (i.e. consents, using the language of the *Planning Act*) also be removed from the tribunal. They raise distinct concerns, especially where the application concerns land in agriculturally protected areas or on private rights of way. Those appeals should continue to go to the provincial tribunal under the Planning Act. However, I understand that the legislature appears to be persuaded to allow them to go to a local appeal body.

I do not have a breakdown of the severance and variance appeals brought together and separately. Whichever is true or not, I do not see a sufficient reason to allow severance appeals to be removed from the Board. Every new residential lot in rural areas and in some urban areas has an impact and can serve, if not as a precedent (because committees and tribunals do not have binding precedents), as an argument for the next one. As in some rural township councils who wonder why they have lost lands to urban areas, someday the diverse land use quality of what used to be a rural municipality can make it vulnerable to being absorbed within the urban boundary on the next review.

4. SECTION 37, PLANNING ACT RECOMMENDATION:

This proposal is one that has been made to the City of Toronto Act Review. Its effect would be to divide the council of 44 ward councillors into 22 councillors elected by the combining each set of two wards into one ward. The other 22 councillors would be elected at large based on the four present community council districts. They would be called District Councillors (DCs):

North District to elect	6 DCs
South District to elect	6 DCs
East District to elect	5 DCs
West District to elect	5DCs

Total 22 DCs

COMMENT

This proposal is brought forward as a corrective to the present ward-based structure in Toronto in order to provide councillors who are elected from a wider area than one ward, and who can bring a wider perspective to bear on all issues that involve the wider city interests. For the issue with which we are concerned – section 37 of the *Planning Act* and bonus height/density benefits, District Councillors(DCs) would be enabled to oversee and scrutinize decisions by the ward councillor, like the one involving funds allocated to the local library garden, in order to ask and answer the question whether the ward councillor's decision would constitute the wisest use of the funds in terms of the public interest in the City as a whole, as well as the area in question. That question is not even asked or considered today beyond the ward level.

This recommendation is made to ensure that those considering this kind of electoral restructuring keep in mind the improved process this would mean to the quantification and allocation of *Planning Act* section 37 funds. This restructuring should be coupled with an OPA setting out the process as to how quantification and allocation would be dealt with in each case under section 37 and that the reasons and the decision must be made public as part of the by-law enabling the project in question. The present OP policy does not address the process with the specificity intended by the *Planning Act*. The public should know that planning is not being done simply on the basis of the cash register or the auction block but that the funds have a direct relation to the proposed development, such as ameliorating an impact from the proposal which could assist those living nearby, or could enable a service of benefit to the ward and the city as a whole.

It is not my intention of preempting in any way the responsibilities of those employed with the City of Toronto Act Review.

5. *APPOINTMENT RECOMMENDATIONS*

(a)There are basically two answers to the remuneration question in relation to the OMB. Both mean an increase in salary because there has to be recognition of this Board's historic role and its present responsibilities for conflict resolution, adjudication, and decisions on a ministerial level directed to the public interest with a sufficient discretion to carry out that responsibility.

One is in response to the present deficit budgeting that is necessary for this and another year. It was Mr. Lee's view that one could run the Board successfully for a time with fewer members, provided you had the number of mediation-trained professionals necessary to bring about a mandatory mediation program. Most of the list would be resolved in this way and the remaining members would preside over the hearings caused by the tough cases that would not settle. Then gradually increase the Board to its optimum size which no longer needs to be in the 30 range, provided a serious effort to appoint mediation-trained professionals from related careers is acted on.

The other response means bringing the OMB up to full strength in full-time members so they can do their jobs effectively, with at least two on any panel where a council's decision is in question and three where required. The members must have regular times when they are off the schedule to write their decisions with time for members to properly consider them and start raiding their salary to the proper level. At least one-quarter to one-third of the 28 members should be trained mediators with conflict resolution experience and with experience in municipal or provincial planning, law, or other related disciplines. This background is vital because settlement terms must meet the tests of consistency with the provincial and local planning policies. More than just settling cases is involved here.

The effects of the decisions of this tribunal last for several generations into the future. Members are entrusted to decide in the public interest and consider issues of long-lasting effect. The one thing that all research critics of the OMB agree is that its decisions have serious and long term consequences. In the early 1980s, the salary was similar to that of the Provincial Court, then in the approximate amount of $80,000 to $90,000 per year. Over subsequent years, the court's salary level became much higher, pulled by the merger of the court system toward the Superior Court scale, and the tribunal's salary scale was frozen much of the time at around $90,000 to $110,000. For members, it is now in the area of $110,000 and over $130,000 for Vice-Chairs. This is, for the range of knowledge, responsibility, and experience required, shockingly low. It is less than a salary scale for a justice of the peace whose jurisdiction is narrowly confined.

I have already dealt with the perennial reply that government always gives – that we have no shortage of applicants when a position with the OMB comes available and is posted. That is a smug and altogether unsatisfactory attitude because it uses the current membership of the Board as satisfactory when it is far from it and the work product shows it, as I have demonstrated earlier from the comments of users of the Board and from some examples of the work itself.

All of this underlines the importance of this tribunal. The consequences become urgent for local and regional planning if they are produced by members who do not reflect the best in their disciplines. It must be made up of good committed and qualified people from a related diversity of professions and at least one member of the interested public who has an affinity and understanding of the work of the tribunal. To get professional persons of stature and ability when they are in their middle years and retain energy and ambition (and not only those retired from public life or older retired professionals), requires a new look at remuneration in context with the benefits offered, and that I have done. I cannot see how good people with at least some recognized contributions to their field can be recruited for the tribunal unless an increase in the salary scale from one below that of a locomotive engineer or an above average plumber to a scale in the range of $175,000 to $200,000 per year, or the corresponding level of salary in the civil service, plus a public service pension and the usual ancillary employee benefits.

(b) I recommend that the term of service be lengthened to six years, to be renewed unless cause is shown for non-renewal. The first two years could be a probationary period, to ensure that the person was as suited to the job as (s)he thought and that the OMB was not surprised by any unexpected eccentricities or problems that were beyond the acceptable. I know of no one knowledgeable of all the requirements of the job who can show that it takes fewer than 5–6 years to become familiar with and confident of one's ability to do all facets of the job required of a member of this tribunal to at least a reasonably acceptable level.

(c) I recommend that any posting or employment with this tribunal must target members of professions related to the wide expanse of knowledge encompassed by the requirements of this tribunal. Comment is to be solicited from the professional society, association or other organization that is responsible for setting the standard of the profession in question. Those areas or experience shall include planning and/or municipal law, mediation (especially associated with law and planning and land valuation), land use planning, municipal engineer, architect, urban design planning, municipal accounting, land appraisal, and one exceptional member of the lay public who can show an adaptability to this kind of public service. All member requirements shall be posted online and updated as required, including vacancies.

(d)I recommend that the Environmental Review Board and the Board of Negotiation merge with the OMB or the new land use/compensation tribunal to become one board, transition time to be 6–12 months.

COMMENT (A) TO (D):

I have considered the salary level of people at the assistant deputy to deputy minister level in ministries like Municipal Affairs and Housing and the Attorney General and a tribunal like the Financial Services Tribunal (FSC). That is a range, according to the 2013 salary levels, made public recently, of between $175,000 at the Assistant Deputy Minister level, and $213,000 at the Deputy Minister level in 2013. Using the increase in the Consumer Price Index, I calculated that these ranges translated to $181,128 and $220,459 per year in 2015. I would recommend a blend of these figures at a conservative level of $175,000 to $200,000.

I am aware that Ontario Court judges are paid a good deal more but they are judges with constitutional recognition. I do not see that this is a realistic expectation for members of any tribunal. Given that people in mid-career in law or in planning often are not in a corporate pension plan provided by employment, I think it would be realistic to suggest remuneration at the $175,000 to $200,000 level. It must be high enough to attract good people who want to change mid-career from planning and mediation, law, architecture or urban design or municipal accounting or engineering to a career in the public service adjudicating a wide range of cases on the tribunal, and, because it involves the benefit of a pension, such people might well find this attractive enough to leave their current careers. It should be stressed that the salary must be up to this level or the tribunal will continue to get more of what it is getting now: largely people whose primary career is over, receiving a pension and can use some extra money for a rather short term.

I strongly suggest to those responsible for selection of members to be demanding. Members with an ability to command respect and with excellent communication skills as well as first-rate mediation skills are, or should be, the priority.

As a temporary alternative in view of the current salary freeze right now, the initial need is for mediation-trained professionals. There are a number of mediation firms that could supply five to six mediators with planning or other related professional qualifications for a limited time as part of a contract, at the end of which the understanding would be that members would be employed at a salary commensurate with the level of responsibility and discretion and governance that the job entails, being the level I have suggested or its equivalent at that time. Or any hiring in the near future would be at current salary levels on the understanding that within three years, the Province will raise members' salaries to the increased remuneration level. That is the approximate time by which Provincial budgeting assumes Ontario will no longer be on a deficit basis. In the end, the OMB's requirements and responsibilities to act in the public interest on zoning and OPA matters, which have lasting consequences, must be recognized in relation to remuneration.

The other alternative is to bring members into line with the ADM/DM blended salary levels but reduce the full-time complement of members to fourteen to fifteen. On the departure dates of the ten-year plus members as their terms end, the selection process priority must be to engage five to six persons with planning or municipal-related experience who are trained mediators. If the recommended restriction on OP appeals is used and minor variances appeals are taken into the municipal process, the reduced level should allow the five to six mediators to deal with the mandatory and voluntary mediation. The remaining members, as they turn over to more qualified persons targeted by the new selection process, would deal with the defended cases.[214]

The recommendations listed above only scrape the surface but they do accomplish that much. These together can represent a re-established land use appeals and compensation tribunal, which can serve the public by dealing with cases in the public interest and by bringing to finality disputes over unreasonable impacts like noise, waste or commercial glare. It will become the prime hub of municipal and planning law jurisprudence and a centre for successful mediation which will keep the hearing delays under control.

The renewed tribunal must be a specialized tribunal with the expertise that the courts expect; that, it has not been in the recent past. It must be a group that has the individual confidence to overcome ego and understand the importance of consultation and discussion of new policy issues within the principle established by *IWA v Consolidated Bathurst*.[215]

If it were not to reach the membership levels of past decades, then the jurisdiction of the Board should be cut back to reduce the workload and keep membership levels to a total of twenty to twenty-four members with remuneration fitting to their responsibilities. Somehow the present assumptions must be destroyed – for instance, that it will take five to ten years for a major city planning document to be approved, or that twelve months for issuance of a compensation decision is acceptable. The OMB must function as an appeal tribunal, no longer *de novo*. By high quality mediation and focused hearings led by knowledgeable members who no longer need to keep hold of files to be assured that at least a brief renewal might occur, this provincial land use tribunal can be the asset to the Province that all stakeholders want and need to see.

The nettle of job security and undistinguished remuneration must be grasped in order to rise above the routine candidates who will settle for less today. Excellence must become the standard and if the planning process in this province is to be all that it can be, that means a great deal more in values of fairness, effectiveness and fact-based policy-consistent decision-making, than those states and provinces without such assets can provide. The government that has the enlightened farsightedness to act will demonstrate what the *Planning Act* means by being "led by provincial policy." The planning and compensation tribunal will indeed assist the province in this goal, instead of several hundred fiefdoms of municipal interpretation of provincial policy without any thought for the broader public interest.

6. FUND TO ASSIST PARTICIPATION

On many appeals, residents, neighbourhood associations and disadvantaged communities need financial assistance to hire a planning expert and legal representation just to be able to participate on a closer to equal footing than is now the case. Funding would have to depend on a low threshold test of merit to the appeal.

The government should arrange, together with the Ontario Professional Planners Institute and other interested groups in the development industry, for the funding of planning assistance to disadvantaged individuals or communities in a manner similar to the assistance given through CELA; that is, to assist low income individuals and disadvantaged communities across Ontario in planning law matters. CELA was established in 1970, funded as an Ontario specialty legal aid clinic since 1978, and incorporated as a not-for-profit corporation without share capital pursuant to the laws of Canada in 1982, providing legal aid services to the community without fees for service. CELA services include environmental law legal services, including representation before a variety of courts and tribunals as well as assistance to individuals representing themselves, summary advice, law reform and public legal education.

It is important to any municipality that cares about equality before the law for its own citizens. The building and urban development industry should especially be involved in seeing that help is available where there is some planning merit to the position of the applicant for funding. It is not necessary or appropriate for me to suggest how this fund could be financed. With all the excellent minds in the executive branch and in the development industry, represented by organizations like the Urban Land Institute, the Building Industry and Land Development Association and the Ontario Homebuilders Association, there should be no shortage of ideas. Certainly the development industry should be able to pay a levy on each development application of a value over a certain base level as part of funding this initiative.

> "It is beyond time that action be taken by government and individuals or organizations on this front. Fundamental principles of the rule of law are involved in this endeavour."

It is beyond time that action be taken by government and individuals or organizations on this front. Fundamental principles of the rule of law are involved in this endeavour.

In the event that the stakeholders are not able to establish an ongoing fund to assist cases with some merit, I recommend that the province give the tribunal the power to order intervener or proponent funding for groups of persons potentially affected by the proposed development, where the case has a reasonable degree of merit.

7. CONSULTATION RECOMMENDATION

The minister, before issuing a Provincial Policy Statement shall confer with the Executive Chair of ELTO, the Associate Chair of the Ontario Municipal Board, and the designated representative of the Association of Municipalities of Ontario (AMO) in addition to any other persons or bodies considered having an interest.

COMMENT

It seems to me that the Minister should always consult with the principal Chairs of ELTO as the heads of the cluster and the tribunal involved in municipal planning issues, and AMO for the Ontario municipal government interest. The tribunal is a valuable resource to the Minister and ministry planning officials in terms of the effective articulation and use of provincial planning statements. It has an institutional memory for the mistakes of the past and for avoiding them; before issuance of a policy statement, mutual consultations by the Minister with the ELTO and tribunal Chairs and AMO concerning new provincial policy statements can only benefit all parties in the execution of their duties in the public interest of this Province.

This in no way implies any diminution of authority of the Minister under the *Planning Act* over provincial policy. It is consistent with the consultative duties of the government with AMO that are set out in the *Municipal Act, 2001*, section 3(1): "... the Province shall consult with municipalities in accordance with a memorandum of understanding entered into between the Province and the Association of Municipalities of Ontario." And this amendment is necessary because the Minister has to this date never taken advantage of the asset that such consultation provides for the making of effective policy.

8. THE MEDIA RECOMMENDATION

This is an urgent need of the OMB because it covers areas of law that few know. It is vital that a media official be briefed before the release of any decision in which there has been more than usual public interest. This will provide the media officer with a chance to read the decision and to talk to the Associate Chair or the duty Vice-Chair about the different levels of decision in the case. The policy issues as well as the external building issues shall be the subject of the briefing. The officer should notify the media office in short order to set a time for a press briefing the following day immediately after the decision is released. The significance of the case to the development of planning or real property or Municipal Law should be front and centre as well as any particular difficulties in arriving at the decision should be highlighted.

The Ministry of Municipal Affairs and Housing seems the more obvious choice because it is more involved in the land use and appraisal world but I don't know what issues this would raise with the Attorney General's Ministry. The OMB is administratively within the Attorney

General's structure but that ministry shows absolutely no interest in the OMB. Its Media Relations site is taken up with court cases and services to victims of crime, not assisting tribunals like the OMB. Yet, it probably affects more people. If at all possible, it is a much better fit to have OMB releases done through the Municipal Affairs and Housing media umbrella.

ACKNOWLEDGEMENTS

This book came out of an invitation to address the Ontario Municipal Board members in 2015. I could not help noticing that the members present, even assuming a few absentees, did not come close to the size of the Board when I had been part of it in the 1980s. I found out from the Associate Chair that the Board was now operating with a membership less than half the full-time strength that it had three decades earlier. I heard of the difficulties this has presented for the current members and for the credibility of this tribunal, causing delays and decision-making problems that were confirmed by a couple of conversations with Board practitioners. I had been looking for a subject to write about and I decided one day in June 2015 to take on what I thought would be a periodical article.

The first person who deserves mention is Ian Lord. Although we have never known each other, he took up the invitation to read and provide comment on the draft manuscript without hesitation and assisted me greatly with his vast knowledge of planning law and mediation, as well as the Board decisions through his work as editor and now Editor-in-Chief of the Ontario Municipal Board Reports. I benefitted from his suggestions and ideas greatly; however, what I have written is my responsibility and mine alone.

I also want to record my thanks to Stanley Makuch for his patience and time taken to read some earlier drafts. It was his helpful direction at a crucial time that set me on a better course.

I record my thanks to Lynda Tanaka, former Executive Chair of ELTO, and Wilson Lee, Associate Chair of the Ontario Municipal Board, now retired, for their input and occasional correction.. Also, the nameless ones who trusted me, and those planners and planning law practitioners who gave me their time and their thoughts for use in this book. Their input was absolutely essential to my understanding of how different and infinitely more detailed the preparation and performance at hearings must be now, given the layers of policy that must be addressed.

I wish to ask the members of the Ontario Municipal Board for their understanding. I realize that some passages in this book will seem unfair to some. I have to provide my view of the Board as I see it and as my research leads me. I am well aware of the great ability of some members but not of enough members. My hope is that this book and other input to the Province will lead to wise decisions in the end, whether it agrees with my recommendations or not. This tribunal's mandate is too important for the Province to continue to treat it as a Trojan horse or an enemy; that sense of respect must go both ways – the Board must treat witnesses from the ministries involved with the same respect as public servants , though that does not mean following their opinions where they are not sound.

.If the necessary investment is made, the members have their duty as well that must be realized, together, every day, with a collegial wisdom and fairness toward all stakeholders. The beneficiaries of the new mediation service, if it should come about, will hopefully multiply and be able to walk away with a sense of contributing to their communities and their own interest. On contested hearings, the losers must know why the case did not go their way. A sense of predictability and consistent principle is owed to the parties that come before this tribunal or its successor for justice, in view of the need for less costly resolutions. Excellence, character and stature in tribunal-related diversity and experience must replace the present laissez-faire standards as the goals of selection, membership and work on this tribunal.

I must express my gratitude and appreciation for the editing and design assistance of the people at Friesen Press. They have been tireless in making this a better product. Astra Crompton, mu file editor, has been especially helpful in seeing me through all the decisions that have been necessary to achieve publication. I thank Emily MacDonald who helped me to get started after being held up and ultimately let down by a Toronto legal publisher. Thank you all from the bottom of my heart.

Finally, I wish to thank my wife, Agnes Wong Howden, for the hours and days she has spent putting the manuscript into a more professional condition. Her help was invaluable and her place in my life is what keeps me going. Without the help of her and all of these people, this book could not have been accomplished.

Peter Haughland Howden
November 2016

LIST OF CASES CITED IN TEXT

114957 Canada Ltée (Spraytech, Société d'arrosage) v. Hudson (Town),
  [2001] 2 S.C.R. 241(S.C.C.)
822403 Ontario Inc. v Oakville (Town), released August 5, 2015(OMB)
109 Ossington Ltd. v Toronto (City), [2014] O.M.B.D. No. 434 (OMB)

Ainsley Financial Corp. v Ontario Securities Commission, [1994] O.J.
  No. 2966; 21 O.R. (3d) 104 (C.A.)

Baker v Canada (Min. of Cit. and Imm.), [1999] 2 SCR 817(S.C.C.)
Bele Himmel Investments Ltd. v. City of Mississauga et al. (1982), 13 O.M.B.R. 17

Caledon (Township) Official Plan, Re, (1973), 2 OMBR 1(OMB)
Campeau Corp. v Gloucester (Twp.) [1979] O.J. No. 3453(C.A.)
Clergy Properties Ltd. v Mississauga (City) (1996) 34 OMBR 277;
    affirmed in *Greater Toronto Airports Authority v Clergy Properties Ltd.*,
    [1997] O.J. no. 6576 [Div. Ct.]; leave to appeal refused
    [1998] O.J. No. 340 (C.A.).
Cloverdale Shopping Centre v Etobicoke (Township), [1966] 2 O.R. 439;
57 D.L.R. (2d) 206 (C.A.)
Council of Canadians with Disabilities v Via Rail Canada Inc.,
    [2007] S.C.J. No.15 (S.C.C.)

Dickinson v Toronto (City) (1999), 37 O.M.B.R. 362 (OMB)
Domtar Inc. v Quebec, [1993] 2 SCR 756
Dunsmuir v New Brunswick, [2008] 1 SCR 190

E.A. Manning v Ontario Securities Commission, [1995] O.J. No.1305 (C.A.)

Friends of Jesus Christ Canada v Toronto (City)
(2010), 68 OMBR 149)

Highway Developments Ltd. v Etobicoke (Twp.) (February 21, 1958, OMB)
Holmes v Jarrett, [1993] O.J. No. 679 (Ont. H.C.J.)
Hopedale Developments Ltd. v Oakville (Town), [1965] 1 O.R. 259 (C,A.)

IWA v Consolidated Bathurst Packaging Ltd., [1990] 1 S.C.R. 282.

J. & R. Rite Holdings (Oshawa) Inc. v Oshawa (City) 1988 CarswellOnt 556 (Co. Ct.).
James Dick Construction Ltd. v Caledon (Township) (2010), 66 O.M.B.R. 263 (OMB)
Jennison Construction Ltd. v Ashfield-Colborne-Wawanosh (Township)
    (2011), 71 O.M.B.R. 195(OMB)
Johnston v Toronto (City), OMB File No. PL 070771, issued March 25, 2008

Kane v Bd. of Governors of U.B.C., [1980] 1 SCR 105

Kelvingrove Investment Corp. v Toronto (City) [2010] 65 OMBR 57
   Material Handling Problem Solvers Inc. v Essex (Town) (2002), 44 OMBR 364
McWilliam v. Morris, [1942] O.W.N. 447(HCJ)
Miller Paving Ltd. v McNab/Braeside (Township) (OMB File No. PL130785,
   Issued October 27, 2015)
Mississauga Golf and Country Club, Re, (1963) 2 OR 625 (C.A.).

Nepean (Twp.) Restricted Area By-law 73–76, Re, (1978) 9 OMBR 36 (OMB)
Newfoundland and Labrador Nurses' Union v Newfoundland and Labrador
   (Treasury Board), [2011] 3 SCR 708
Northern Electric Co., R v, [1955] O.R. 431; 3 D.L.R. 449; 111 C.C.C. 241(HCJ)

Ottawa (City) v. Minto Communities Inc. [2009] O.J. No.4913 (Div. Ct.)
Ottawa Carleton (Reg. Mun.) Official Plan Amendment 8,
   Re, (1991), 26 OMBR 132) (OMB)
Ottawa(City) Official Plan Amendment 76: *Friends of the Greenspace Alliance*
   v Ottawa (City), File PL120109, released Dec. 22, 2010

Richmond Hill (Town) v Elgin Bay Corp. 2015 ONSC 4979 (SCJ)
Ron Forbes Enterprises Ltd. v Bruce (County), [2006] O.M.B.D.
   No. 1328 (OMB)

Scarborough (Township) v Bondi, [1959] SCR 44.
Sentinel Broadway Holdings Inc. v Toronto (City), file MM 130048,
   released June 19, 2014
Shell Canada Products Ltd. v. Vancouver (City), [1994] 1 S.C.R. 231
Sifton Properties Ltd. and Grandview Ravines Inc. v Brantford (City),
   (OMB File PL 100472-3, released June 26, 2014)
Sorauren Developments Inc. v Toronto (City), OMB File No. PL 130568,
   issued January 6, 2014
Southwold (Twp.) v Caplice, (1978), 22 O.P.R. (2d) 804 (Div. Ct.),
Sutton Place Developments Ltd. v Toronto (City), (March 7, 1958, OMB)

Toronto Transit Commission and Metro Toronto v Toronto (City), COMPLETE
Toronto (City) v. Goldlist Properties Inc. (2003), 67 O.R. (3d) 441 (C.A.).

Uniform Urban Developments Inc v Ottawa (City), File PL120109,
   released Feb. 14, 2014

Waterloo (Reg. Mun.) Official Plan and Lea Silvestri Investments
   Ltd. et al., Re, (OMB File PL110080, Phase 1 decision on land
   inventory issues, January 21, 2013)
Westminster (Township) v London (City) (1974), 5 O.R. (2d) 401 (Div. Ct.).

ENDNOTES

(Endnotes)

1   John G. Chipman, *A Law Unto Itself: How The Ontario Municipal Board Has Developed And Applied Land Use Planning Policy* (Toronto, University of Toronto Press, 2002); Aaron A. Moore, *Planning Politics in Toronto: The OMB and Urban Development* (Toronto, University of Toronto Press, 2013).

2   Gene Desfor, Roger Keil, Stefan Kipfer, and Gerda Wekerle. "Surf to Turf: No Limits to Growth in Toronto." *Studies in Political Economy,* Vol. 77, 2006, 131–155.

3   *Planning Act,* R.S.O. 1990, c. P.13.

4   Section 16(1) and (2) of the *Planning Act* does not use the word "define" in saying what an OP is meant to be. It describes the sort of document meant by the *Planning Act* by its contents:
    (1) An official plan shall contain,
       (a)   goals, objectives and policies established primarily to manage and direct physical change and the effects on the social, economic and natural environment of the municipality or part of it, or an area that is without municipal organization; and
       (b)   such other matters as may be prescribed.
    (2) An official plan may contain,
       (a)   a description of the measures and procedures proposed to attain the objectives of the plan;
       (b)   a description of the measures and procedures for informing and obtaining the views of the public in respect of a proposed amendment to the official plan or proposed revision of the plan or in respect of a proposed zoning by-law; and
    (c) such other matters as may be prescribed. 2006, c. 23, s. 8.

5   There is a statutory obligation imposed upon a municipality to amend its by-laws and in the interim the municipality should refuse any application for a building permit, even though such application complies with its by-law if the by-law does not conform to the official plan of the regional municipality. *Campeau Corp. v Gloucester (Twp.)* [1979] O.J. No. 3453(C.A.); *J. & R. Rite Holdings (Oshawa) Inc. v Oshawa (City)* 1988 Carswell Ont 556 (Co. Ct.). As well, recent *Planning Act* amendments (in 2002 and 2006, to sections 26 and 27) require zoning to be brought into conformity with local (and regional) official plans within one year (for a regional plan) and three years (local O.P.). These relatively recent inputs water down somewhat the *Southwold (Twp.) v Caplice,* (1978), 22 O.P.R. (2d) 804 (Div. Ct.), dictum that 'official pans are not effective land use control instruments.'

6   R.S.O. 1990, c.O.28. Sections 34 to 37 grant full and exclusive jurisdiction to decide matters under any Act of the Legislature and section 87 grants generous authority to issue tailor-made orders that are enforceable in a court of record. They read:
    34. The Board for all purposes of this Act has all the powers of a court of record and shall have an official seal which shall be judicially noticed.
    35. The Board, as to all matters within its jurisdiction under this Act, has authority to hear and determine all questions of law or of fact.
    36. The Board has exclusive jurisdiction in all cases and in respect of all matters in which jurisdiction is conferred on it by this Act or by any other general or special Act.

37. The Board has jurisdiction and power (a) to hear and determine all applications made, proceedings instituted and matters brought before it under this Act or any other general or special Act...

87. <u>The Board may direct in any order that the order,</u> or any portion or provision thereof, <u>shall come into force at a future fixed time,</u> or upon the happening of any contingency, event or condition specified in the order, or <u>upon the performance, to the satisfaction of the Board or person named by it, of any terms which the Board may impose upon any party interested,</u> and the Board may direct that the whole, or any portion of the order, shall have force for a limited time, or until the happening of any specified event. [Emphasis added]

7   Chipman, *A Law Unto Itself,* 10.

8   Leo Longo, "Correcting the Record: The Ontario Municipal Board's Upcoming Centenary and its Legislative Roots" (2006), 19 M.P.L.R. (4th) 22.

9   *Ibid,* 22.

10   Robert G. Doumani and Patricia A. Foran. *2016 Ontario Planning Act & Commentary* (Markham: LexisNexis Canada, 2015).

11   Ian Milligan. "This Board Has a Duty to Intervene: Challenging the Spadina Expressway through the Ontario Municipal Board, 1963–1971." *Urban History Review*, Vol. 39, No. 2 (Spring, 2011), 25–37.

12   Before 1998, the present city was divided between the city, governed by city council and five boroughs with their own councils. Metropolitan Toronto was the level of government that had jurisdiction over roads and traffic and certain other services throughout the city and the boroughs. The 1997 *City of Toronto Act* amalgamated the parts into one whole, and the Metro level of government disappeared.

13   Report of the Select Committee on the Ontario Municipal Board, tabled in the Legislative Assembly by the chairman of the Committee John P. MacBeth, 2d session, 29th Legislature, 21 Eliz. 11. Toronto: Legislative Assembly, 1972, 12–14.

14   Peter H. Howden. "Environmental Jurisdiction of the OMB." Draft Notes. Speech by the author to Insight Conference in the mid-1980s.

15   *Westminster (Township) v London (City)* (1974), 5 O.R. (2d) 401 (Div. Ct.).

16   "Environmental Assessment: A Vision Lost." [Evolution of the *Environmental Assessment Act* since 1976] 2007–2008 ECO Annual Report by the Environmental Commissioner submitted to the Legislative Assembly on October 21, 2008

17   *Clergy Properties Ltd. v Mississauga (City)* (1996) 34 OMBR 277; affirmed in *Greater Toronto Airports Authority v Clergy Properties Ltd.,* [1997] O.J. no. 6576 [Div. Ct.]; leave to appeal refused [1998] O.J. no. 340 (C.A.).

18   *Domtar Inc. v Quebec,* [1993] 2 SCR 756.

19   Ontario Ministry of Agriculture and Food. *Food Land Guidelines: a policy statement of the government of Ontario on planning for agriculture* (Toronto: Government of Ontario, 1978).

20   P. Scargall, interview by the author on November 6, 2015.

21   Re Township of Caledon Official Plan (1974) 2 OMBR 1, 3.

22   *Re Township of Caledon Official Plan* (1973), 2 OMBR 1, 2.

23   Ontario general election, 1967:
Conservative
Thomas Wells
11,968
42.9%

New Democrat
John Brewin
10,435
37.4%

Liberal
Milne Freeman
5,505
19.7%

24   M. Melling, interview by the author on August 19, 2015.

25   J. Davies, interview by the author on August 13, 2015.

26   L. Dale-Harris, interview by the author on August 12, 2015.

27   R. Doumani, interview by the author on August 20, 2015.

28   S. Zakem, interview by the author on October 7, 2015.

29   A. Patton, interview by the author on September 30, 2015.

30   J. Park, interview by the author on October 6, 2015.

31   S. Makuch, interview by the author on August 12, 2015.

32   M. Melling , interview by the author on October 15, 2015.

33   M. McQuaid, interview by the author on August 20, 2015.

34   A. Patton, see note 29.

35   L. Dale-Harris, see note 26.

36   R. Doumani, see note 26.

37   J. Pepino, interview by the author on August 13, 2016.

38   *Shell Canada Products Ltd. v. Vancouver (City)*, [1994] 1 S.C.R. 231.

39   *114957 Canada Ltée (Spraytech, Société d'arrosage) v. Hudson (Town)*, [2001] 2 S.C.R. 241, para 23.

40   *Toronto (City) v. Goldlist Properties Inc.* (2003), 67 O.R. (3d) 441 (C.A.).

41   *Municipal Act, 2001*, S.O. 2001, c.75, sections 2 and 3.

42   They were added by amendments in S.C. 2006, c.32, Sched. A sections 71 to 84 (licensing and environmental provisions).

43   Christina Blizzard, "Time to Take Some of OMB's Power Away," *Toronto Sun*, Sept. 2014 http://www.torontosun.com/2014/09/27/time-to-take-some-of-ontario-municipal-boards-power-away. Accessed October 10, 2016.

44   https://www.thestar.com/news/queenspark/2013/08/27/how_the_omb_stifles_democracy_in_ontario_cohn.html. Accessed October 10, 2016.

45   http://torontolife.com/real-estate/ossington-strip-getting-condo-mid-rise/. Accessed October 10, 2016

46   http://www.therecord.com/news-story/4030168-region-alleges-bias-in-omb-decision-on-future-development/. Accessed October 10, 2016.

47   http://www.waterloochronicle.ca/news-story/5893500-proper-planning/. Accessed October 10, 2016.

48   https://www.cpsa-acsp.ca/papers-2009/Moore.pdf. Accessed October 10, 2016.

49   Chipman, *A Law Unto Itself*, 202.

50   Former Toronto Planning Director Paul Bedford, urban planner Ken Greenberg, and developer Steven Diamond (in his early career, a planning and development lawyer who practiced before the OMB) put together a paper entitled "Rethinking the Role of the OMB in the Planning and Development Process in Toronto". They proposed that there be a local Planning Advisory Committee (PAC) for each planning area in Toronto and that those committees be composed of knowledgeable persons with skill sets from business, architecture, planning, resident and real estate backgrounds should be proposed by the Province and formally appointed by City Council. When each development proposal goes through the process, the planning staff, the local PAC and City Council would in turn examine it and vote to reject or allow it. Provided that all three agree,

there would be no appeal to the OMB. If all three accept the proposal, no appeal would be allowed to the OMB. If all three voted to reject it, that would be the end of it – there would be no appeal allowed to the OMB. Only where one or two of the three do not agree, would an appeal be allowed to proceed to the OMB. The independence of the PAC from the council and the professionally related and diverse composition of the PAC were vital to the success of this program.

51   *Waterloo (Reg. Mun.) Official Plan and Lea Silvestri Investments Ltd. et al. Re:* OMB File PL110080, Phase 1 decision on land inventory issues, January 21, 2013.

52   The OMB panel continued the excerpt from Justice Aston where he had cited a prior Board decision written by a member of the panel responsible for the Waterloo decision on the matter of deference to a council decision and the meaning of the phrase that the Board is "to have regard to ... that decision." That excerpt was omitted in the text as not necessary to the point being made; however I am including it here because it shows how limited the Board's attention has given to its own jurisprudence. Aston J: "However, in the context of the *Planning Act*, and balancing the public interest mandates of both the Board and the municipality, I would agree with Member Stefanko in Keswick Sutherland that the Board has an obligation to at least scrutinize and carefully consider the Council decision as well as the information and material that was before Council ... However, the Board does not have to find that the Council's decision is demonstrably unreasonable to arrive at a different conclusion."

53   *Material Handling Problem Solvers Inc. v Essex (Town)* (2002), 44 OMBR 364 [Member Krushelnicki, as he then was; now the Executive Chair of ELTO and Chair of the OMB].

54   *Toronto (City) v Goldlist Properties Inc.* (2003), 67 O.R. (3d) 441 (C.A.), at para 49. The Court stated, in regard to the kind of instrument that an OP is, that,

"In this regard, it is important to bear in mind that the purpose of an official plan is to set out a framework of 'goals, objectives and policies' to shape and discipline specific operative planning decisions."

55   See *Waterloo (Reg. Mun.) Official Plan and Silvestri Investments et al*, Re, OMB File No. PL110080, Final Approval as Modified, July 14, 2015.

56   Paige Desmond. "OMB accepts settlement of regional land dispute." *Waterloo Record*, June 18, 2015) http://www.therecord.com/news-story/5685221-omb-accepts-settlement-of-regional-land-dispute/. Accessed October 10, 2016.

57   *Cloverdale Shopping Centre v Etobicoke (Township)*, [1966] 2 O.R. 439; 57 D.L.R. (2d) 206 (C.A.).

58   *Kane v Bd. of Governors of U.B.C.*, [1980] 1 SCR 105 at pars. 21–22 and 44; *Baker v Canada (Min. of Cit. and Imm.)*, [1999] 2 SCR 817, at paras. 21–22 and 44.

59   Eli Comay (1910–2010) was the Metro Toronto Planning Commissioner between 1962 and 1966. He established a professional practice in 1966. At the local level, Mr. Comay conducted studies that led to the establishment of planning departments in the regions of Ottawa-Carleton and Niagara. Mr. Comay's work with the private sector included an appointment as planning coordinator for the development of the Erin Mills community in Mississauga where he worked closely with

planner John Bousfield. Housing was a particularly important area of practice, and Comay was involved with several committees and task forces devoted to this issue. He served as Chairman of the Ontario Advisory Task Force on Housing Policy, 1972–1973. It was the report of this task force that led to the formation of the Ministry of Housing. This is the Comay report cited in the text and suggested by comments by Ian Lord on the issues surrounding the OMB's discretionary powers.

60   The *St. Catharines Standard*, May 18, 2016 edition. The councillor from Welland who is on the working group and reported on the rapid growth of support to reform the OMB is Coun. Mary Ann Grimaldi, and the councillors who were mentioned in the article as supporting the reform movement were Coun. Joyce Morocco and Coun. Jim Collard from Niagara municipalities. The suggestion about a better selection and recruitment program for the OMB is one shared strongly by this writer.

61   The information in this section is from Moore, *Planning Politics in Toronto* and Barry Cullingworth and Roger Caves, *Planning in the U.S.A.*, 3rd ed. (London and New York: Routledge, 2013), and the websites of the various boards and tribunals cited.

62   Section 17 (50.1) of the *Planning Act* provides: "For greater certainty, subsection (50) (allowing modifications) does not give the Municipal Board power to approve or modify any part of the plan that, (a) is in effect; and (b) was not dealt with in the decision of council to which the notice of appeal relates."

63   On objection to a Development Plan, the Minister may refer the plan to the Manitoba Municipal Board and after a hearing, the Board may recommend to the Minister to either to approve, alter or reject the plan. The Minister, after consulting the Executive Council, makes the final decision. On objection to a zoning by-law, the Board convenes a hearing and may decide to confirm, alter or refuse to approve the by-law (sections 44(1) and 45(3)). *Planning Act of Manitoba*, RSM, 1987, c.P80.

64   M. Green, interview by the author on September 17, 2015.

65   Stephen Hamilton. *The Ontario Municipal Board and Regulatory Capture*. (Halifax: Dalhousie University, 2007).

66   R. Houser, interview by the author on August 19, 2015.

67   W. D. "Rusty" Russell, interview by the author on July 29, 2015.

68   J. Park, see note 30.

69   *Scarborough (Township) v Bondi*, [1959] SCR 44. *Bondi* stands for the proposition that in planning law, the fact that one lot is zoned differently from others in the area (i.e. residential, single-family but irregular size meant the lot areas when it was divided into two lots were less than the zoning otherwise allowed) does not mean it is void as discriminatory where the resulting two lots are in keeping with the overall scale and character of the area. However, the by-law was ruled null and void because OMB approval to the exercise of the power had not been provided before passage of the by-law and the authorizing statute required approval before the power to zone was exercised.

70   *Hopedale*, [1965] 1 OR 259 (C.A.).

71   *Mississauga Golf and Country Club*, [1963] 2 OR 625 (C.A.).

72   The Court of Appeal in *Hopedale* referred to the two OMB decisions as being from cases titled *Highway Developments Ltd. v Etobicoke (Twp.)*, February 21, 1958 and *Sutton Place Developments Ltd. v Toronto (City)*, March 7, 1958. The two cases do not seem to be reported and the OMB website requires file numbers, which are unknown.

73   *Baker,* para. 28.

74   Sumeet Tandon. "Evolution and Contradiction of Ontario's Land-Use Oversight Mechanisms" (Ottawa: Carleton University School of Public Policy and Administration, 2014). *CURE Policy Brief*, May, 2011 [ISSN-925-5780], 5–6.

75   S. Waqué, interview by the author on October 5, 2015.

76   1972 Select Committee Report, General Observations and Conclusions, "J. T. WEIR, with leave of the Committee, will speak to these headings". Legislature of Ontario Library, Toronto, 1 and 17.

77   M. McQuaid, interview by the author on August 20, 2015

78   C. MacDougall was one of the counsel on the Minto (Yonge-Eglinton, Toronto) case; interview by the author on October 2, 2015.

79   A. Patton, see note 29.

80   London Fog, reprint of article by Jonathan Sher in the *London Free Press*, May 4, 2004.

81   J. Pepino, see note 37.

82   L. Longo, interview by the author on August 31, 2015.

83   M. McQuaid, see note 33; he added the comment on intensification by letter to the author dated February 19, 2016, enclosing an article stating that at the November 2015 meeting, the York regional council rejected staff's preferred growth scenario and directed staff to compare the implications of the recommended 45% intensification rate and the provincially mandated rate of 40%. The 40% rate has been described by researchers on urban sprawl as "little more than business as usual, compared to the target set by Vancouver of 70%." See notes 153 and 155 with associated text.

84   J. Park, see note 30.

85   L. Dale-Harris, see note 26.

86   *Baker,* para. 22.

87   Jamie Bradburn. "Ghost City: The Bayview Ghost." *The Grid* (ceased publication 2014) and *Pad To Pad*, www.padtopad.ca, based on material from *The Leaside* and from the *Globe & Mail* and The *Toronto Star* 1961–1981.

88   Cullingworth and Cave, *Planning in the USA*, 100.

89   Christina Blizzard, "Time to Take Some of OMB's Power Away," *Toronto Sun*, Sept. 2014.

90   J. Park, see note 30.

91   M. Melling, see note 32.

92   L. Longo, see note 73; S. Makuch, see note 31.

93   K. Greenberg, interview by the author on November 10, 2015.

94   *Cloverdale Shopping Centre*, see note 57.

95   This idea is based on a proposal conceived by development executive, Stephen Diamond, former City Planning Director, Paul Bedford, and planner, Ken Greenberg.

96   *Spraytech*, para 23.

97   *Toronto (City) v Goldlist Properties Inc. et al.* (2003) 67 O.R. (3d) 441 (C.A.),para 49

98   *Planning Act*, section 3(5) and section 26(21).

99   *Re Mississauga Golf and Country Club*, 630-631.

100   Edward LaRusic, *Towards A More 'Reasonable' Ontario Municipal Board: Looking to Nova Scotia* (Toronto: Ryerson University, 2012).

101   Aaron Moore, *Passing The Buck: The OMB and Local Politicians in Toronto*, 2000–06, a paper presented in May 2009 to the Canadian Political Science Association Conference, 1.

102   *Moore, Passing The Buck*, 3–4 and 10.

103   *Ibid*, 4.

104   Chipman, *A Law Unto Itself*, 9 (Table I.I).

105   *Ibid*, 28.

106   *Ibid*, 28.

107 *Ibid*, 28–9.

108 *Ibid*, 36.

109 *Ibid*, 37.

110 *Ibid*, 36.

111 *Ibid*, 36–7.

112 *OPA C-65686: The Motel Strip Secondary Plan*, at p. 53.

113 *Re Nepean (Twp.) Restricted Area By-law 73-76*, (1978) 9 OMBR 36.

114 *Dickinson v Toronto (City)* (1999), 37 O.M.B.R. 362, paras. 8–9.

115 Chipman, *A Law Unto Itself*, 95 and 134.

116 *Ibid*, 133.

117 C. MacDougall, interview by the author on October 2, 2015.

118 Ontario Ministry of Agriculture and Food. *Food Land Guidelines: a policy statement of the government of Ontario on planning for agriculture.* (Toronto: Government of Ontario, 1976).

119 *Re Township of Caledon Official Plan*, 2

120 Chipman, *A Law Unto Itself*, 95.

121 Stanley Makuch, *Public Interest, Private Property Law and Planning Policy in Canada* edited by A. Smith and M. Valiante, (Vancouver: UBC Press 2015), Chapter 3: "The Disappearance of Planning Law in Ontario", 96–7.

122 Moore, *Passing the Buck*, 4.

123 *Ibid*, 3.

124 2009, S.O. 2009, c. 33, Sched. 5.

125 Lorne Sossin and Jamie Baxter. "Ontario's Administrative Tribunal Clusters: A Glass Half-Full or Half-Empty for Administrative Justice?" (2012) 12 Oxford University *Commonwealth Law Journal* 157; http://papers.ssrn.com/abstract=2099751.

126 L. Tanaka, interview by the author on December 4, 2015.

127 *Adjudicative Tribunals Accountability, Governance and Appointments Act 2009*, S.O. 2009, c. 33, Sched. 5, section 15.

128 Kevin Whitaker, *Final Report of the Agency Cluster Facilitator for the Municipal, Environment and Land Planning Tribunals* (Toronto: Queen's Printer, 2007).

129 L. Tanaka, see note 126.

130 *Ibid.*

131 *Ibid.*

132 Whitaker, *Final Report of the Agency Cluster Facilitator*, 6.

133 *Ibid*, 25.

134 The source of these statements must remain confidential.

135 S. Makuch, see note 31.

136 P. Scargall, interview by the author on November 6, 2015.

137 ELTO Facilitator's Report, 6.

138 Ontario Tribunal Clusters, 42.

139 Whitaker, *Final Report of the Agency Cluster Facilitator*, p. 8, "Features of a Modern Tribunal," August 22, 2007.

140 William Lahey, "The Contributions of Utilities Regulation to Electrical Systems Transformation: The Case of Nova Scotia", *Energy Regulation Quarterly*, Nov. 2014, Vol.2, Fall/14.

141 Kevin Latimer, managing partner of Cox and Palmer, Halifax, Nova Scotia, interview with the author.

142 The OMB decision dealt with policies proposed for Richmond Hill's official plan. Their objective is to guide future decisions about parkland conveyances to the Town as a condition of development (section 42, *Planning Act*). That decision is *Elginbay Corp., Signature Developments Inc. et al v Richmond Hill (Town)* (OMB File No. PL110189, released January 15, 2015). The OMB approved the policies of the Town but imposed a cap of 25% of land proposed for development or its equivalent. The Town, supported by four intervener municipalities, appealed, asserting that the OMB has no jurisdiction to impose the cap. The municipality's by-law setting a park rate or levy, is not reviewable by the Board and therefore it lacks jurisdiction to impose an overall limit on this municipal power.

     The appeal was heard by the Divisional Court on August 24, 2016 and the decision issued on September 6, 2016 allowing the appeal. The court set aside the OMB-ordered cap. The court stated that the OMB had available to it a number of policy directives that it could have placed on the Town, including a policy discouraging undue restriction on high-density development by use of the park rate powers: "What the OMB could not do", Justice Nordheimer wrote on behalf of a unanimous court, "is adopt an unreasonable interpretation of its statutory authority and thereby accord to itself the right to impose a cap on the Town's use of a mechanism expressly granted to municipalities by the Legislature."

The court tacitly followed *Goldlist* in applying the court's line of authorities that started with the 1994 dissent of McLachlin J, now CJC, in *Shell Canada Products Ltd.*, and continued with its adoption by a majority of the Supreme Court in *Spraytech*, and more recently by the Ontario Court of Appeal in *Croplife Canada v Toronto (City)* (2005),75 O.R. (3d)1, to land use policy issues: "... the powers given to municipalities are to be interpreted 'broadly and generously within their context and statutory limits, to achieve the legitimate interests of the municipality and its inhabitants'"(*Richmond Hill*, at para 48). This is the continuing development of the law in the planning area of which I wrote in the concluding section of Chapter II.

143   P. Scargall, see note 136.

144   S. Makuch, see note 31.

145   L. Longo, see note 73.

146   M. Melling, see note 32.

147   1972 Select Committee Report, pp. 13-14.

148   Provincial Policy Statement, 2005 (PPS) was issued and in effect on March 1, 2005, replacing the 1996–7 Statement. This excerpt is taken from the PPS, 2014, issued and in effect on April 30, 2014.

149   *Niagara Escarpment Planning and Development Act*, R.S.O. 1990, c. N.2; for ORMCA, see S.O. 2001, c.31.

150   Excerpts from the PPS, 2014, sections 1.1, 1.2, 1.3, 1.6, 1.7, and Part IV.

151   It is the staff planning report that normally gives form to the proposal and lists and comments on the relevant OP sections, servicing and other issues raised by the proposal and usually a recommendation for action by council. It is that planning report that development lawyers often try very hard to obtain in favour of their client's proposal.

152   *Kelvingrove Investment Corp. v Toronto (City)* [2010] 65 OMBR 57 at paras. 5 and 62–65.

153   *The Canadian Oxford Dictionary*, K. Barber, ed. (Toronto: Oxford University Press, 2004), 97.

154   Makuch, *Public Interest, Private Property*, 912.

155   Development lawyer P. Devine proposed this idea as one that he and former City Planning Director, Paul Bedford, had conceived. The submission dated August 21, 2015 is before the Municipal Legislation Review of the *City of Toronto Act* as a reform to improve governance by the

Province as the council is unlikely to voluntarily give up the power that the present system gives each ward councillor. The reason for the use of districts is that running an election campaign across the entire city for half the Councillors would be too expensive for many candidates. The use of districts is a compromise between half the council being elected at large and continuing with strict ward system for all purposes.

156   A. Patton, see note 29.

157   M. Green, see note 55.

158   "905" refers to the large area on the fringes of Toronto from Hamilton to Oshawa.

159   R. Houser, see note 57.

160   The AMO website gives 444 as the total number of municipalities now in Ontario.

161   Tandon, *The Evolution and Contradiction of Ontario's Land Use Oversight Mechanisms*, 2.

162   Cherise Burda. *Getting Tough on Urban Sprawl: Solutions to Meet Ontario's Climate Control Targets*, (Calgary: Pembina Institute, 2008), 16.

163   Damilare Adeola. *The Effect of Provincial and Municipal Sustainability Policies on Urban Development Patterns in Markham* (Kingston: Queen's University, 2011), iv and 389.

164   *Ibid*, 46–7.

165   *Ibid*, 47.

166   Tandon, *Evolution and Contradiction of Ontario's Land-use Mechanisms*, 5.

167   *Ibid*, 5.

168   *Ibid*, 5.

169   Adeola, *The Effect of Provincial and Municipal Sustainability Policies*, 60.

170   2005, c. 13, section 9(1).

171   2015, c. 26, section 24(1), introducing a new section 26(1), not yet in effect.

172   Makuch, *Public Interest, Private Property*, 91–92.

173   *Baker v Canada (Min. of Cit. and Imm.)* [1999] 2 S.C.R. 817, at para. 22: "I emphasize that underlying all these factors is the notion that the purpose of the participatory rights contained within the duty of procedural fairness is to ensure that administrative decisions are made using a fair and

open procedure, appropriate to the decision being made and its statutory, institutional, and social context, with an opportunity for those affected by the decision to put forward their views and evidence fully and have them considered by the decision-maker."

174 Simon Frith. Chapter 7 in *Questions of Cultural Identity*, ed. by Stuart Hall and Paul du Gay, (London: Sage Publications Ltd., 1996) (reprinted 2011).

175 *Phase 1, Environmental Site Assessment*, Genivar Inc. for 822403c Ontario Inc., Oakville: September 2012, at ES 1; www.oakville.ca/assets.

176 Cynthia MacDougall was counsel on this case. Her complete comment is illuminating for purposes of considering the need for a provincial tribunal in the land use planning process:

"What bothered me was that she (the City planner) did not seem to be aware that there was a basic principle involved. That is, that you cannot take away the use of land without paying compensation. There seems to be an 'end justifies the means' mentality among the younger staff and the Board is very important to correct that kind of thinking."

177 Dickinson v Toronto (City), 8–9.

178 Makuch, *Public Policy, Private Property*, 93.

179 The 'methodology attack' notion on a Provincial Policy comes from planning law counsel, Ian Lord, in his generous editorial comments on this book.

180 Tandon, "Evolution and Contradiction of Ontario's Land Use Mechanisms", 5.

181 Burda, *Getting Tough on Urban Sprawl: Solutions to meet Ontario climate change targets*, 40.

182 *Dunsmuir v New Brunswick*, [2008] 1 SCR 190; *Newfoundland and Labrador Nurses' Union v Newfoundland and Labrador (Treasury Board)*, [2011] 3 SCR 708, paras. 9-13.

183 Report of the Select Committee on the Ontario Municipal Board, 14–15; 30–31.

184 Re Township of Caledon Official Plan (1974) 2 OMBR 1, 3.

185 The Rule of Law has been given content by several principles developed by the World Justice Project (WJP), originally formed as a presidential initiative of the American Bar Association. It is now a non-profit organization in Washington. Its sponsors research into justice issues and are engaged in pragmatic solving of local rule of law issues. The WJP developed a nine-point list of factors that make up the Rule of Law. The fourth factor is the equal application of the law.

186 40 D.L.R. (2d) 673 at pp. 677–8, [1963] 2 O.R. 625 at pp. 629–30.

187 Bryan Finlay. "Consistency in Tribunal Decision Making," *Canadian Journal of Administrative Law and Practice* (2012), 25 CJALP 277–288.

188 [1990] 1 S.C.R. 282.

189 The maxim *audi alteram partem* is defined as: "the parties are to be given adequate notice and opportunity to be heard." J.M. Evans, *de Smith's Judicial Review of Administrative Action* (4th ed. 1980) 156, cited in *IWA v Consolidated Bathurst Packaging Ltd.*, see note 181.

190 [1955] O.R. 431; 111 C.C.C. 241.

191 *McWilliam v Morris* [1942] O.W.N. 447 [H.C.J.].

192 (2011) 71 OMBR 195 at paras. 44-5, 71-74 and 140.

193 (2010), 66 OMBR 263.

194 OMB File No. PL130785, issued October 27, 2015.

195 See *IWA v Consolidated Bathurst Packaging Ltd.*, see note 189.

196 John Caliendo, ABC Residents' Association, and Andrew Biggart, a prominent municipal lawyer, *The OMB: We Come to Reform, Not to Bury You*; a paper sent to the author in April 2016. Excerpt published as "Making the OMB a True Appellate Body." (Toronto: Novae Res Urbis, April 22, 2016), edition, 6.

197 *Holmes v Jarrett*, [1993] O.J. No. 679 (Ont. H.C.J.).

198 *R. ex rel. McWilliam v. Morris*, [1942] O.W.N. 447, cited with approval by McRuer CJHC in *R v Northern Electric Co.*, [1955] O.R. 431; 3 D.L.R. 449; 111 C.C.C. 241(HCJ).

199 For the citation to Granger J.'s judgment in *Holmes v Jarrett*, see note 197 above.

200 *Saskatchewan Municipal Board, About The Board: How Does The Board Fulfill Its Mandate?* www.smb.gov.sk.ca.

201 Ken Greenberg, *What's Wrong with the OMB's Involvement in Toronto?* (Toronto: Wellington Place Newsletter, April 10, 2014) www.wellingtonplace.org.

202 Makuch, *Public Interest, Private Property*, 93.

203 The Law Dictionary.com and Black's Law Dictionary Free 2nd ed. www.thelawdictionary.org.

204 David Mullan, *Administrative Law* (Toronto: Irwin Law Inc., February, 2001) cited in *The Canadian Online Legal Dictionary*, Irwin Law: www.Irwinlaw.com.

205 L. Dale-Harris, see note 26.

206 K. Greenberg, see note 93.

207 The quoted reminders came from Ian Lord, counsel and mediator, who assisted me greatly with editing.

208 *Metro Toronto and Toronto Transit Commission v Toronto (City)*, COMPLETE

209 Statistics Canada, historic population figures for Barrie, ON.

210 David L. Cooperrider and Diana Whitney. *Appreciative Inquiry: A Positive Revolution in Change.* (Oakland: Berrett-Kohler, 2005).

211 Edward LaRusic, *Towards A More Reasonable Ontario Municipal Board: Looking to Nova Scotia* (Toronto: Ryerson University, 2012).

212 *Hopedale Development Ltd. v Oakville (Town)*, [1965] 1 O.R. 259; 47 D.L.R. (2d) 482 (C.A.).

213 W.D. "Rusty" Russell, see note 67, and Alan Patton, see note 29.

214 This idea for reform of the planning process could further reduce the workload if it could be brought into operation – no easy task. For a more complete description of this initiative, see Note 50.

215 The *Consolidated Bathurst* principle includes the following:

> Full board meetings are a practical means of calling upon the accumulated experience of board members when making an important policy decision and obviate the possibility of different panels inadvertently deciding similar issues in a different way. The rules of natural justice should reconcile the characteristics and exigencies of decision making by specialized tribunals with the procedural rights of the parties.
>
> The members of a panel who actually participate in the decision must have heard both the evidence and the arguments presented by the parties. The presence of other Board members at the full board meeting does not, however, amount to "participation" in the final decision. Discussion with a person who has not heard the evidence does not necessarily vitiate the resulting decision because this discussion might "influence the decision maker.
>
> Decision makers cannot be forced or induced to adopt positions they do not agree with by means of some formalized consultation process. A discussion does not prevent a decision maker from adjudicating in accordance with his own conscience and does not constitute an obstacle to this freedom. The ultimate decision, whatever discussion may take place, is that of the decision maker and he or she must assume full responsibility for that decision.